UNCANNY X-MEN

THE DRACO

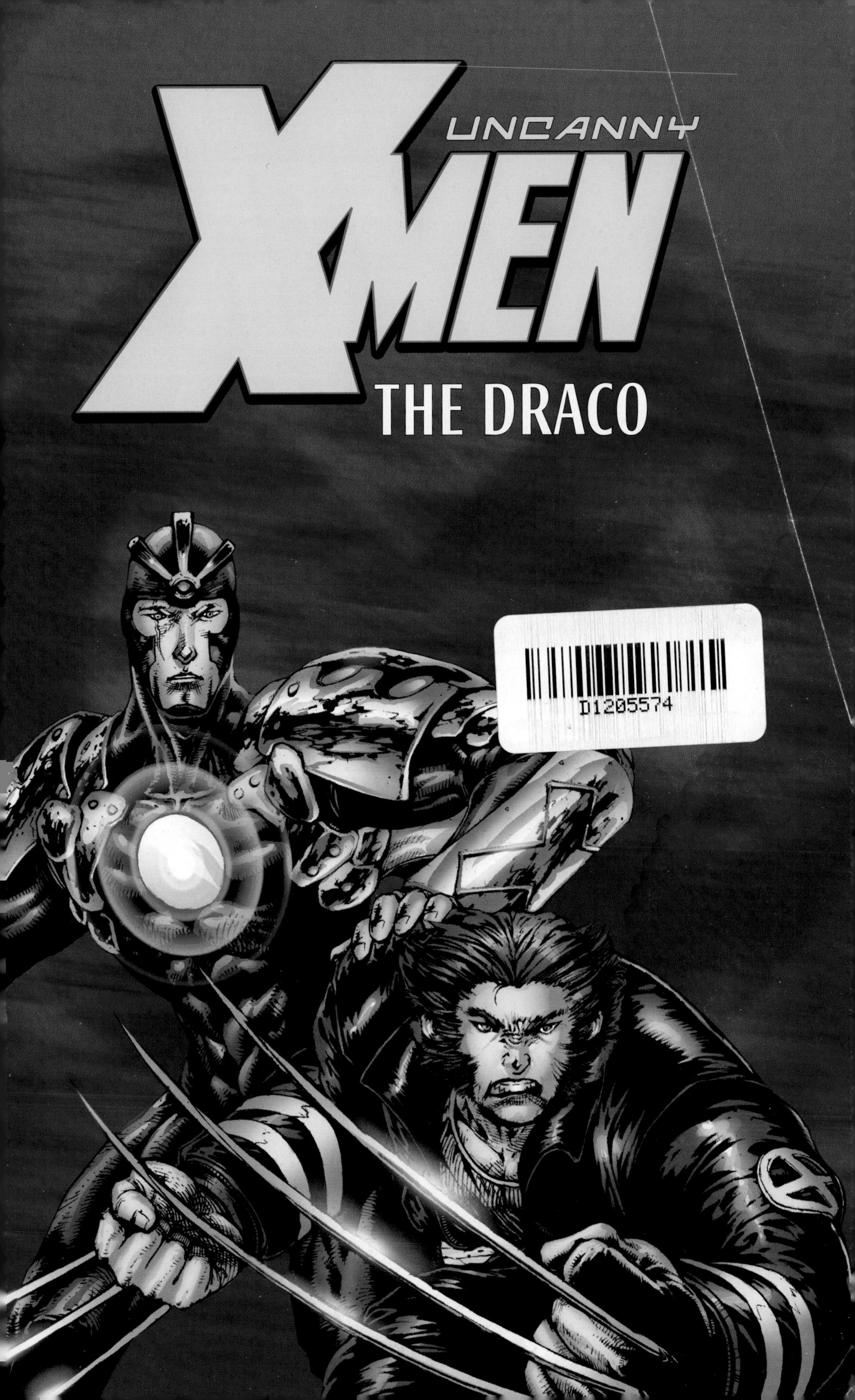

UNCANNY X-MEN
THE DRACO

Writer: CHUCK AUSTEN
Artists: PHILLIP TAN, SEAN PHILLIPS
and TAKESHI MIYAZAWA
with CRAIG YEUNG & SCOTT ELMER

Colors: AVALON STUDIOS and DAVE McCAIG
Letters: VIRTUAL CALLIGRAPHY'S RUS WOOTON
Cover Art: PHILLIP TAN
Assistant Editors: WARREN SIMONS, ANNIE THORNTON,
CORY SEDLMEIER and STEPHANIE MOORE
Editor: MIKE MARTS

Collections Editor: JEFF YOUNGQUIST
Assistant Editor: JENNIFER GRÜNWALD
Book Designer: MEGHAN KERNS
Editor in Chief: JOE QUESADA
Publisher: DAN BUCKLEY

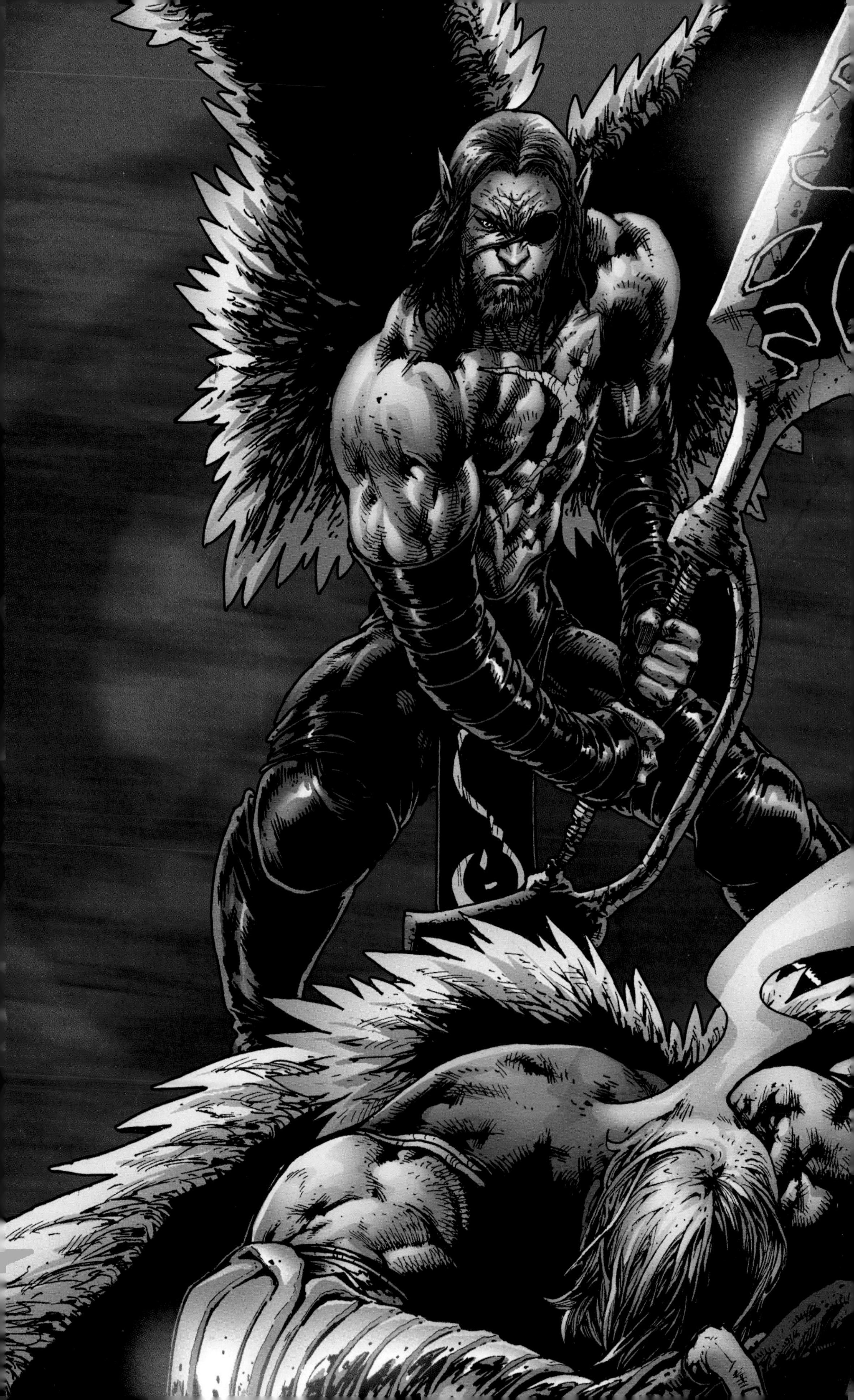

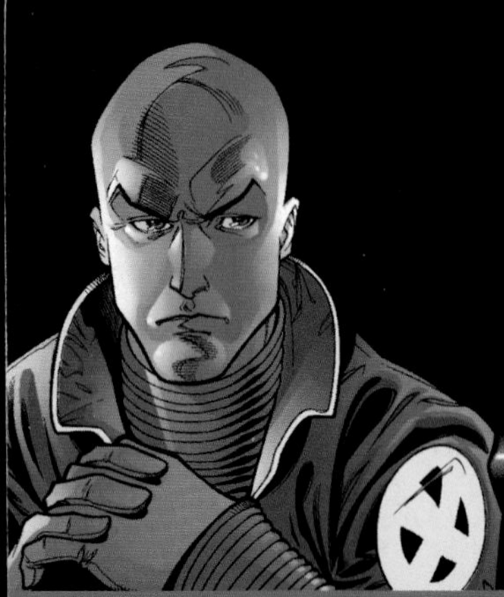

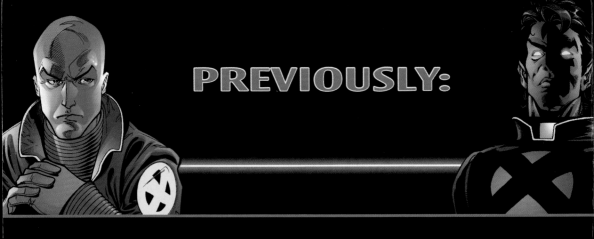

PREVIOUSLY:

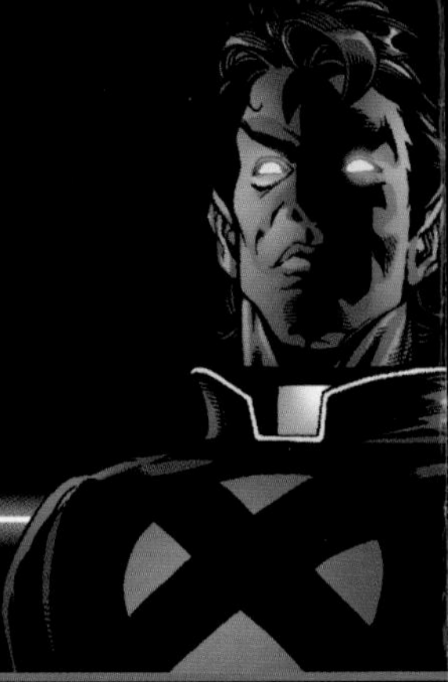

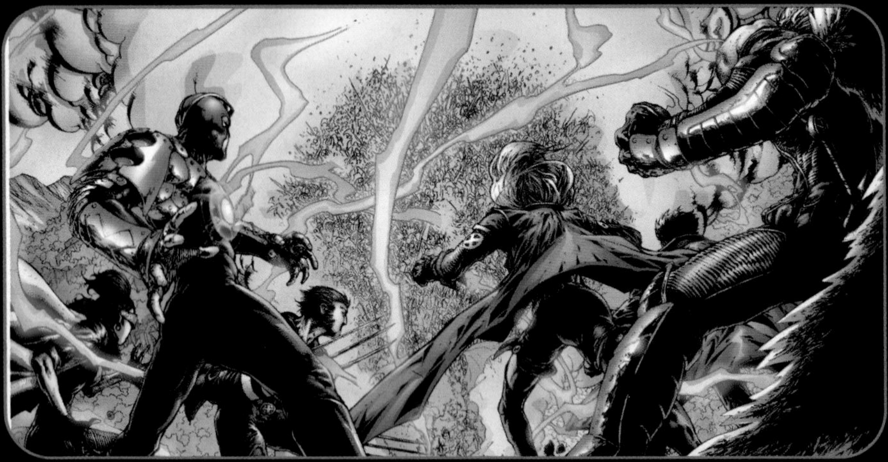

MYSTIQUE...little is known about this woman save that her life has always been shrouded in mystery. With the uncanny ability to morph her body into any form she desires, Mystique can perfectly impersonate other people and create new identities at will.

Mutant terrorist, government employee, international spy or European aristocrat—throughout her illustrious career, Mystique has worn many faces, answered to many names and assumed many guises.

But if there is one item of Mystique's puzzling past that stands out above all others, one enigma that mystifies more than anything else, it is her family history. She is strangely connected to several notable mutants, most of them associated in one way or another with the X-Men, her longtime arch-rivals. She is ex-wife to the notoriously dangerous Weapon X agent SABRETOOTH. Foster mother to X-Treme X-Men member ROGUE. But most importantly, she has long been rumored to be the true blood mother of X-Men member Kurt Wagner, otherwise known as NIGHTCRAWLER.

Are the rumors true? Is Mystique truly Nightcrawler's mother, as she has claimed to be in the past? And if so, who is Kurt's father? How and when was Kurt born? What were the circumstances? And why would Mystique abandon her son to the life of an orphan at such an early age?

The truth, the real reasons, the answers, can all be found where they have always been—secretly locked away and hidden in a tiny corner of one person's mind. Mystique's.

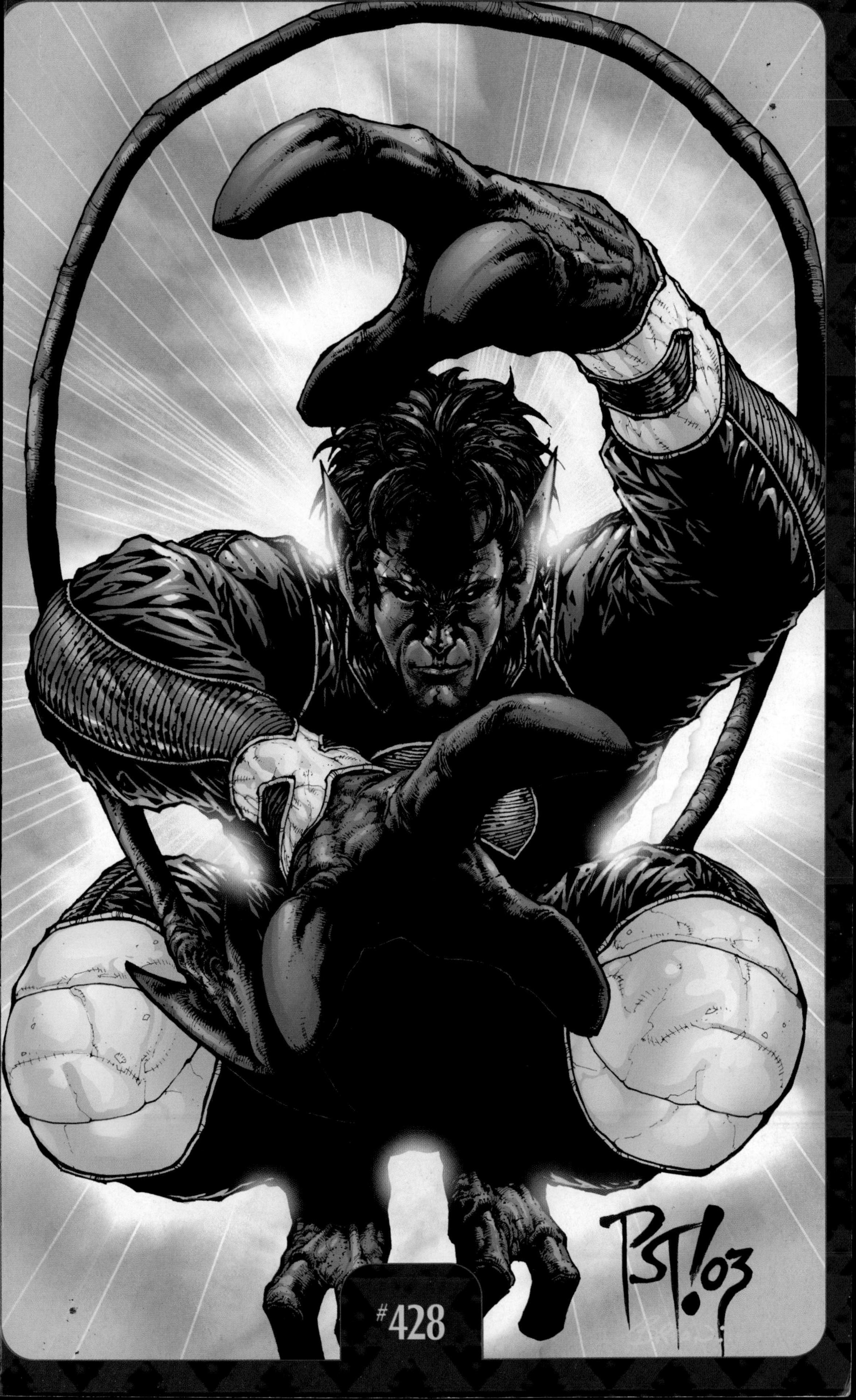
#428

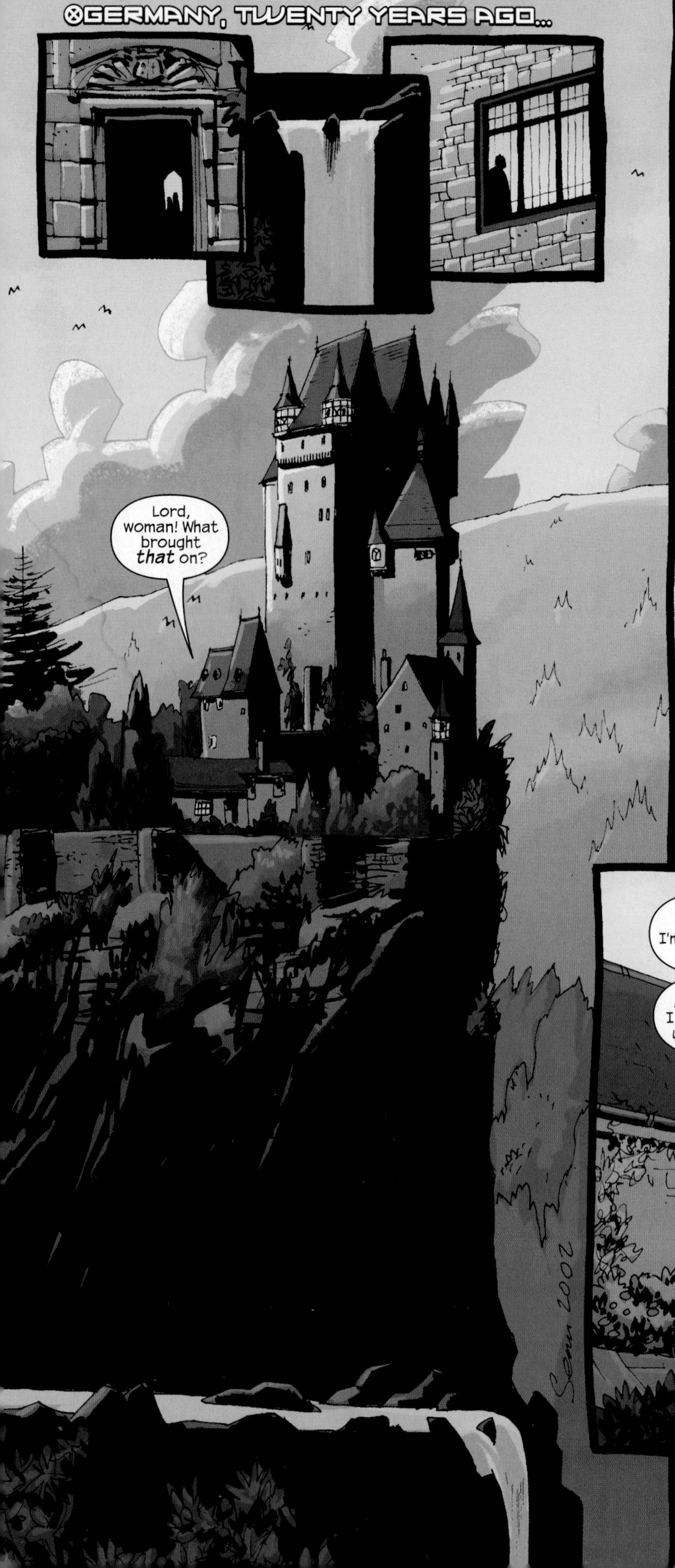

GERMANY, TWENTY YEARS AGO...
Lord, woman! What brought *that* on?
Seán 2002

How Did I Get Here?

A prelude to The DRACO

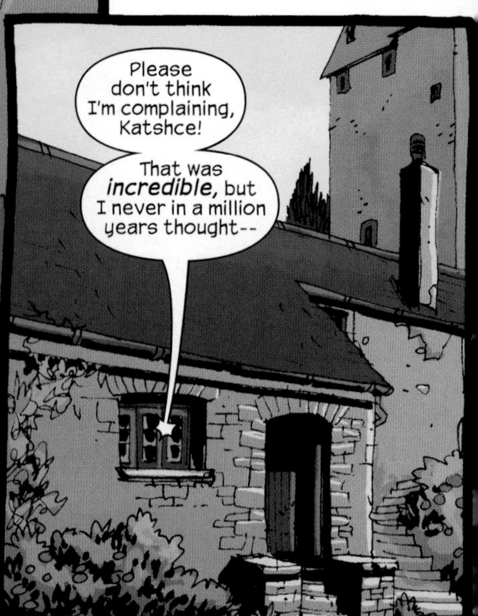

Please don't think I'm complaining, Katshce!
That was *incredible*, but I never in a million years thought--

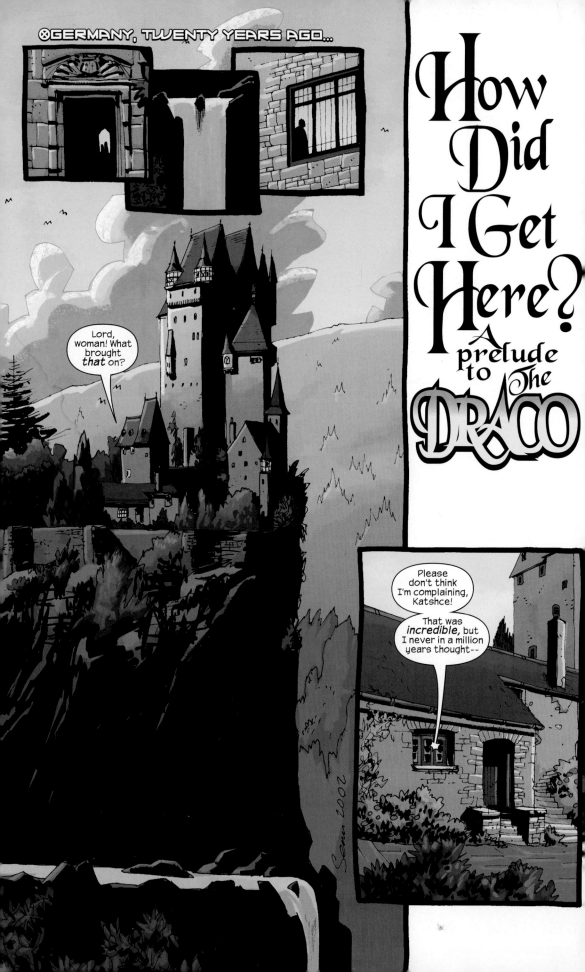

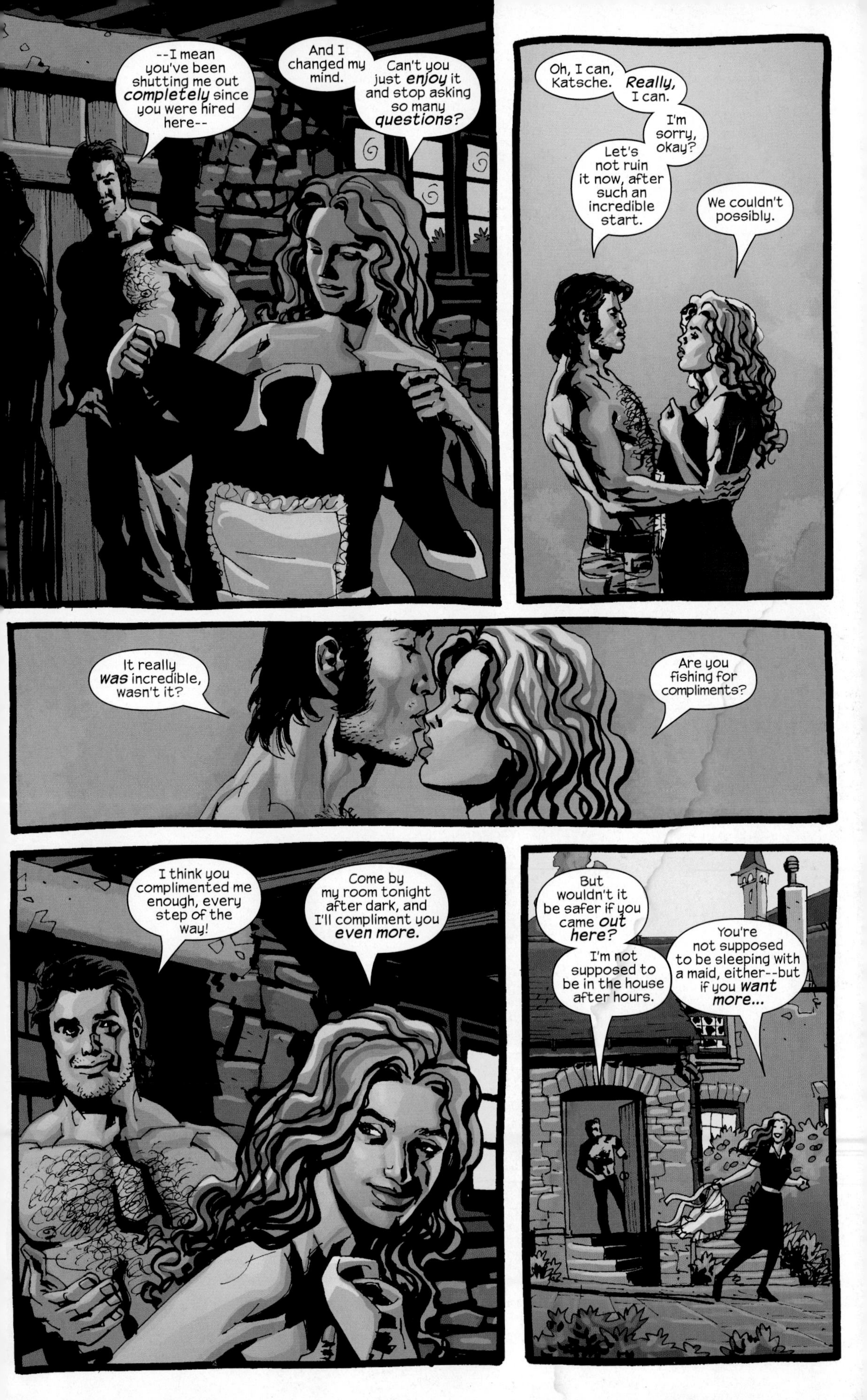
--I mean you've been shutting me out *completely* since you were hired here--
And I changed my mind.
Can't you just *enjoy* it and stop asking so many *questions?*
Oh, I can, Katsche. *Really,* I can.
I'm sorry, okay?
Let's not ruin it now, after such an incredible start.
We couldn't possibly.
It really *was* incredible, wasn't it?
Are you fishing for compliments?
I think you complimented me enough, every step of the way!
Come by my room tonight after dark, and I'll compliment you *even more.*
But wouldn't it be safer if you came *out here?*
I'm not supposed to be in the house after hours.
You're not supposed to be sleeping with a maid, either--but if you *want more...*

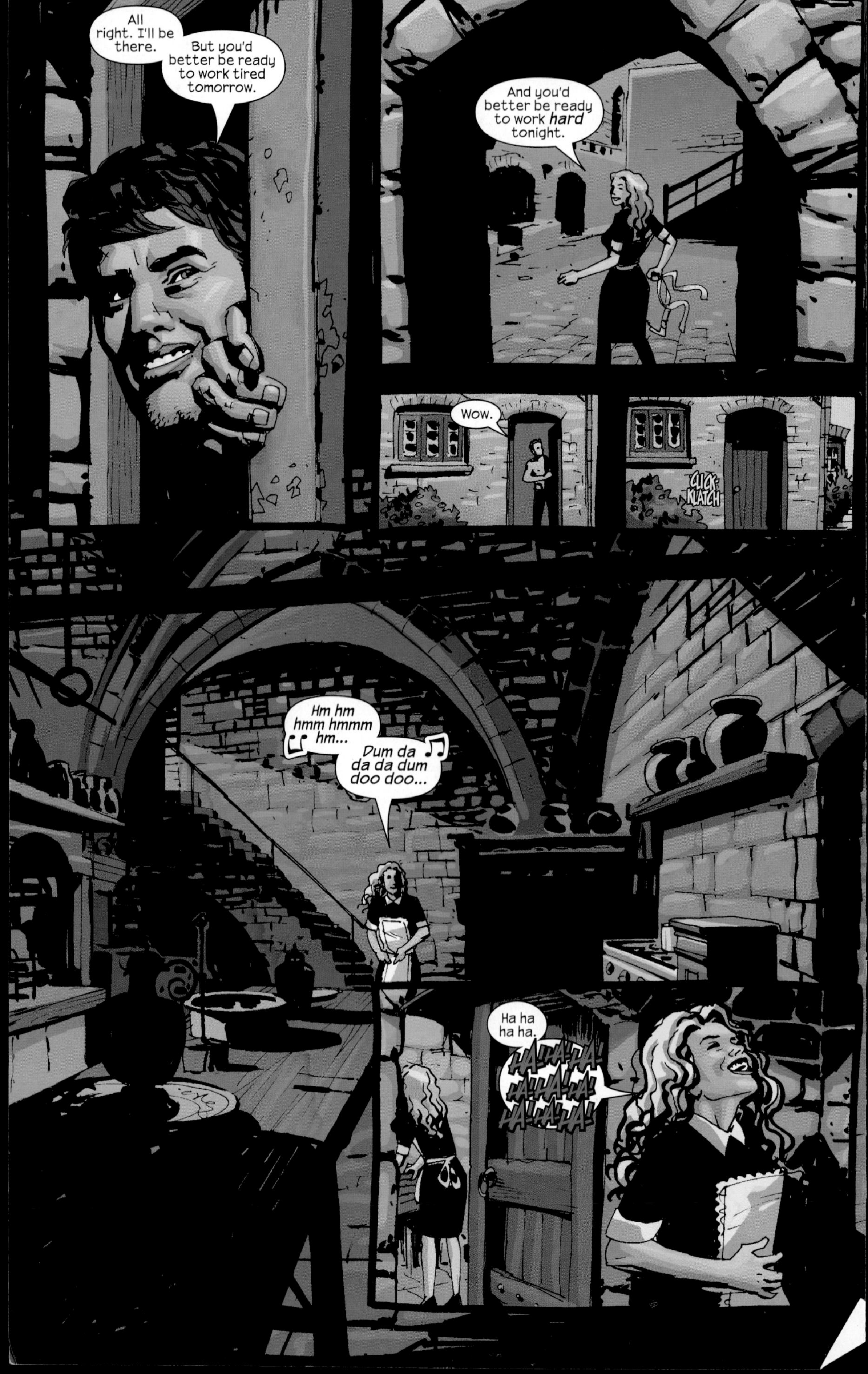
All right. I'll be there.
But you'd better be ready to work tired tomorrow.
And you'd better be ready to work *hard* tonight.
Wow.
CLICK-KLATCH
Hm hm hmm hmmm hm...
Dum da da da dum doo doo...
Ha ha ha ha.
HA! HA-HA! HA! HA-HA! HA! HA-HA!

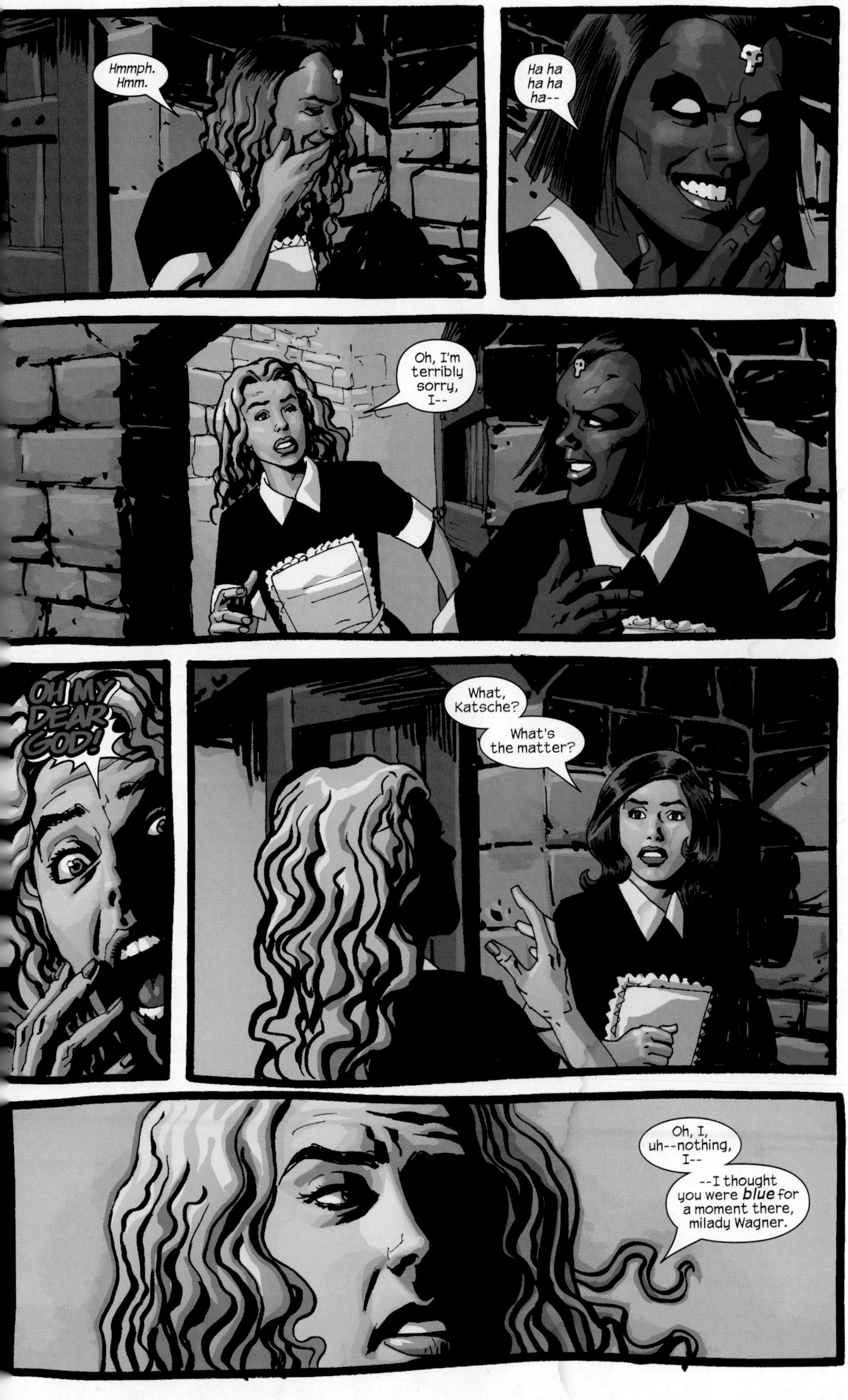
Hmmph. Hmm.
Ha ha ha ha ha--
Oh, I'm terribly sorry, I--
OH MY DEAR GOD!
What, Katsche?
What's the matter?
Oh, I, uh--nothing, I--
--I thought you were *blue* for a moment there, milady Wagner.

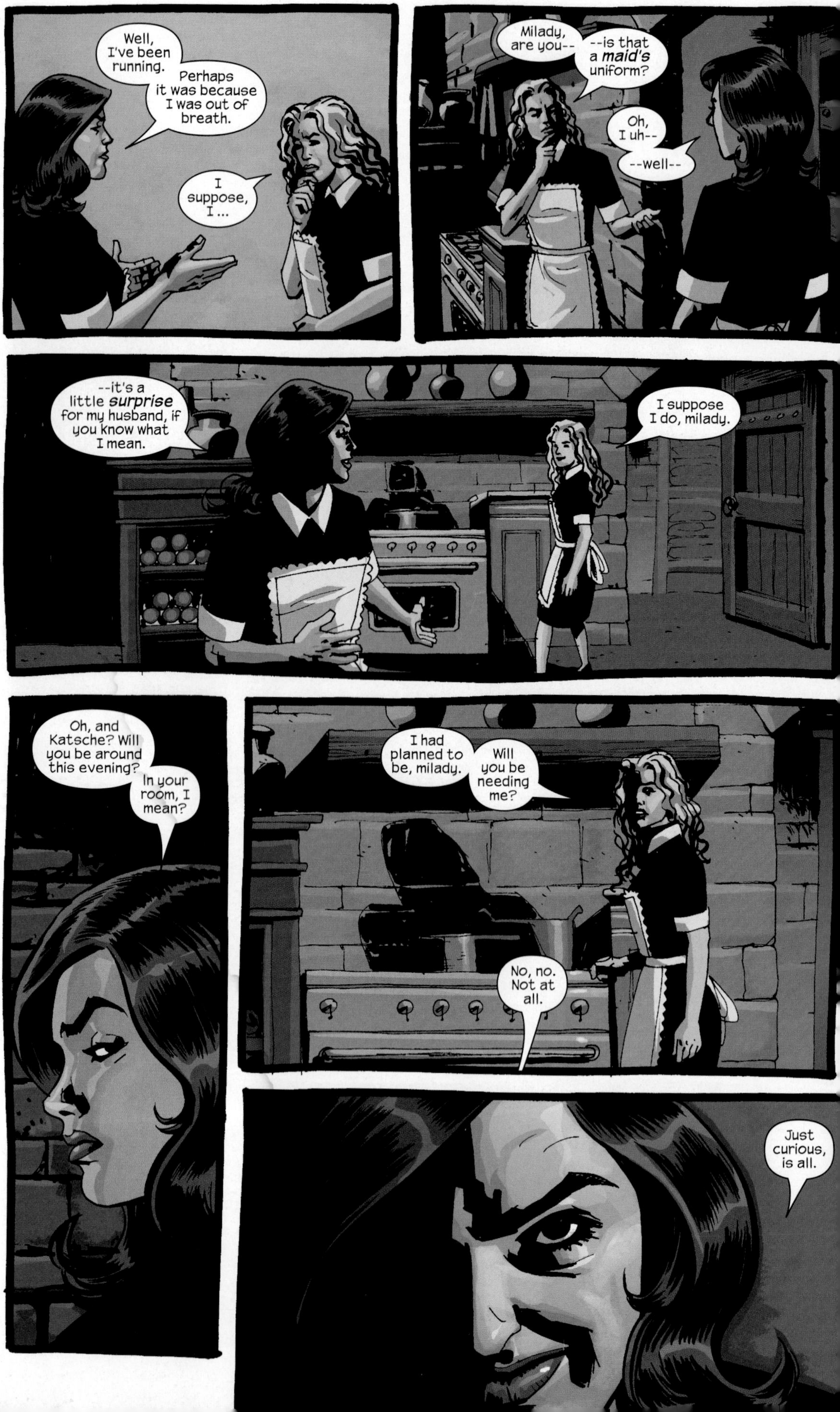
Well, I've been running.
Perhaps it was because I was out of breath.
I suppose, I...
Milady, are you--
--is that a *maid's* uniform?
Oh, I uh--
--well--
--it's a little *surprise* for my husband, if you know what I mean.
I suppose I do, milady.
Oh, and Katsche? Will you be around this evening?
In your room, I mean?
I had planned to be, milady.
Will you be needing me?
No, no. Not at all.
Just curious, is all.

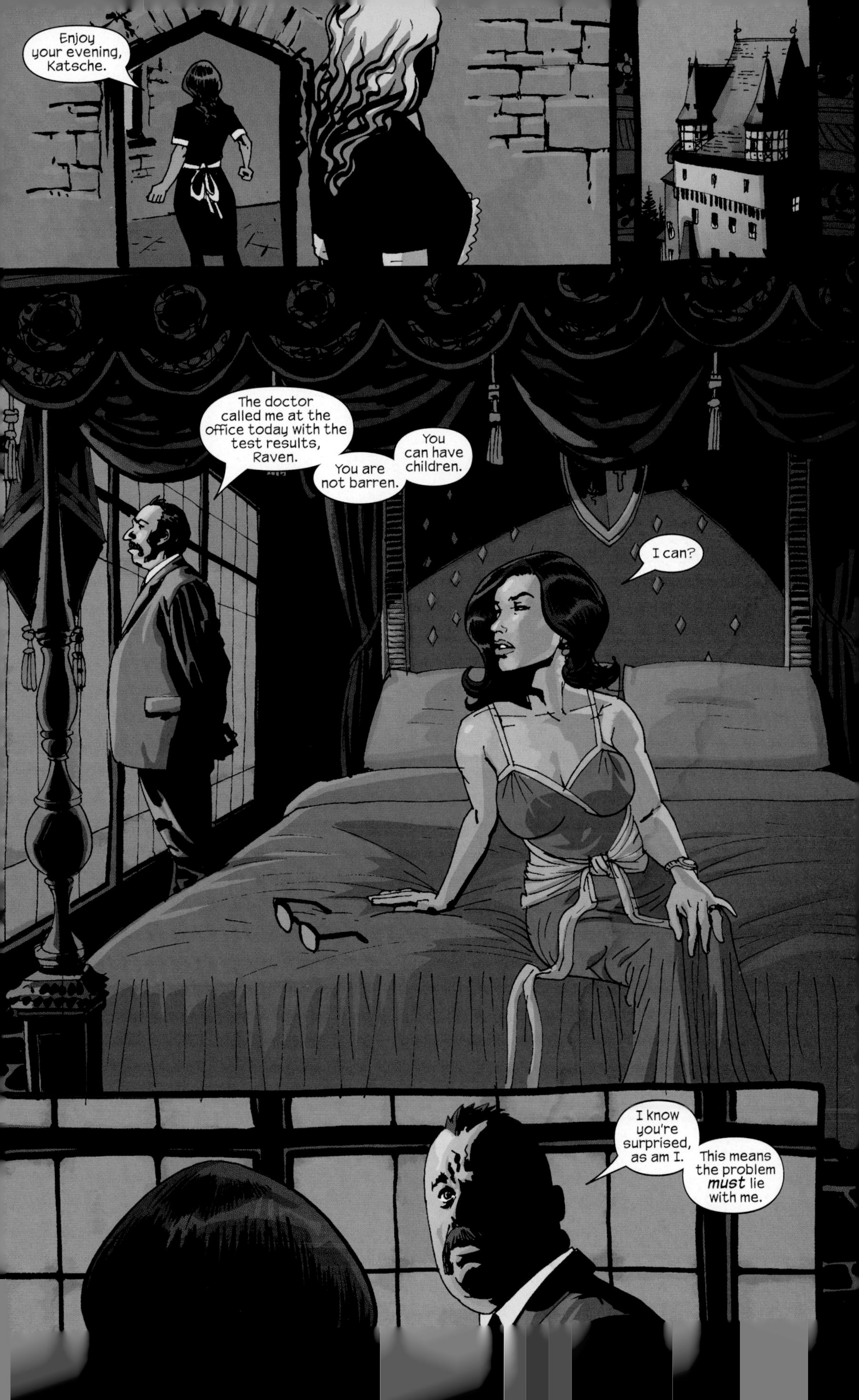

Enjoy your evening, Katsche.
The doctor called me at the office today with the test results, Raven.
You are not barren.
You can have children.
I can?
I know you're surprised, as am I.
This means the problem *must* lie with me.

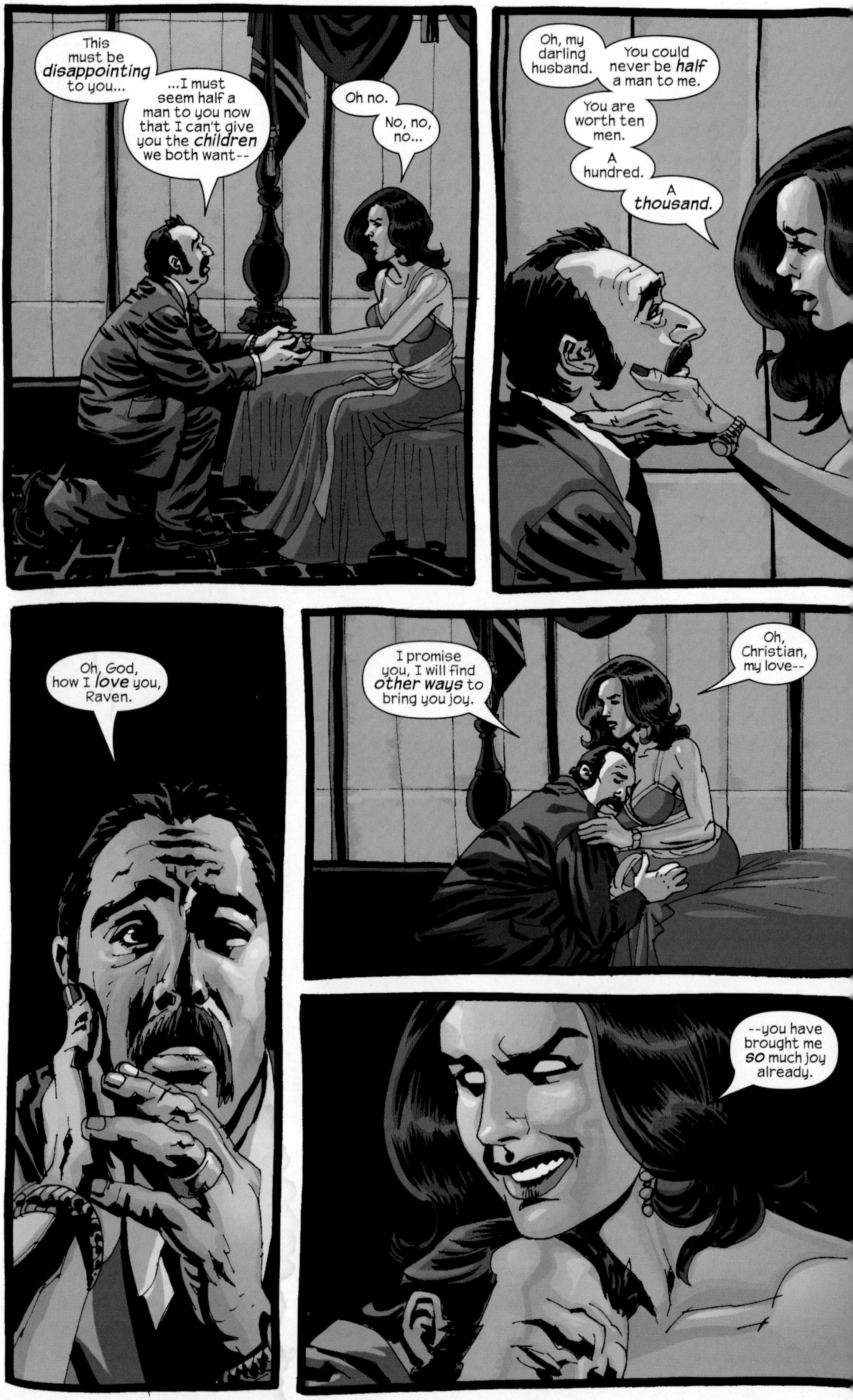
This must be *disappointing* to you...
...I must seem half a man to you now that I can't give you the *children* we both want--
Oh no.
No, no, no...
Oh, my darling husband.
You could never be *half* a man to me.
You are worth ten men.
A hundred.
A *thousand.*
Oh, God, how I *love* you, Raven.
I promise you, I will find *other ways* to bring you joy.
Oh, Christian, my love--
--you have brought me *so* much joy already.

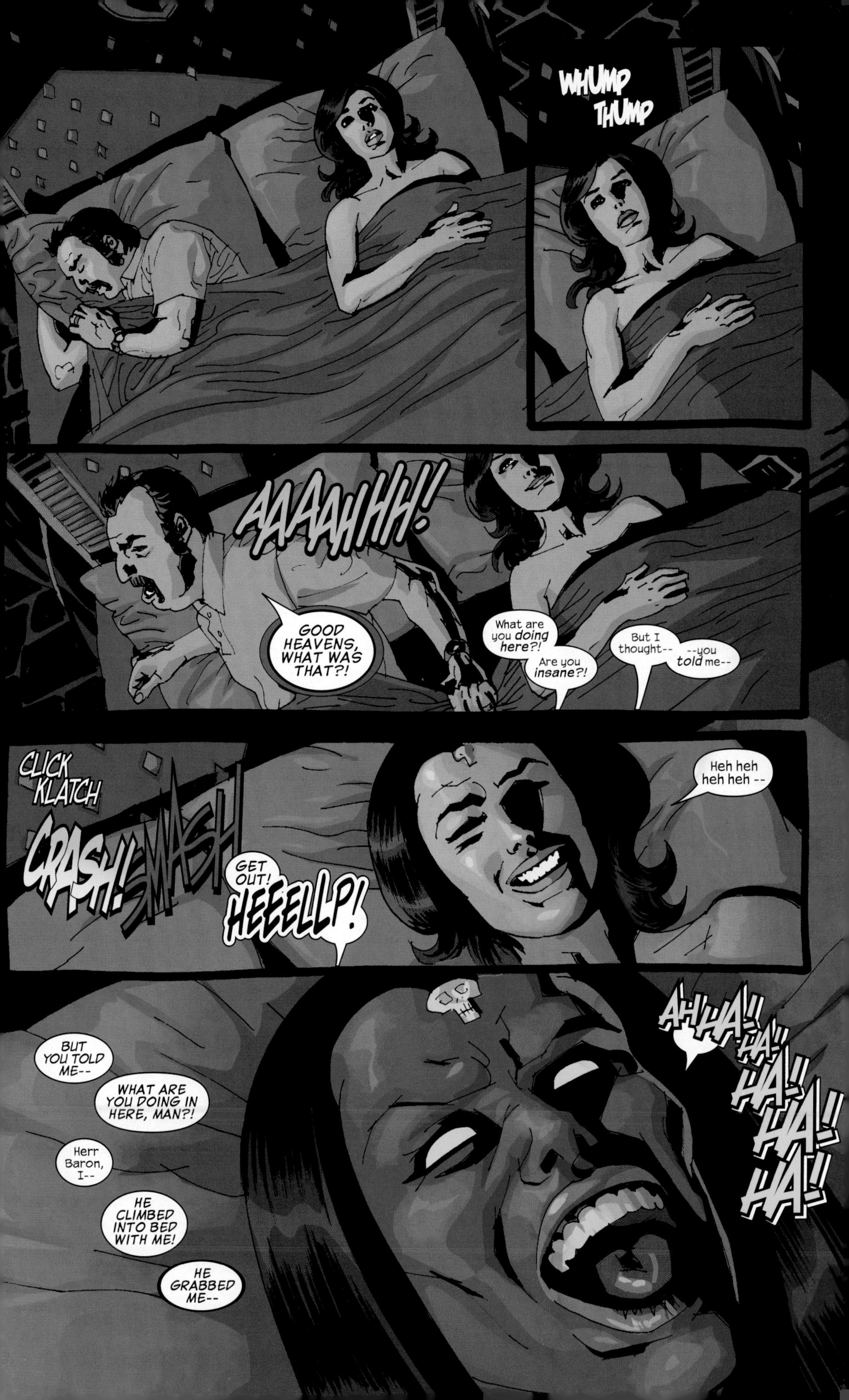
WHUMP
THUMP
AAAAHHH!
GOOD HEAVENS, WHAT WAS THAT?!
What are you doing here?!
Are you insane?!
But I thought--
--you told me--
CLICK
KLATCH
CRASH! SMASH
GET OUT! HEEELLP!
Heh heh heh heh --
AH HA! HA! HA! HA! HA!
BUT YOU TOLD ME--
WHAT ARE YOU DOING IN HERE, MAN?!
Herr Baron, I--
HE CLIMBED INTO BED WITH ME!
HE GRABBED ME--

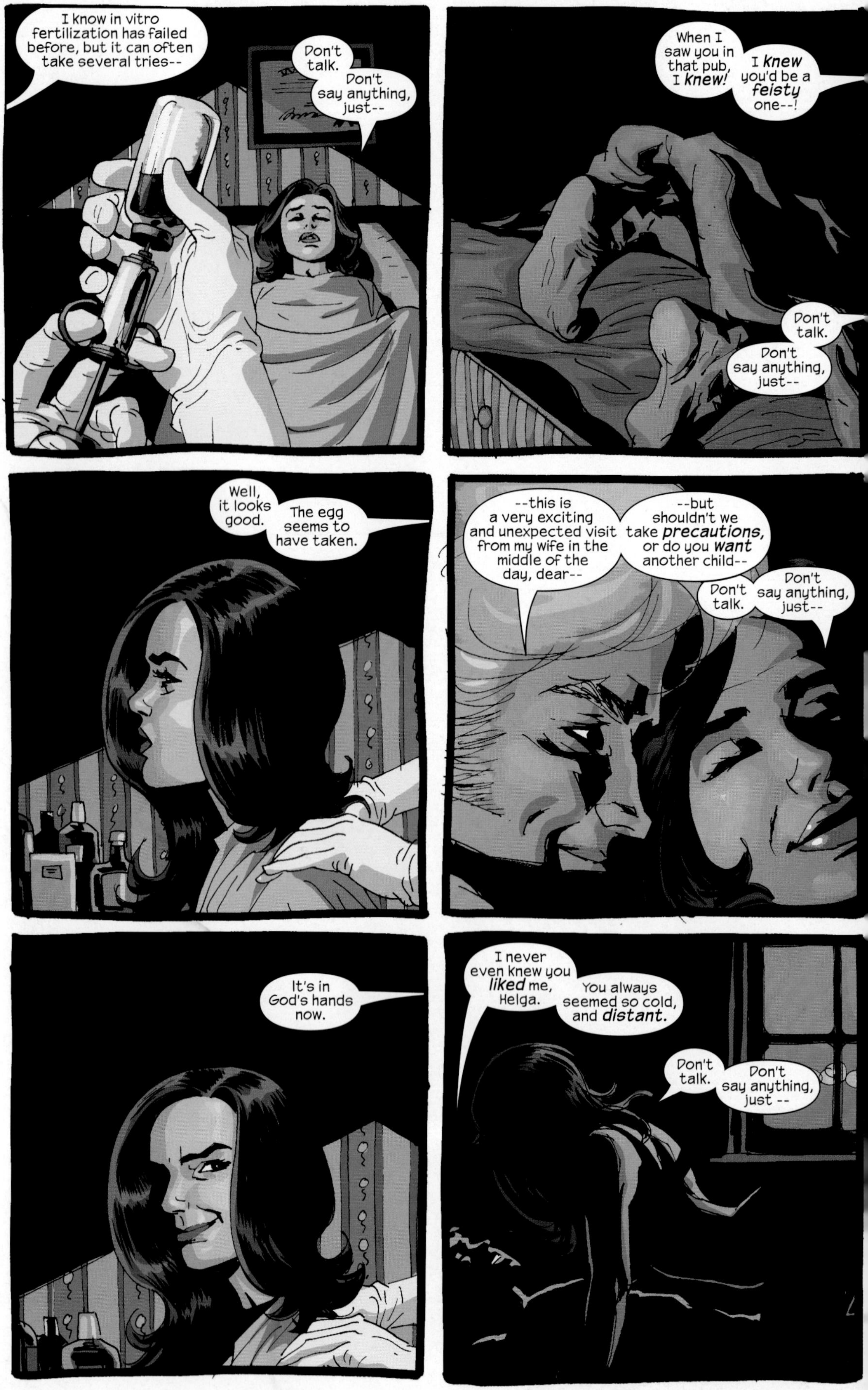
I know in vitro fertilization has failed before, but it can often take several tries--
Don't talk.
Don't say anything, just--
When I saw you in that pub, I *knew!*
I *knew* you'd be a *feisty* one--!
Don't talk.
Don't say anything, just--
Well, it looks good.
The egg seems to have taken.
--this is a very exciting and unexpected visit from my wife in the middle of the day, dear--
--but shouldn't we take *precautions,* or do you *want* another child--
Don't talk.
Don't say anything, just--
It's in God's hands now.
I never even knew you *liked* me, Helga.
You always seemed so cold, and *distant.*
Don't talk.
Don't say anything, just --

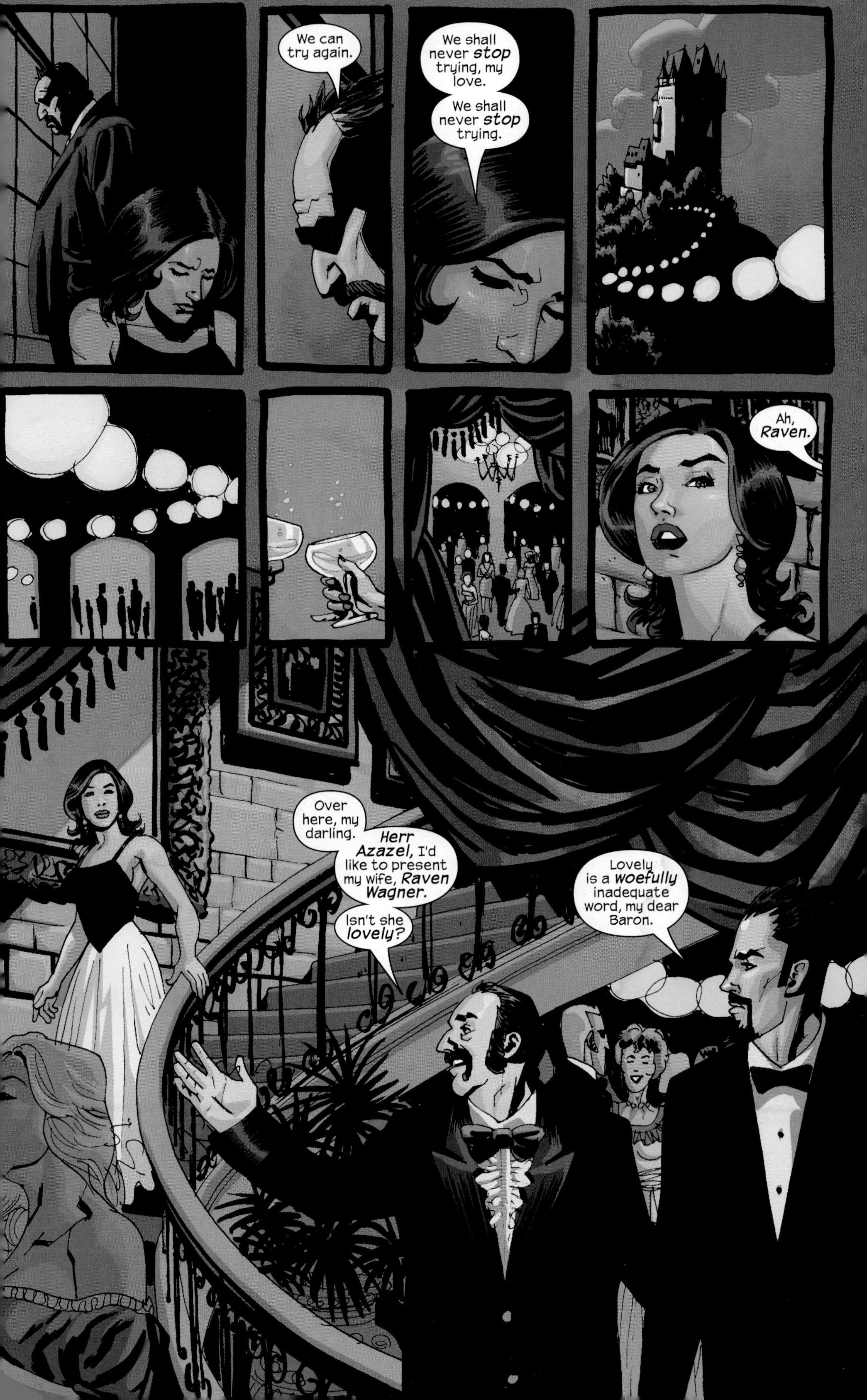
We can try again.
We shall never stop trying, my love.
We shall never stop trying.
Ah, Raven.
Over here, my darling.
Herr Azazel, I'd like to present my wife, Raven Wagner.
Isn't she lovely?
Lovely is a woefully inadequate word, my dear Baron.

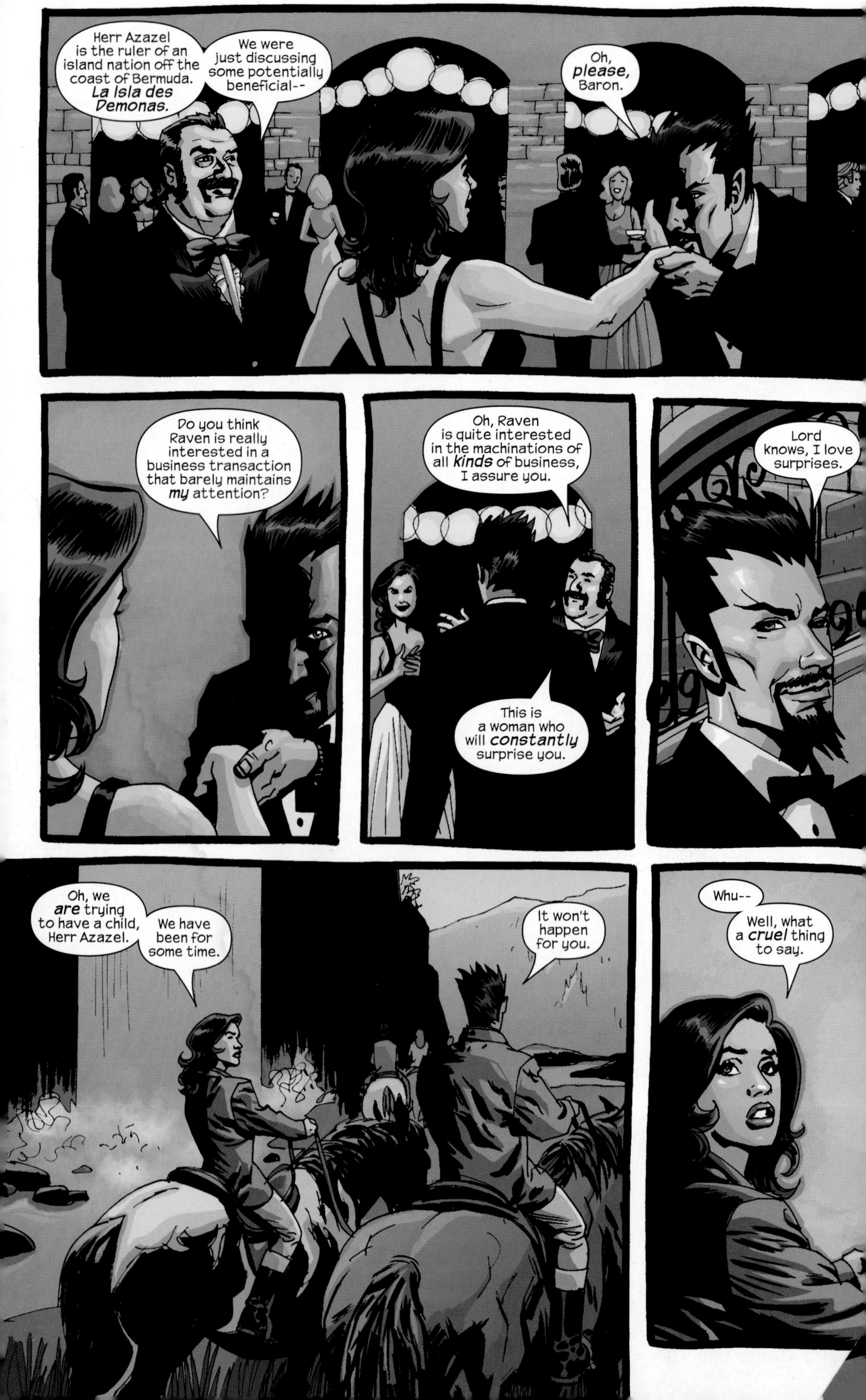
Herr Azazel is the ruler of an island nation off the coast of Bermuda. *La Isla des Demonas.*
We were just discussing some potentially beneficial--
Oh, *please,* Baron.
Do you think Raven is really interested in a business transaction that barely maintains *my* attention?
Oh, Raven is quite interested in the machinations of all *kinds* of business, I assure you.
This is a woman who will *constantly* surprise you.
Lord knows, I love surprises.
Oh, we *are* trying to have a child, Herr Azazel.
We have been for some time.
It won't happen for you.
Whu--
Well, what a *cruel* thing to say.

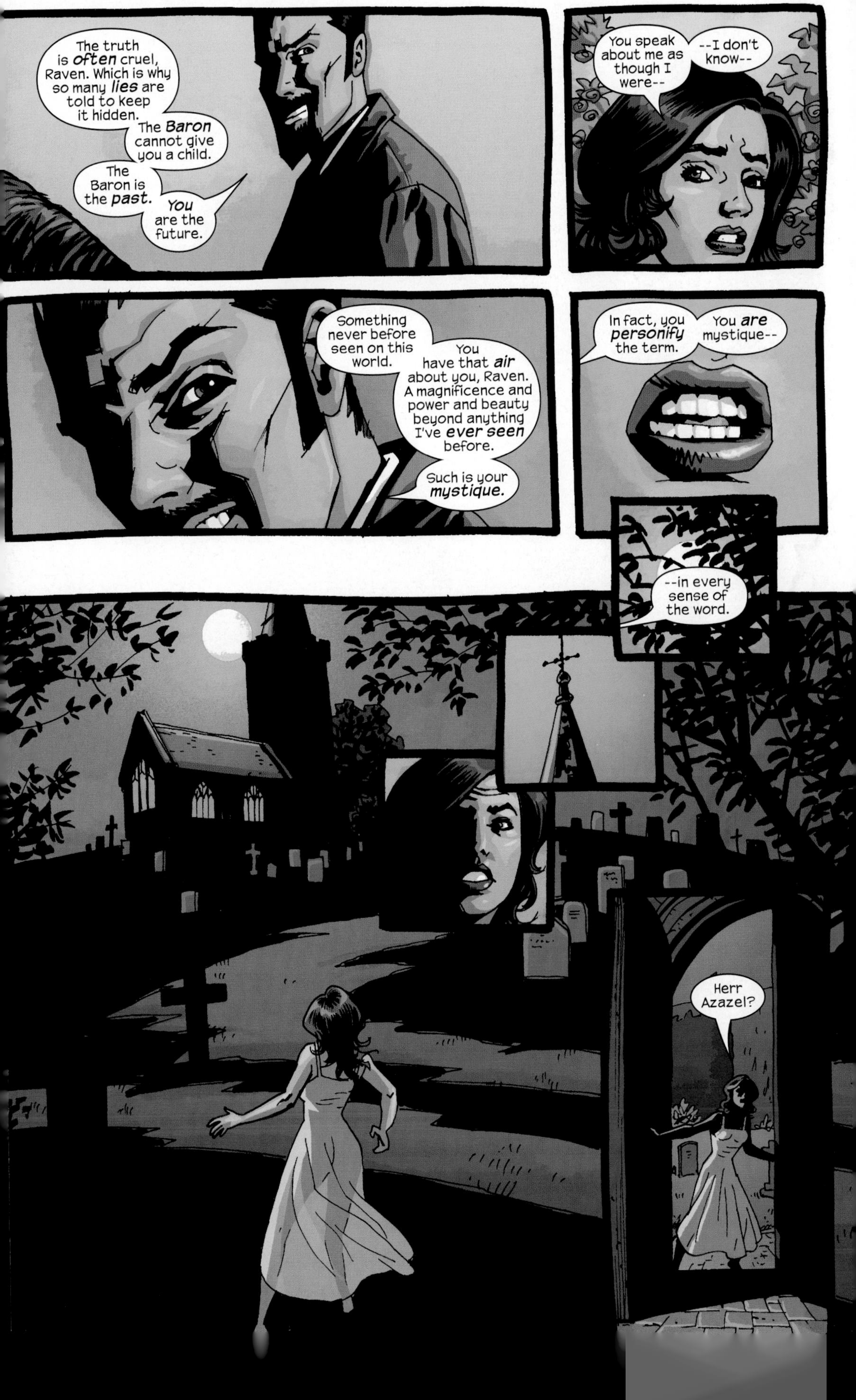
The truth is *often* cruel, Raven. Which is why so many *lies* are told to keep it hidden.
The *Baron* cannot give you a child.
The Baron is the *past.*
You are the future.
You speak about me as though I were--
--I don't know--
Something never before seen on this world.
You have that *air* about you, Raven. A magnificence and power and beauty beyond anything I've *ever seen* before.
Such is your *mystique.*
In fact, you *personify* the term.
You *are* mystique--
--in every sense of the word.
Herr Azazel?

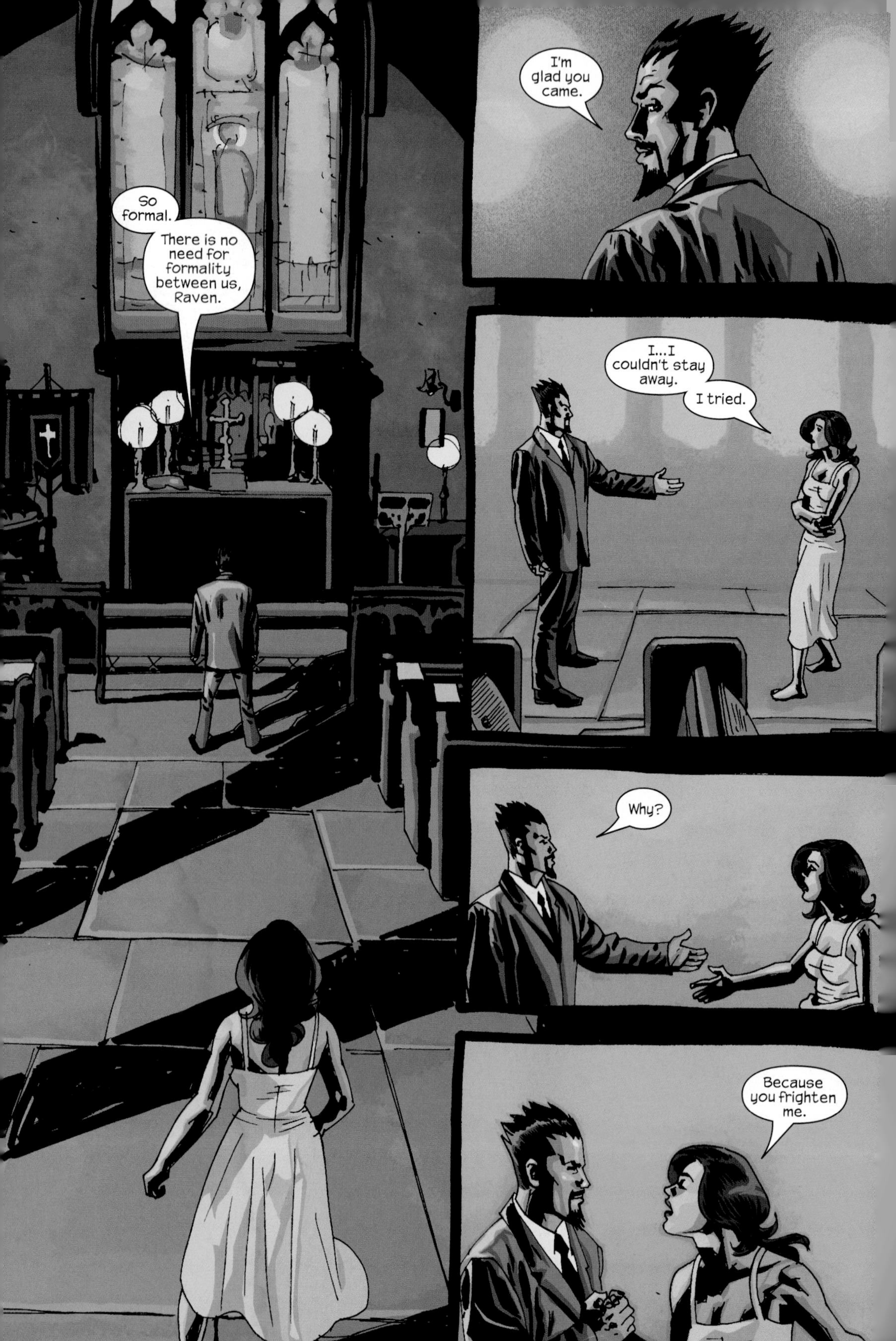
I'm glad you came.
So formal.
There is no need for formality between us, Raven.
I...I couldn't stay away.
I tried.
Why?
Because you frighten me.

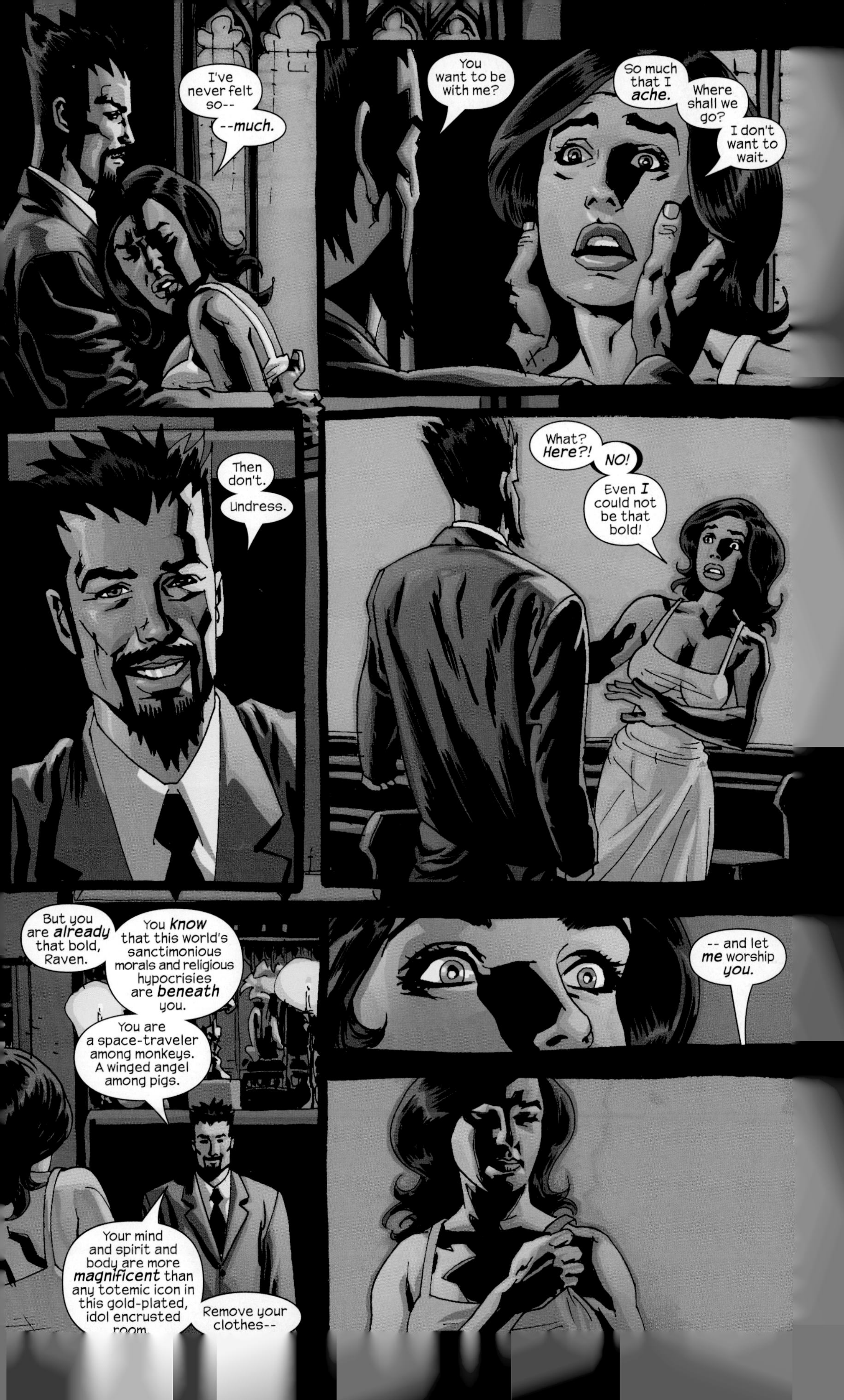

I've never felt so--
--*much.*
You want to be with me?
So much that I *ache.*
Where shall we go?
I don't want to wait.
Then don't.
Undress.
What? *Here?!*
NO!
Even *I* could not be that bold!
But you are *already* that bold, Raven.
You *know* that this world's sanctimonious morals and religious hypocrisies are *beneath* you.
You are a space-traveler among monkeys. A winged angel among pigs.
Your mind and spirit and body are more *magnificent* than any totemic icon in this gold-plated, idol encrusted room.
Remove your clothes--
-- and let *me* worship *you.*

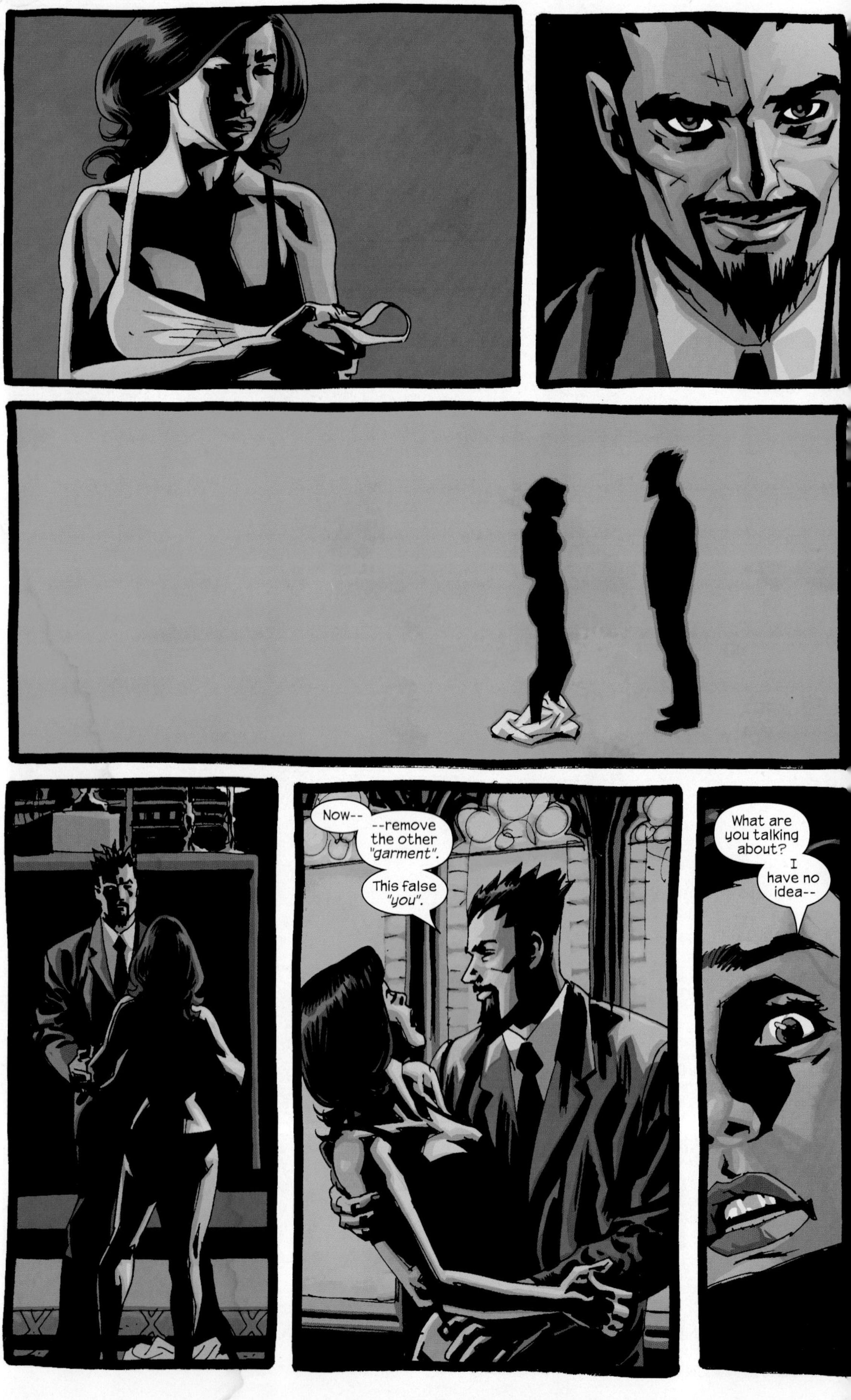
Now--
--remove the other "garment".
This false "you".
What are you talking about?
I have no idea--

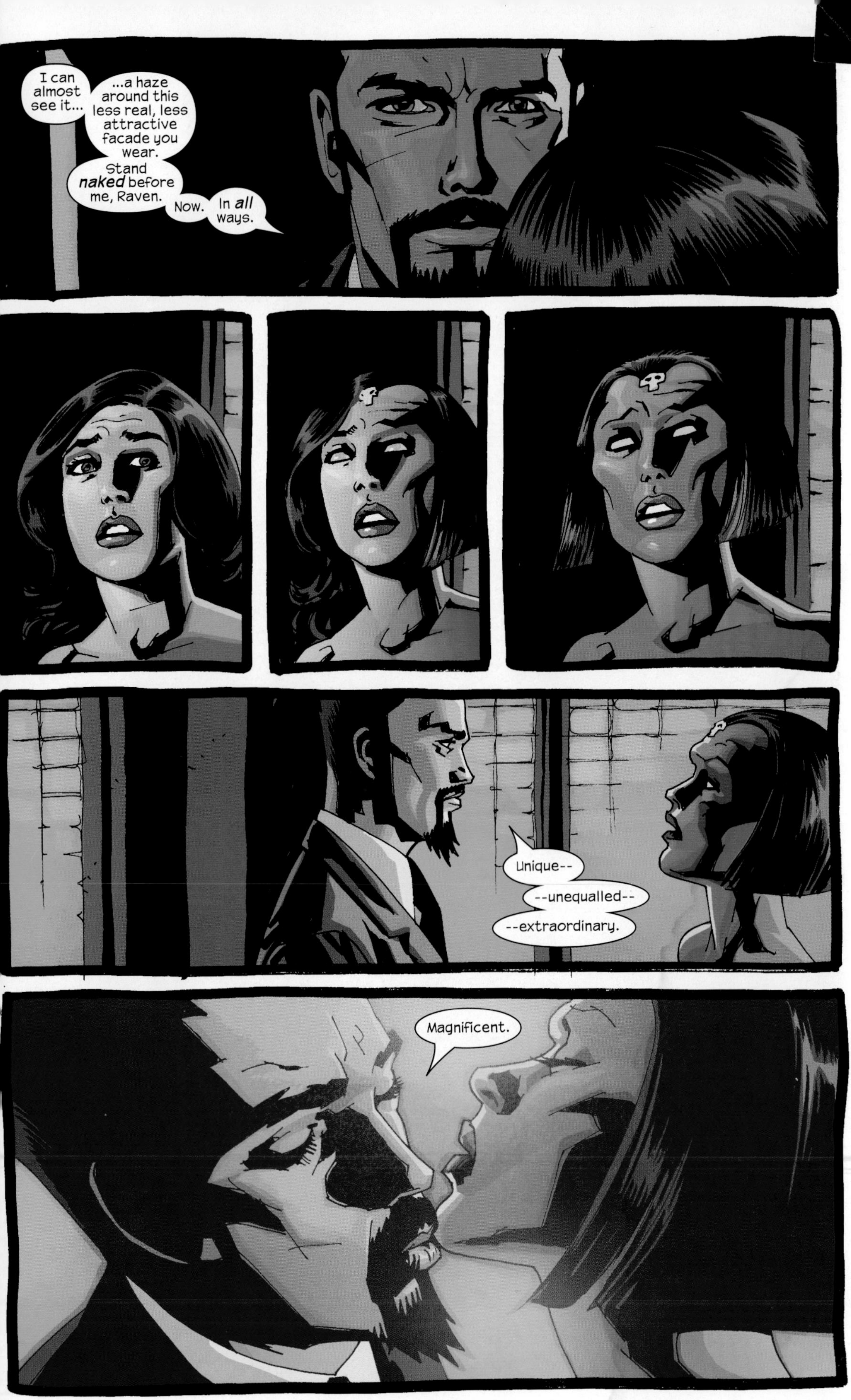
I can almost see it...
...a haze around this less real, less attractive facade you wear.
Stand *naked* before me, Raven.
Now.
In *all* ways.
Unique--
--unequalled--
--extraordinary.
Magnificent.

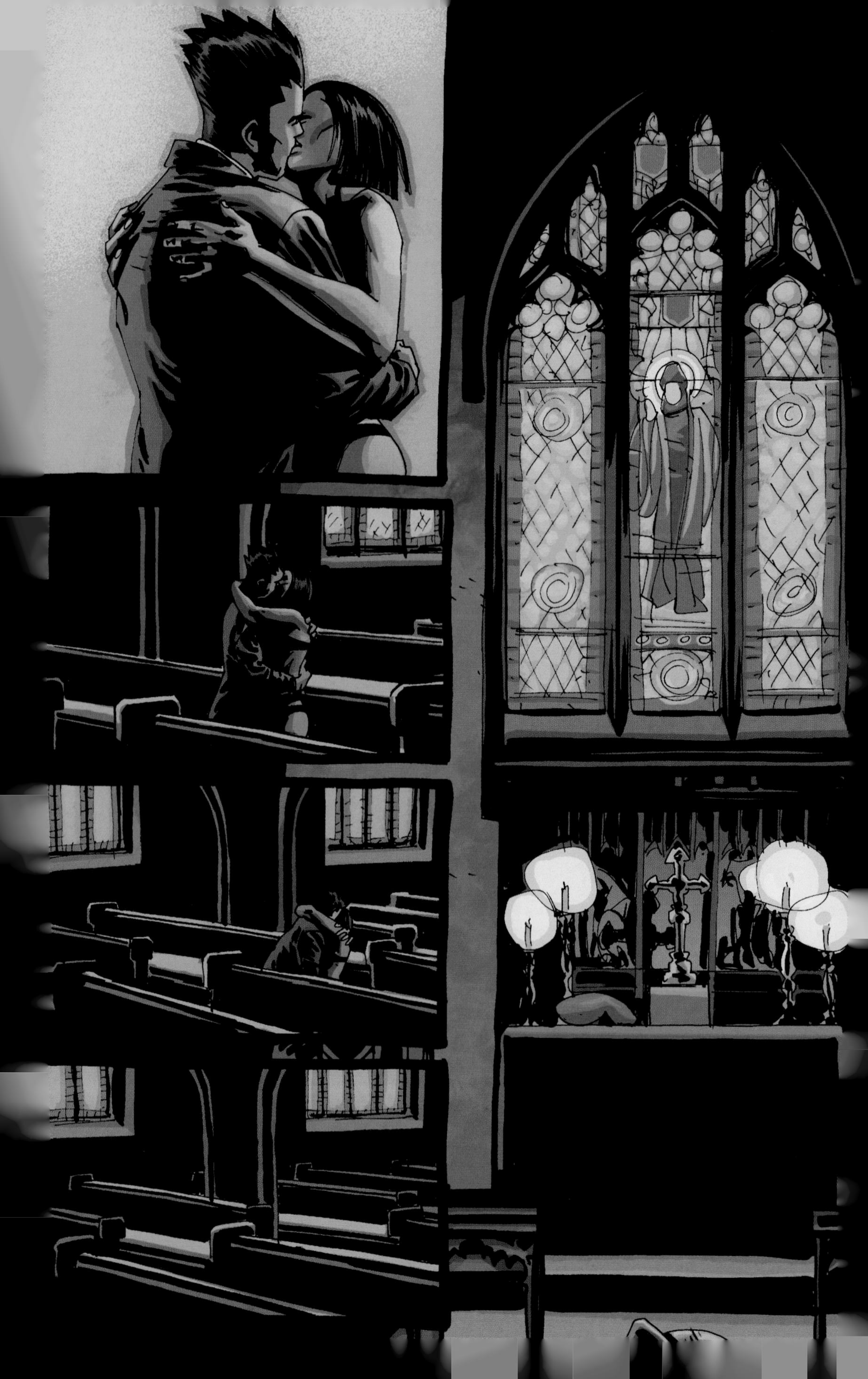

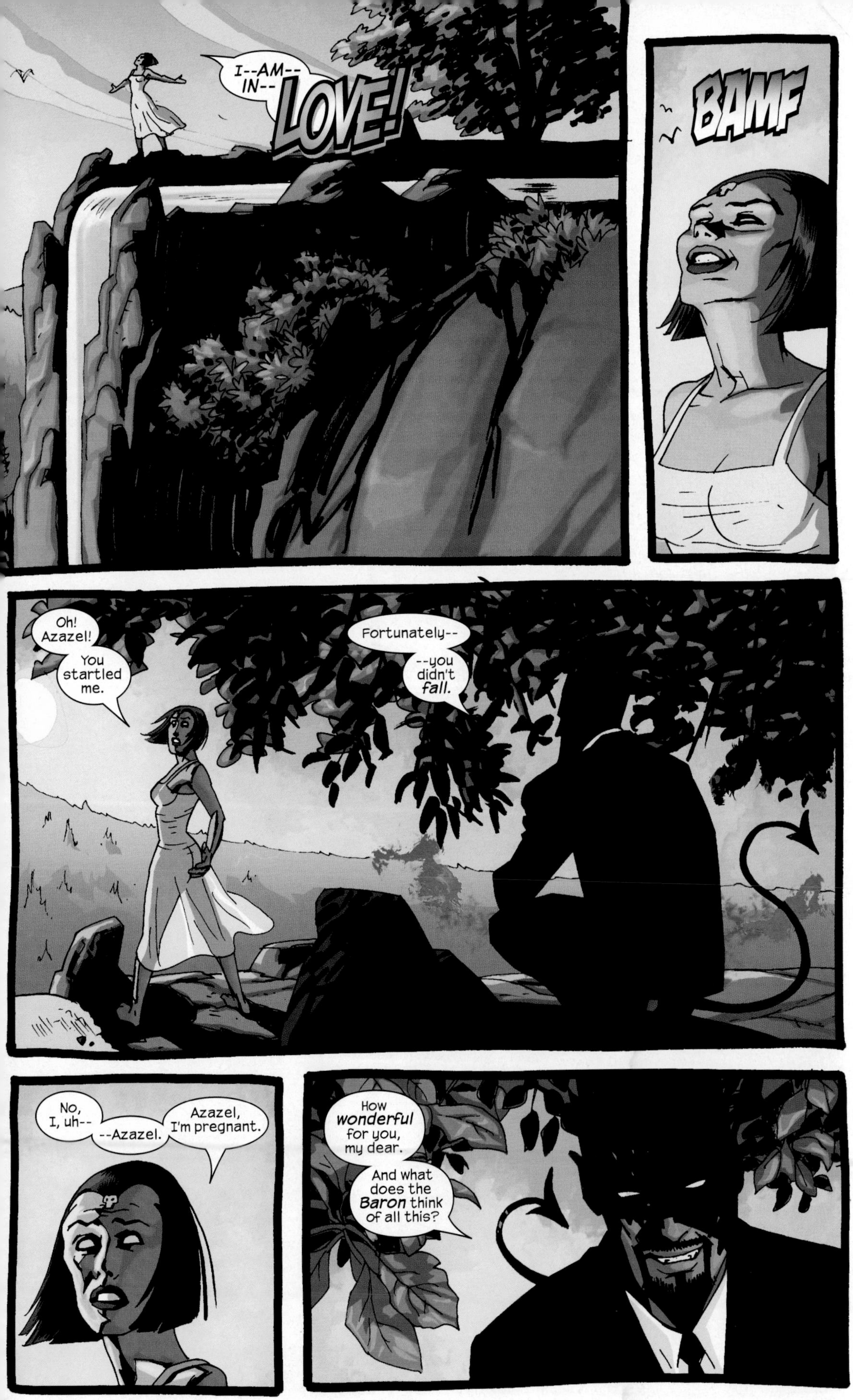

I--AM-- IN--
LOVE!
BAMF
Oh! Azazel!
You startled me.
Fortunately--
--you didn't fall.
No, I, uh--
--Azazel.
Azazel, I'm pregnant.
How wonderful for you, my dear.
And what does the Baron think of all this?

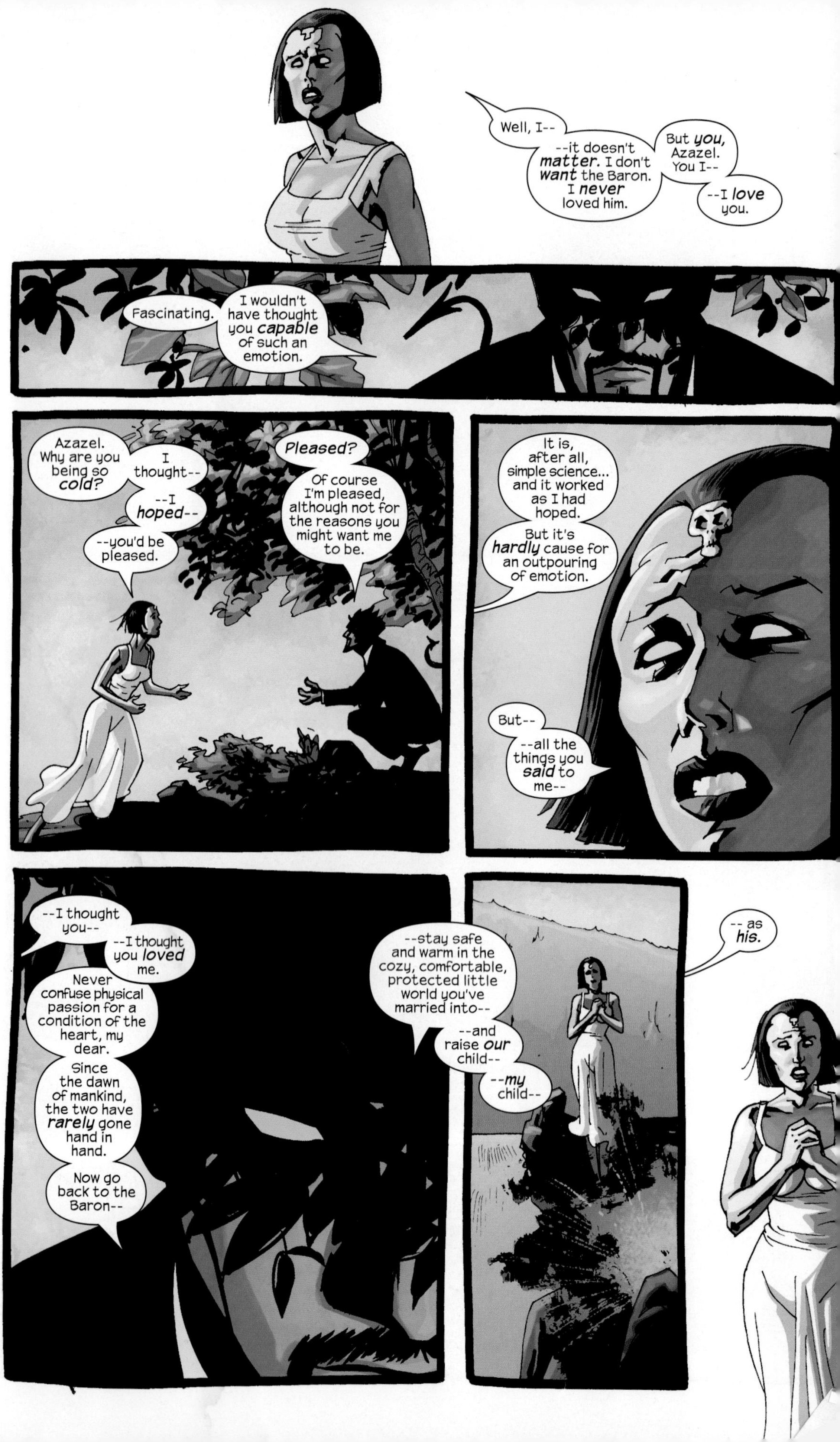
Well, I--
--it doesn't matter. I don't want the Baron. I never loved him.
But you, Azazel. You I--
--I love you.
Fascinating.
I wouldn't have thought you capable of such an emotion.
Azazel. Why are you being so cold?
I thought--
--I hoped--
--you'd be pleased.
Pleased?
Of course I'm pleased, although not for the reasons you might want me to be.
It is, after all, simple science... and it worked as I had hoped.
But it's hardly cause for an outpouring of emotion.
But--
--all the things you said to me--
--I thought you--
--I thought you loved me.
Never confuse physical passion for a condition of the heart, my dear.
Since the dawn of mankind, the two have rarely gone hand in hand.
Now go back to the Baron--
--stay safe and warm in the cozy, comfortable, protected little world you've married into--
--and raise our child--
--my child--
-- as his.

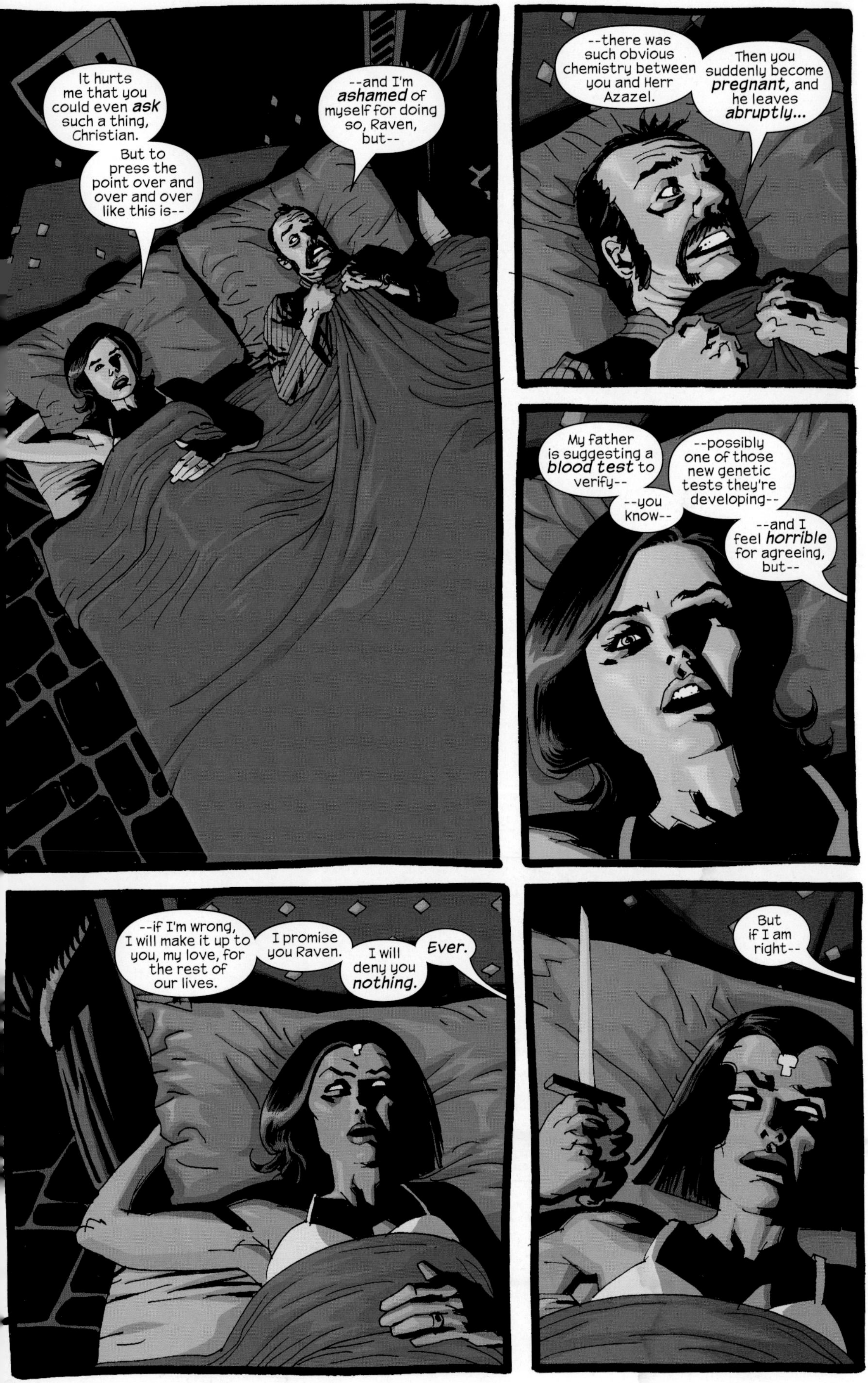
It hurts me that you could even ask such a thing, Christian.
But to press the point over and over and over like this is--
--and I'm ashamed of myself for doing so, Raven, but--
--there was such obvious chemistry between you and Herr Azazel.
Then you suddenly become pregnant, and he leaves abruptly...
My father is suggesting a blood test to verify--
--you know--
--possibly one of those new genetic tests they're developing--
--and I feel horrible for agreeing, but--
--if I'm wrong, I will make it up to you, my love, for the rest of our lives.
I promise you Raven.
I will deny you nothing.
Ever.
But if I am right--

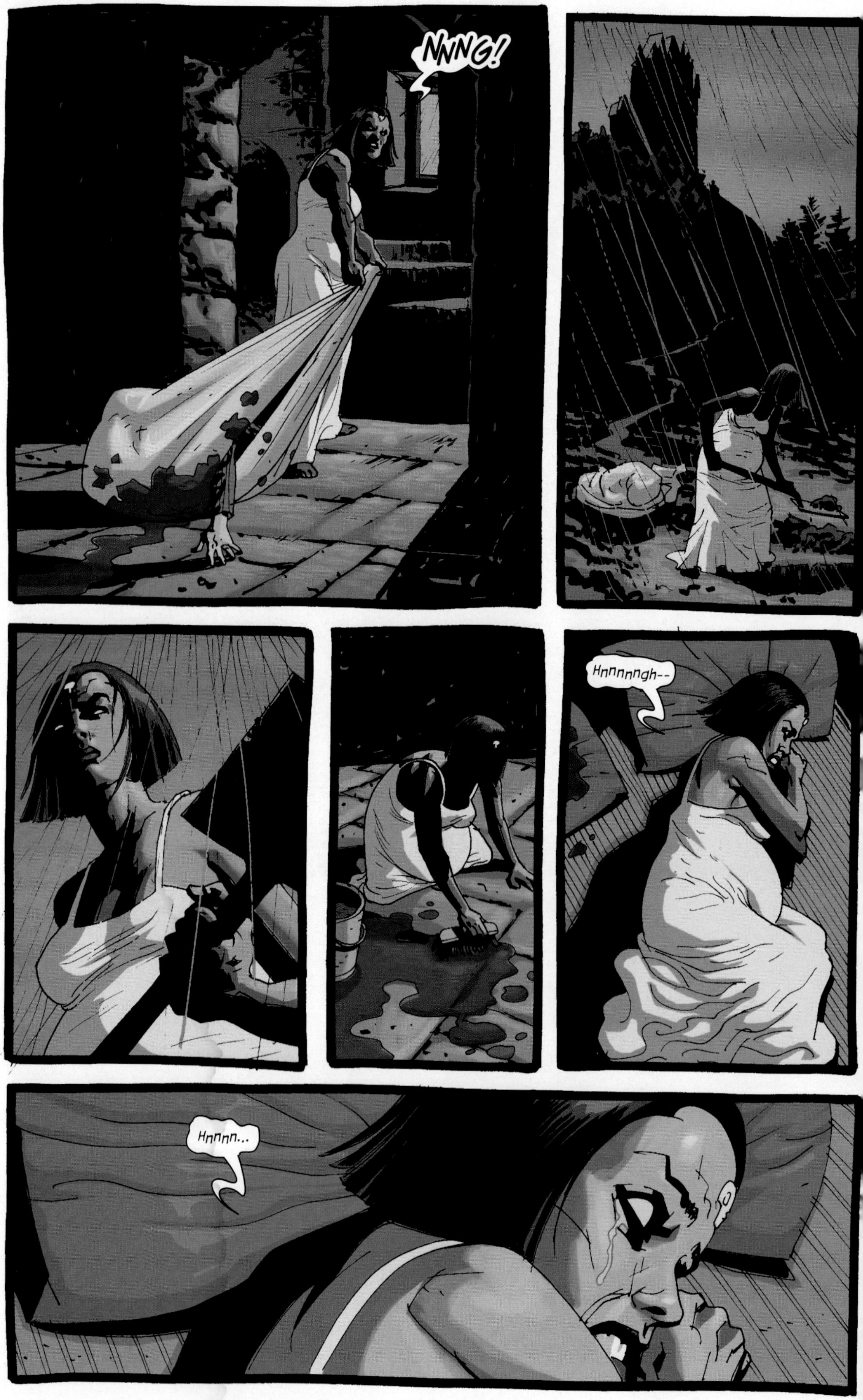
NNNG!
Hnnnnngh--
Hnnnn...

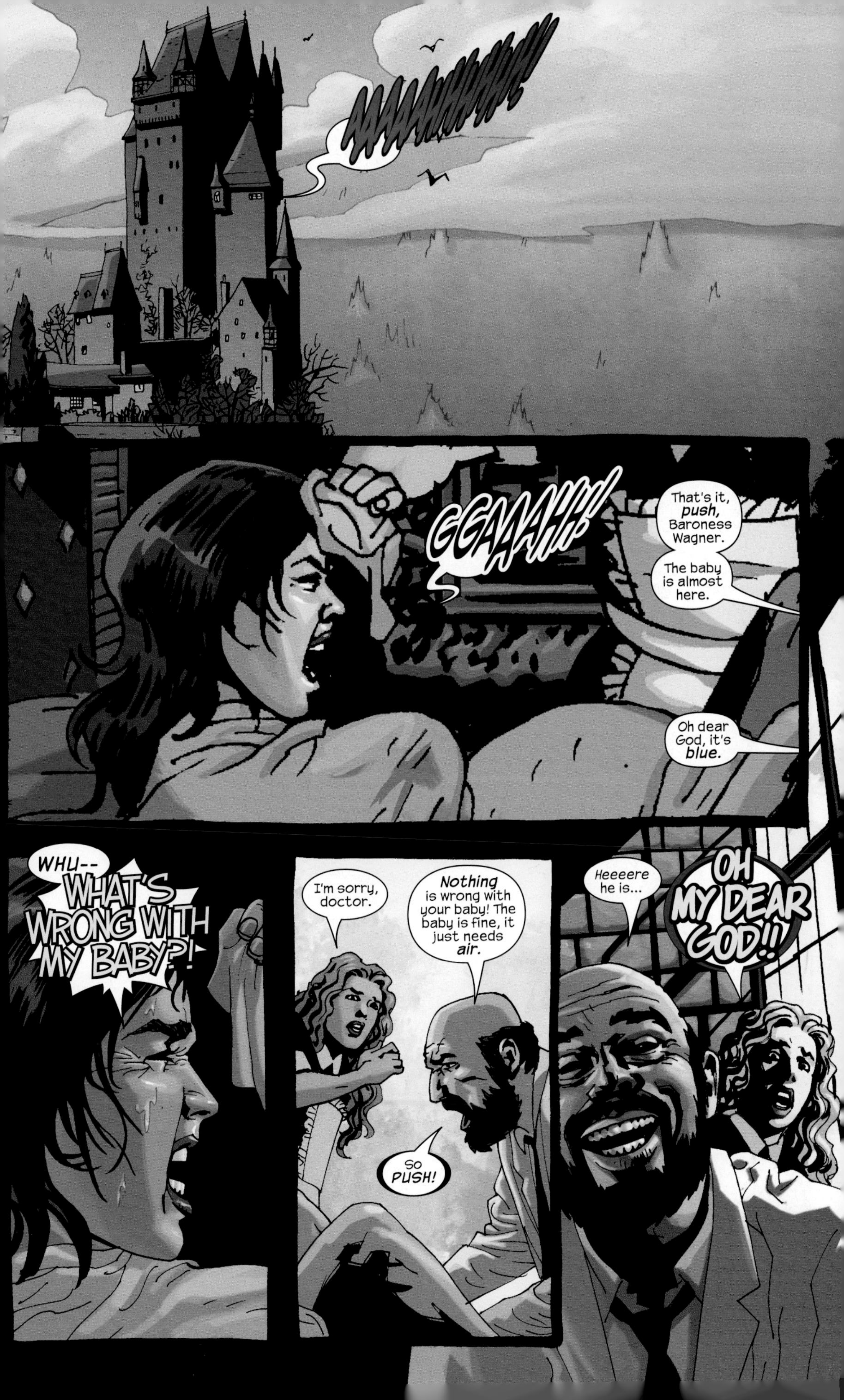
AAAAAHHHHH!!
GGAAAH!!
That's it, *push,* Baroness Wagner.
The baby is almost here.
Oh dear God, it's *blue.*
WHU-- WHAT'S WRONG WITH MY BABY?!
I'm sorry, doctor.
Nothing is wrong with your baby! The baby is fine, it just needs *air.*
SO *PUSH!*
Heeeere he is...
OH MY DEAR GOD!!

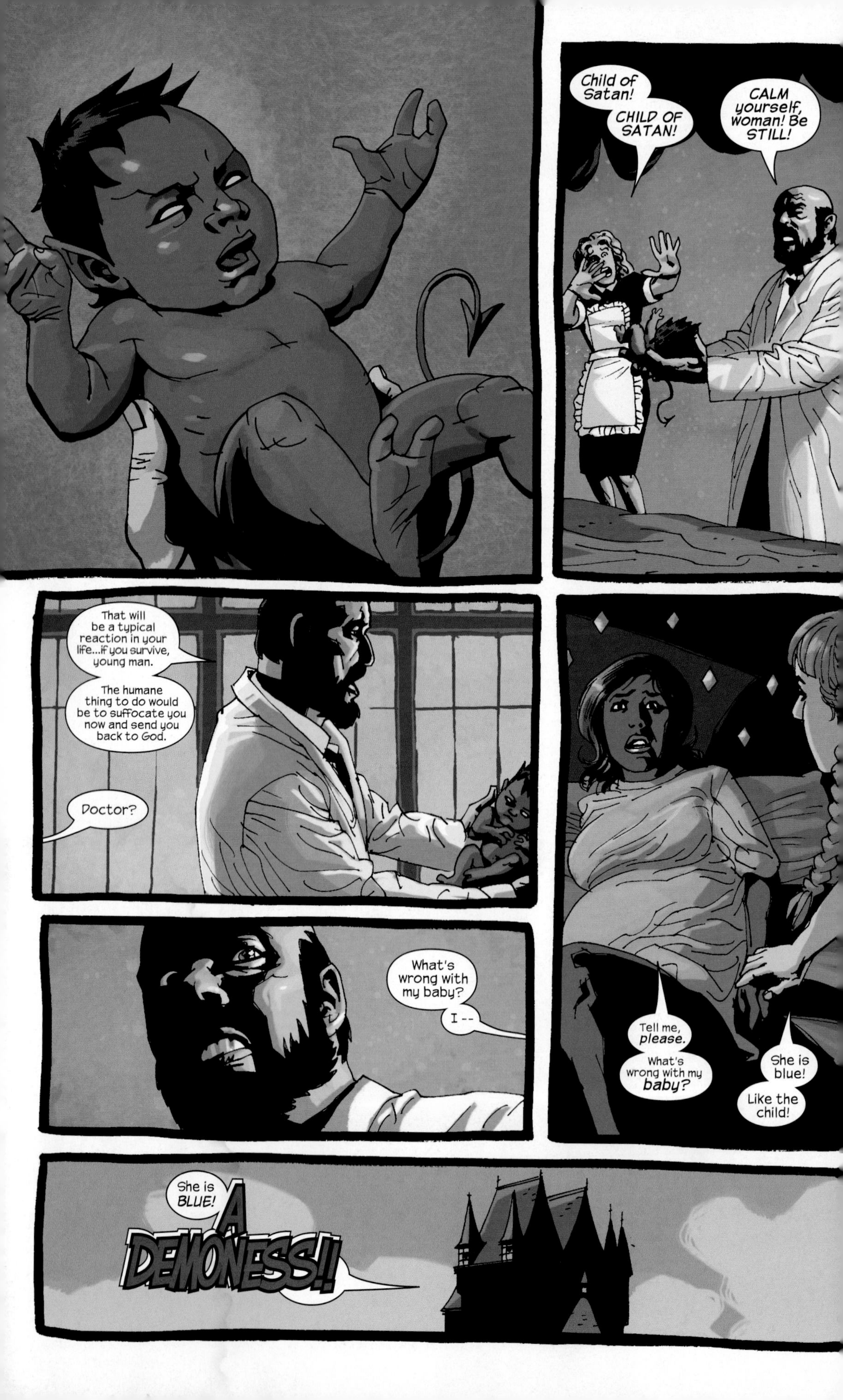
Child of Satan!
CHILD OF SATAN!
CALM yourself, woman! Be STILL!
That will be a typical reaction in your life...if you survive, young man.
The humane thing to do would be to suffocate you now and send you back to God.
Doctor?
What's wrong with my baby?
I --
Tell me, please.
What's wrong with my baby?
She is blue!
Like the child!
She is BLUE!
A DEMONESS!!

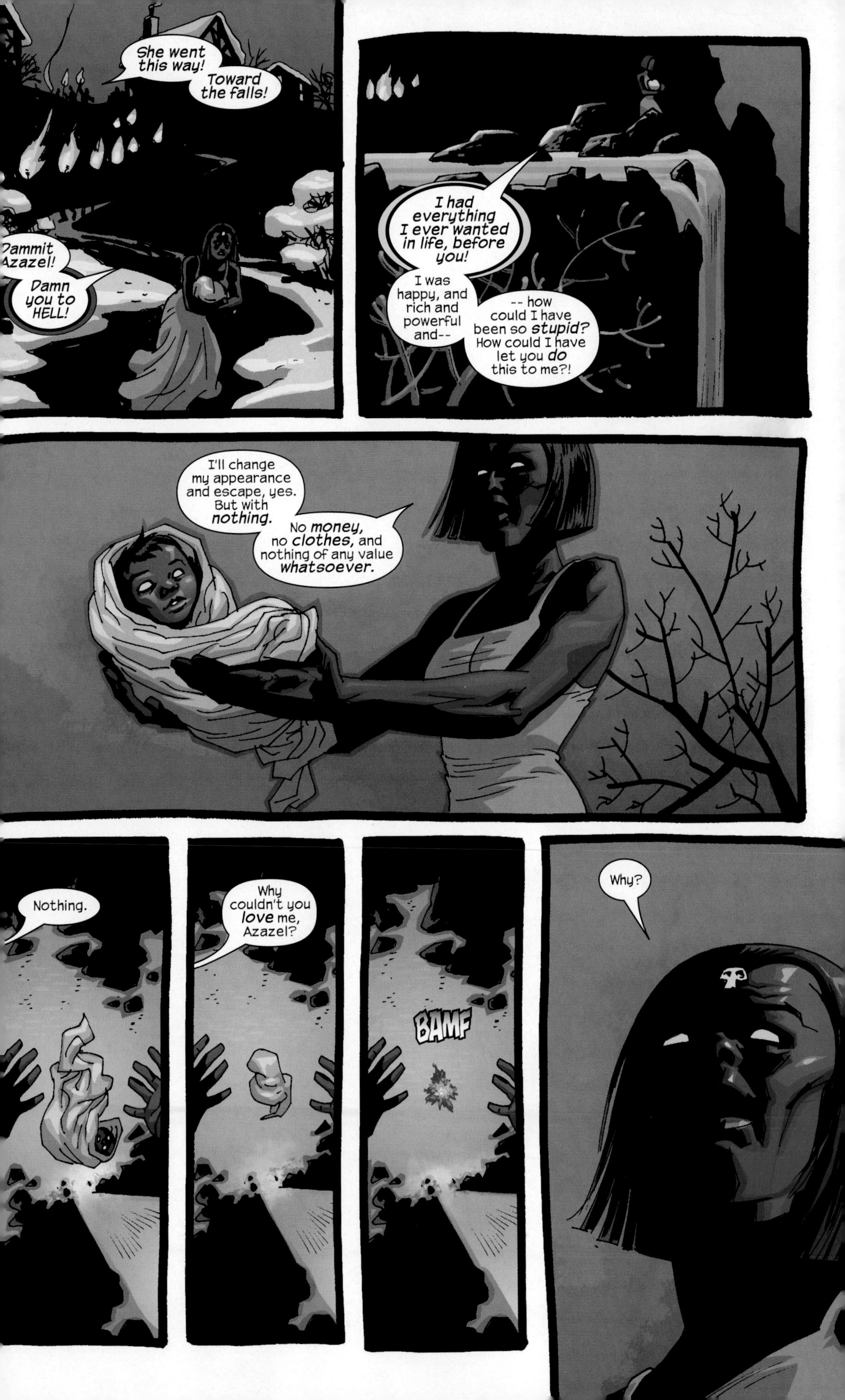
She went this way!
Toward the falls!
Dammit Azazel!
Damn you to HELL!
I had everything I ever wanted in life, before you!
I was happy, and rich and powerful and--
-- how could I have been so stupid? How could I have let you do this to me?!
I'll change my appearance and escape, yes. But with nothing.
No money, no clothes, and nothing of any value whatsoever.
Nothing.
Why couldn't you love me, Azazel?
BAMF
Why?

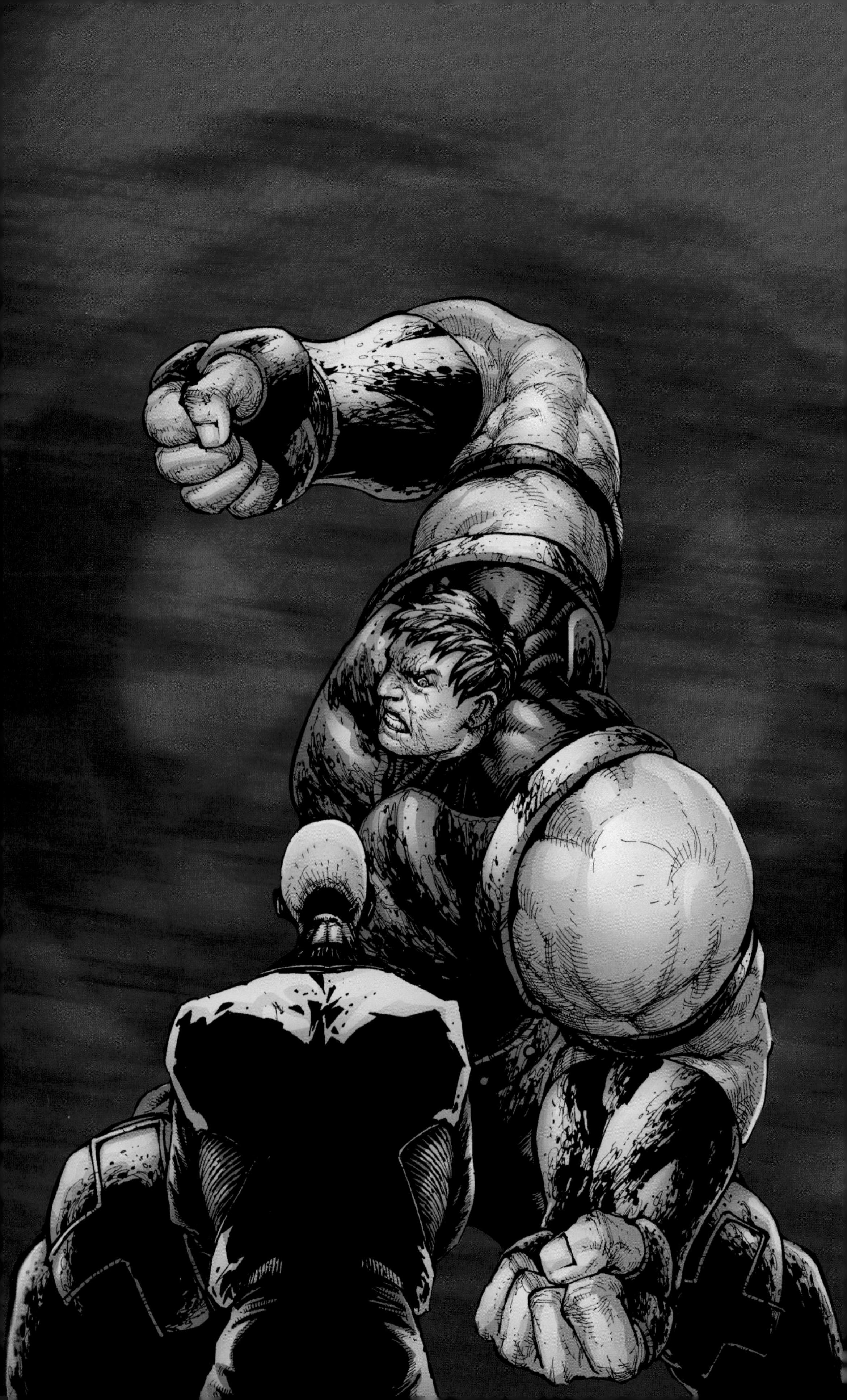

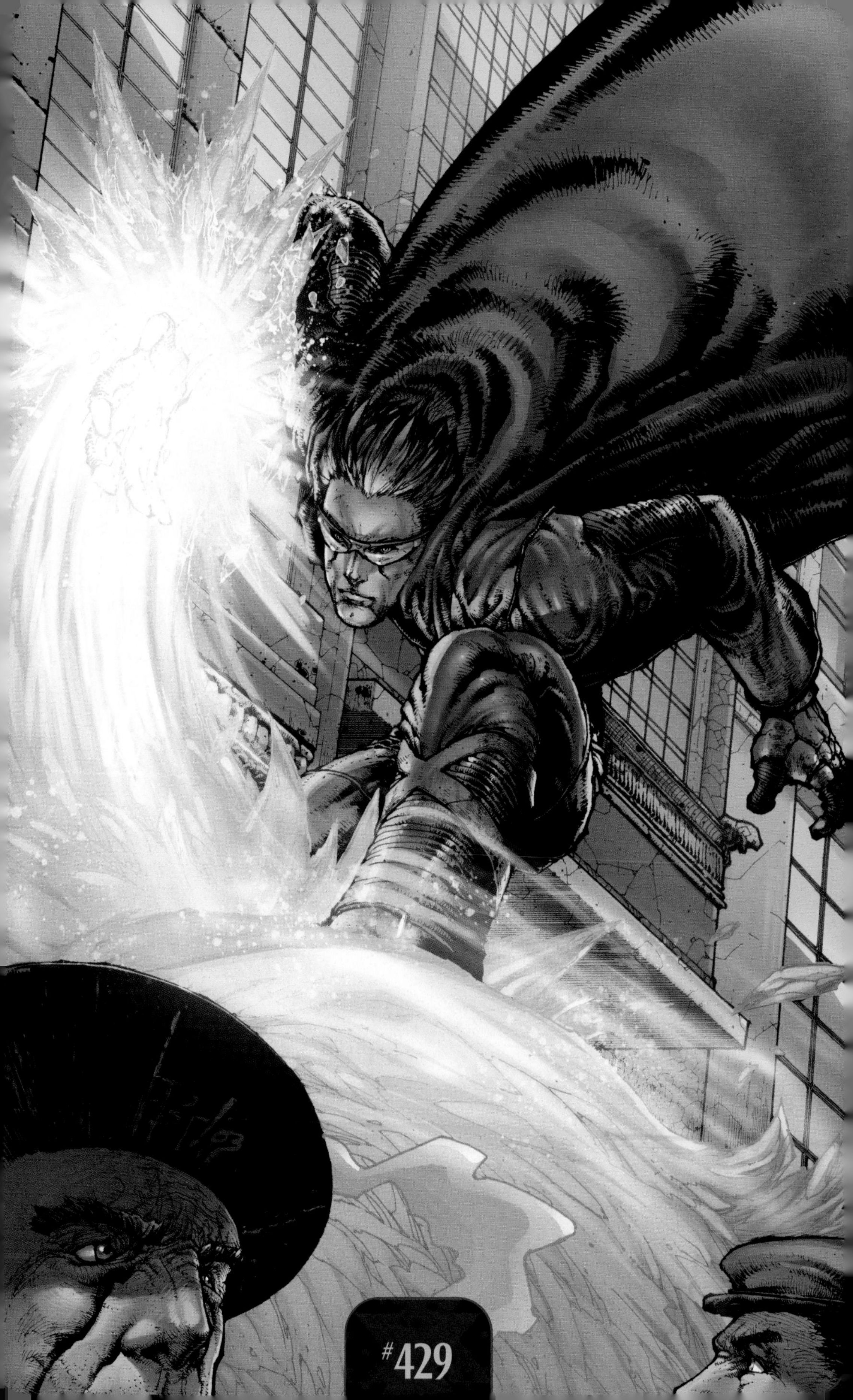
#429

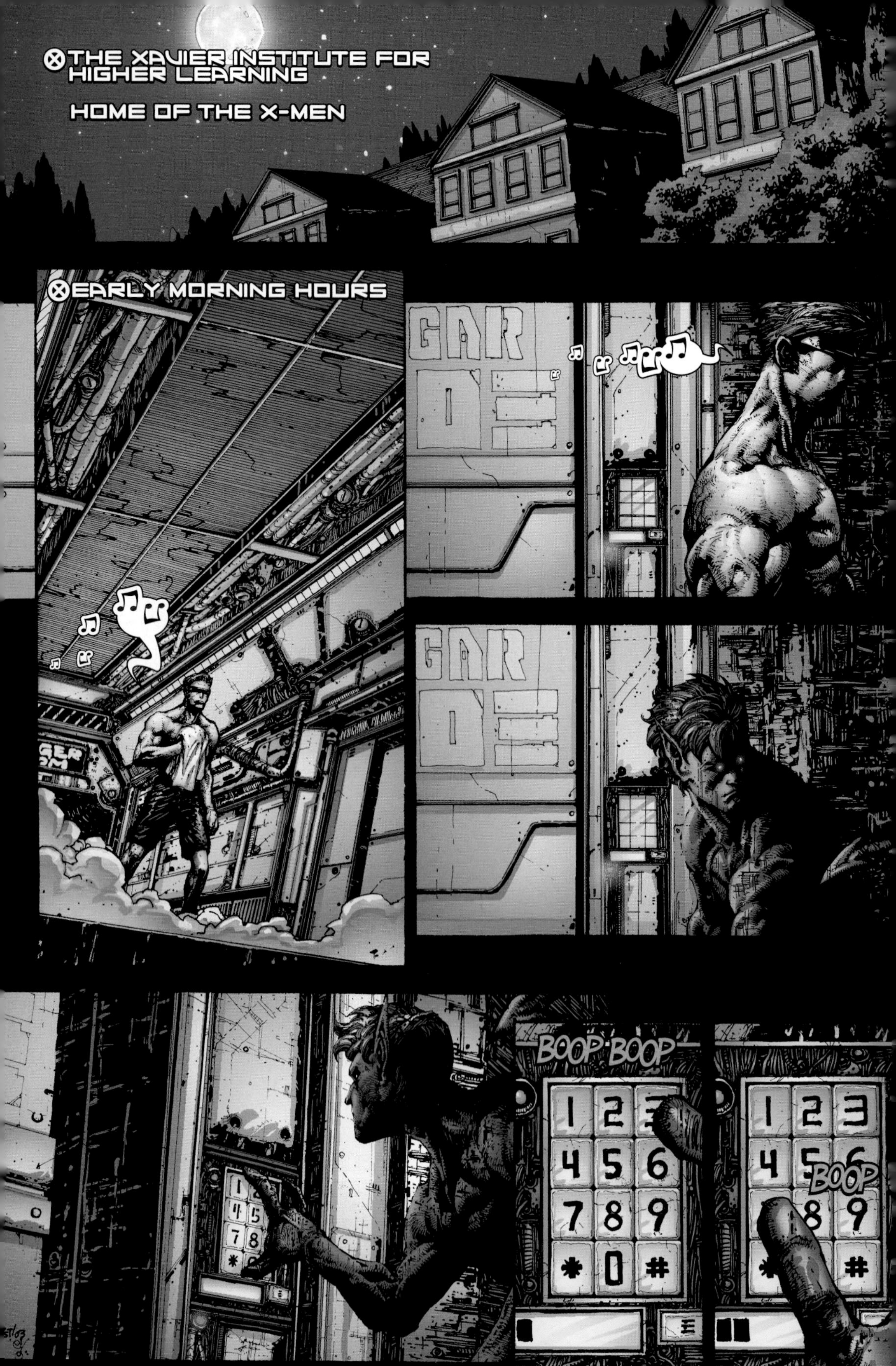
THE XAVIER INSTITUTE FOR HIGHER LEARNING
HOME OF THE X-MEN
EARLY MORNING HOURS
BOOP BOOP
BOOP

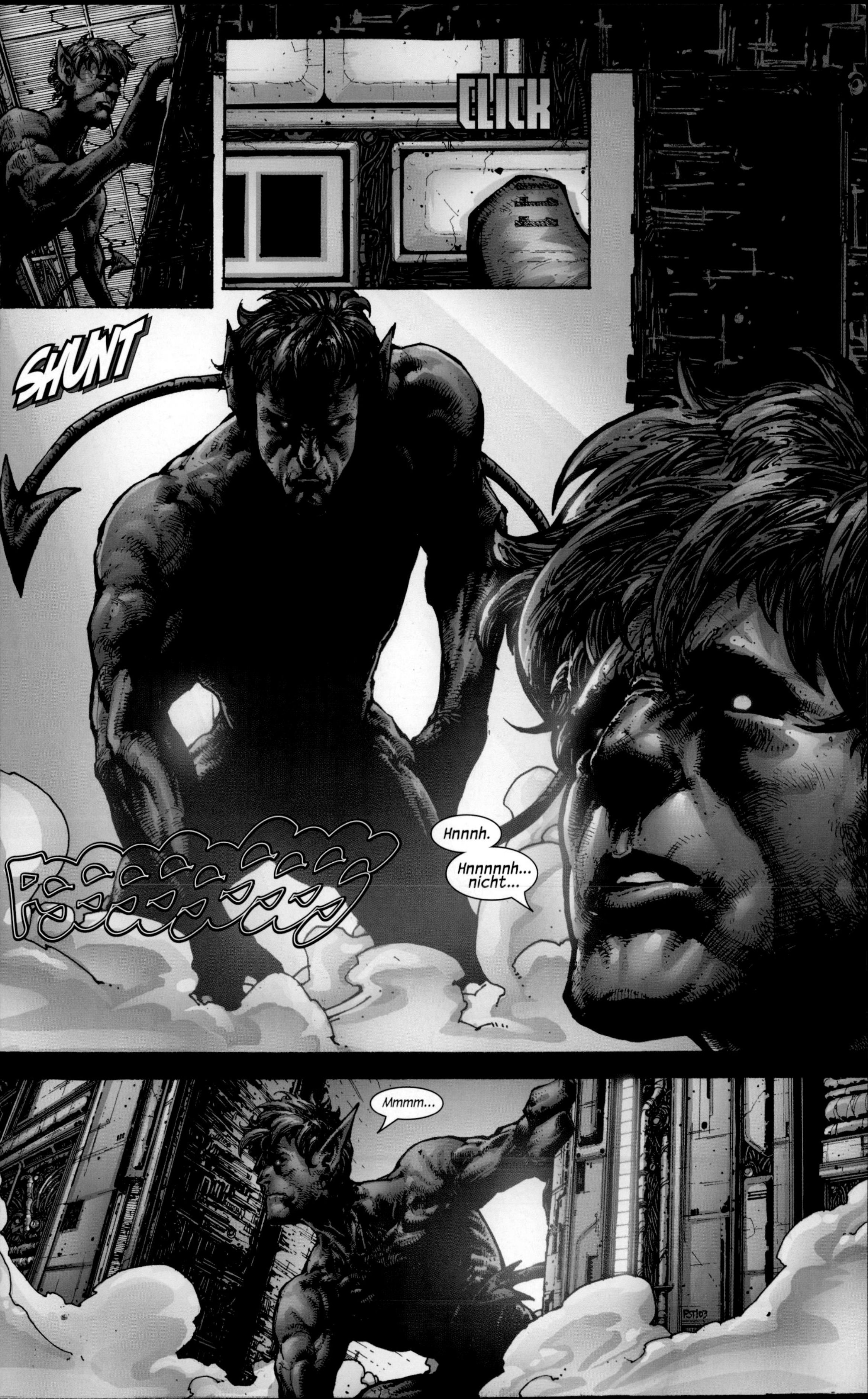

CLICK
SHUNT
Hnnnh.
Hnnnnnh... nicht...
Mmmm...

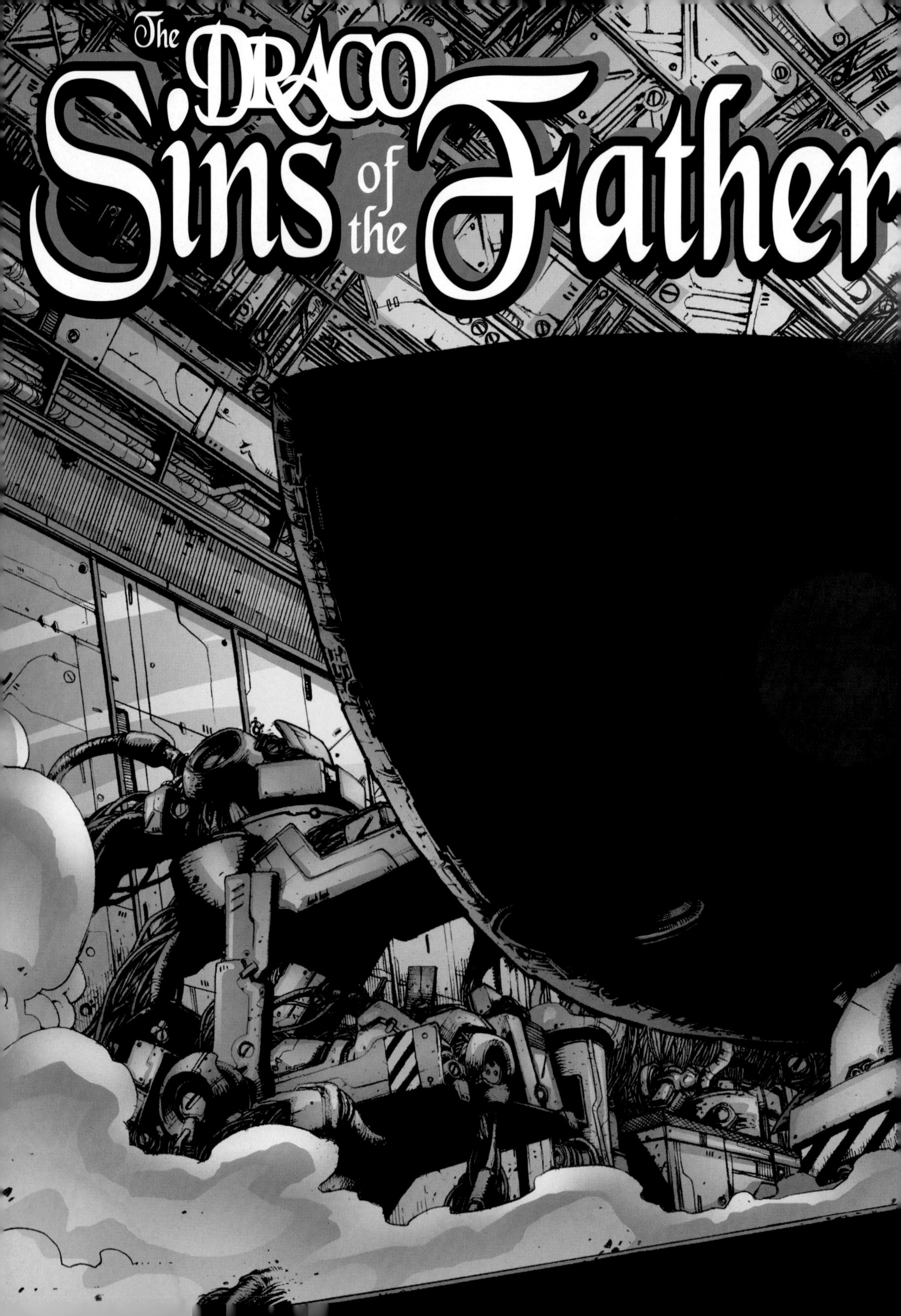
The DRACO
Sins of the Father

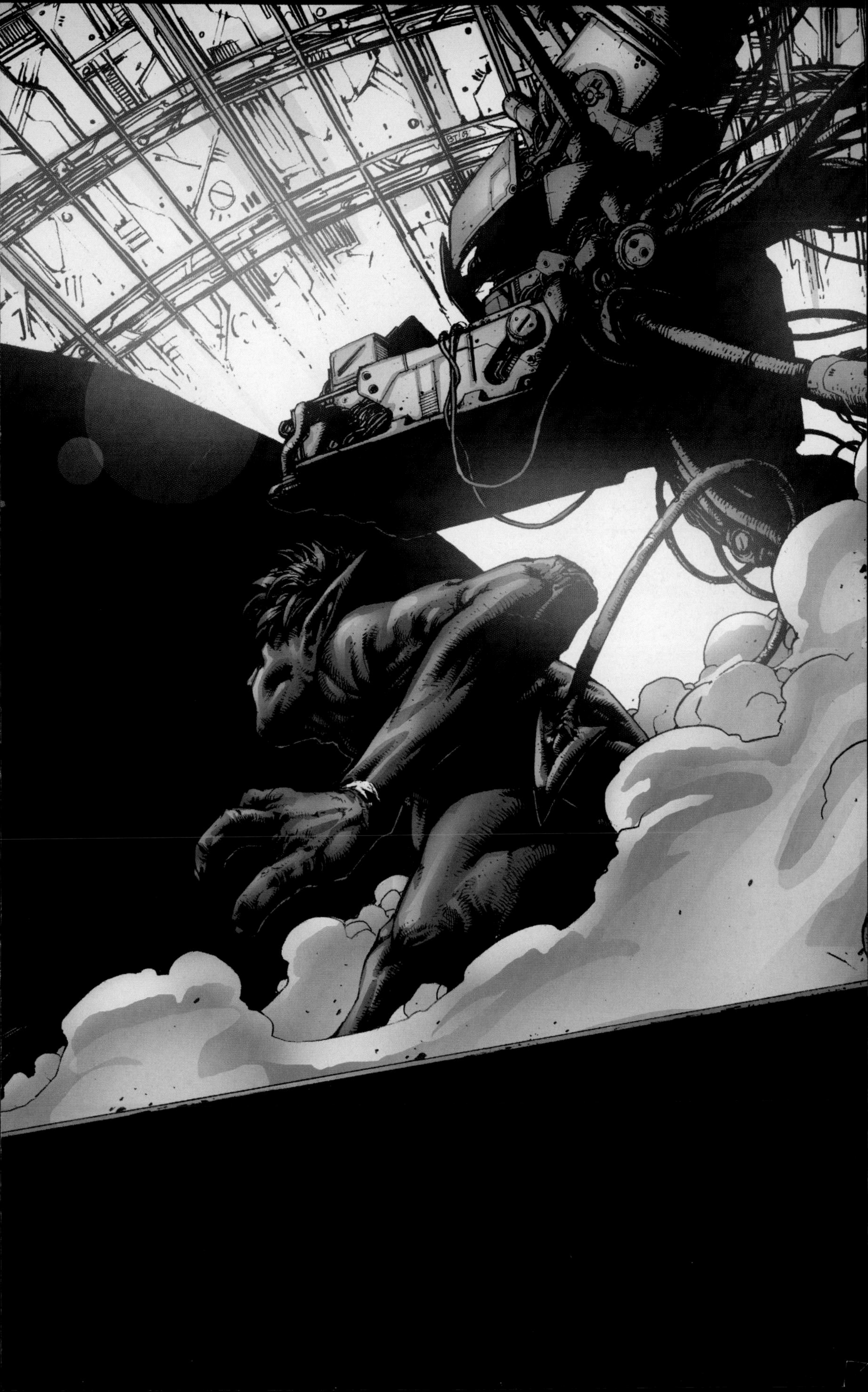

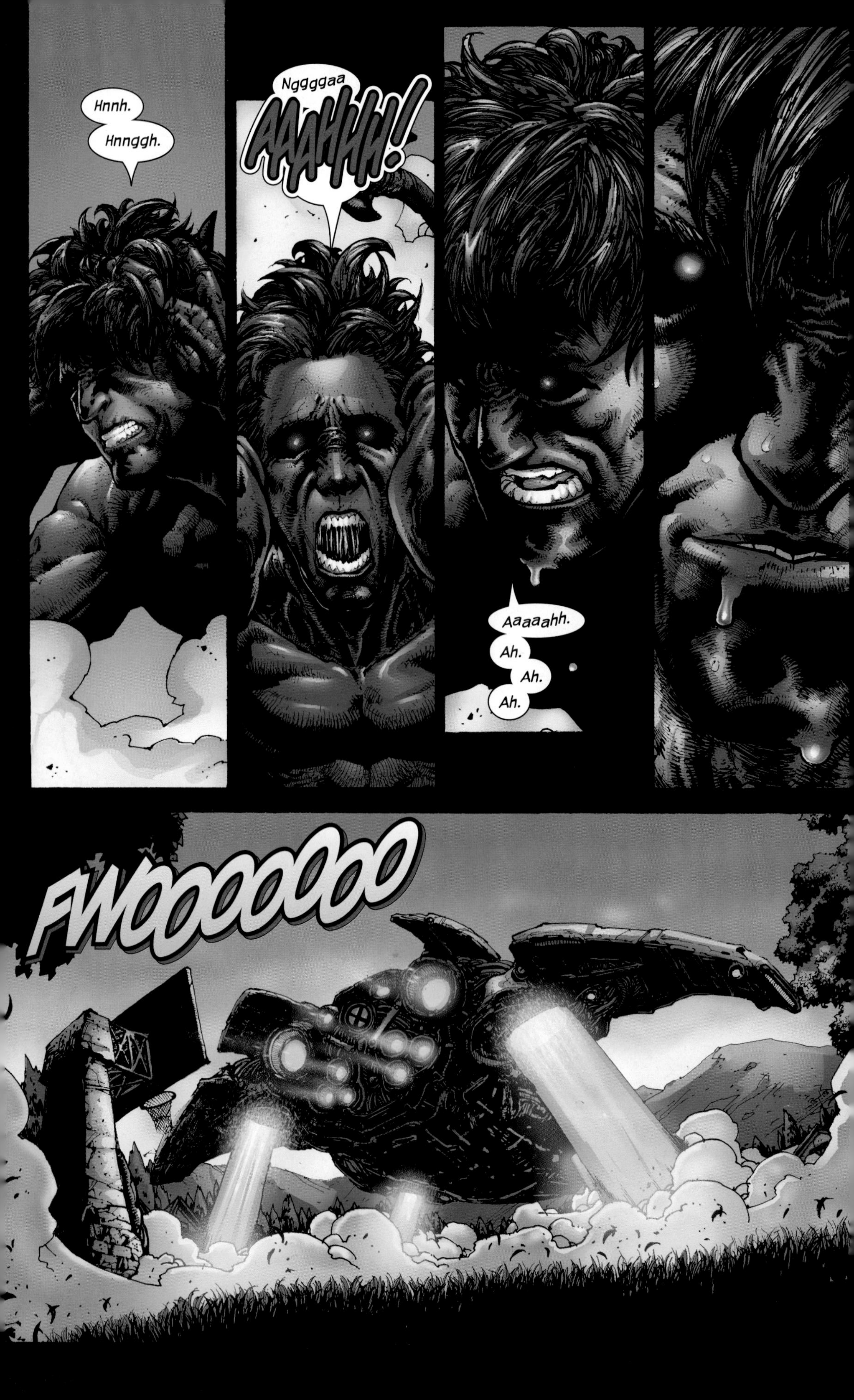
Hnnh.
Hnnggh.
Ngggaa
AAAHHH!
Aaaaahh.
Ah.
Ah.
Ah.
FWOOOOOOO

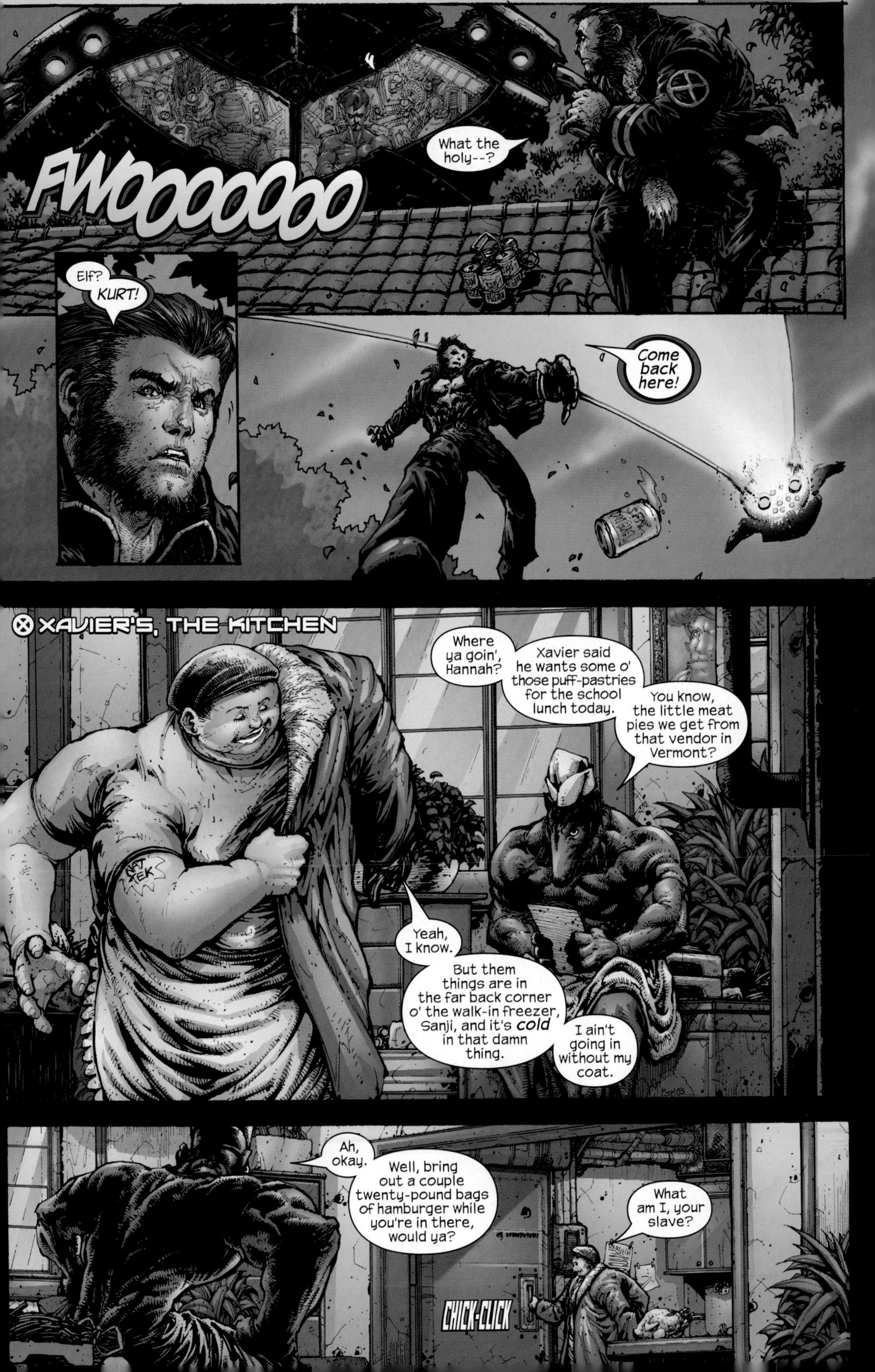
What the holy--?
FWOOOOOOO
Elf? KURT!
Come back here!
XAVIER'S, THE KITCHEN
Where ya goin', Hannah?
Xavier said he wants some o' those puff-pastries for the school lunch today.
You know, the little meat pies we get from that vendor in Vermont?
Yeah, I know.
But them things are in the far back corner o' the walk-in freezer, Sanji, and it's *cold* in that damn thing.
I ain't going in without my coat.
Ah, okay.
Well, bring out a couple twenty-pound bags of hamburger while you're in there, would ya?
What am I, your slave?
CHICK-CLICK

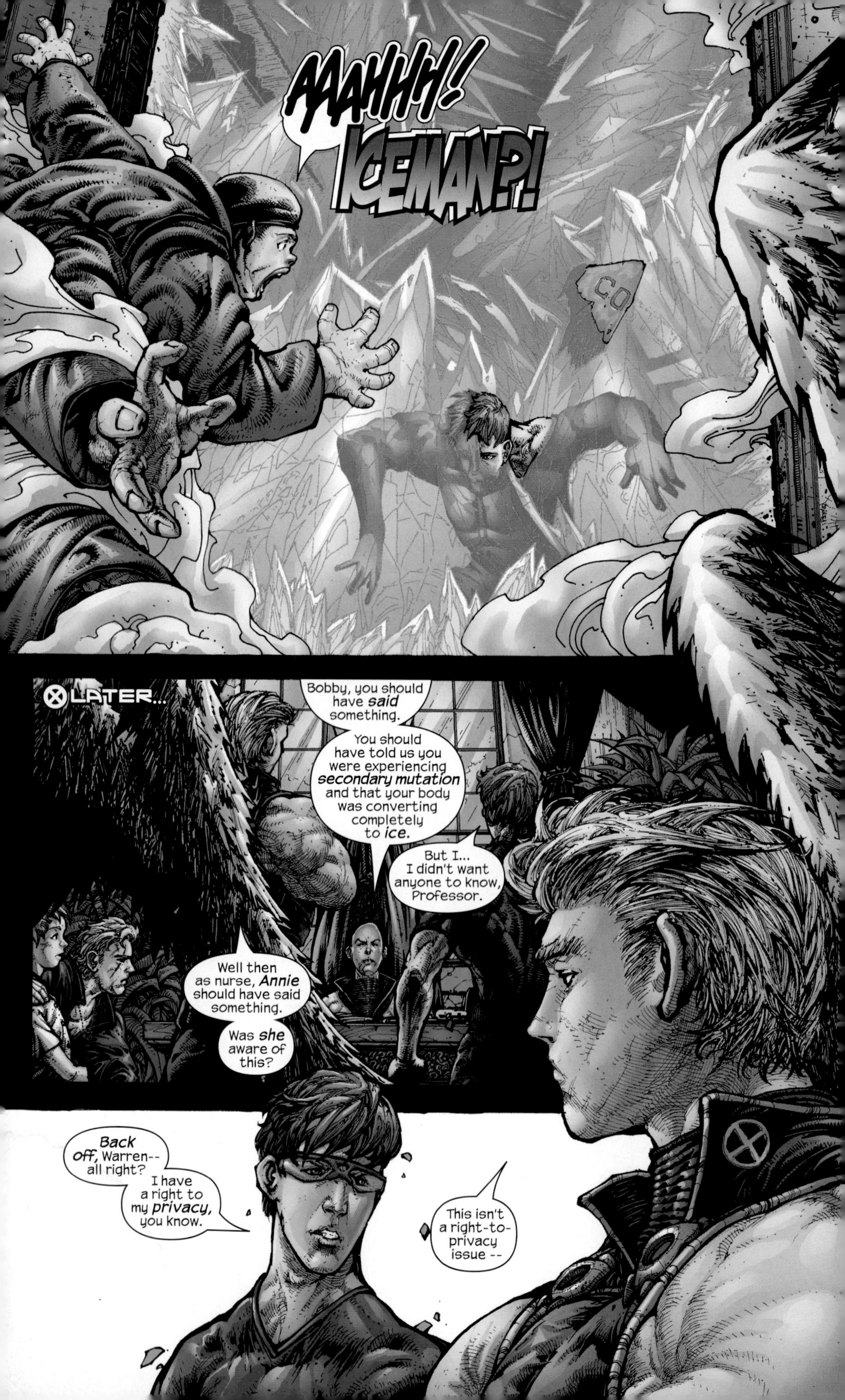
AAAHHH! ICEMAN?!
LATER...
Bobby, you should have said something.
You should have told us you were experiencing secondary mutation and that your body was converting completely to ice.
But I... I didn't want anyone to know, Professor.
Well then as nurse, Annie should have said something.
Was she aware of this?
Back off, Warren-- all right? I have a right to my privacy, you know.
This isn't a right-to-privacy issue --

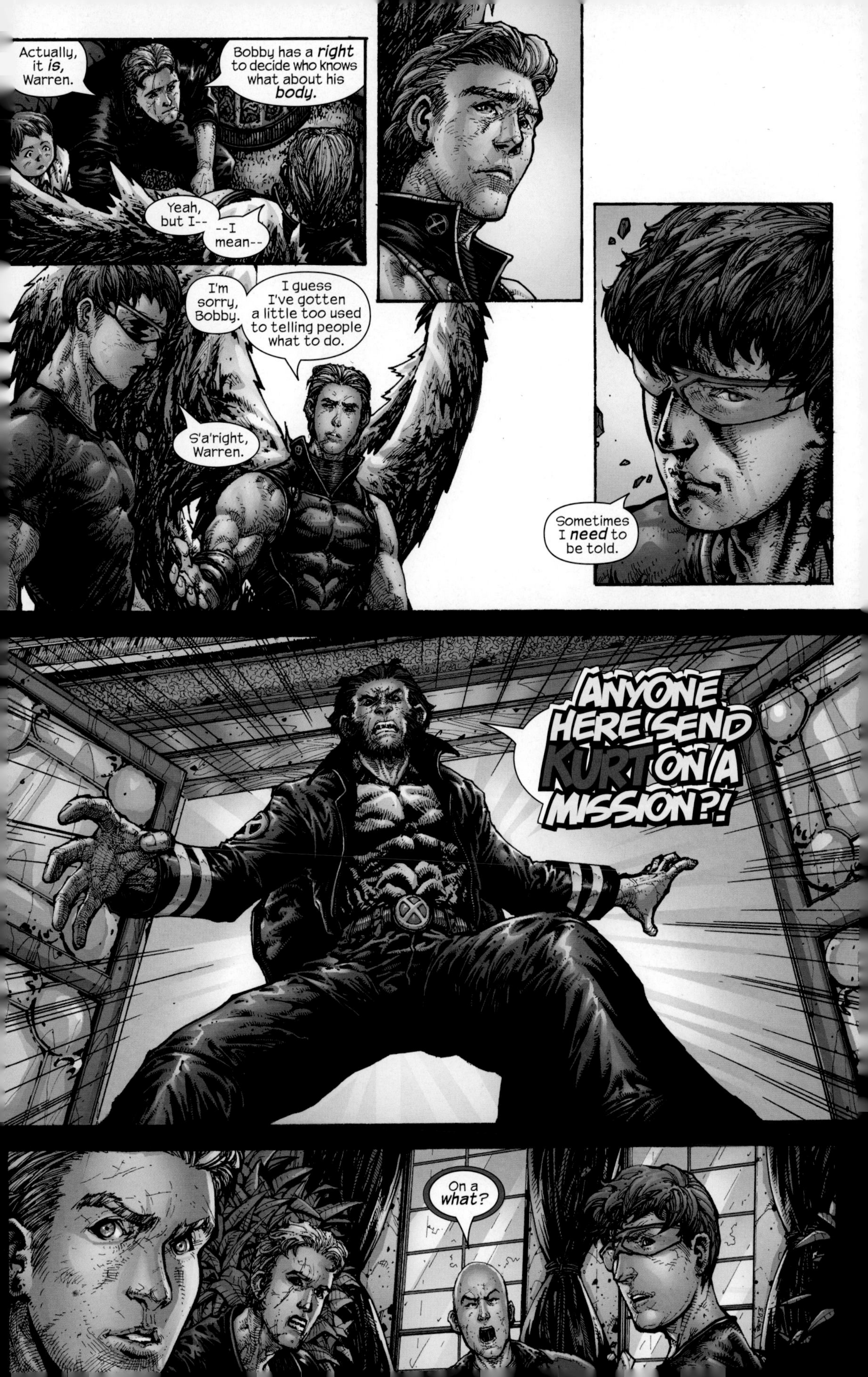
Actually, it *is*, Warren.
Bobby has a *right* to decide who knows what about his *body*.
Yeah, but I--
--I mean--
I'm sorry, Bobby.
I guess I've gotten a little too used to telling people what to do.
S'a'right, Warren.
Sometimes I *need* to be told.
ANYONE HERE SEND KURT ON A MISSION?!
On a *what*?

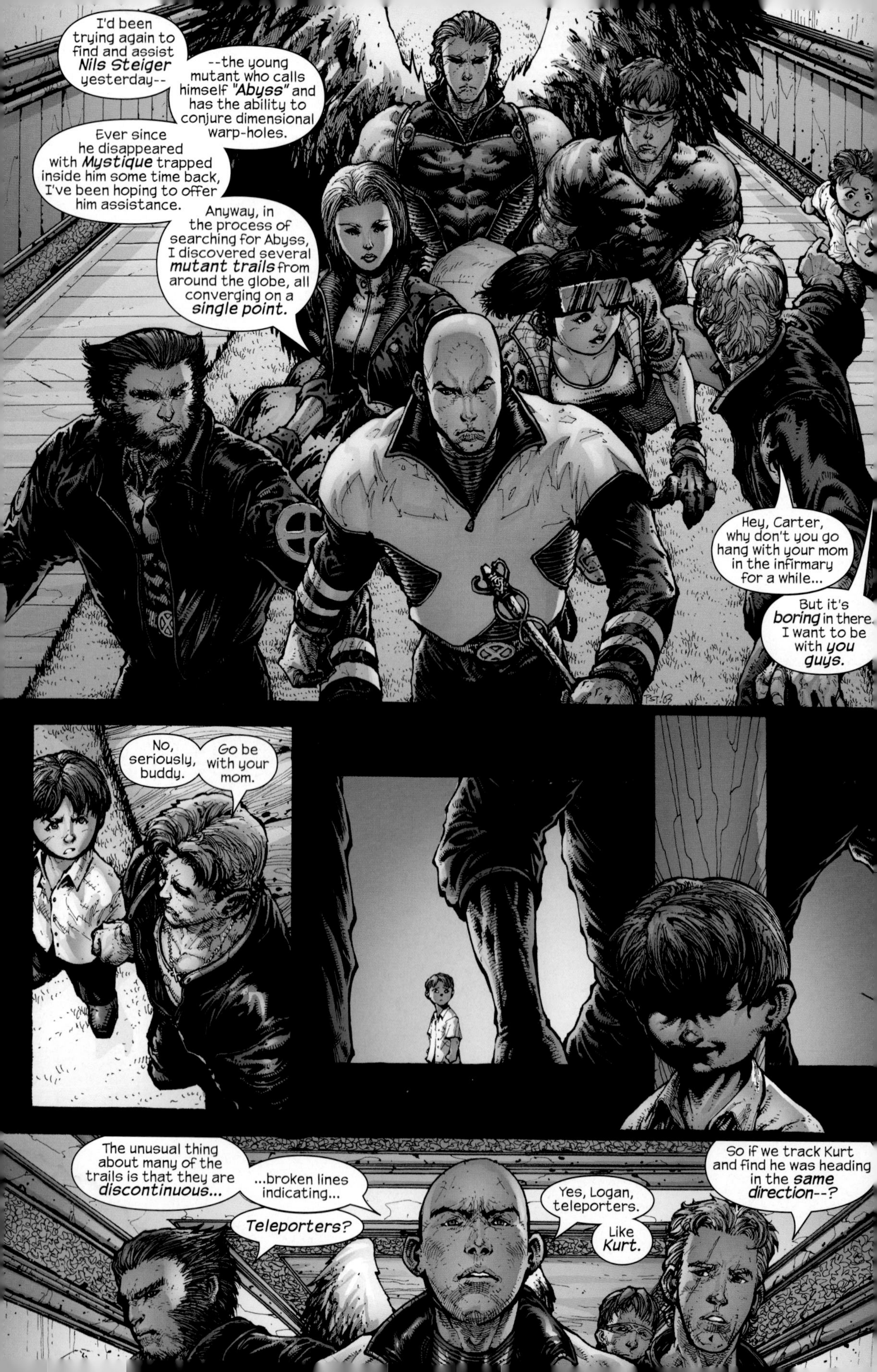
I'd been trying again to find and assist Nils Steiger yesterday--
--the young mutant who calls himself "Abyss" and has the ability to conjure dimensional warp-holes.
Ever since he disappeared with Mystique trapped inside him some time back, I've been hoping to offer him assistance.
Anyway, in the process of searching for Abyss, I discovered several mutant trails from around the globe, all converging on a single point.
Hey, Carter, why don't you go hang with your mom in the infirmary for a while...
But it's boring in there. I want to be with you guys.
No, seriously, buddy.
Go be with your mom.
The unusual thing about many of the trails is that they are discontinuous...
...broken lines indicating...
Teleporters?
Yes, Logan, teleporters.
Like Kurt.
So if we track Kurt and find he was heading in the same direction--?

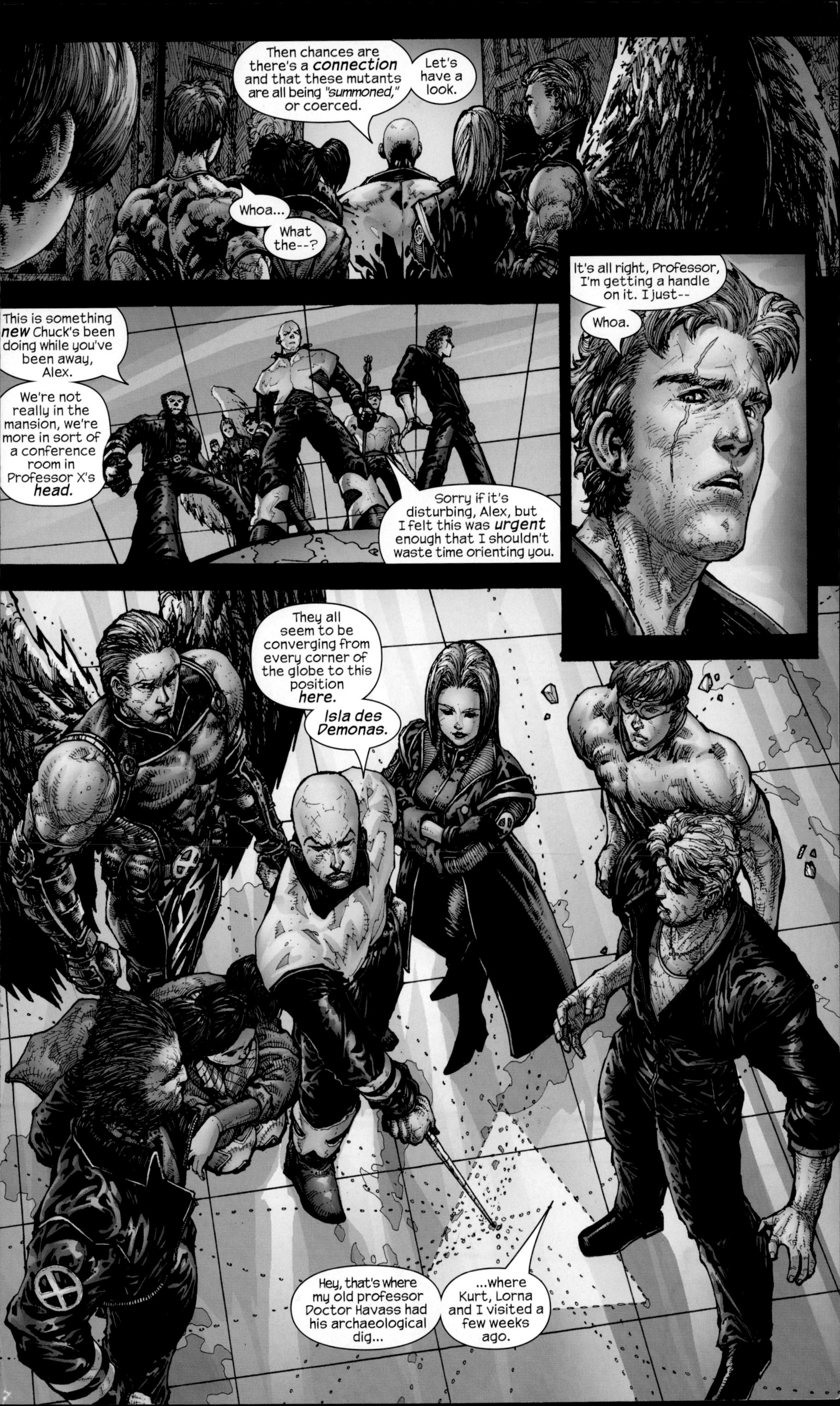

Then chances are there's a *connection* and that these mutants are all being *"summoned,"* or coerced.
Let's have a look.
Whoa...
What the--?
This is something *new* Chuck's been doing while you've been away, Alex.
We're not really in the mansion, we're more in sort of a conference room in Professor X's *head.*
Sorry if it's disturbing, Alex, but I felt this was *urgent* enough that I shouldn't waste time orienting you.
It's all right, Professor, I'm getting a handle on it. I just--
Whoa.
They all seem to be converging from every corner of the globe to this position *here.*
Isla des Demonas.
Hey, that's where my old professor Doctor Havass had his archaeological dig...
...where Kurt, Lorna and I visited a few weeks ago.

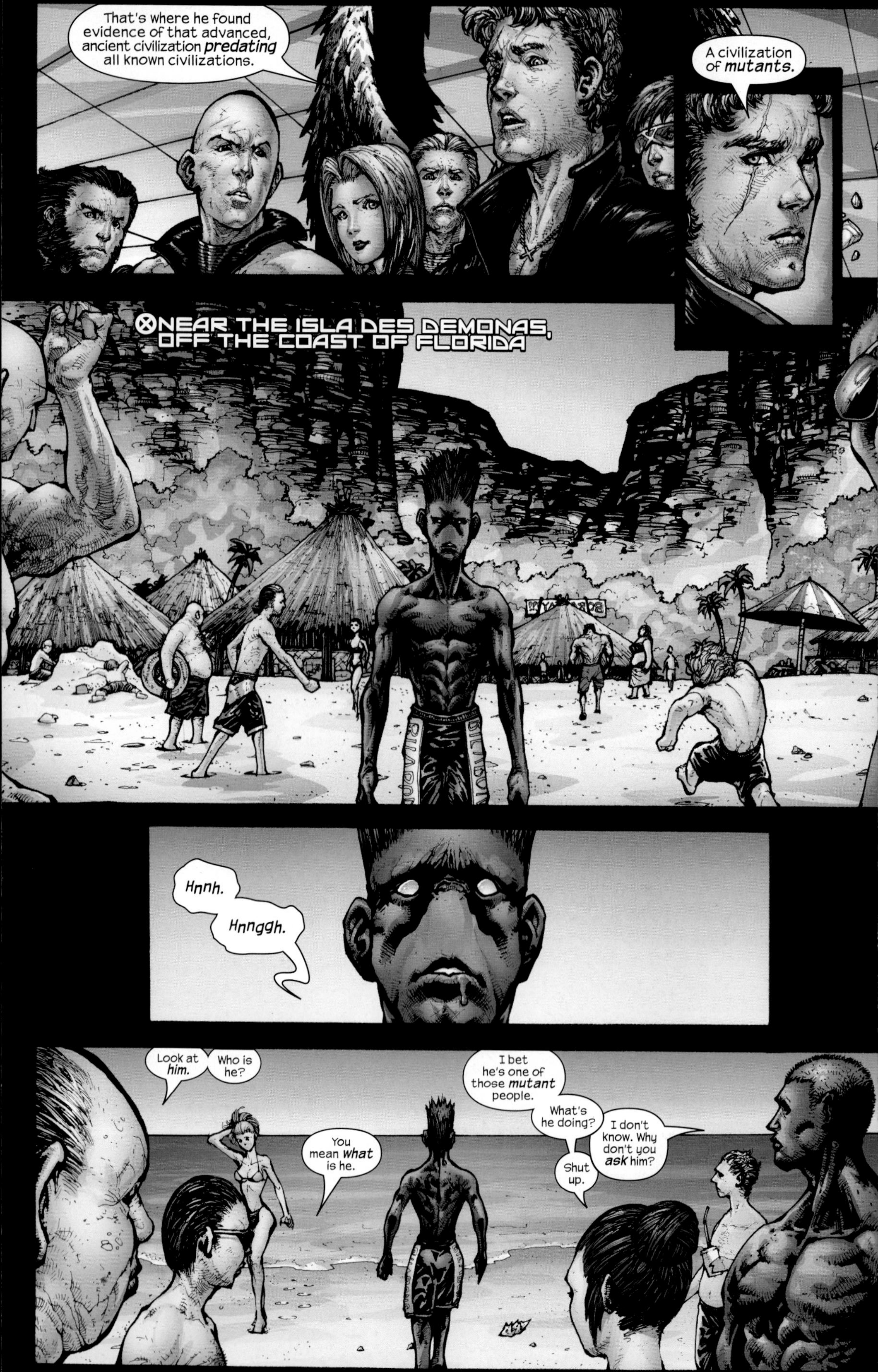
That's where he found evidence of that advanced, ancient civilization *predating* all known civilizations.
A civilization of *mutants.*
NEAR THE ISLA DES DEMONAS, OFF THE COAST OF FLORIDA
Hnnh.
Hnnggh.
Look at *him.*
Who is he?
You mean *what* is he.
I bet he's one of those *mutant* people.
What's he doing?
Shut up.
I don't know. Why don't you *ask* him?

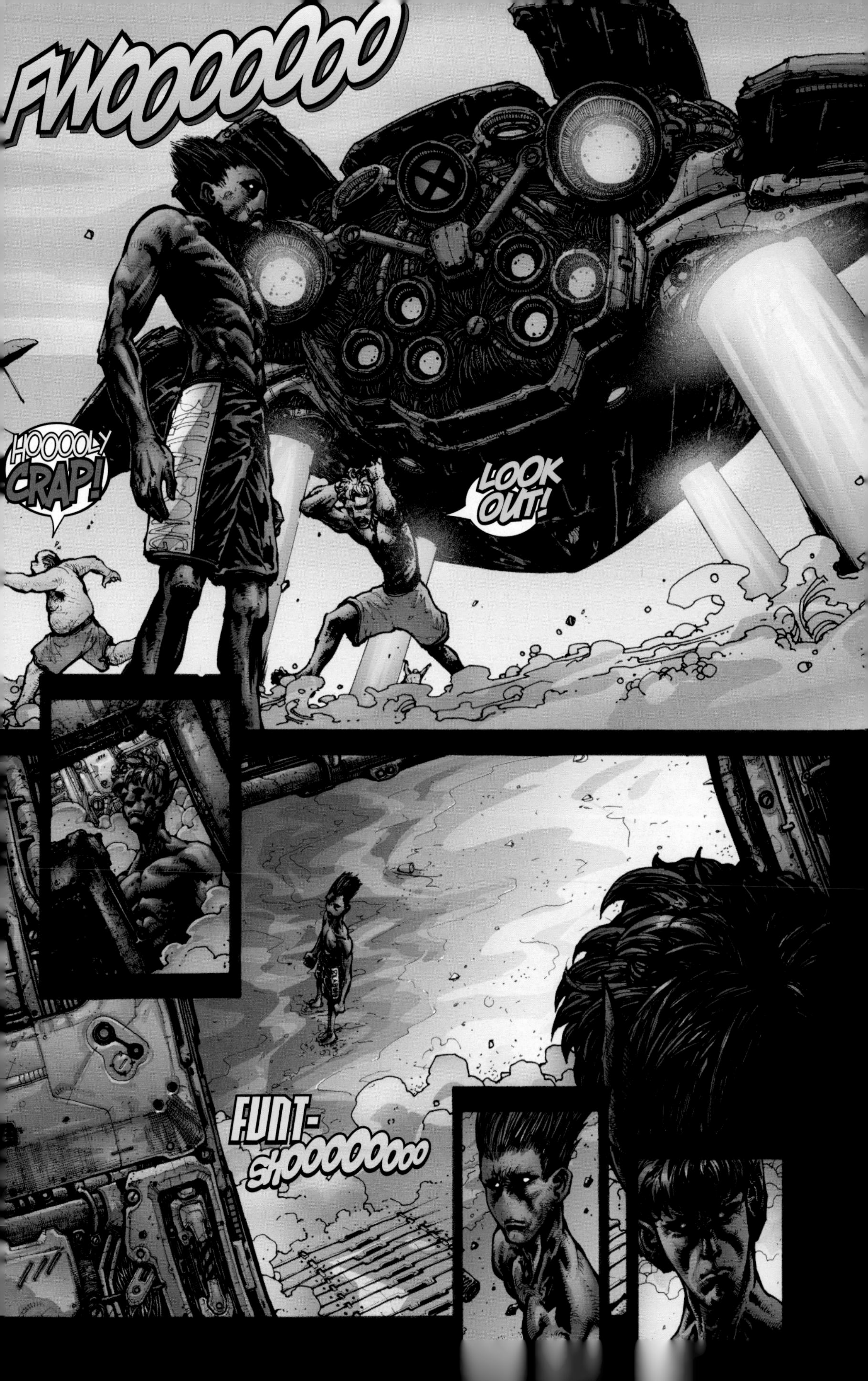
FWOOOOOOO
HOOOOLY CRAP!
LOOK OUT!
FUNT-SHOOOOOooo

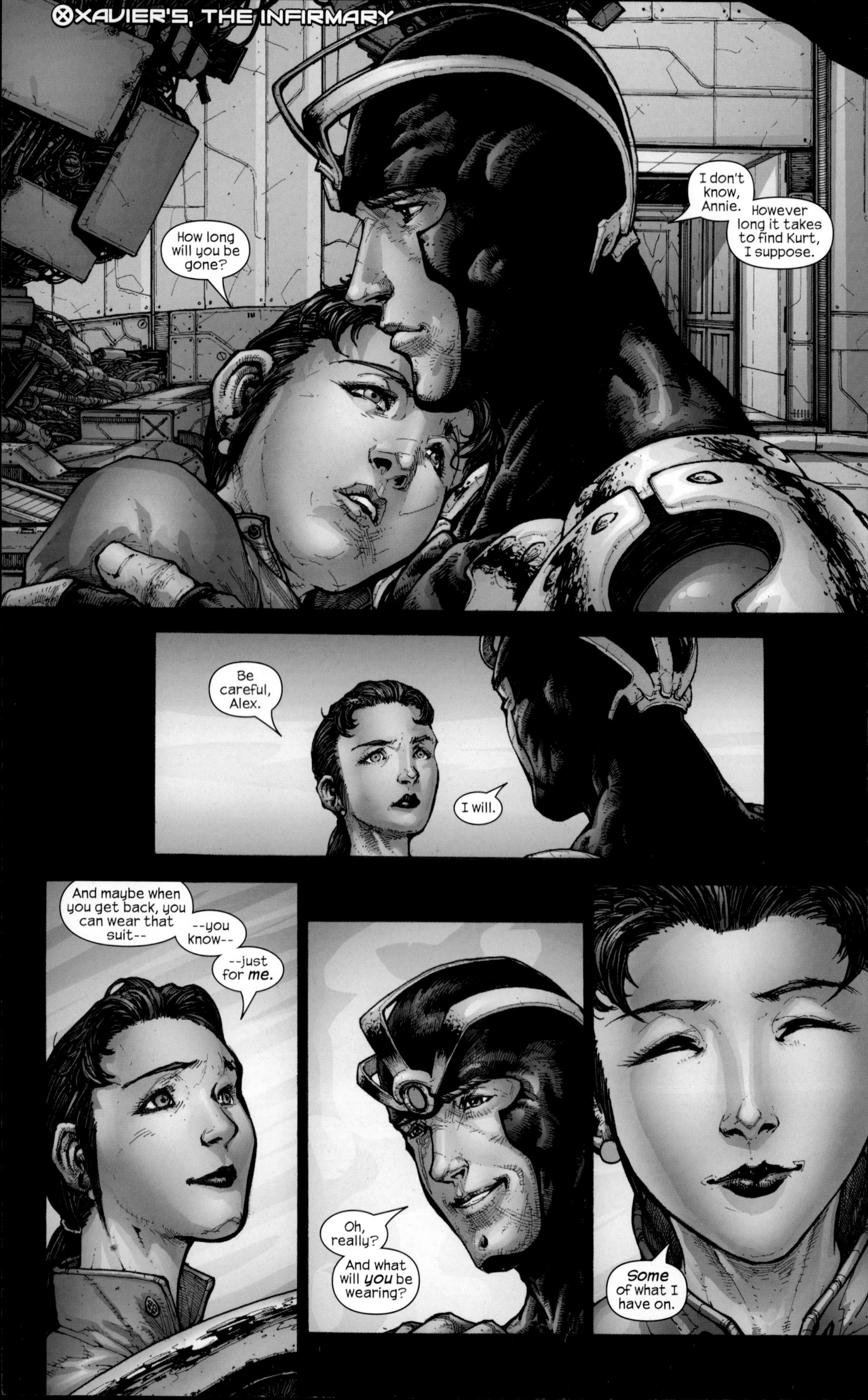
XAVIER'S, THE INFIRMARY
How long will you be gone?
I don't know, Annie.
However long it takes to find Kurt, I suppose.
Be careful, Alex.
I will.
And maybe when you get back, you can wear that suit--
--you know--
--just for *me.*
Oh, really?
And what will *you* be wearing?
Some of what I have on.

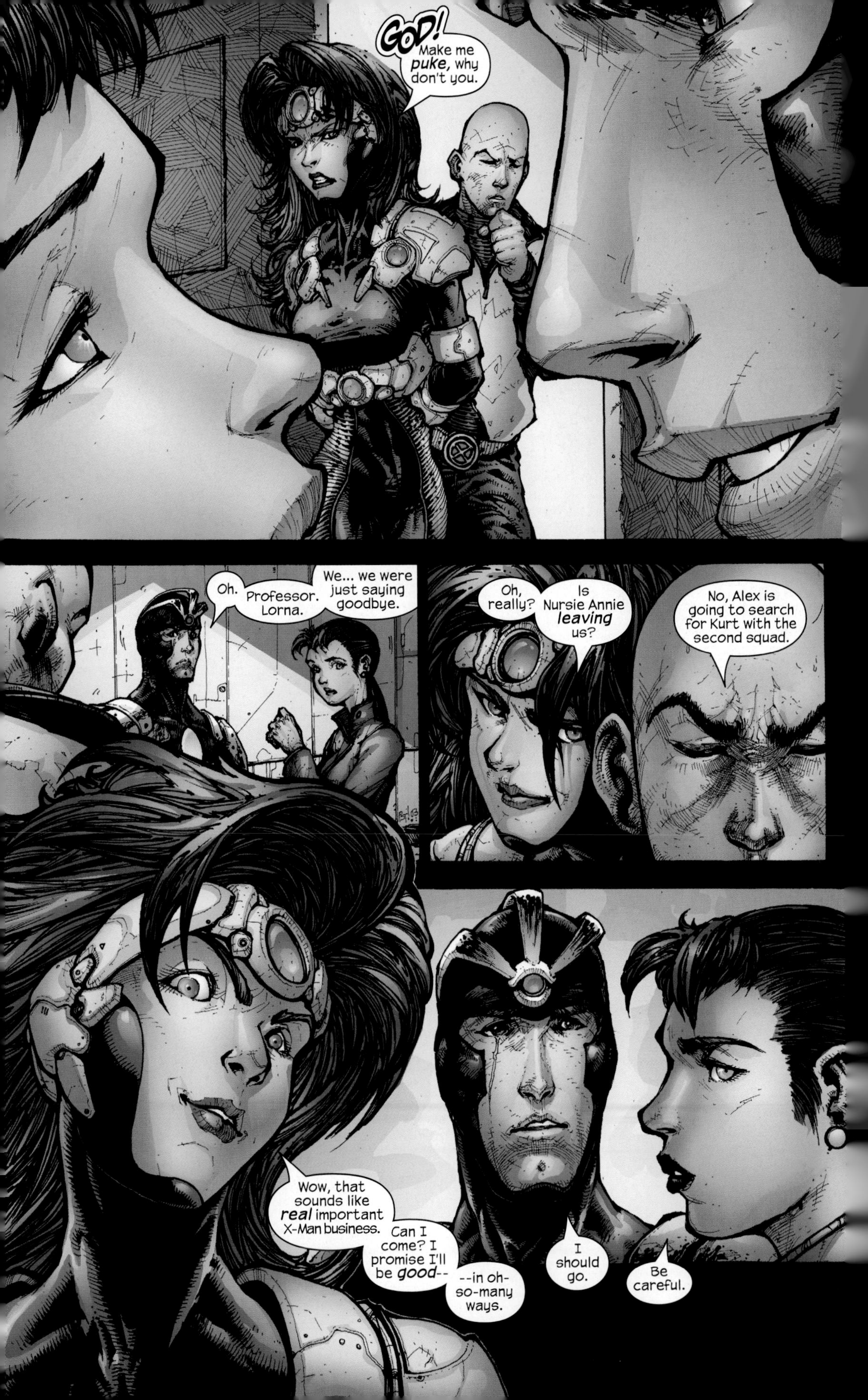
GOD!
Make me puke, why don't you.
Oh.
Professor. Lorna.
We... we were just saying goodbye.
Oh, really?
Is Nursie Annie leaving us?
No, Alex is going to search for Kurt with the second squad.
Wow, that sounds like real important X-Man business.
Can I come? I promise I'll be good--
--in oh-so-many ways.
I should go.
Be careful.

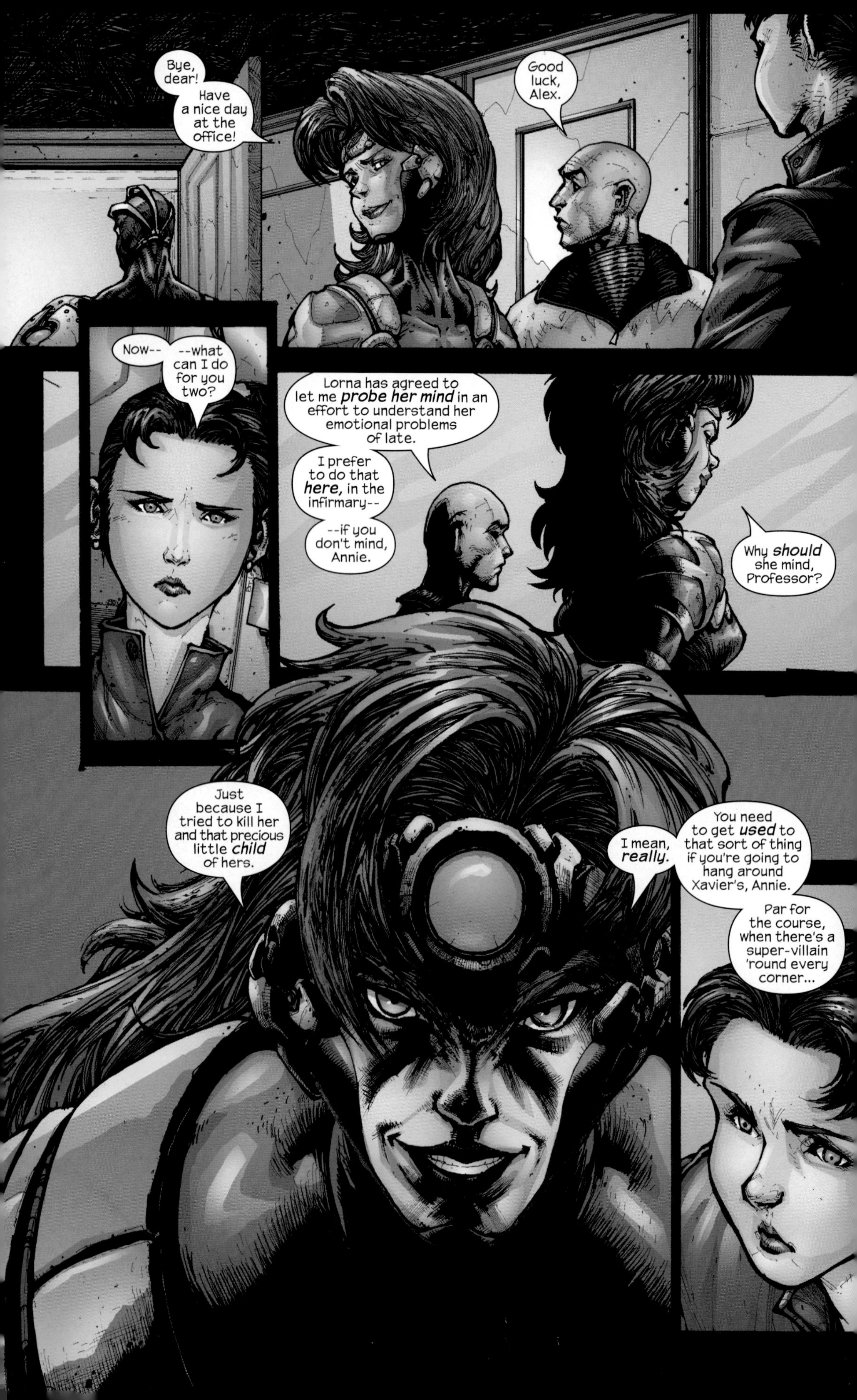

Bye, dear!
Have a nice day at the office!
Good luck, Alex.
Now--
--what can I do for you two?
Lorna has agreed to let me probe her mind in an effort to understand her emotional problems of late.
I prefer to do that here, in the infirmary--
--if you don't mind, Annie.
Why should she mind, Professor?
Just because I tried to kill her and that precious little child of hers.
I mean, really.
You need to get used to that sort of thing if you're going to hang around Xavier's, Annie.
Par for the course, when there's a super-villain 'round every corner...

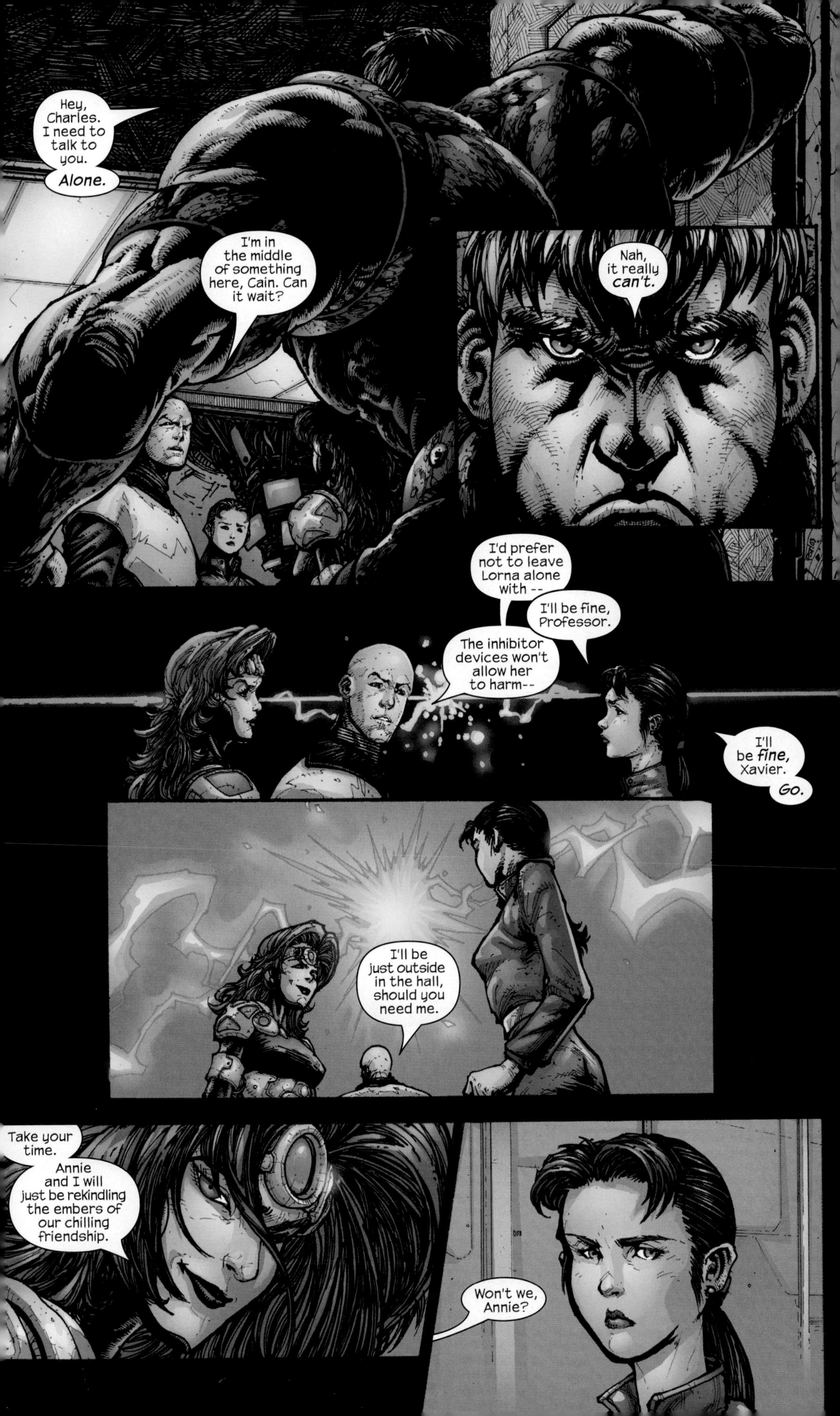

Hey, Charles. I need to talk to you. Alone.
I'm in the middle of something here, Cain. Can it wait?
Nah, it really can't.
I'd prefer not to leave Lorna alone with --
I'll be fine, Professor.
The inhibitor devices won't allow her to harm--
I'll be fine, Xavier. Go.
I'll be just outside in the hall, should you need me.
Take your time.
Annie and I will just be rekindling the embers of our chilling friendship.
Won't we, Annie?

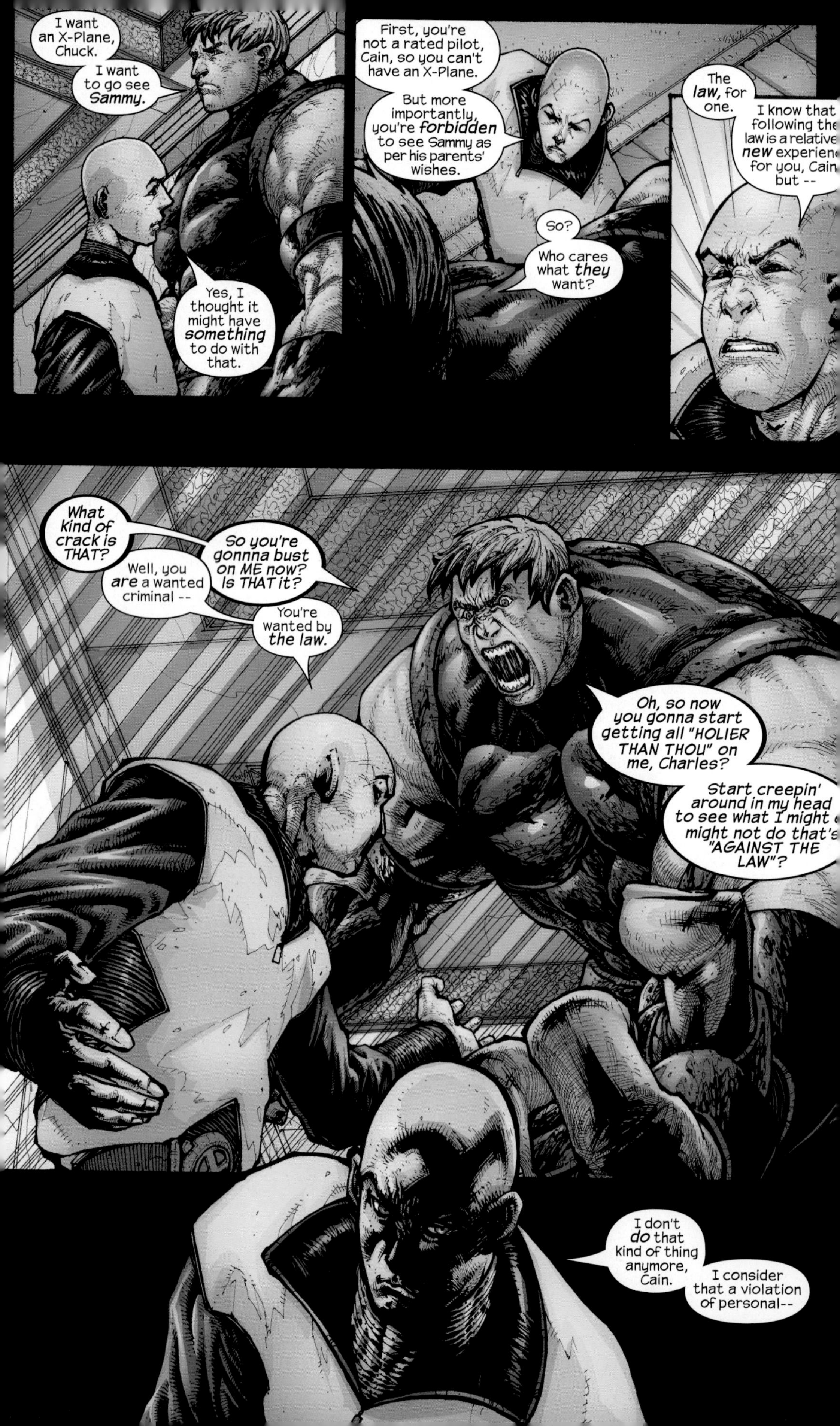

I want an X-Plane, Chuck.
I want to go see Sammy.
Yes, I thought it might have something to do with that.
First, you're not a rated pilot, Cain, so you can't have an X-Plane.
But more importantly, you're forbidden to see Sammy as per his parents' wishes.
So?
Who cares what they want?
The law, for one.
I know that following the law is a relative new experien for you, Cain but --
What kind of crack is THAT?
So you're gonna bust on ME now? Is THAT it?
Well, you are a wanted criminal --
You're wanted by the law.
Oh, so now you gonna start getting all "HOLIER THAN THOU" on me, Charles?
Start creepin' around in my head to see what I might might not do that's "AGAINST THE LAW"?
I don't do that kind of thing anymore, Cain.
I consider that a violation of personal--

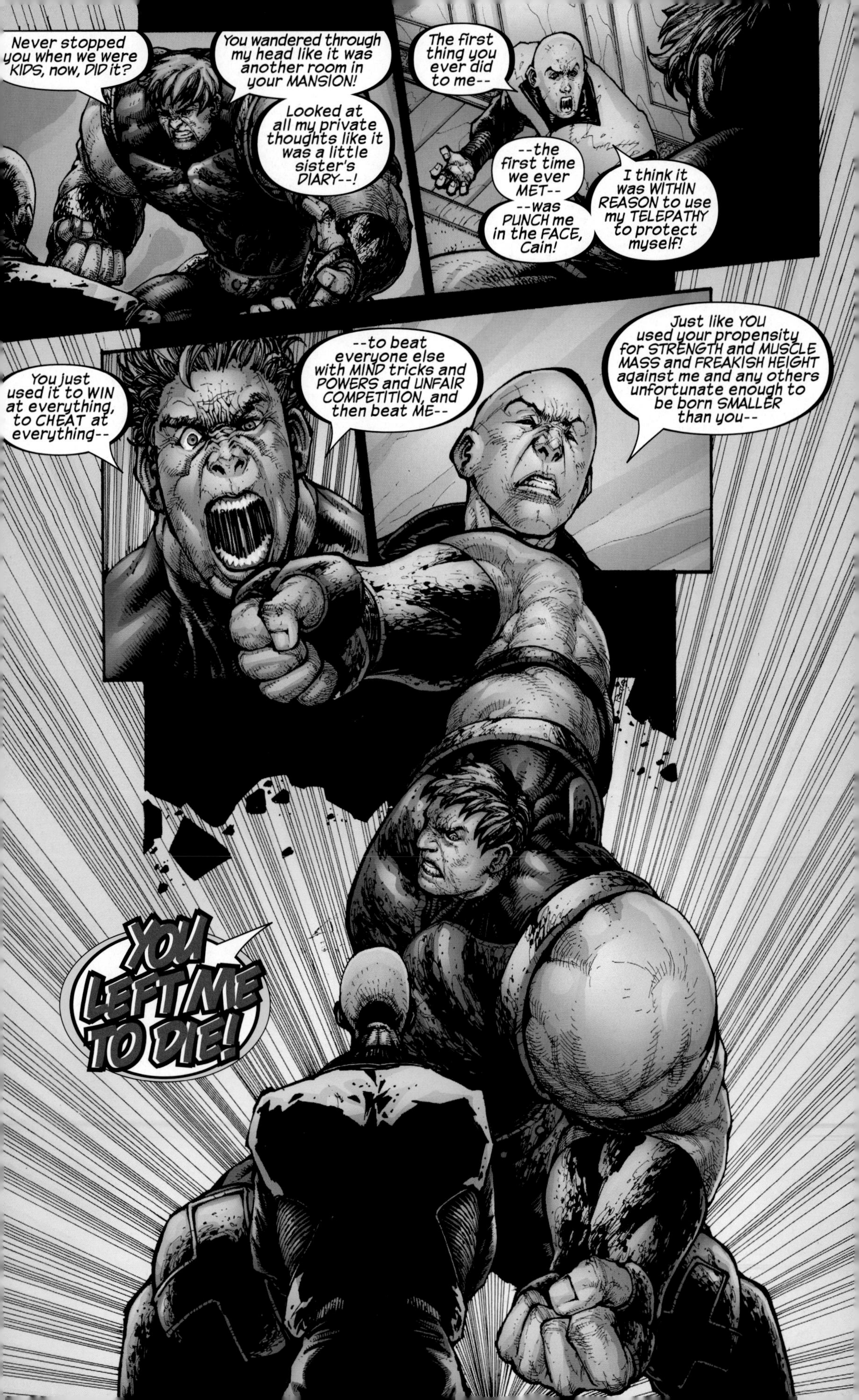
Never stopped you when we were KIDS, now, DID it?
You wandered through my head like it was another room in your MANSION!
Looked at all my private thoughts like it was a little sister's DIARY--!
The first thing you ever did to me--
--the first time we ever MET--
--was PUNCH me in the FACE, Cain!
I think it was WITHIN REASON to use my TELEPATHY to protect myself!
You just used it to WIN at everything, to CHEAT at everything--
--to beat everyone else with MIND tricks and POWERS and UNFAIR COMPETITION, and then beat ME--
Just like YOU used your propensity for STRENGTH and MUSCLE MASS and FREAKISH HEIGHT against me and any others unfortunate enough to be born SMALLER than you--
YOU LEFT ME TO DIE!

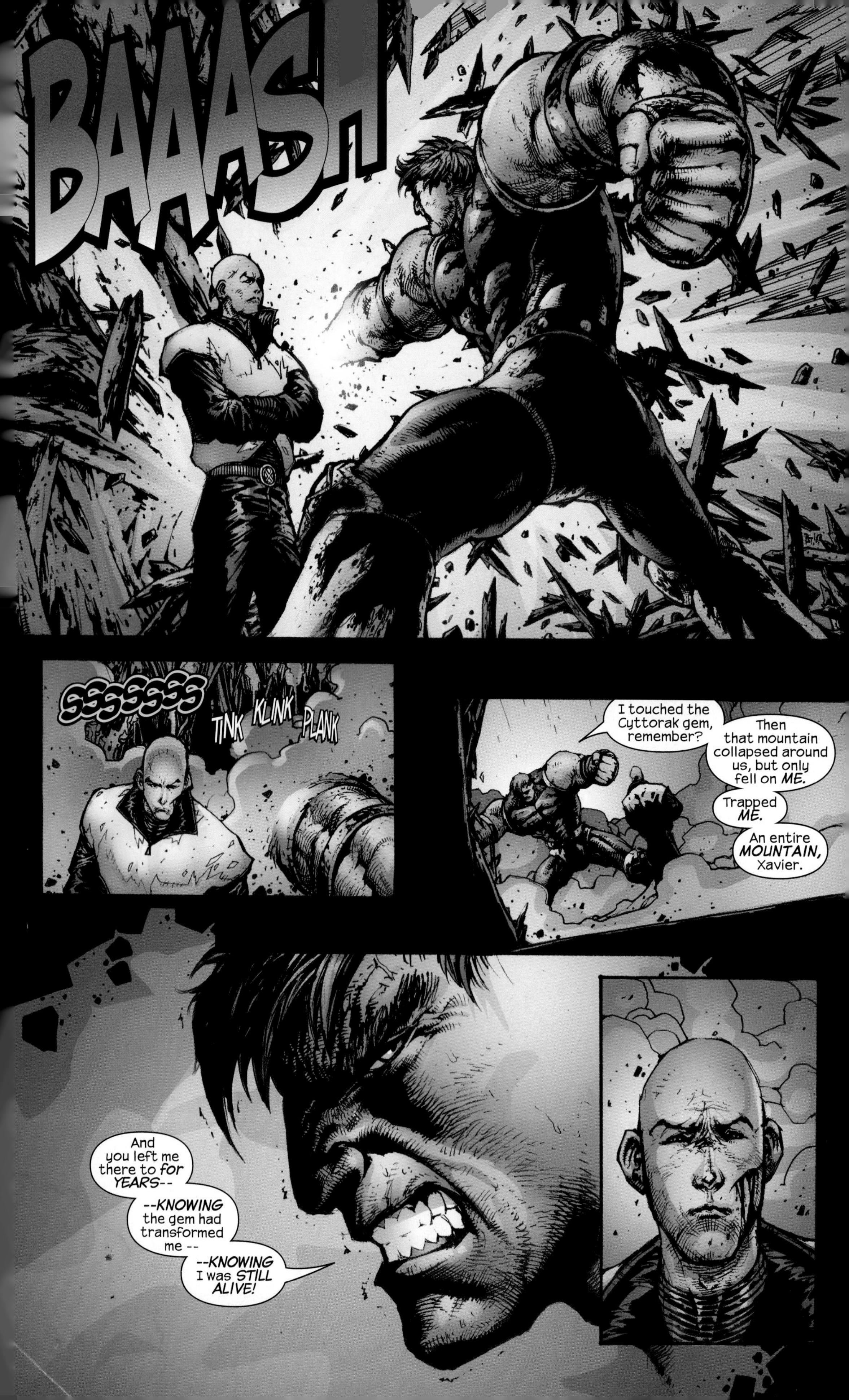
BAAASH
SSSSSSS
TINK
KLINK
PLANK
I touched the Cyttorak gem, remember?
Then that mountain collapsed around us, but only fell on ME.
Trapped ME.
An entire MOUNTAIN, Xavier.
And you left me there to for YEARS--
--KNOWING the gem had transformed me --
--KNOWING I was STILL ALIVE!

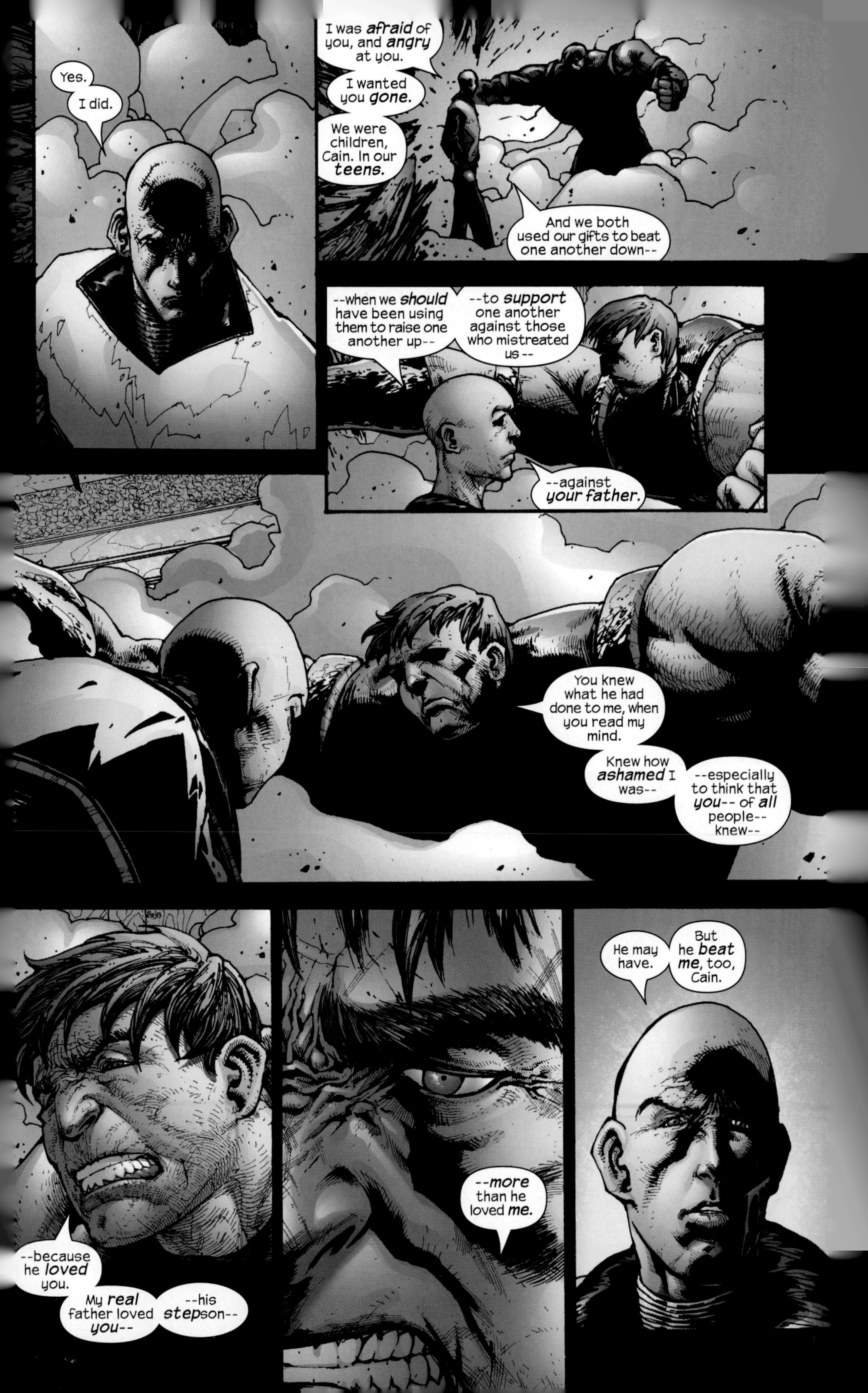
Yes.
I did.
I was afraid of you, and angry at you.
I wanted you gone.
We were children, Cain. In our teens.
And we both used our gifts to beat one another down--
--when we should have been using them to raise one another up--
--to support one another against those who mistreated us--
--against your father.
You knew what he had done to me, when you read my mind.
Knew how ashamed I was--
--especially to think that you-- of all people-- knew--
--because he loved you.
My real father loved you--
--his stepson--
--more than he loved me.
He may have.
But he beat me, too, Cain.

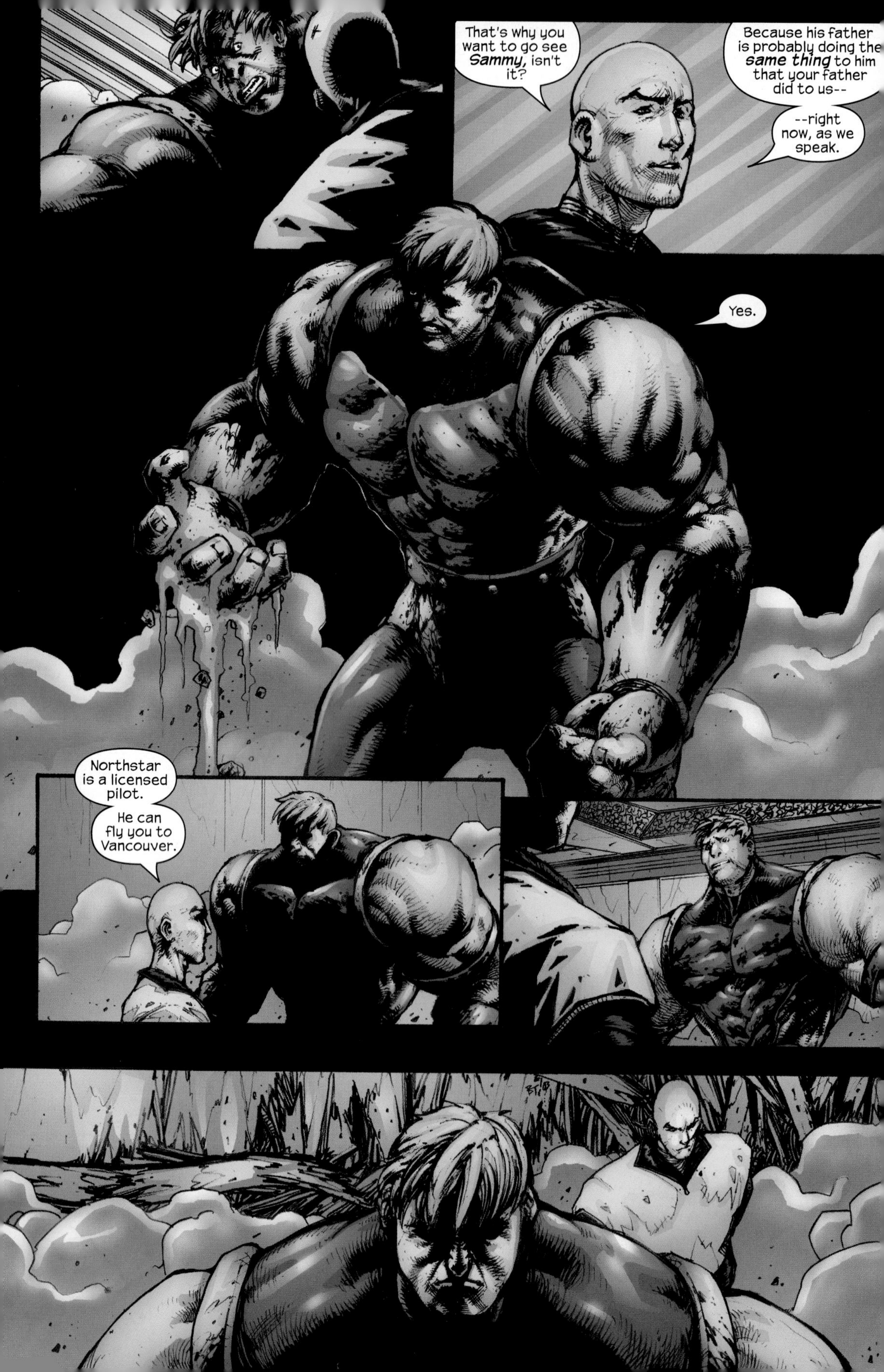

That's why you want to go see *Sammy*, isn't it?
Because his father is probably doing the ***same thing*** to him that your father did to us--
--right now, as we speak.
Yes.
Northstar is a licensed pilot.
He can fly you to Vancouver.

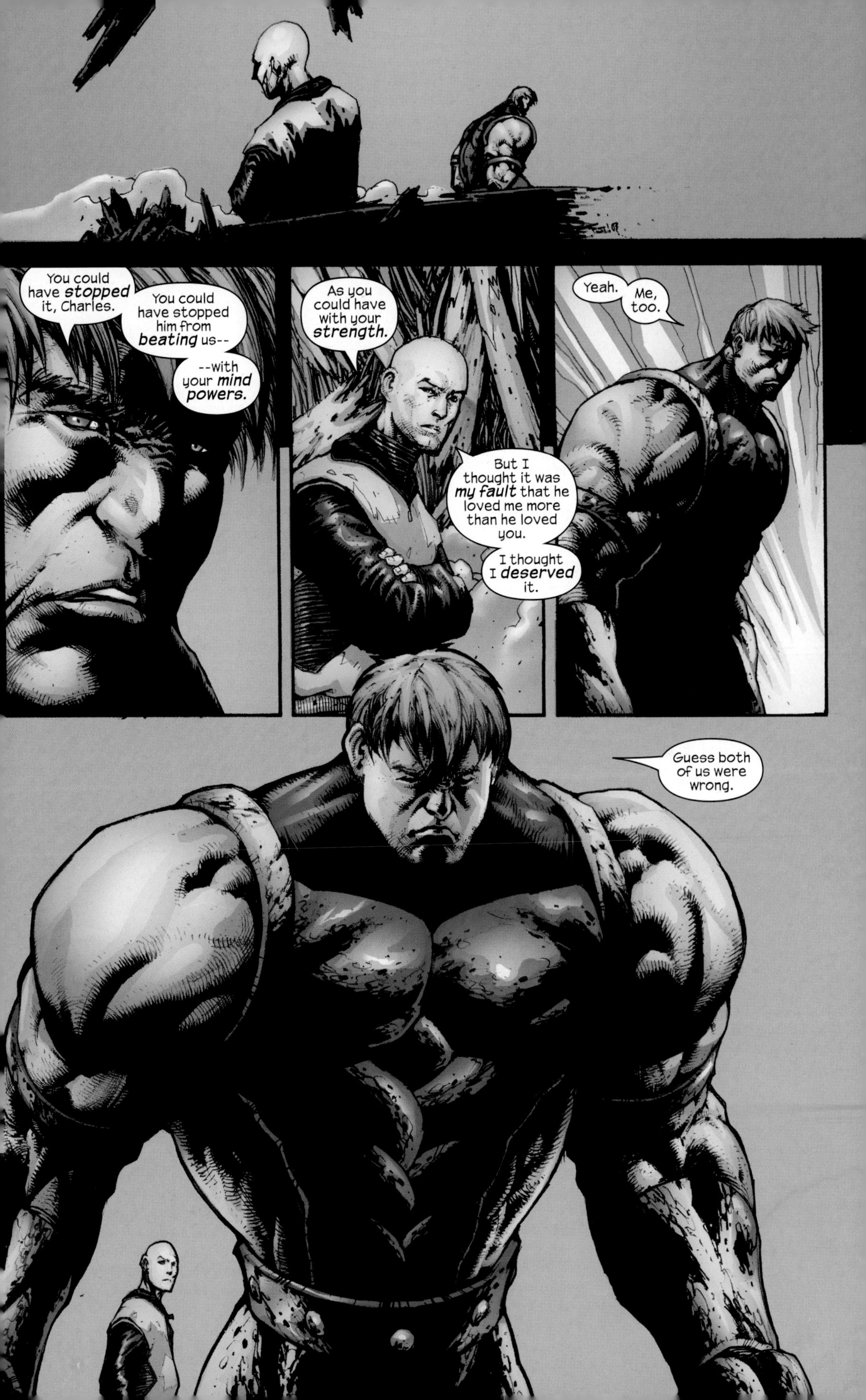
You could have stopped it, Charles.
You could have stopped him from beating us--
--with your mind powers.
As you could have with your strength.
But I thought it was my fault that he loved me more than he loved you.
I thought I deserved it.
Yeah.
Me, too.
Guess both of us were wrong.

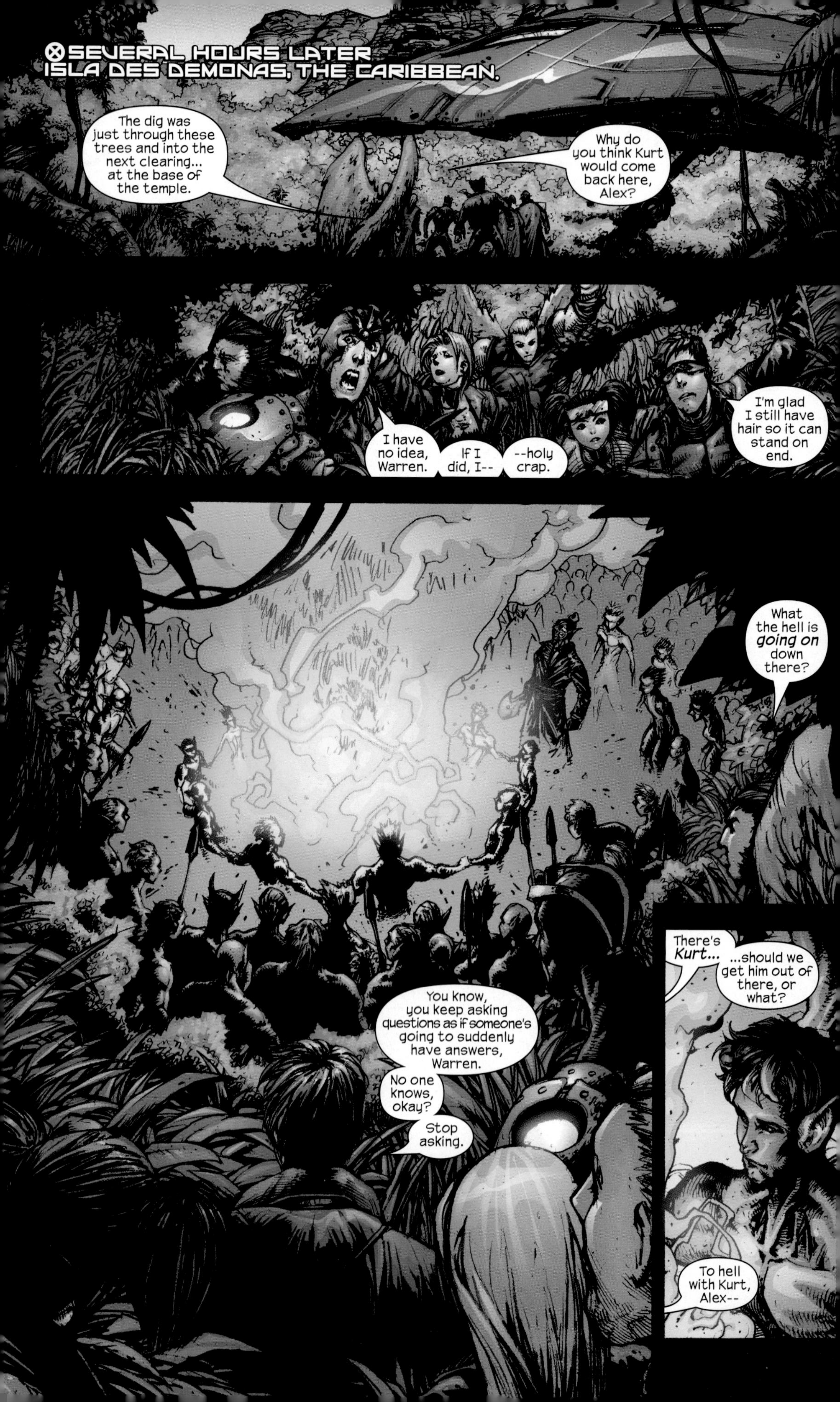
SEVERAL HOURS LATER
ISLA DES DEMONAS, THE CARIBBEAN.
The dig was just through these trees and into the next clearing... at the base of the temple.
Why do you think Kurt would come back here, Alex?
I have no idea, Warren.
If I did, I--
--holy crap.
I'm glad I still have hair so it can stand on end.
What the hell is *going on* down there?
You know, you keep asking questions as if someone's going to suddenly have answers, Warren.
No one knows, okay?
Stop asking.
There's *Kurt*...
...should we get him out of there, or what?
To hell with Kurt, Alex--

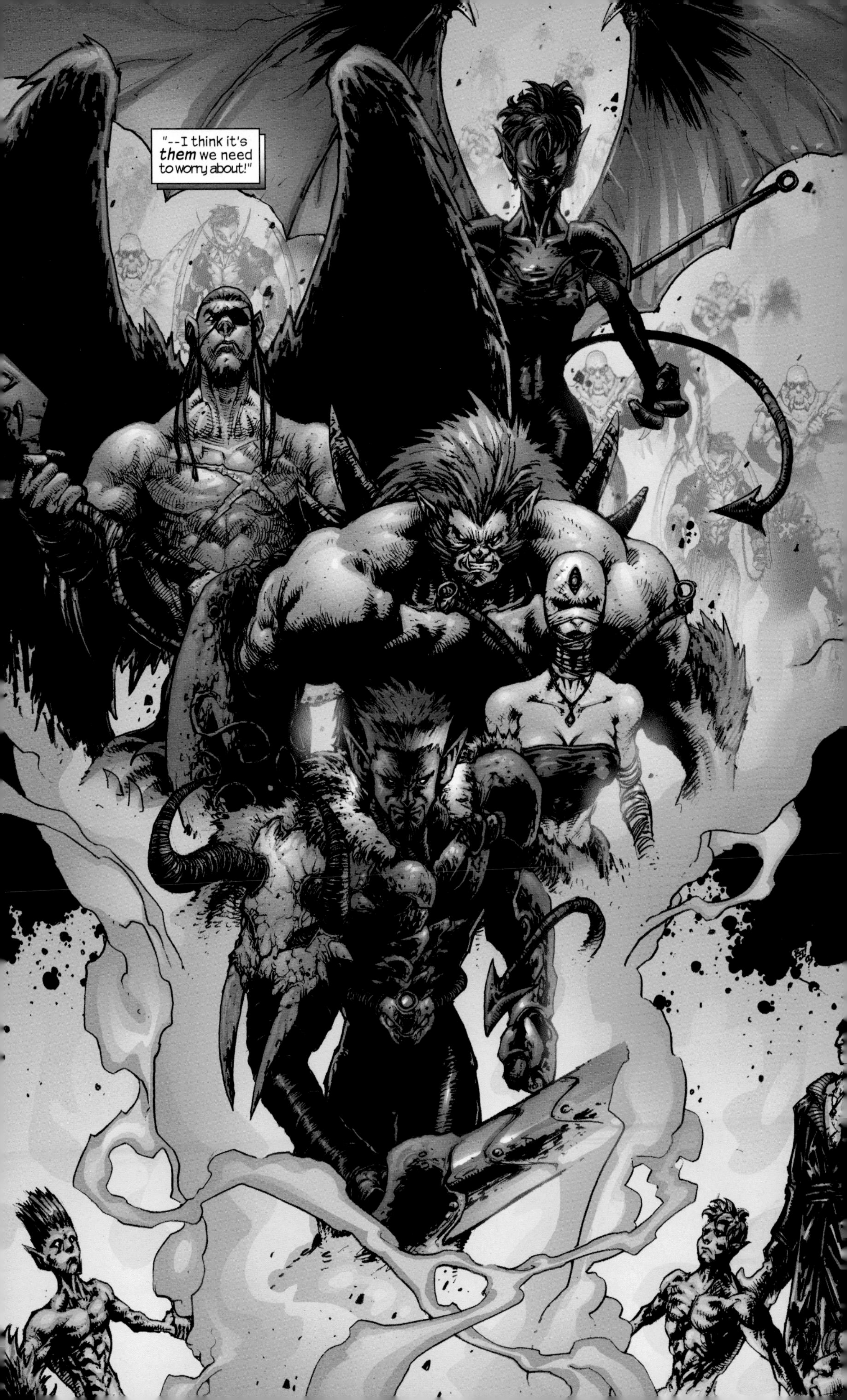
"--I think it's *them* we need to worry about!"

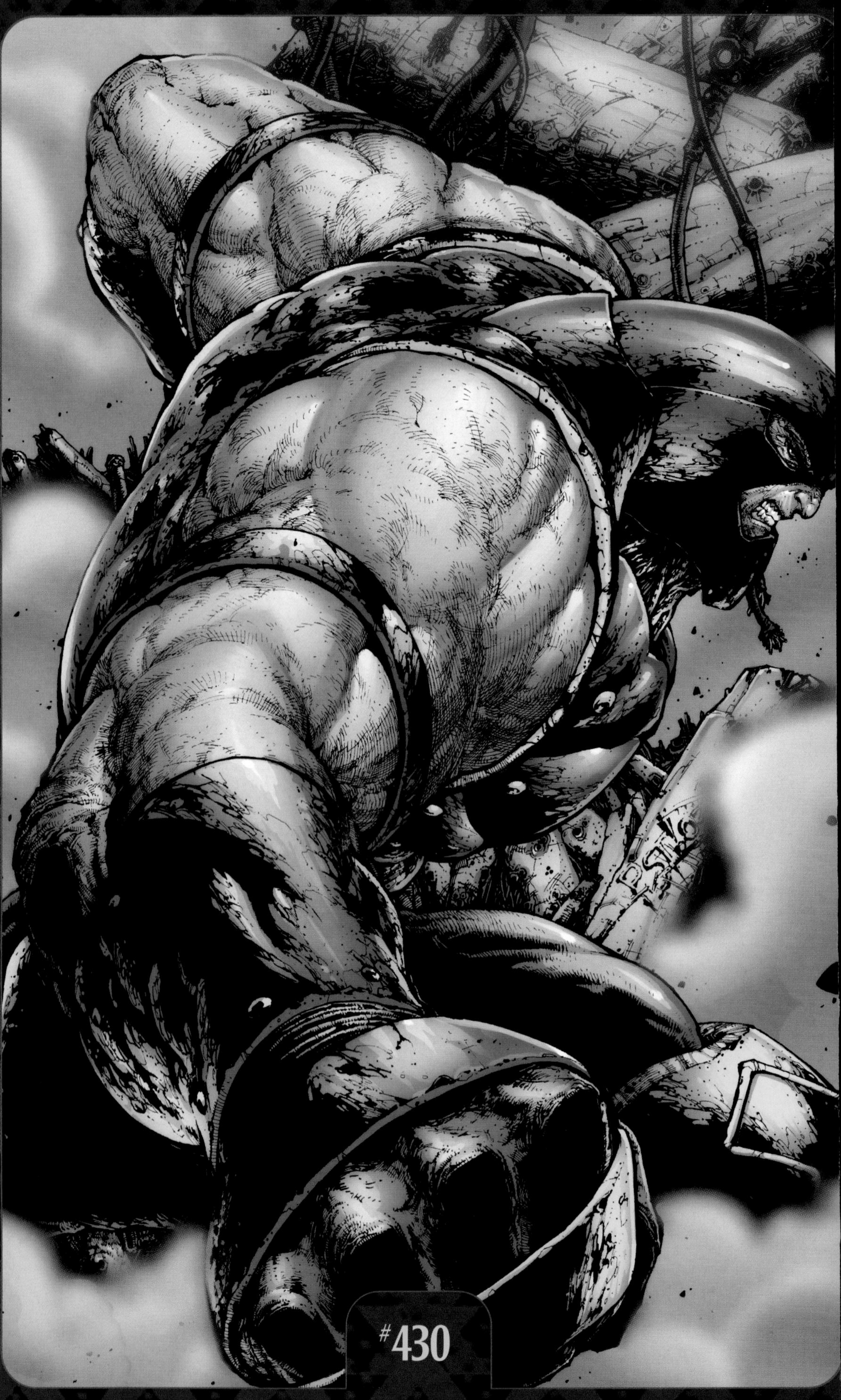

#430

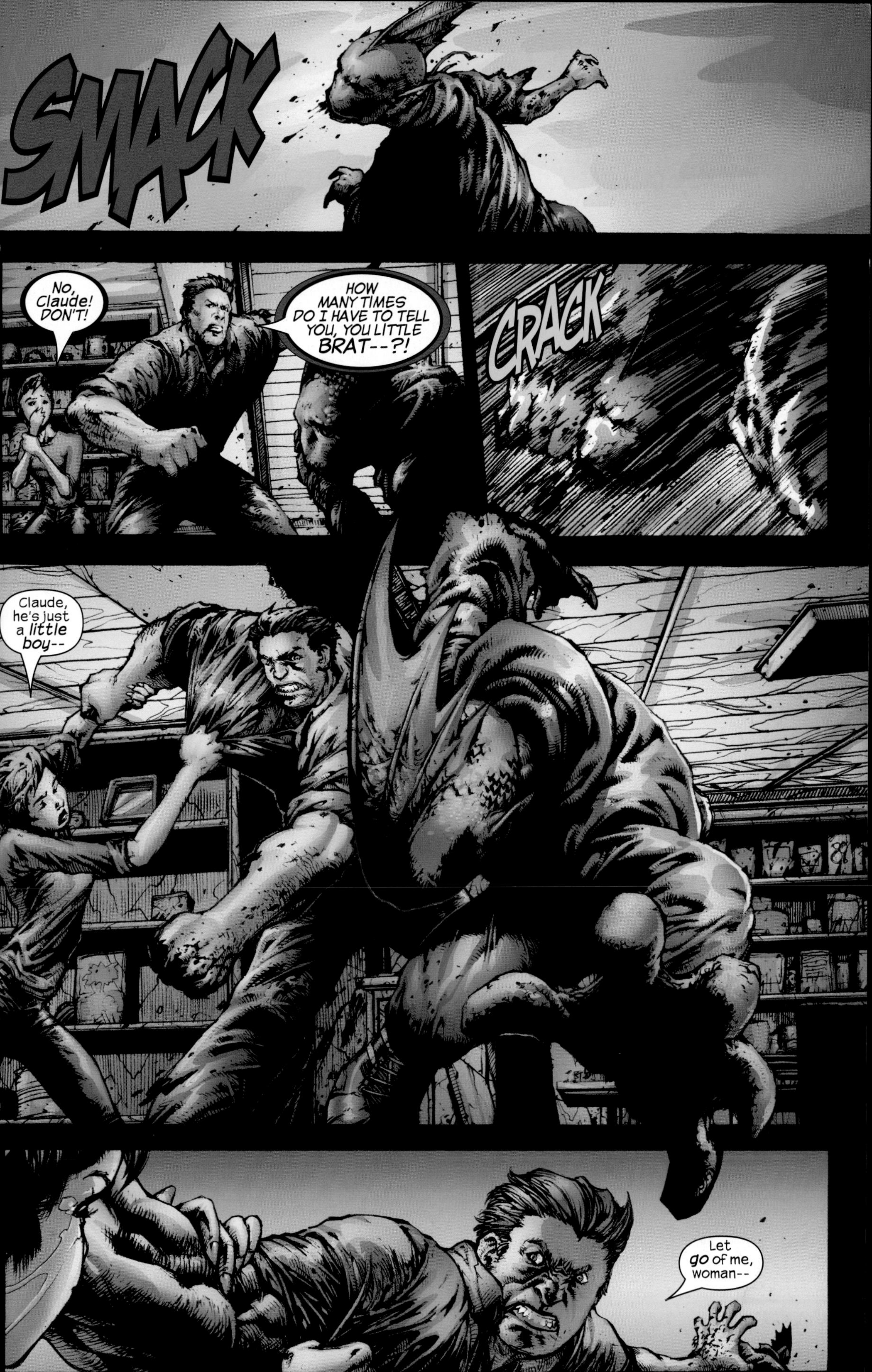
SMACK
No, Claude! DON'T!
HOW MANY TIMES DO I HAVE TO TELL YOU, YOU LITTLE BRAT--?!
CRACK
Claude, he's just a little boy--
Let go of me, woman--

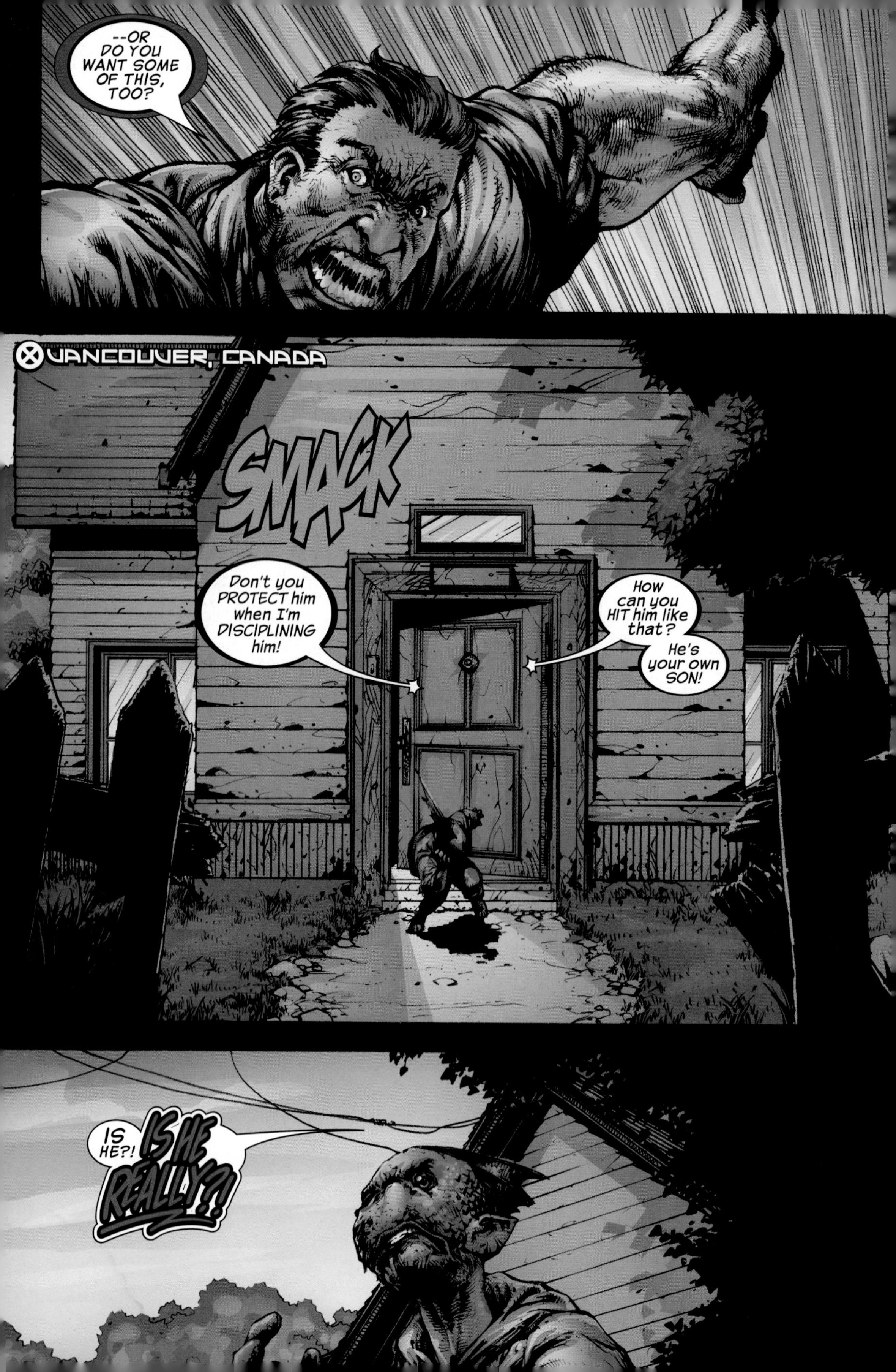
--OR DO YOU WANT SOME OF THIS, TOO?
VANCOUVER, CANADA
SMACK
Don't you PROTECT him when I'm DISCIPLINING him!
How can you HIT him like that?
He's your own SON!
IS HE?!
IS HE REALLY?!

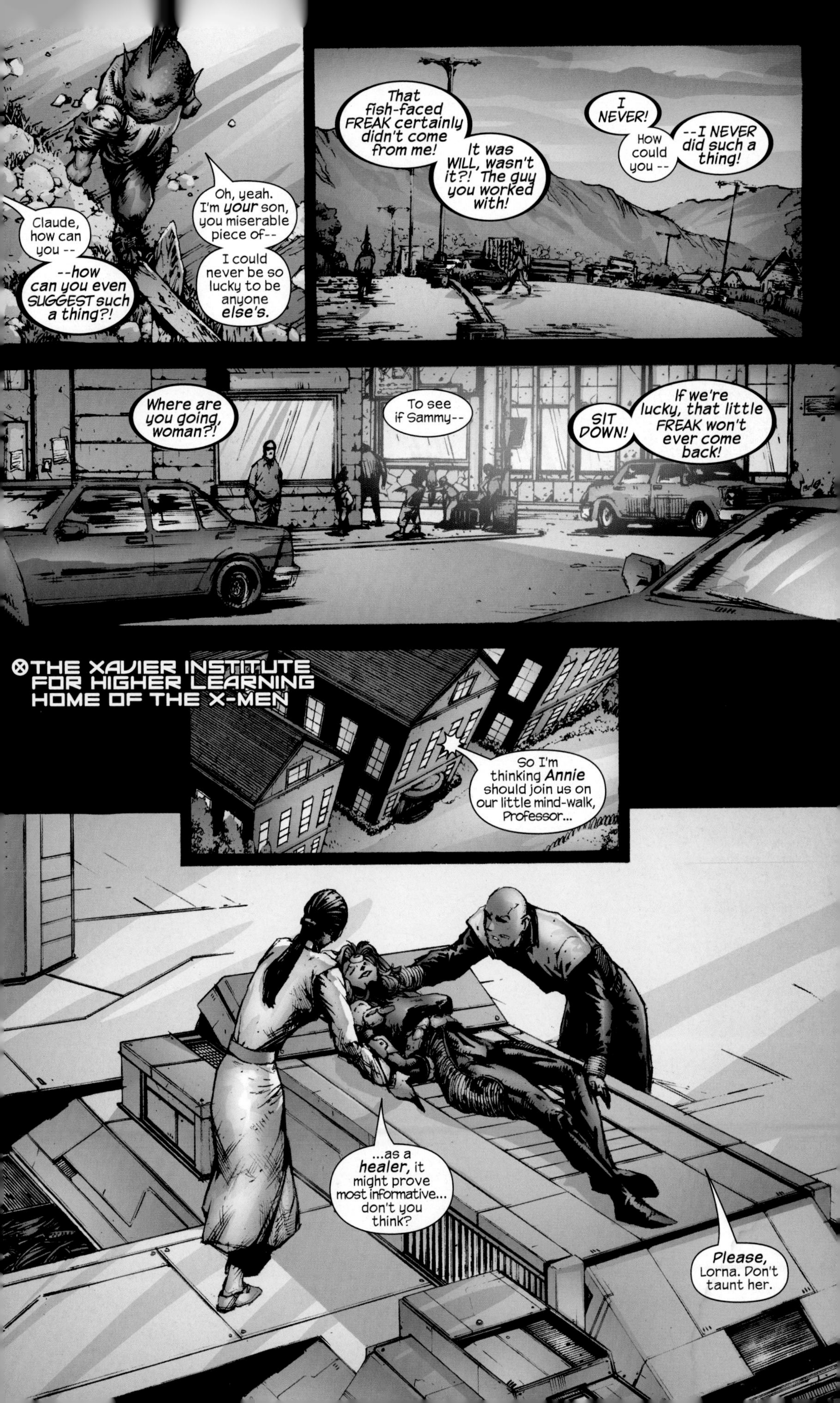

Claude, how can you --
--how can you even SUGGEST such a thing?!
Oh, yeah. I'm your son, you miserable piece of--
I could never be so lucky to be anyone else's.
That fish-faced FREAK certainly didn't come from me!
It was WILL, wasn't it?! The guy you worked with!
I NEVER!
How could you --
--I NEVER did such a thing!
Where are you going, woman?!
To see if Sammy--
SIT DOWN!
If we're lucky, that little FREAK won't ever come back!
THE XAVIER INSTITUTE FOR HIGHER LEARNING HOME OF THE X-MEN
So I'm thinking Annie should join us on our little mind-walk, Professor...
...as a healer, it might prove most informative... don't you think?
Please, Lorna. Don't taunt her.

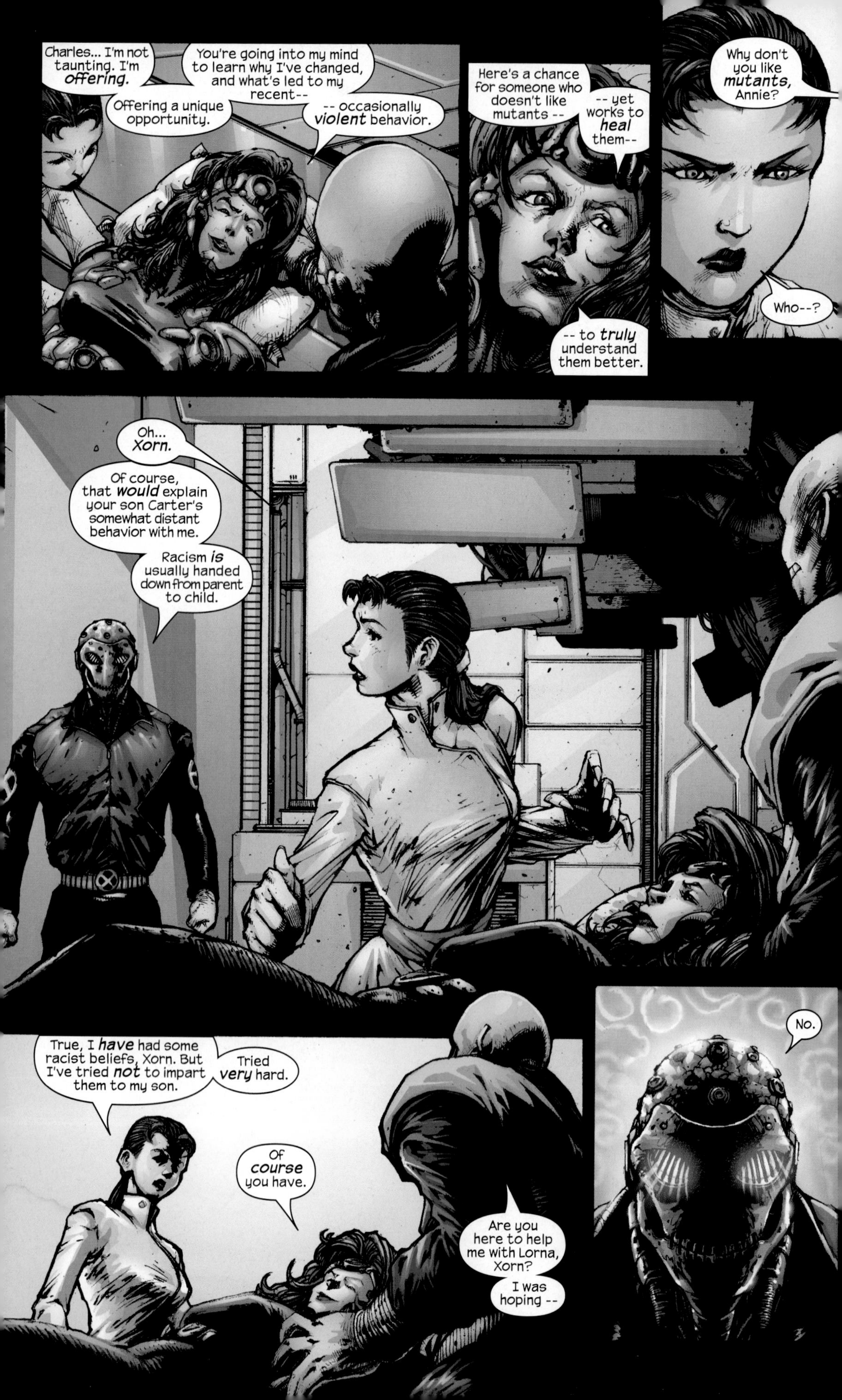

Charles... I'm not taunting. I'm *offering.*
Offering a unique opportunity.
You're going into my mind to learn why I've changed, and what's led to my recent--
-- occasionally *violent* behavior.
Here's a chance for someone who doesn't like mutants --
-- yet works to *heal* them--
-- to *truly* understand them better.
Why don't you like *mutants,* Annie?
Who--?
Oh... *Xorn.*
Of course, that *would* explain your son Carter's somewhat distant behavior with me.
Racism *is* usually handed down from parent to child.
True, I *have* had some racist beliefs, Xorn. But I've tried *not* to impart them to my son.
Tried *very* hard.
Of *course* you have.
Are you here to help me with Lorna, Xorn?
I was hoping --
No.

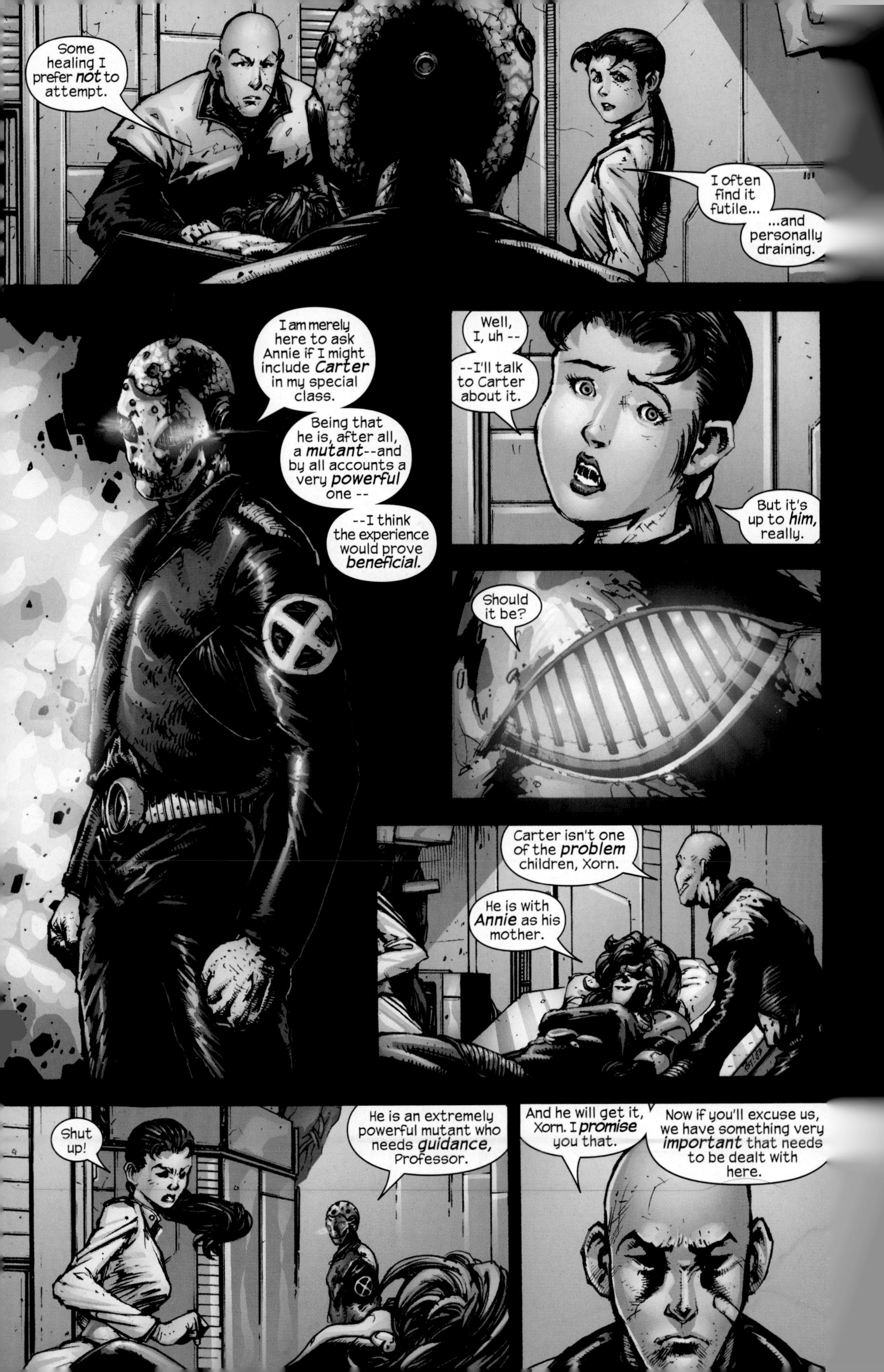

Some healing I prefer *not* to attempt.
I often find it futile...
...and personally draining.
I am merely here to ask Annie if I might include *Carter* in my special class.
Being that he is, after all, a *mutant*--and by all accounts a very *powerful* one --
--I think the experience would prove *beneficial.*
Well, I, uh --
--I'll talk to Carter about it.
But it's up to *him,* really.
Should it be?
Carter isn't one of the *problem* children, Xorn.
He is with *Annie* as his mother.
Shut up!
He is an extremely powerful mutant who needs *guidance,* Professor.
And he will get it, Xorn. I *promise* you that.
Now if you'll excuse us, we have something very *important* that needs to be dealt with here.

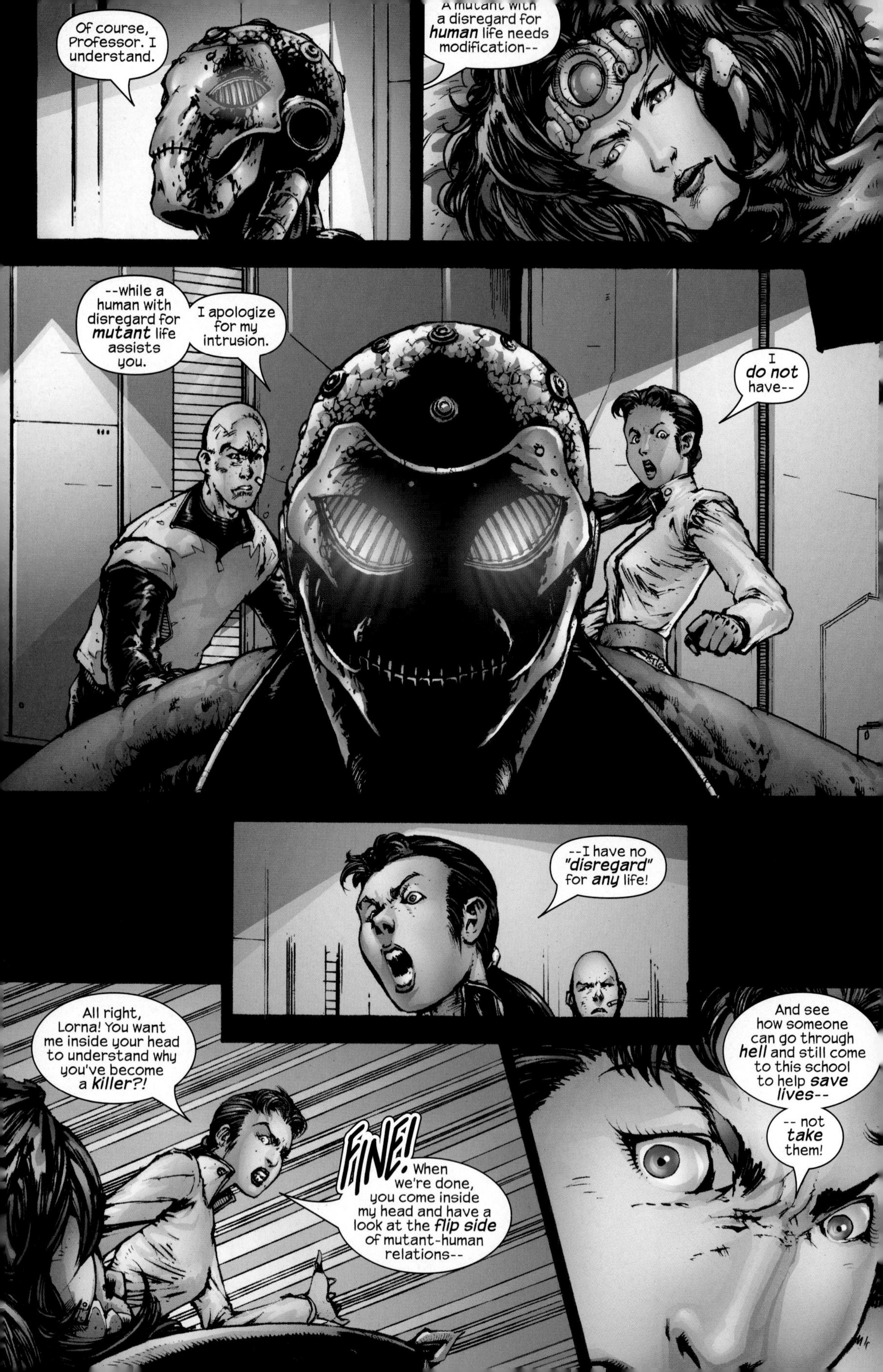

Of course, Professor. I understand.
A mutant with a disregard for *human* life needs modification--
--while a human with disregard for *mutant* life assists you.
I apologize for my intrusion.
I *do not* have--
--I have no *"disregard"* for *any* life!
All right, Lorna! You want me inside your head to understand why you've become a *killer?!*
FINE! When we're done, you come inside my head and have a look at the *flip side* of mutant-human relations--
And see how someone can go through *hell* and still come to this school to help *save lives*--
-- not *take* them!

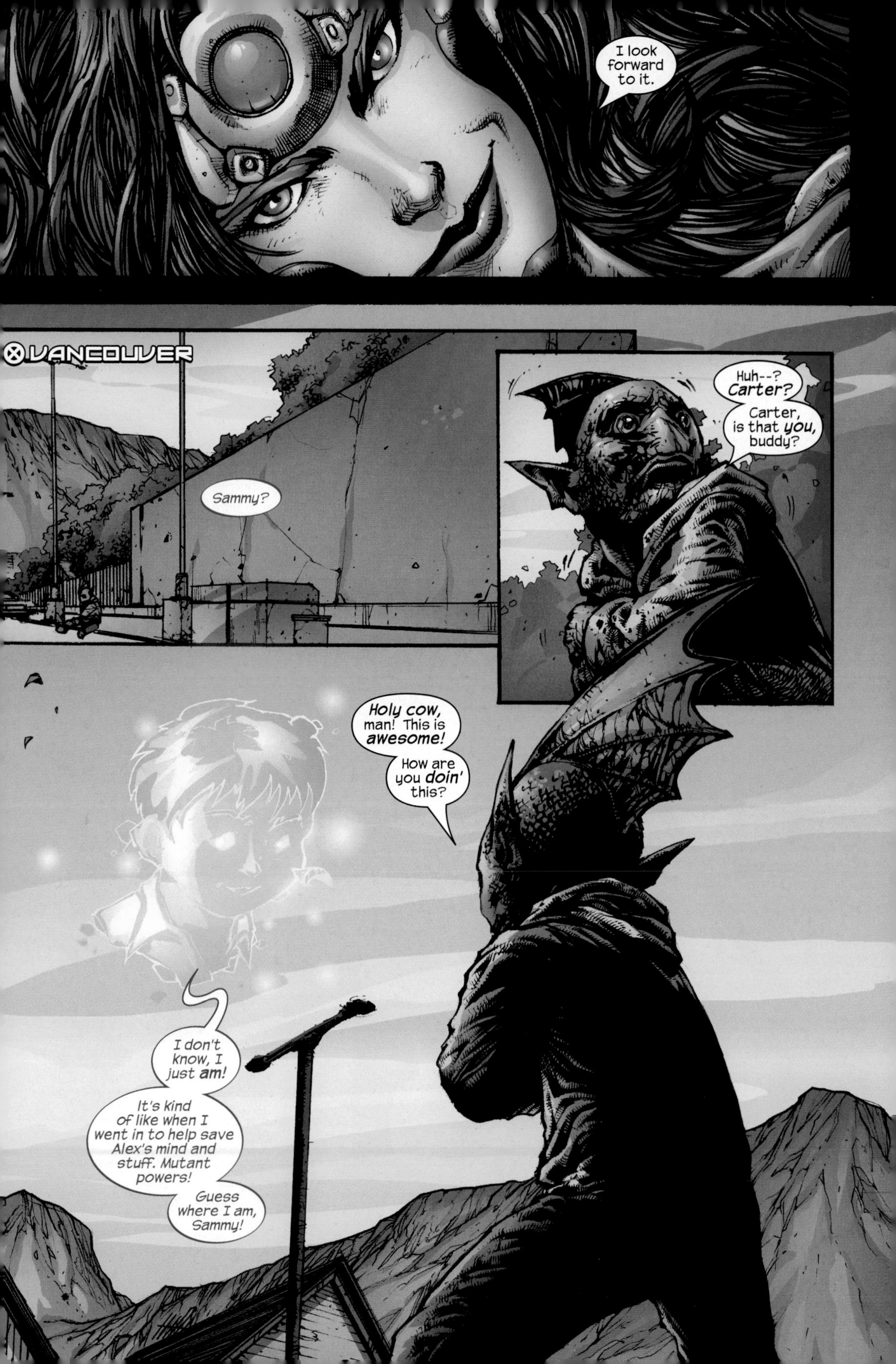

I look forward to it.
VANCOUVER
Sammy?
Huh--? Carter?
Carter, is that you, buddy?
Holy cow, man! This is awesome!
How are you doin' this?
I don't know, I just am!
It's kind of like when I went in to help save Alex's mind and stuff. Mutant powers!
Guess where I am, Sammy!

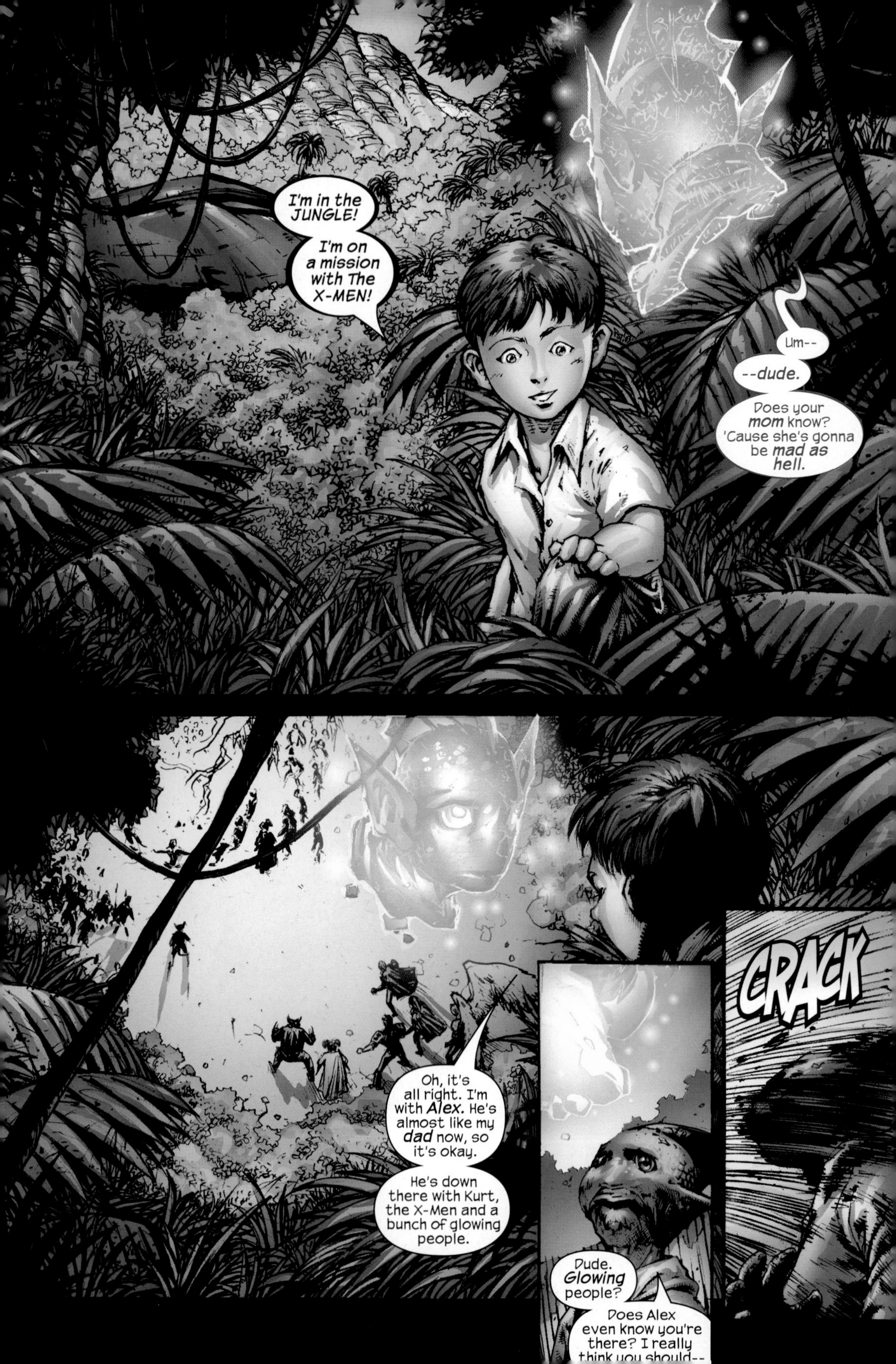

I'm in the JUNGLE!
I'm on a mission with The X-MEN!
Um--
--dude.
Does your mom know? 'Cause she's gonna be mad as hell.
Oh, it's all right. I'm with Alex. He's almost like my dad now, so it's okay.
He's down there with Kurt, the X-Men and a bunch of glowing people.
CRACK
Dude. Glowing people?
Does Alex even know you're there? I really think you should--

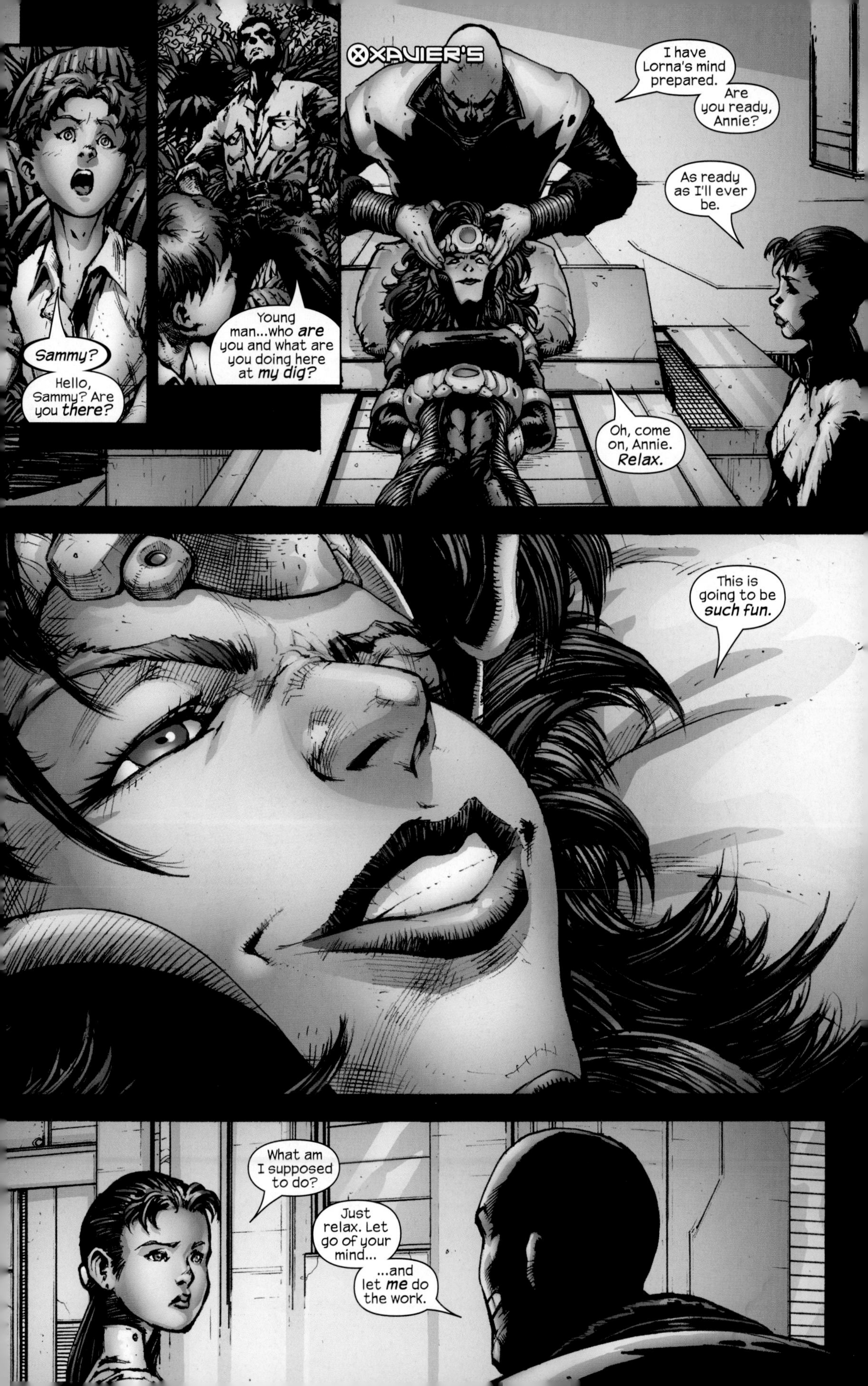
Sammy?
Hello, Sammy? Are you there?
Young man...who are you and what are you doing here at my dig?
XAVIER'S
I have Lorna's mind prepared.
Are you ready, Annie?
As ready as I'll ever be.
Oh, come on, Annie. Relax.
This is going to be such fun.
What am I supposed to do?
Just relax. Let go of your mind...
...and let me do the work.

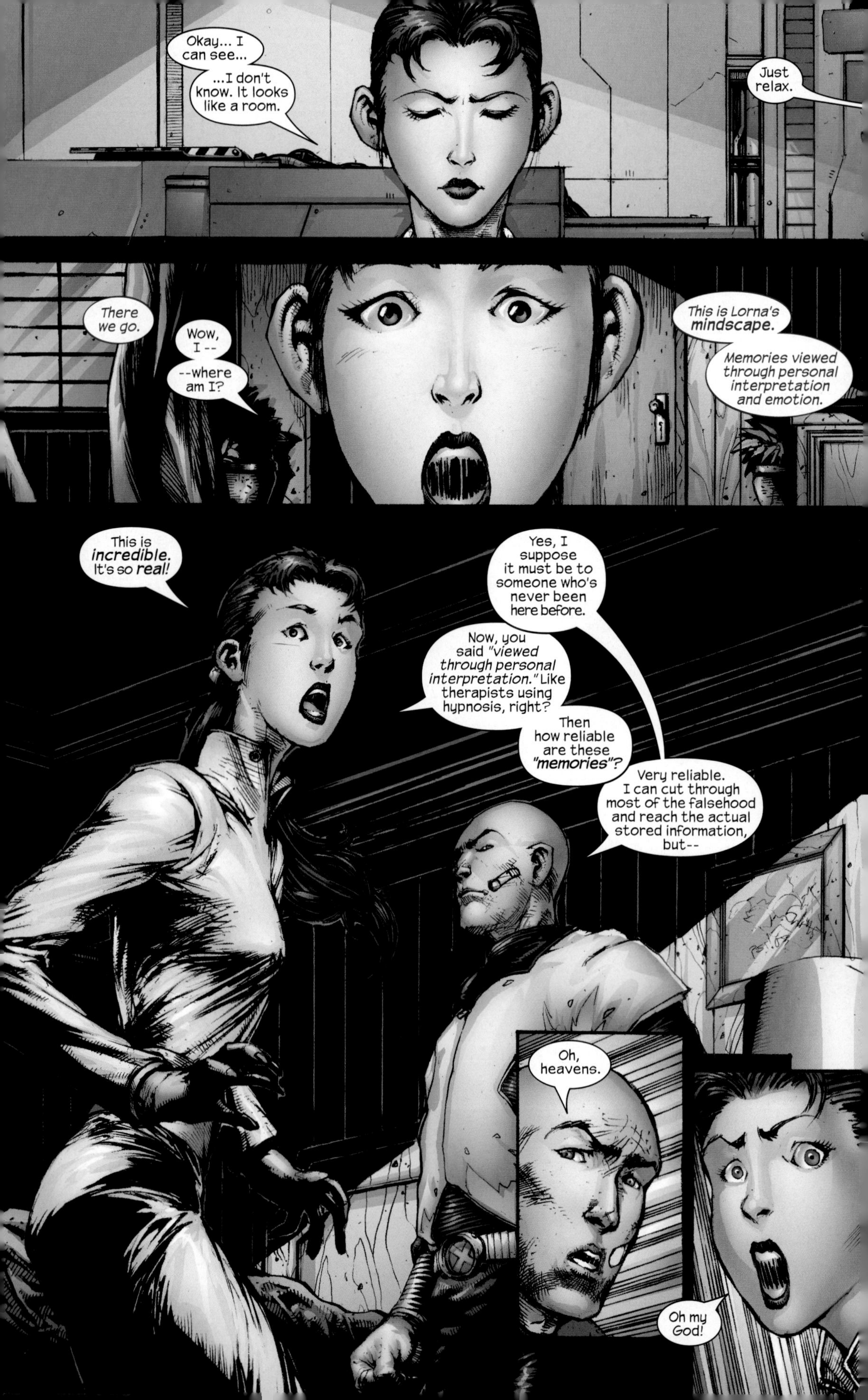
Okay... I can see...
...I don't know. It looks like a room.
Just relax.
There we go.
Wow, I --
--where am I?
This is Lorna's mindscape.
Memories viewed through personal interpretation and emotion.
This is incredible. It's so real!
Yes, I suppose it must be to someone who's never been here before.
Now, you said "viewed through personal interpretation." Like therapists using hypnosis, right?
Then how reliable are these "memories"?
Very reliable. I can cut through most of the falsehood and reach the actual stored information, but--
Oh, heavens.
Oh my God!

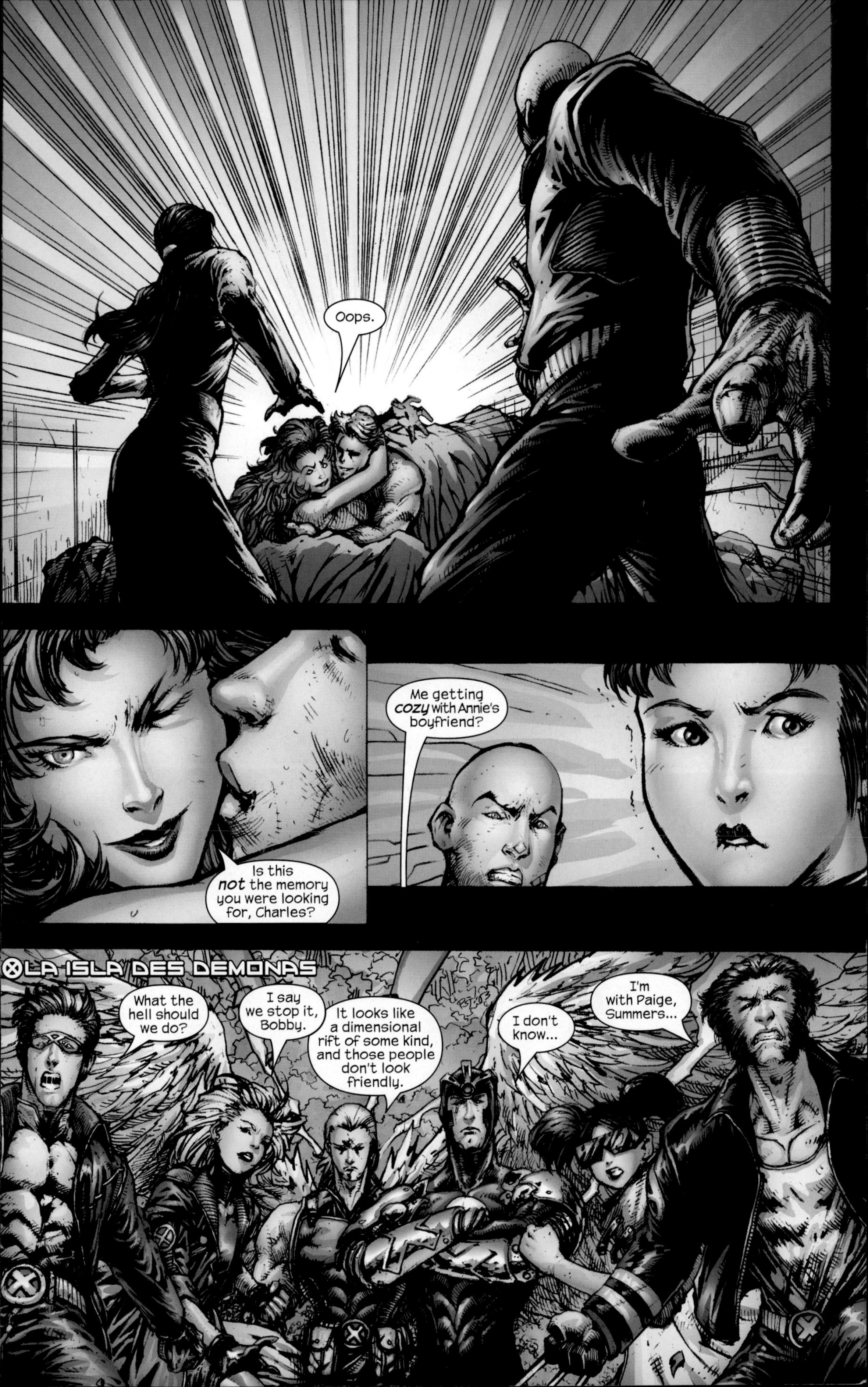
Oops.
Is this *not* the memory you were looking for, Charles?
Me getting *cozy* with Annie's boyfriend?
LA ISLA DES DEMONAS
What the hell should we do?
I say we stop it, Bobby.
It looks like a dimensional rift of some kind, and those people don't look friendly.
I don't know...
I'm with Paige, Summers...

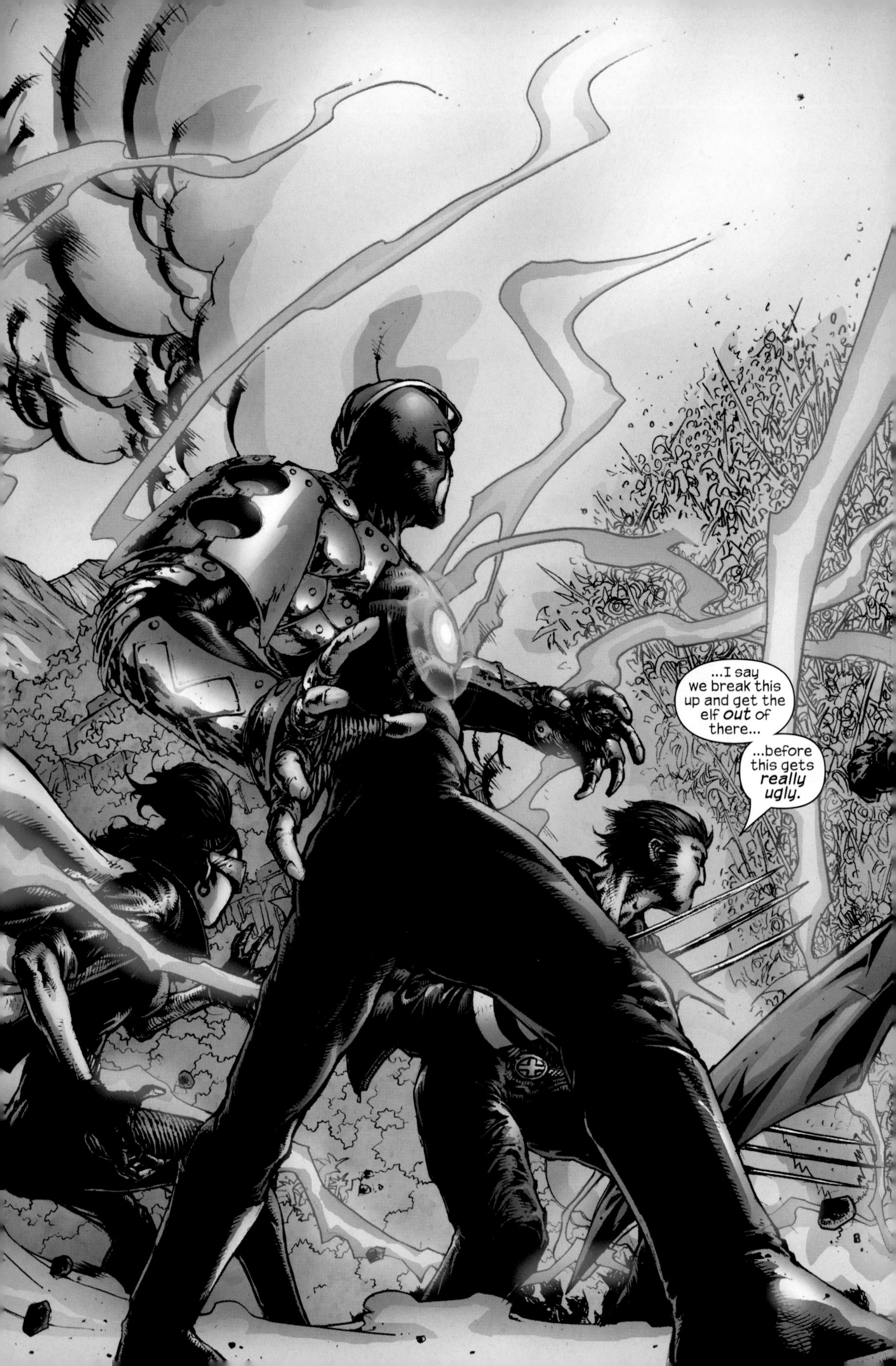
...I say we break this up and get the elf out of there...
...before this gets really ugly.

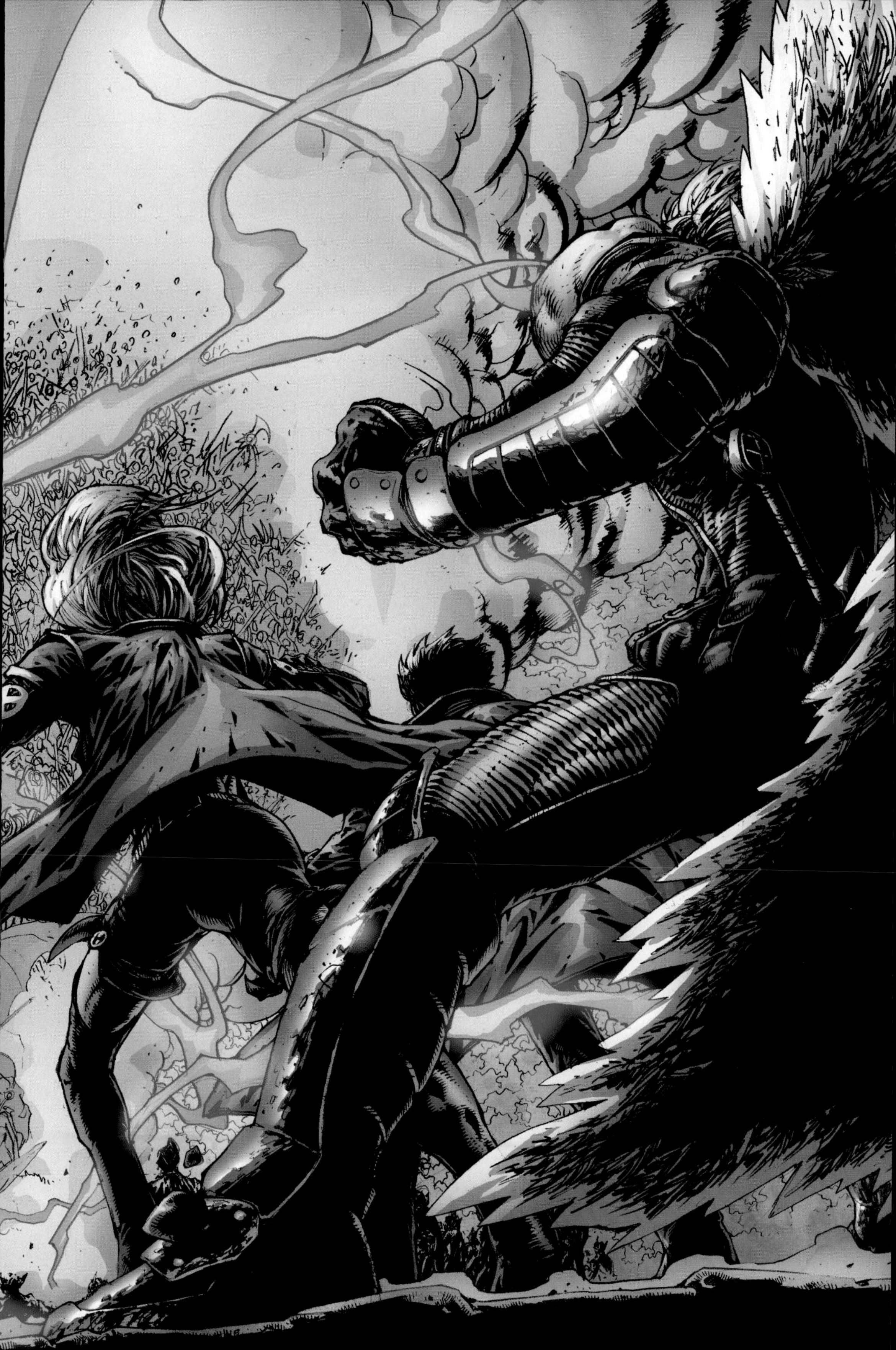

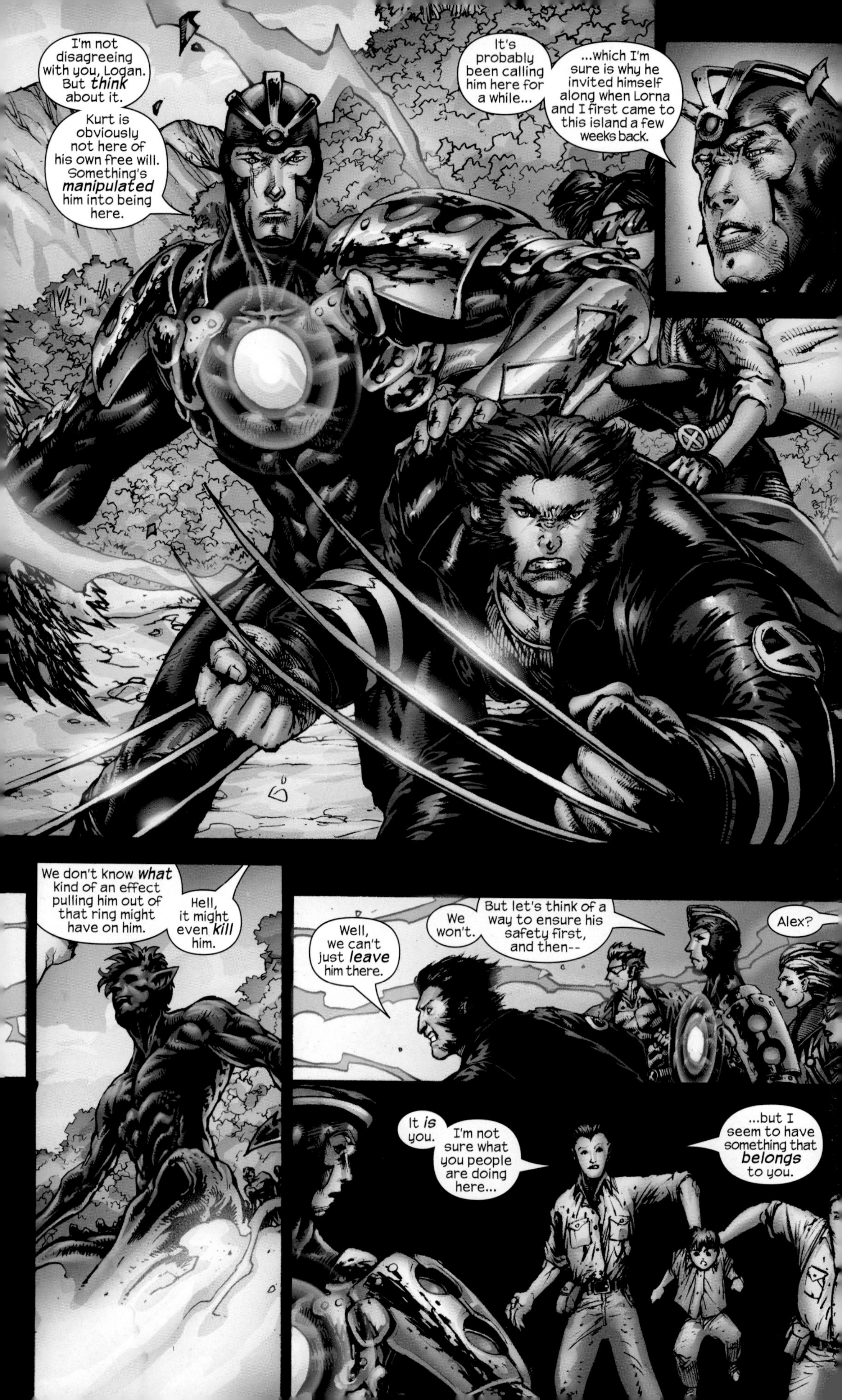

I'm not disagreeing with you, Logan. But *think* about it.
Kurt is obviously not here of his own free will. Something's *manipulated* him into being here.
It's probably been calling him here for a while...
...which I'm sure is why he invited himself along when Lorna and I first came to this island a few weeks back.
We don't know *what* kind of an effect pulling him out of that ring might have on him.
Hell, it might even *kill* him.
Well, we can't just *leave* him there.
We won't.
But let's think of a way to ensure his safety first, and then--
Alex?
It *is* you.
I'm not sure what you people are doing here...
...but I seem to have something that *belongs* to you.

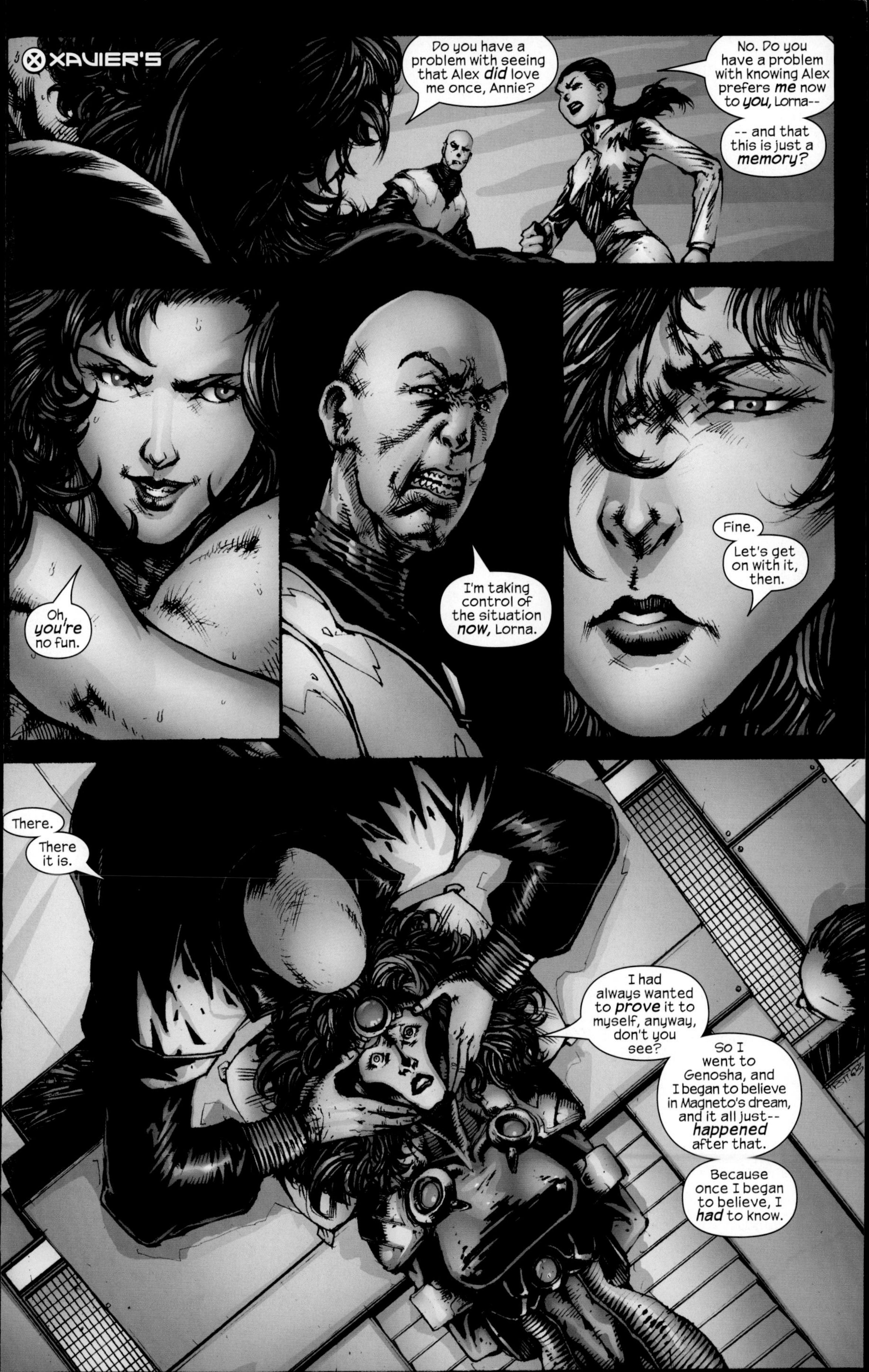
XAVIER'S
Do you have a problem with seeing that Alex did love me once, Annie?
No. Do you have a problem with knowing Alex prefers me now to you, Lorna--
-- and that this is just a memory?
Oh, you're no fun.
I'm taking control of the situation now, Lorna.
Fine.
Let's get on with it, then.
There.
There it is.
I had always wanted to prove it to myself, anyway, don't you see?
So I went to Genosha, and I began to believe in Magneto's dream, and it all just-- happened after that.
Because once I began to believe, I had to know.

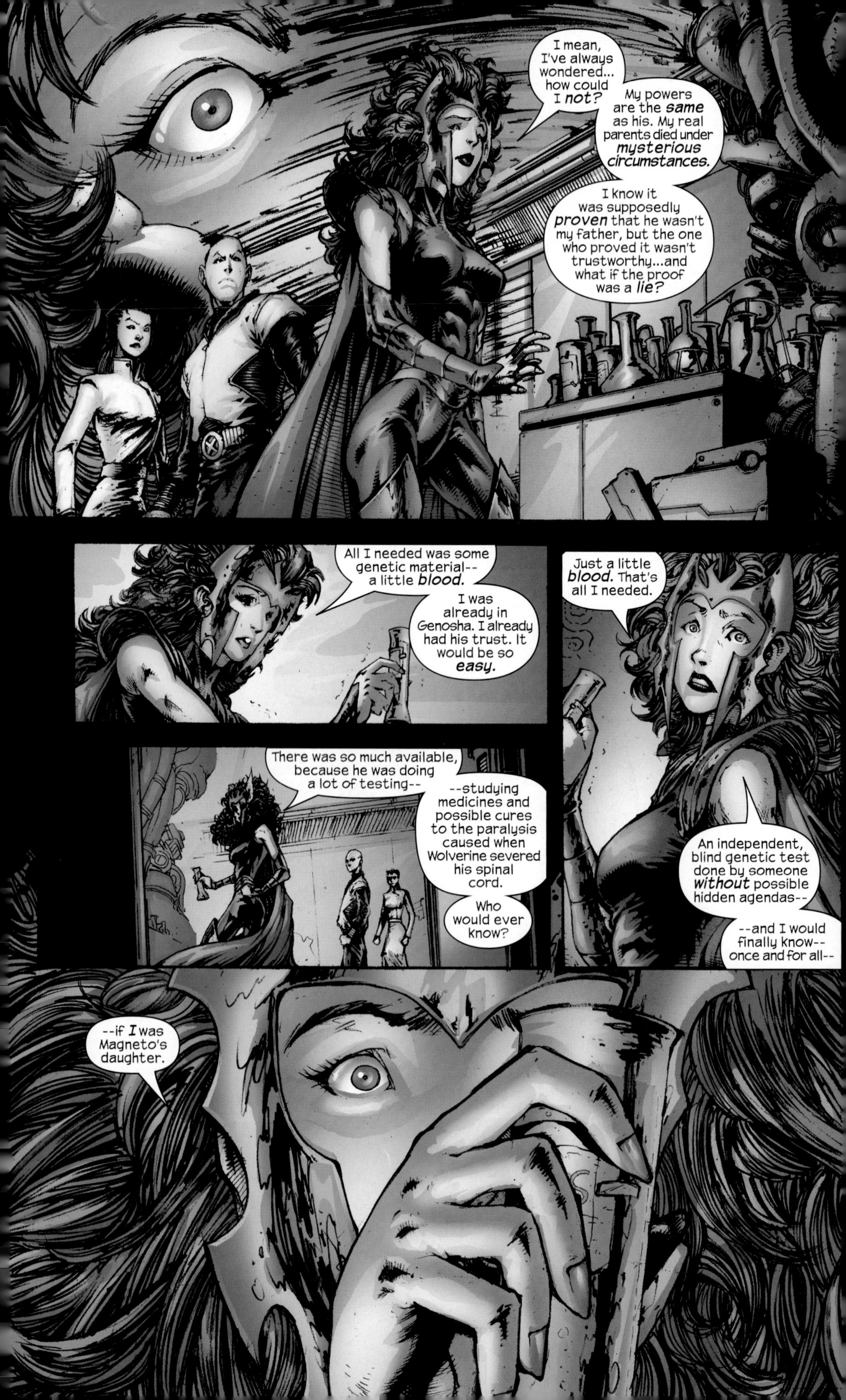
I mean, I've always wondered... how could I *not?*
My powers are the *same* as his. My real parents died under *mysterious circumstances.*
I know it was supposedly *proven* that he wasn't my father, but the one who proved it wasn't trustworthy...and what if the proof was a *lie?*
All I needed was some genetic material-- a little *blood.*
I was already in Genosha. I already had his trust. It would be so *easy.*
Just a little *blood.* That's all I needed.
There was so much available, because he was doing a lot of testing--
--studying medicines and possible cures to the paralysis caused when Wolverine severed his spinal cord.
Who would ever know?
An independent, blind genetic test done by someone *without* possible hidden agendas--
--and I would finally know-- once and for all--
--if *I* was Magneto's daughter.

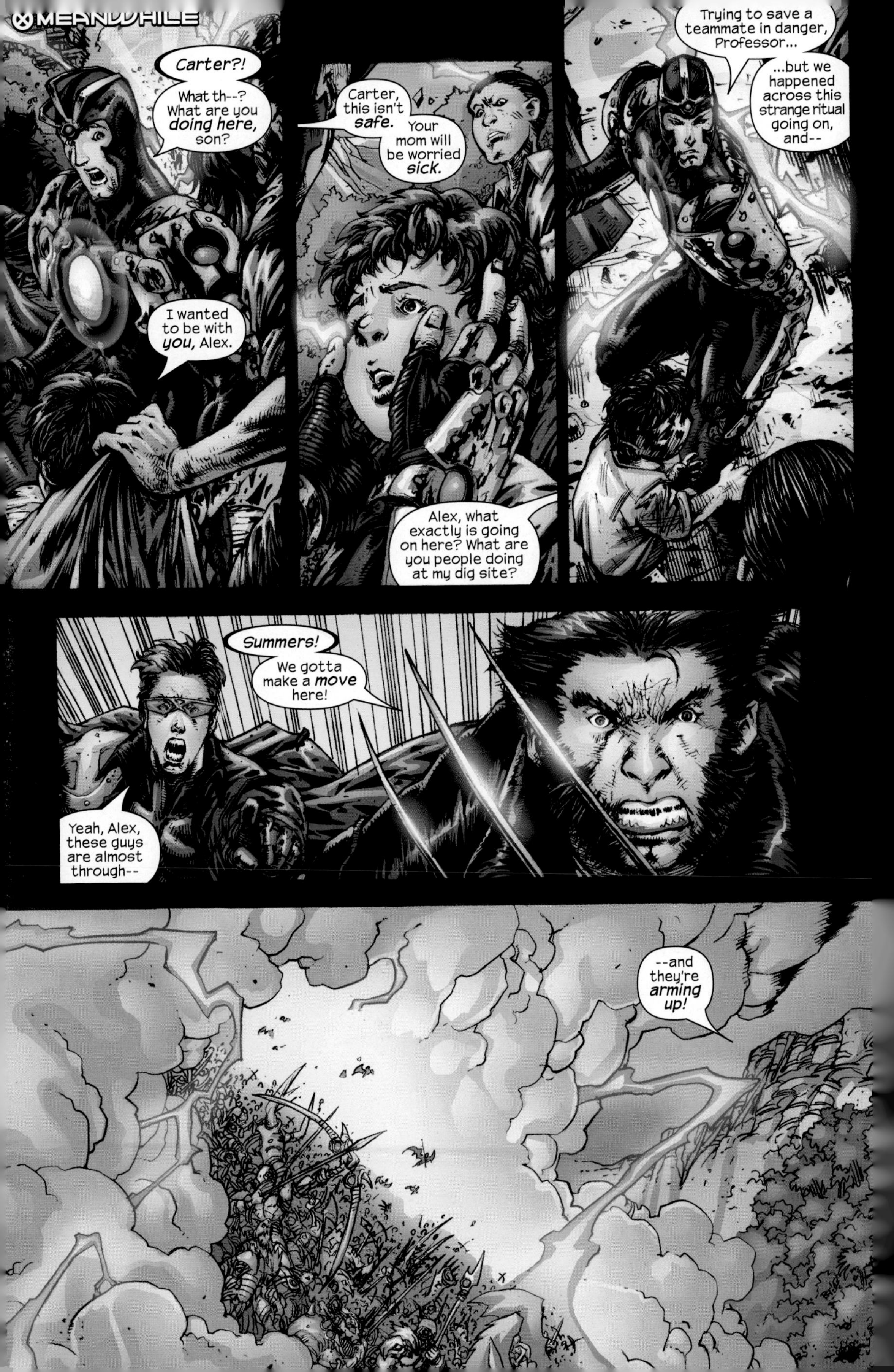
MEANWHILE
Carter?!
What th--? What are you doing here, son?
I wanted to be with you, Alex.
Carter, this isn't safe.
Your mom will be worried sick.
Alex, what exactly is going on here? What are you people doing at my dig site?
Trying to save a teammate in danger, Professor...
...but we happened across this strange ritual going on, and--
Summers!
We gotta make a move here!
Yeah, Alex, these guys are almost through--
--and they're arming up!

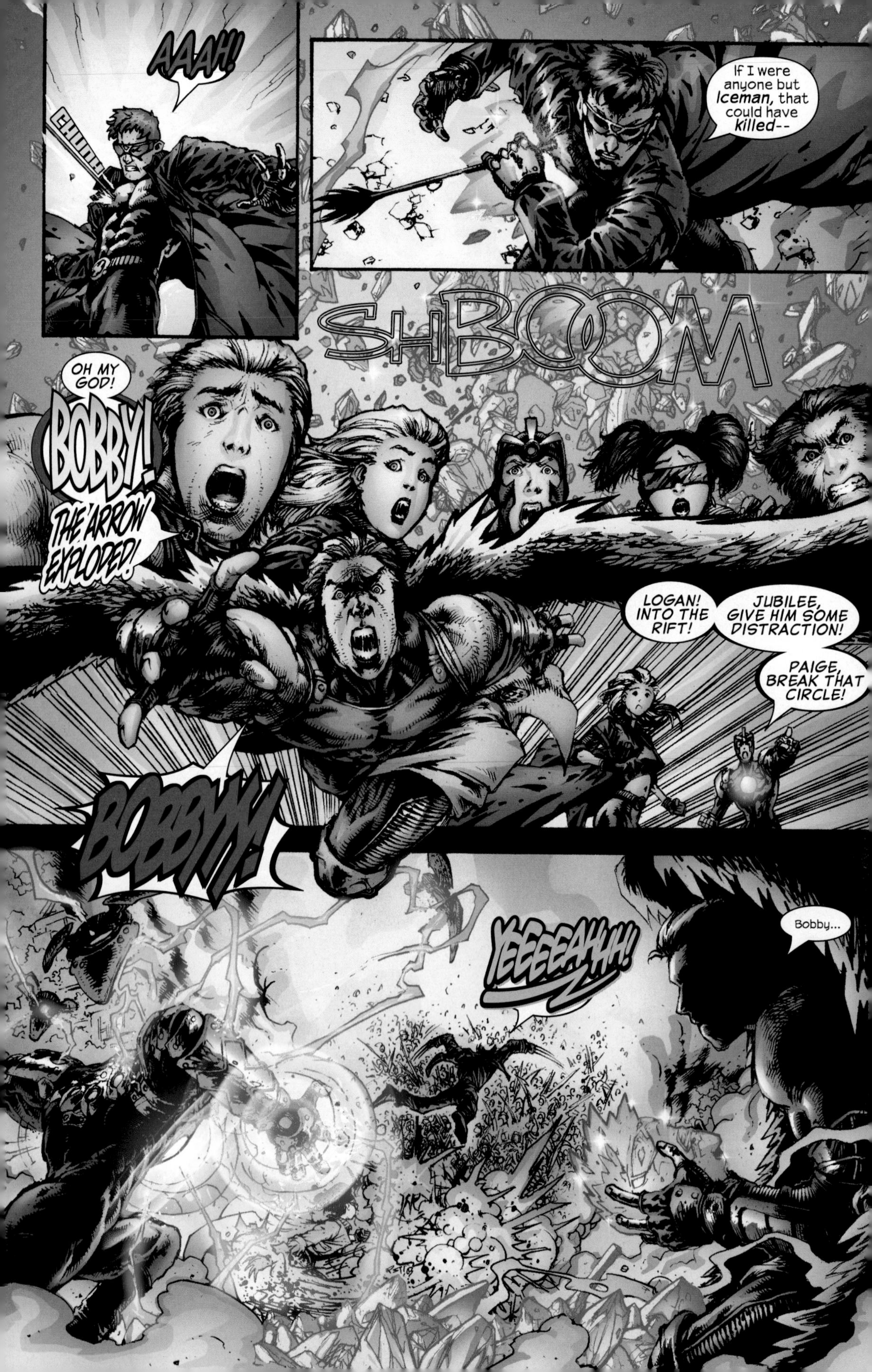

AAAH!
CHUNK
If I were anyone but Iceman, that could have killed--
SHBOOM
OH MY GOD!
BOBBY!
THE ARROW EXPLODED!
LOGAN! INTO THE RIFT!
JUBILEE, GIVE HIM SOME DISTRACTION!
PAIGE, BREAK THAT CIRCLE!
BOBBYY!
YEEEEAHHH!
Bobby...

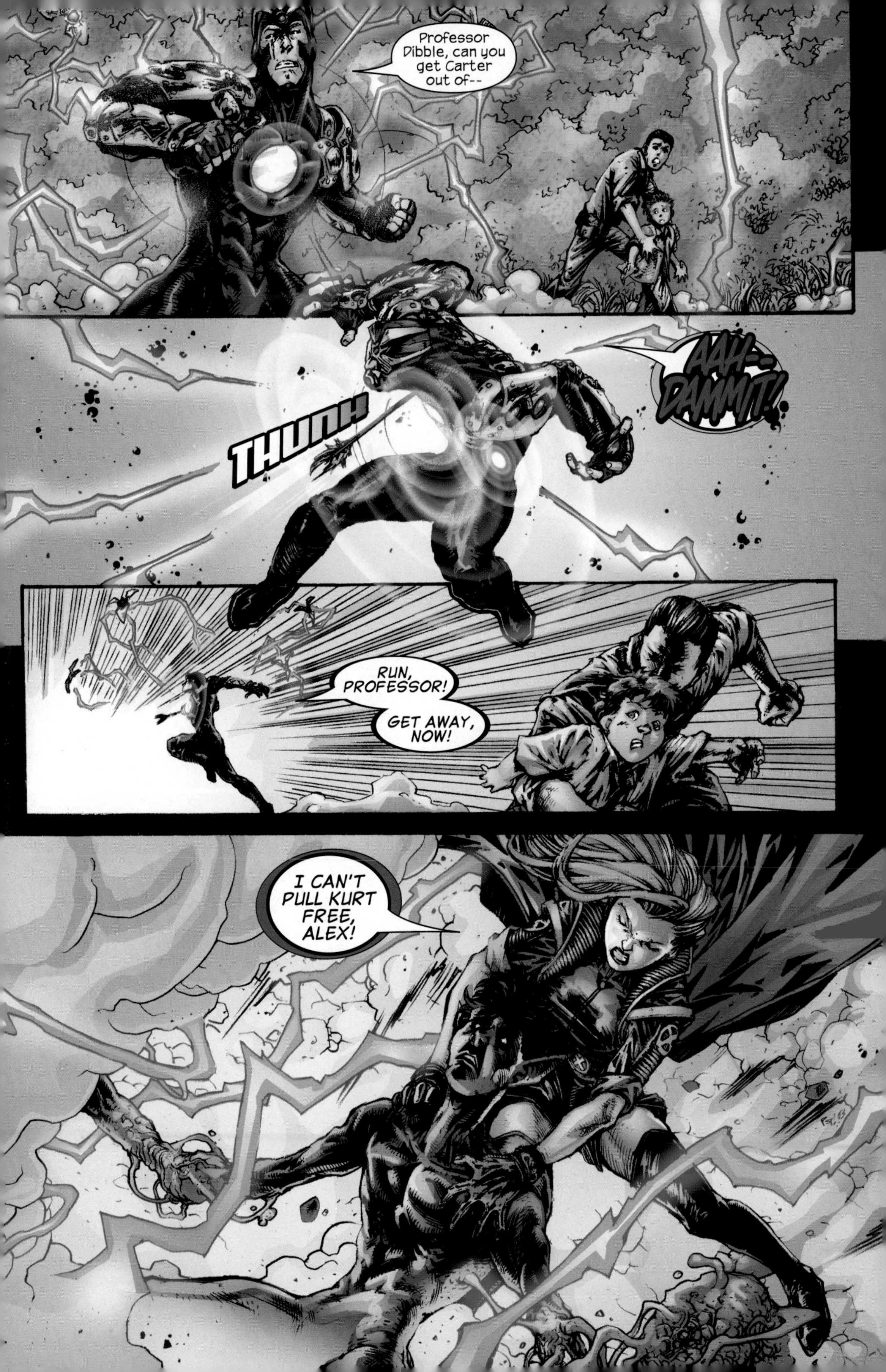
Professor Dibble, can you get Carter out of--
THUNK
AAH--DAMMIT!
RUN, PROFESSOR!
GET AWAY, NOW!
I CAN'T PULL KURT FREE, ALEX!

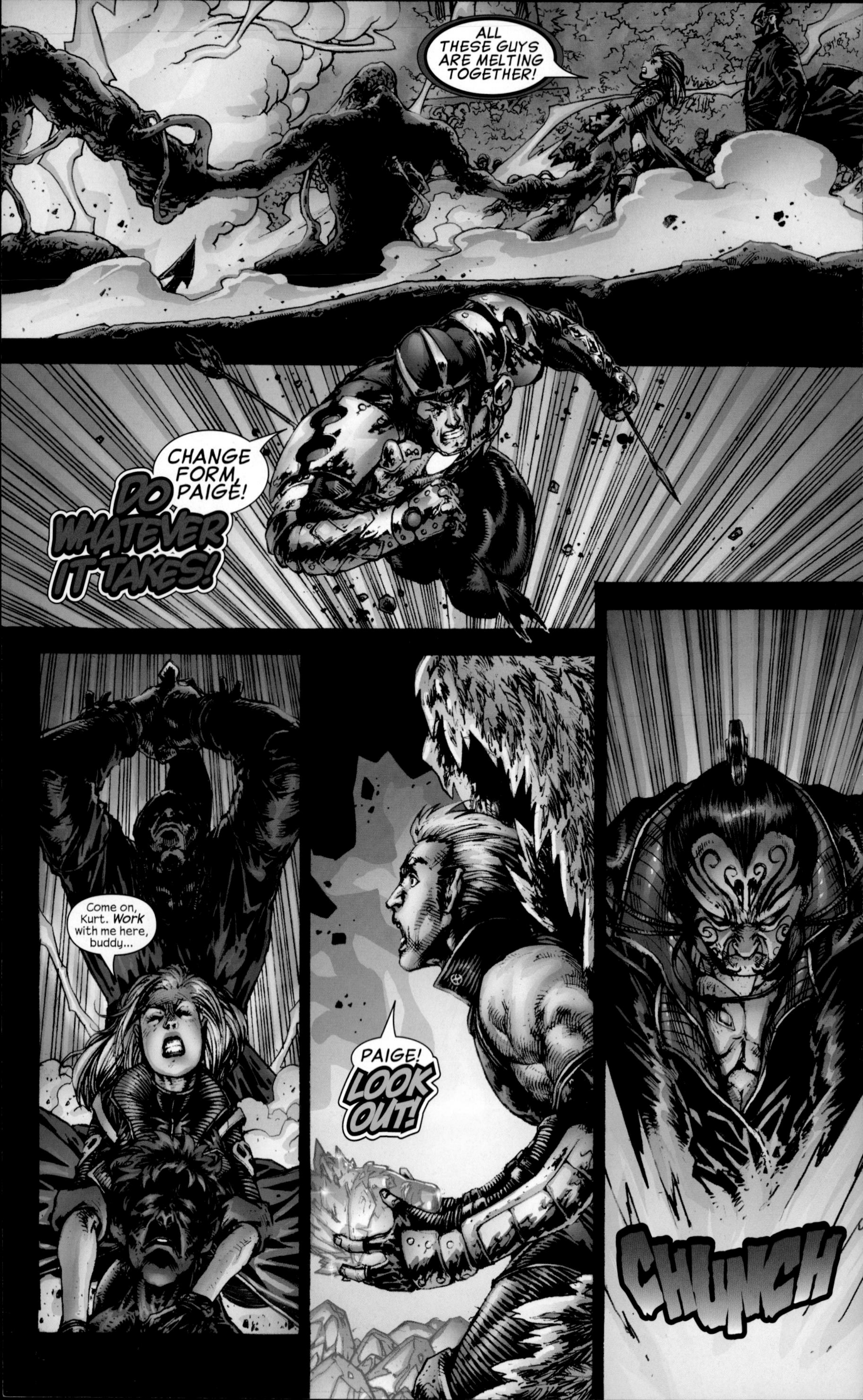
ALL THESE GUYS ARE MELTING TOGETHER!
CHANGE FORM, PAIGE!
DO WHATEVER IT TAKES!
Come on, Kurt. **Work** with me here, buddy...
PAIGE! LOOK OUT!
CHUNCH

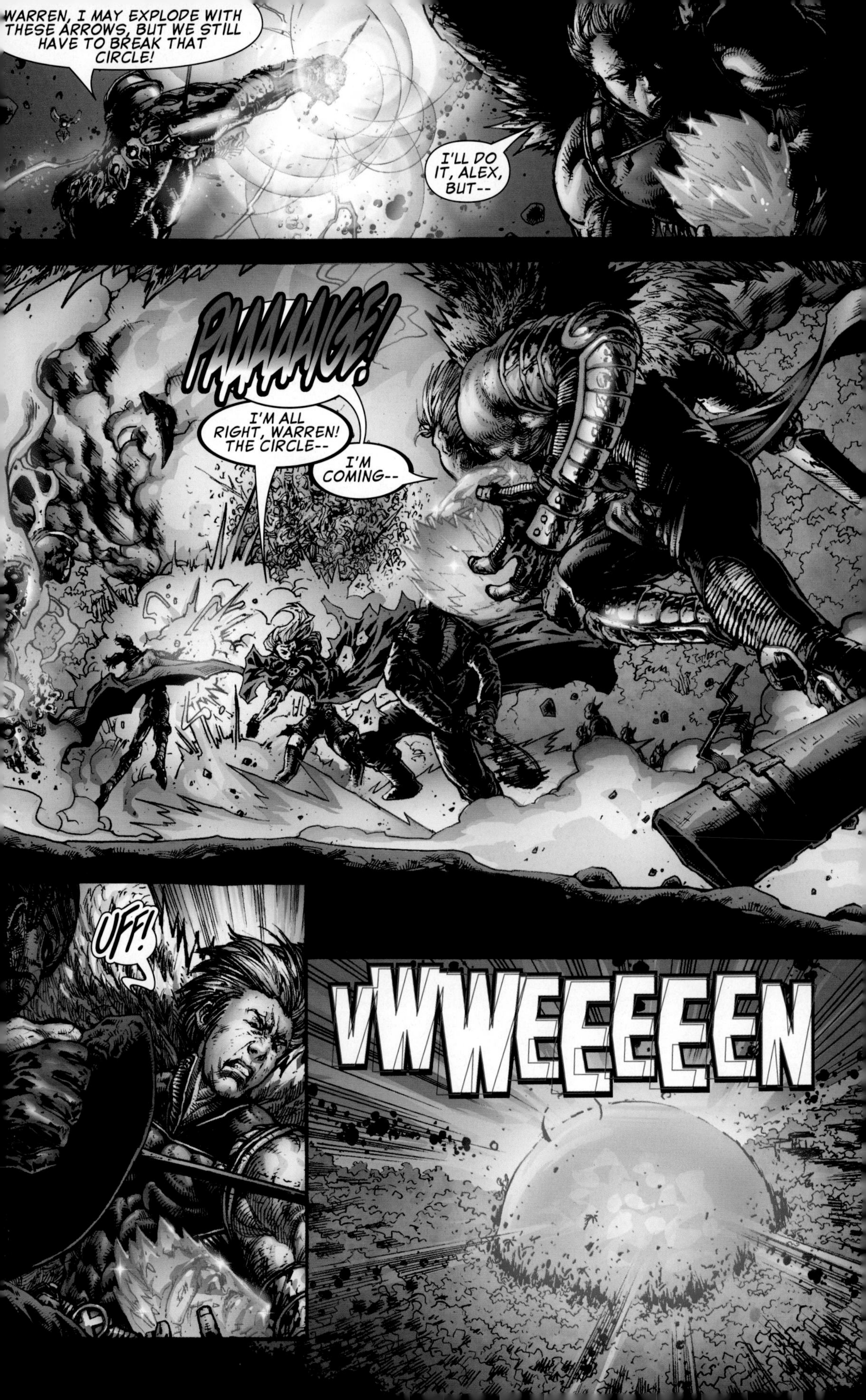
WARREN, I MAY EXPLODE WITH THESE ARROWS, BUT WE STILL HAVE TO BREAK THAT CIRCLE!
I'LL DO IT, ALEX, BUT--
PAAAAAIGE!
I'M ALL RIGHT, WARREN! THE CIRCLE--
I'M COMING--
UFF!
VWWEEEEEN

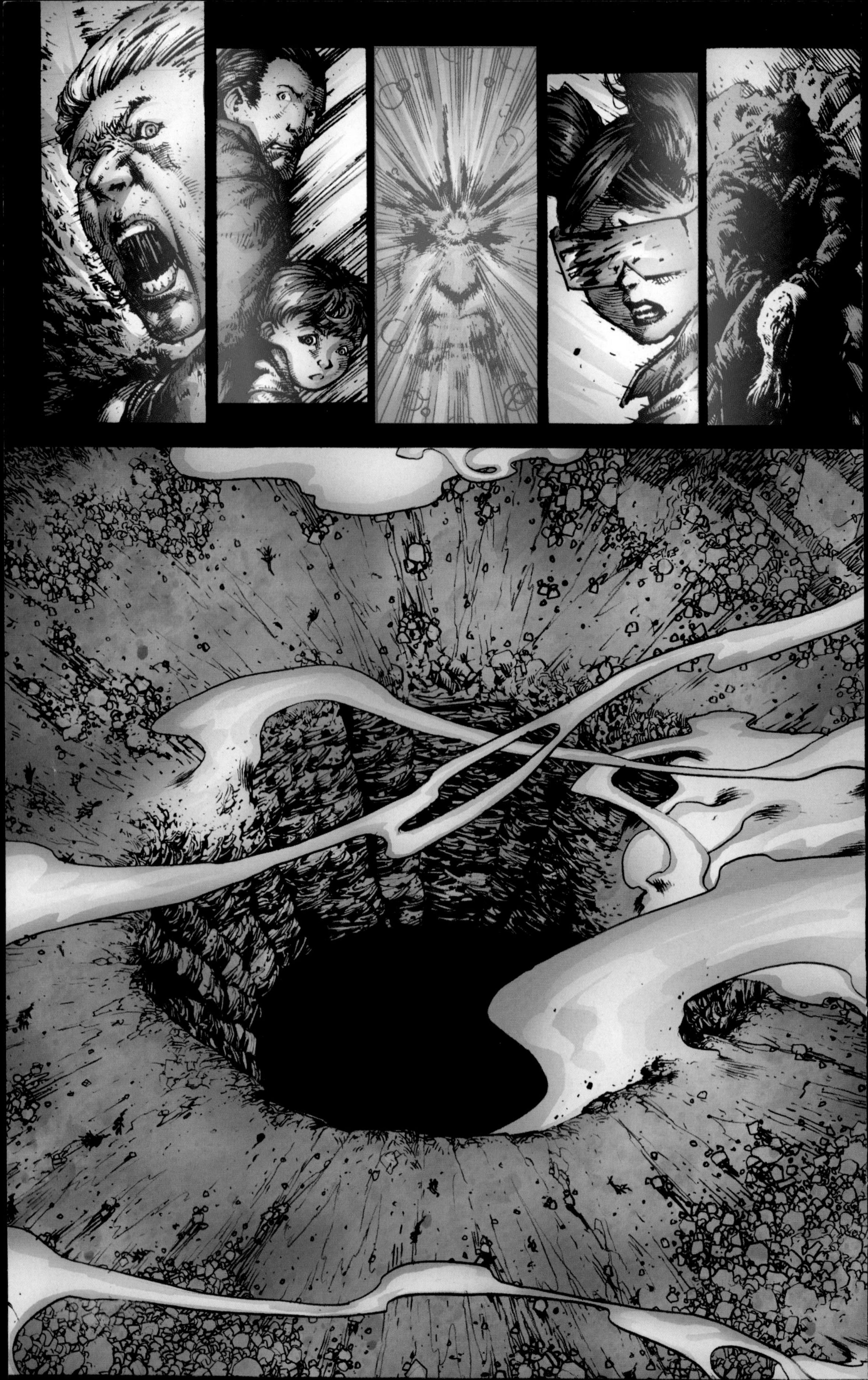

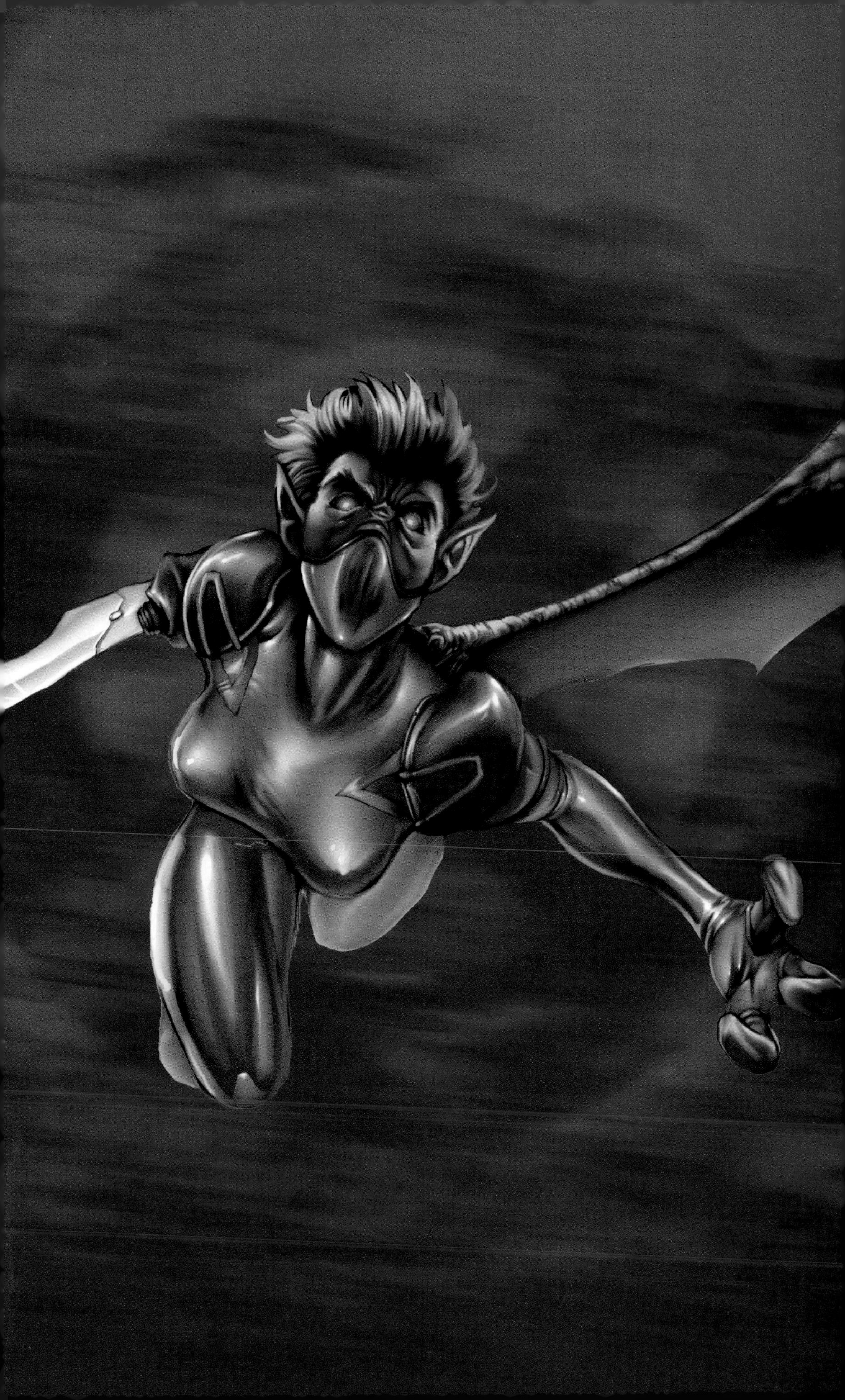

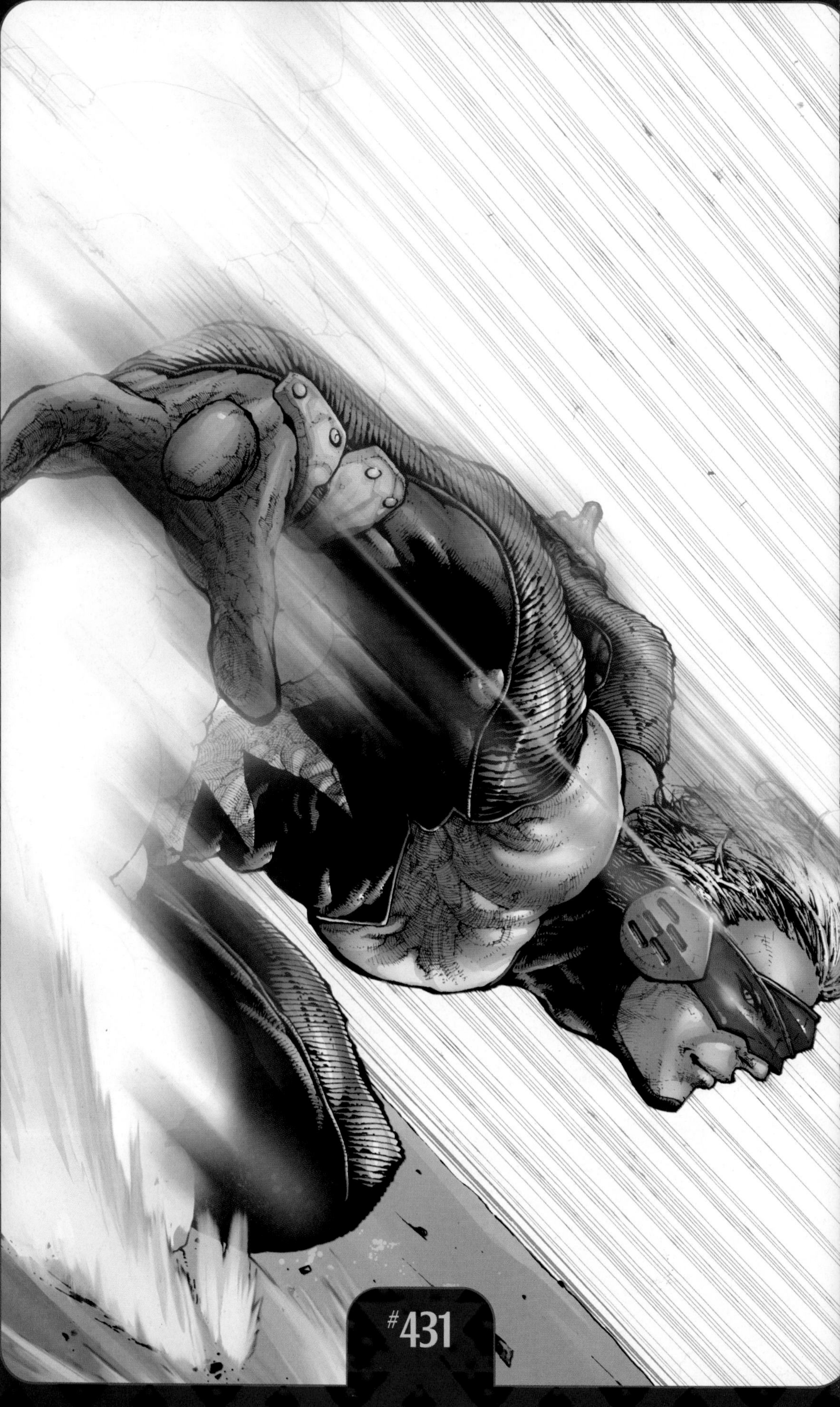

#431

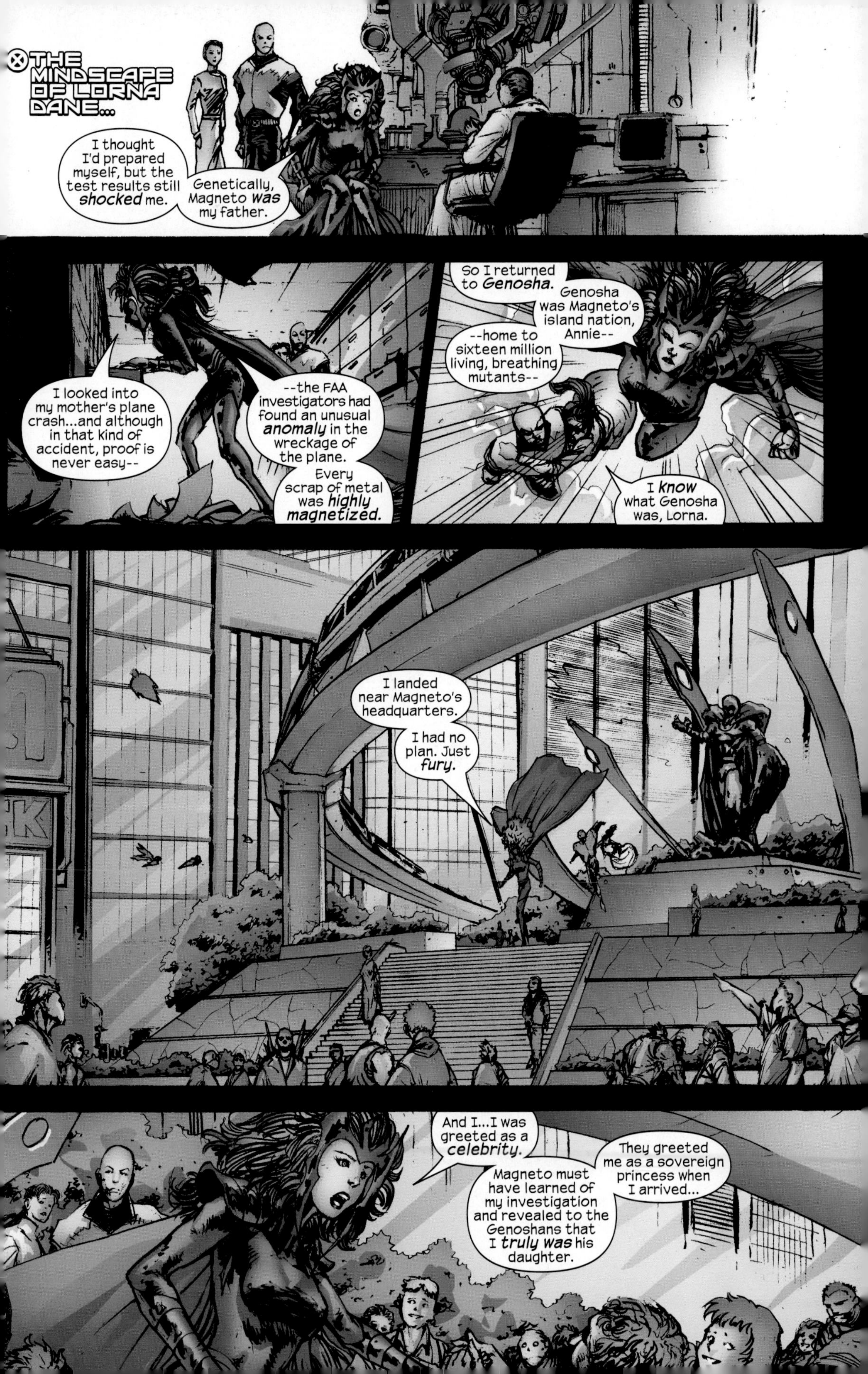
THE MINDSCAPE OF LORNA DANE...
I thought I'd prepared myself, but the test results still shocked me.
Genetically, Magneto was my father.
I looked into my mother's plane crash...and although in that kind of accident, proof is never easy--
--the FAA investigators had found an unusual anomaly in the wreckage of the plane.
Every scrap of metal was highly magnetized.
So I returned to Genosha.
Genosha was Magneto's island nation, Annie--
--home to sixteen million living, breathing mutants--
I know what Genosha was, Lorna.
I landed near Magneto's headquarters.
I had no plan. Just fury.
And I...I was greeted as a celebrity.
They greeted me as a sovereign princess when I arrived...
Magneto must have learned of my investigation and revealed to the Genoshans that I truly was his daughter.

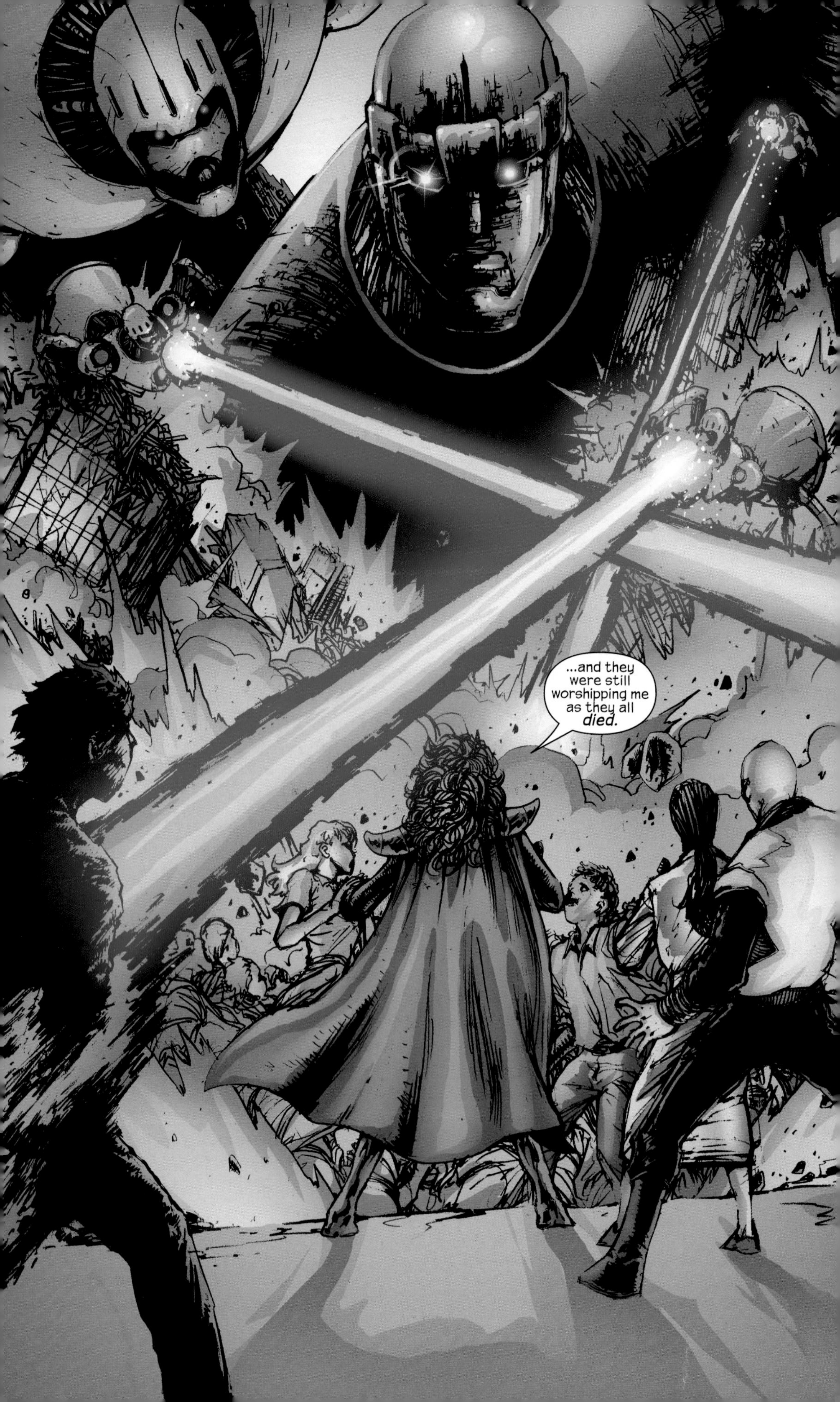
...and they were still worshipping me as they all *died.*

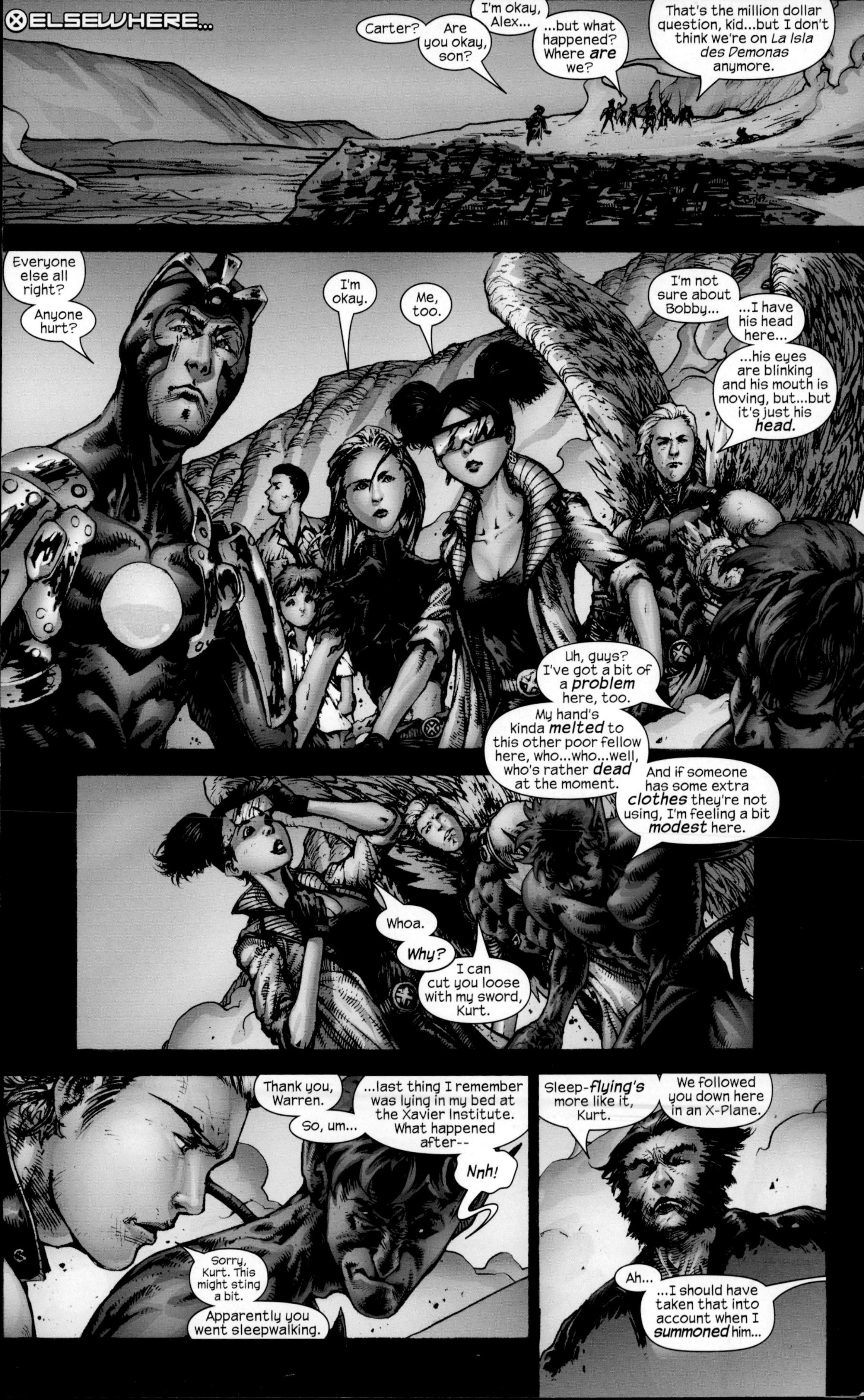
ELSEWHERE...
Carter?
Are you okay, son?
I'm okay, Alex...
...but what happened? Where *are* we?
That's the million dollar question, kid...but I don't think we're on *La Isla des Demonas* anymore.
Everyone else all right?
Anyone hurt?
I'm okay.
Me, too.
I'm not sure about Bobby...
...I have his head here...
...his eyes are blinking and his mouth is moving, but...but it's just his **head.**
Uh, guys? I've got a bit of a **problem** here, too.
My hand's kinda **melted** to this other poor fellow here, who...who...well, who's rather **dead** at the moment.
And if someone has some extra **clothes** they're not using, I'm feeling a bit **modest** here.
Whoa.
Why?
I can cut you loose with my sword, Kurt.
Thank you, Warren.
So, um...
...last thing I remember was lying in my bed at the Xavier Institute. What happened after--
Nnh!
Sorry, Kurt. This might sting a bit.
Apparently you went sleepwalking.
Sleep-**flying's** more like it, Kurt.
We followed you down here in an X-Plane.
Ah...
...I should have taken that into account when I **summoned** him...

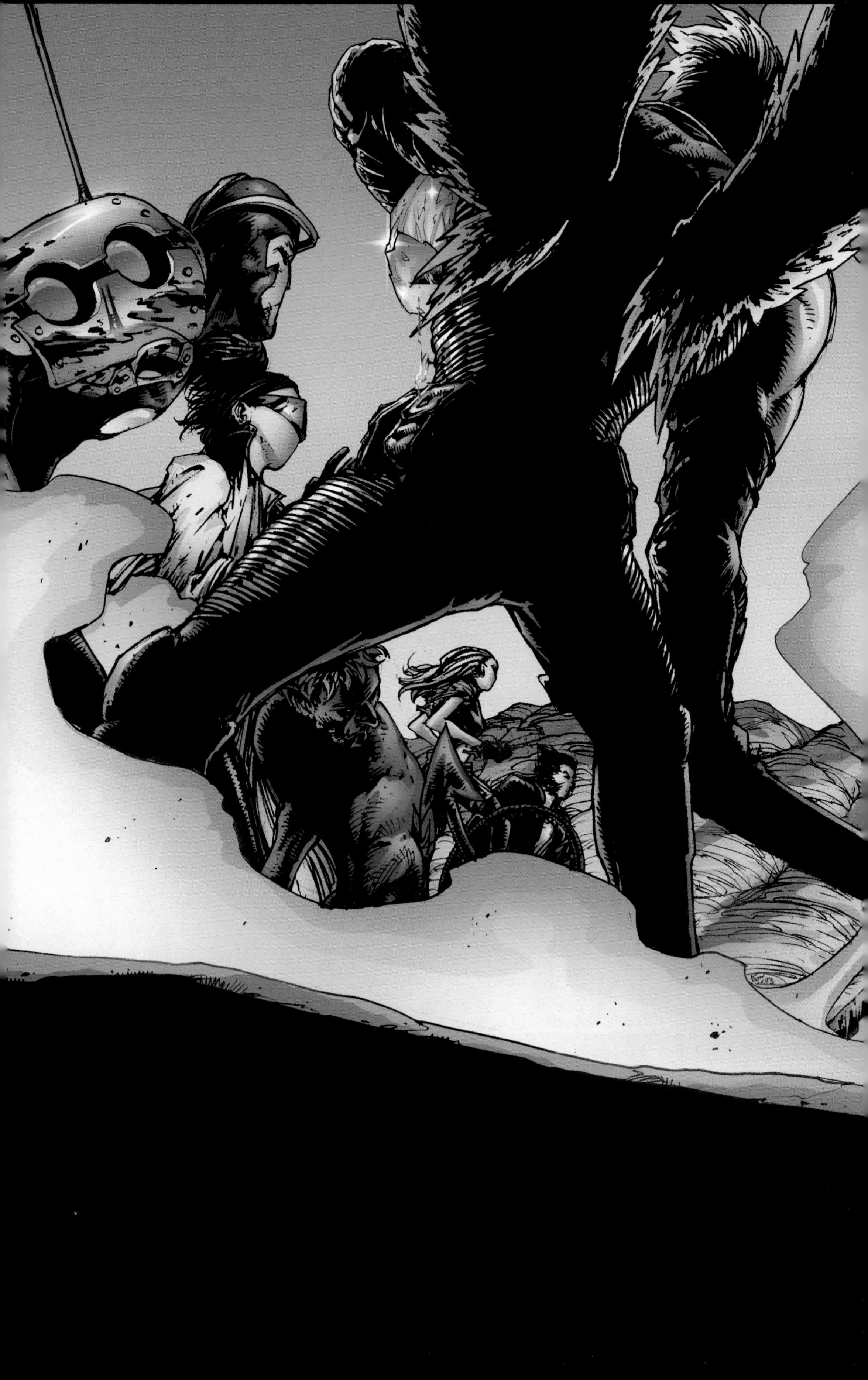

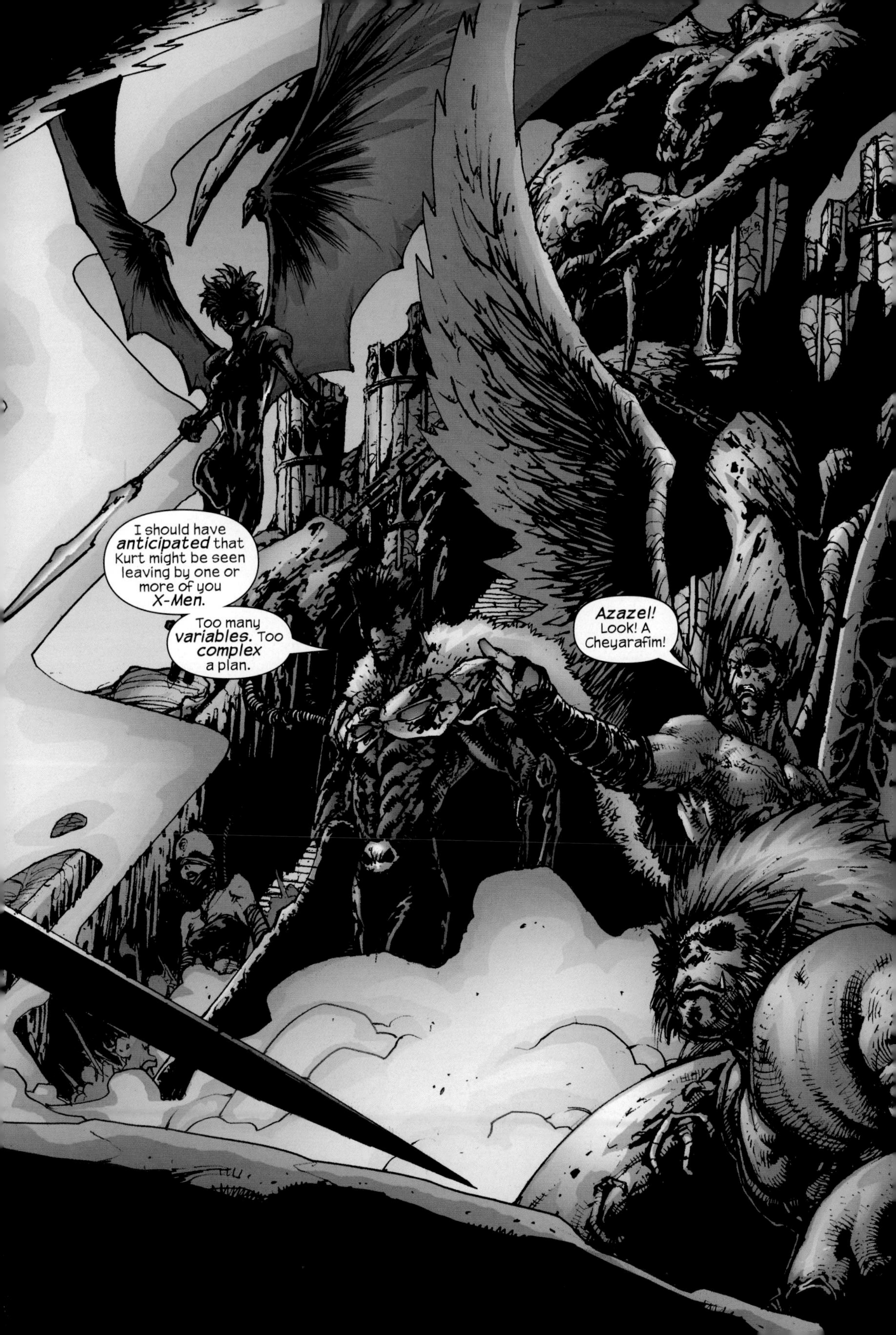
I should have *anticipated* that Kurt might be seen leaving by one or more of you *X-Men*.
Too many *variables.* Too *complex* a plan.
Azazel! Look! A Cheyarafim!

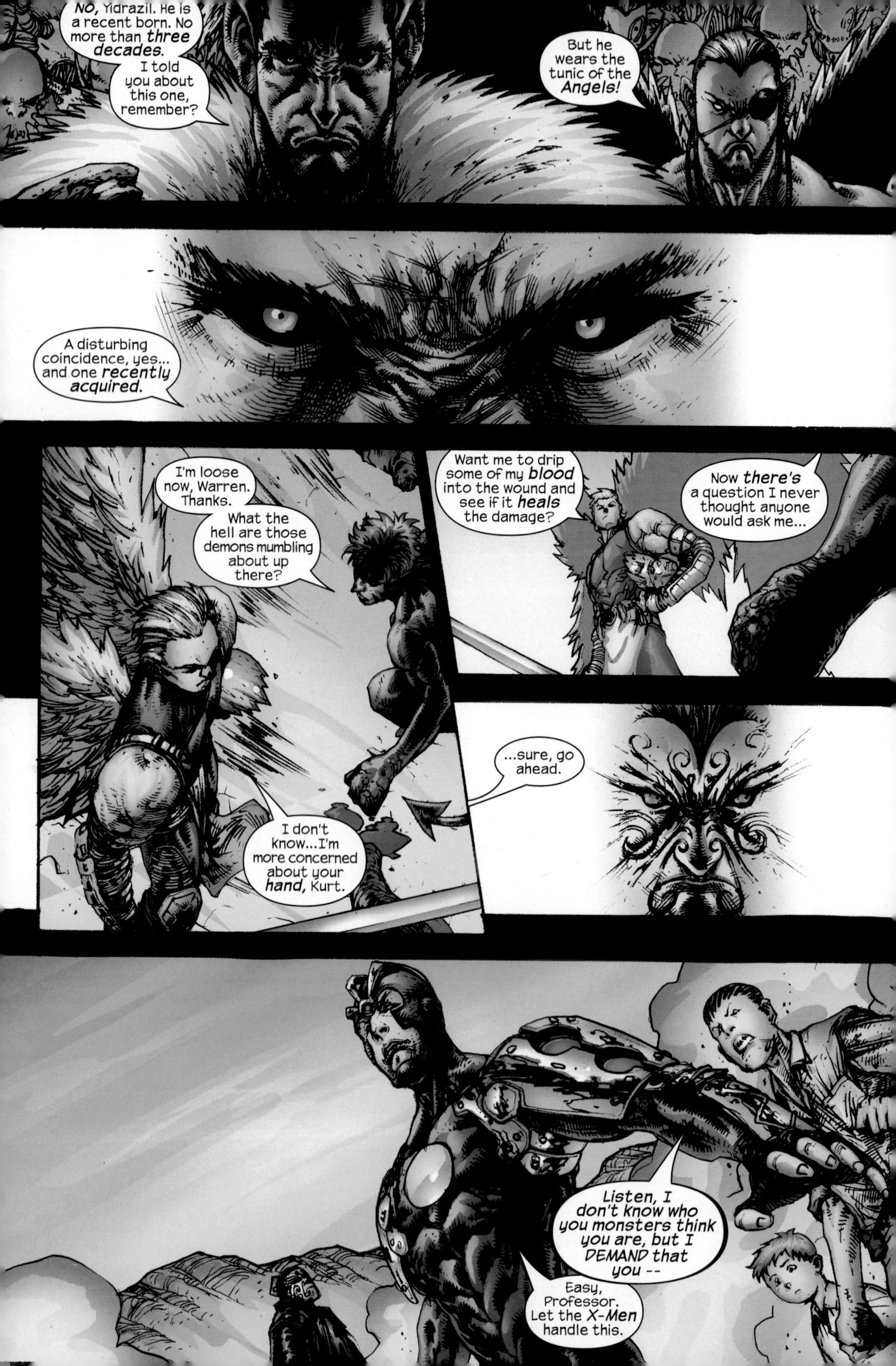
NO, Yidrazil. He is a recent born. No more than three decades.
I told you about this one, remember?
But he wears the tunic of the Angels!
A disturbing coincidence, yes... and one recently acquired.
I'm loose now, Warren. Thanks.
What the hell are those demons mumbling about up there?
I don't know...I'm more concerned about your hand, Kurt.
Want me to drip some of my blood into the wound and see if it heals the damage?
Now there's a question I never thought anyone would ask me...
...sure, go ahead.
Listen, I don't know who you monsters think you are, but I DEMAND that you --
Easy, Professor. Let the X-Men handle this.

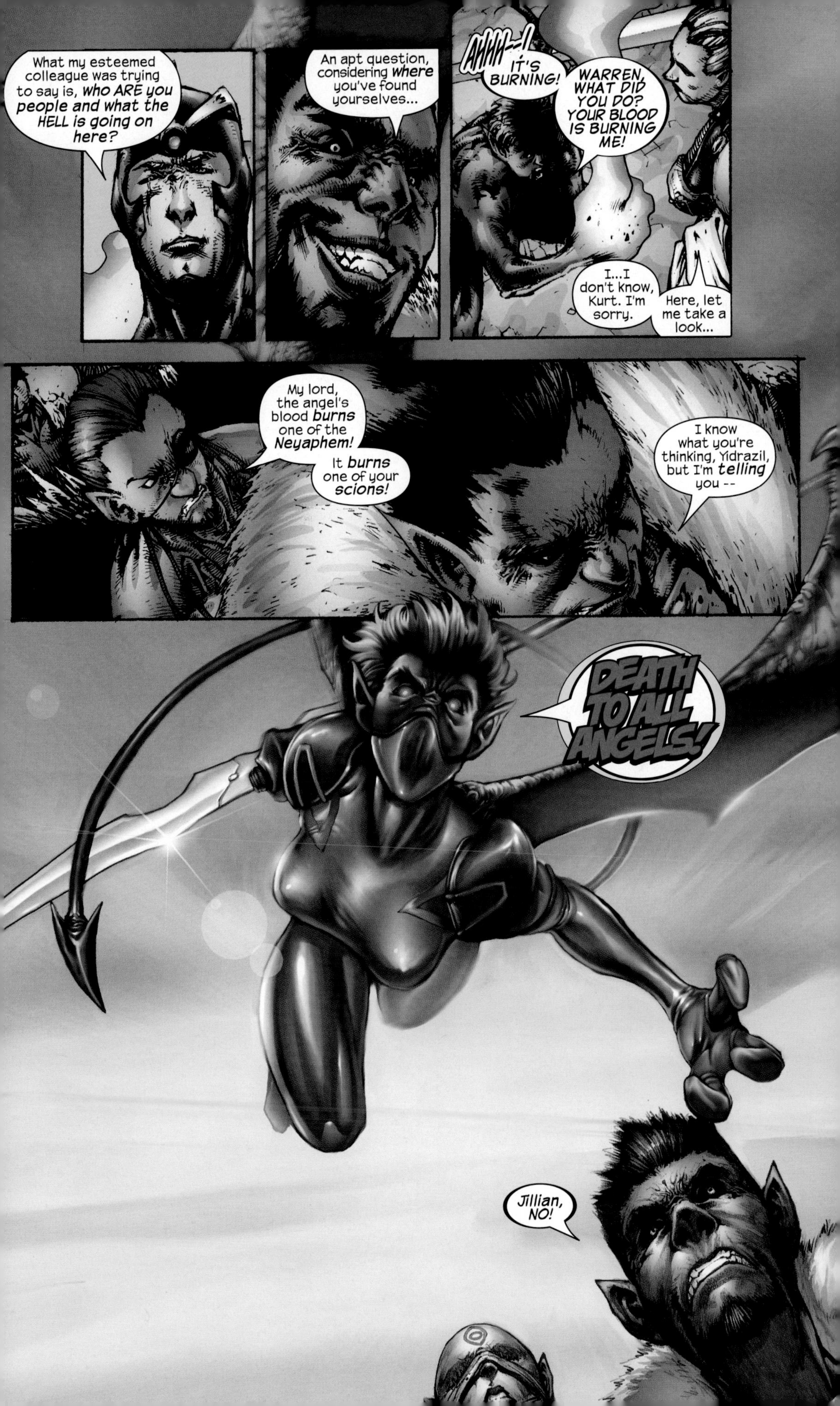
What my esteemed colleague was trying to say is, WHO ARE you people and what the HELL is going on here?
An apt question, considering where you've found yourselves...
AHHH--!
IT'S BURNING!
WARREN, WHAT DID YOU DO? YOUR BLOOD IS BURNING ME!
I...I don't know, Kurt. I'm sorry.
Here, let me take a look...
My lord, the angel's blood burns one of the Neyaphem!
It burns one of your scions!
I know what you're thinking, Yidrazil, but I'm telling you --
DEATH TO ALL ANGELS!
Jillian, NO!

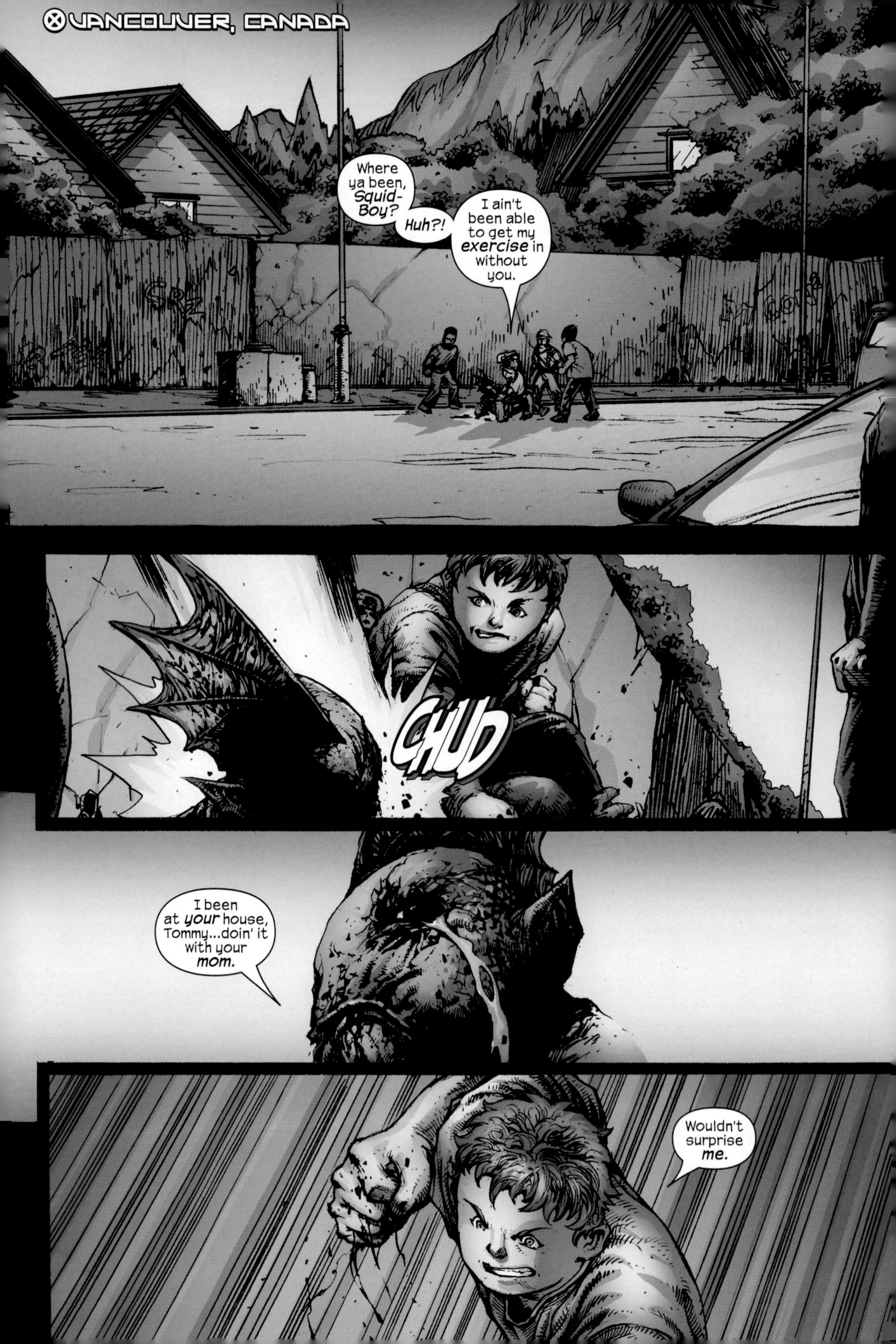
VANCOUVER, CANADA
Where ya been, Squid-Boy?
Huh?!
I ain't been able to get my exercise in without you.
CHUD
I been at your house, Tommy...doin' it with your mom.
Wouldn't surprise me.

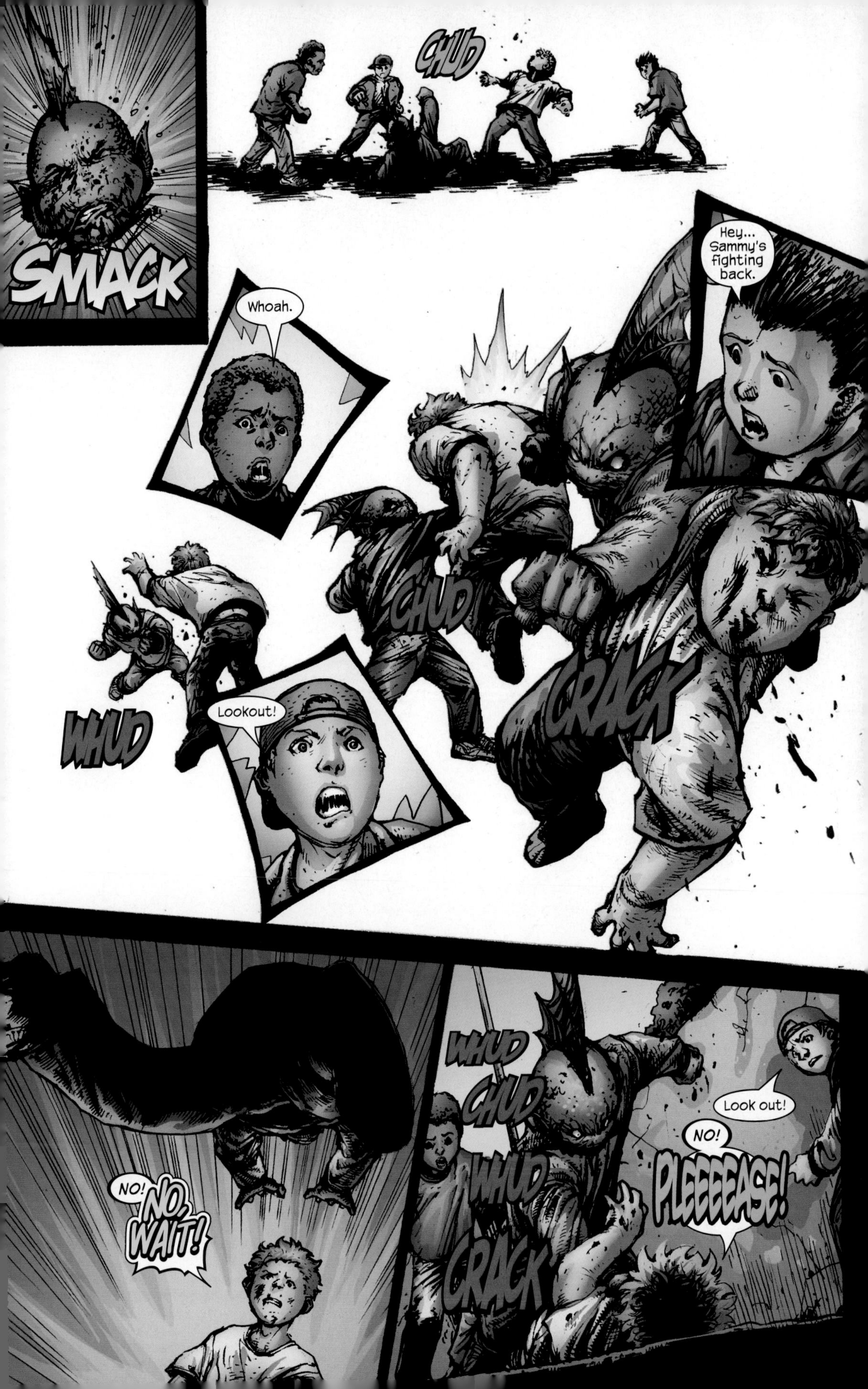
SMACK
CHUD
Hey... Sammy's fighting back.
Whoah.
CHUD
CRACK
WHUD
Lookout!
NO!
NO, WAIT!
WHUD
CHUD
WHUD
CRACK
Look out!
NO!
PLEEEEASE!

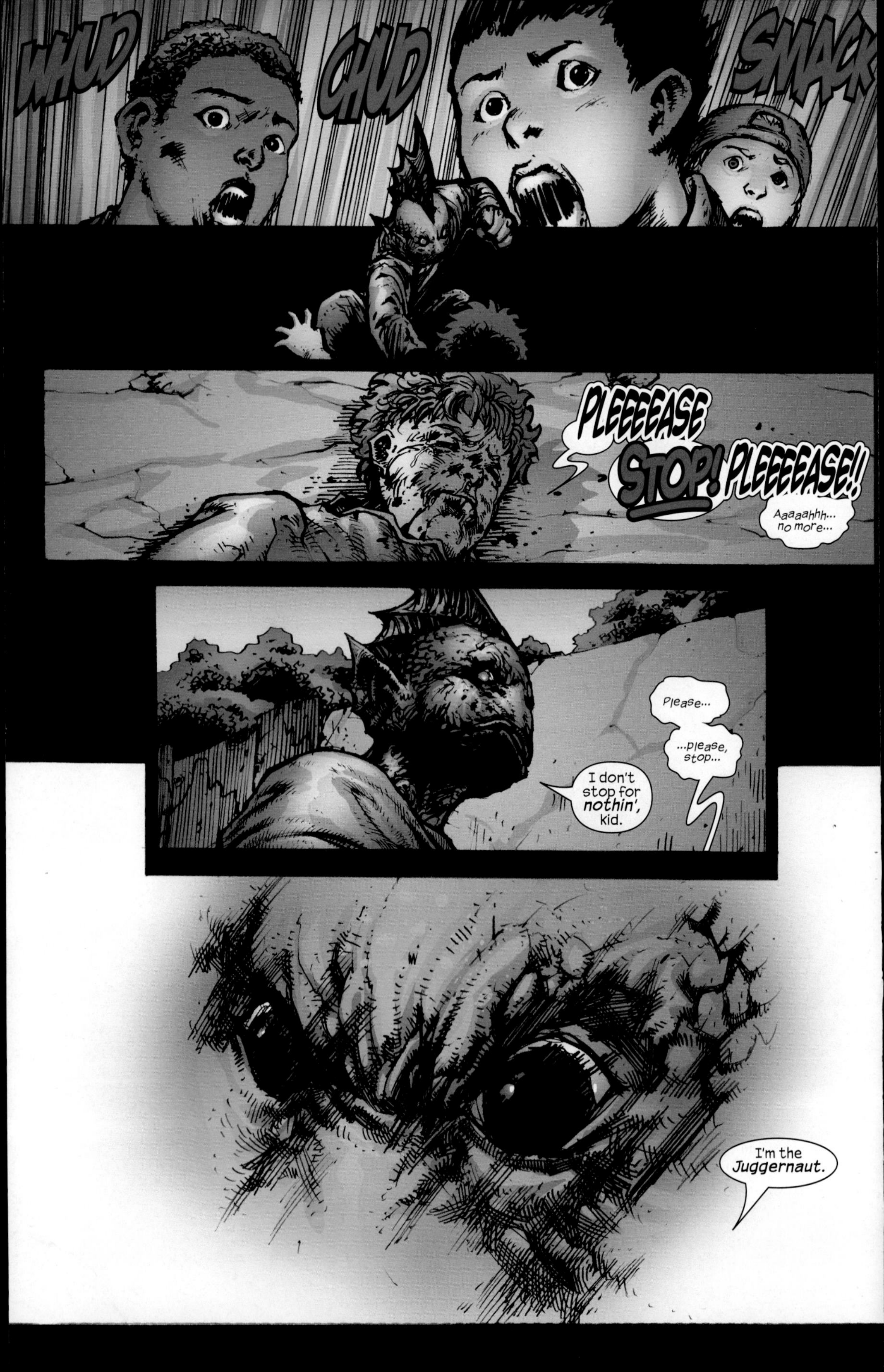
WHUD
CHUD
SMACK
PLEEEEASE STOP! PLEEEEASE!!
Aaaaahhh... no more...
Please...
...please, stop...
I don't stop for nothin', kid.
I'm the Juggernaut.

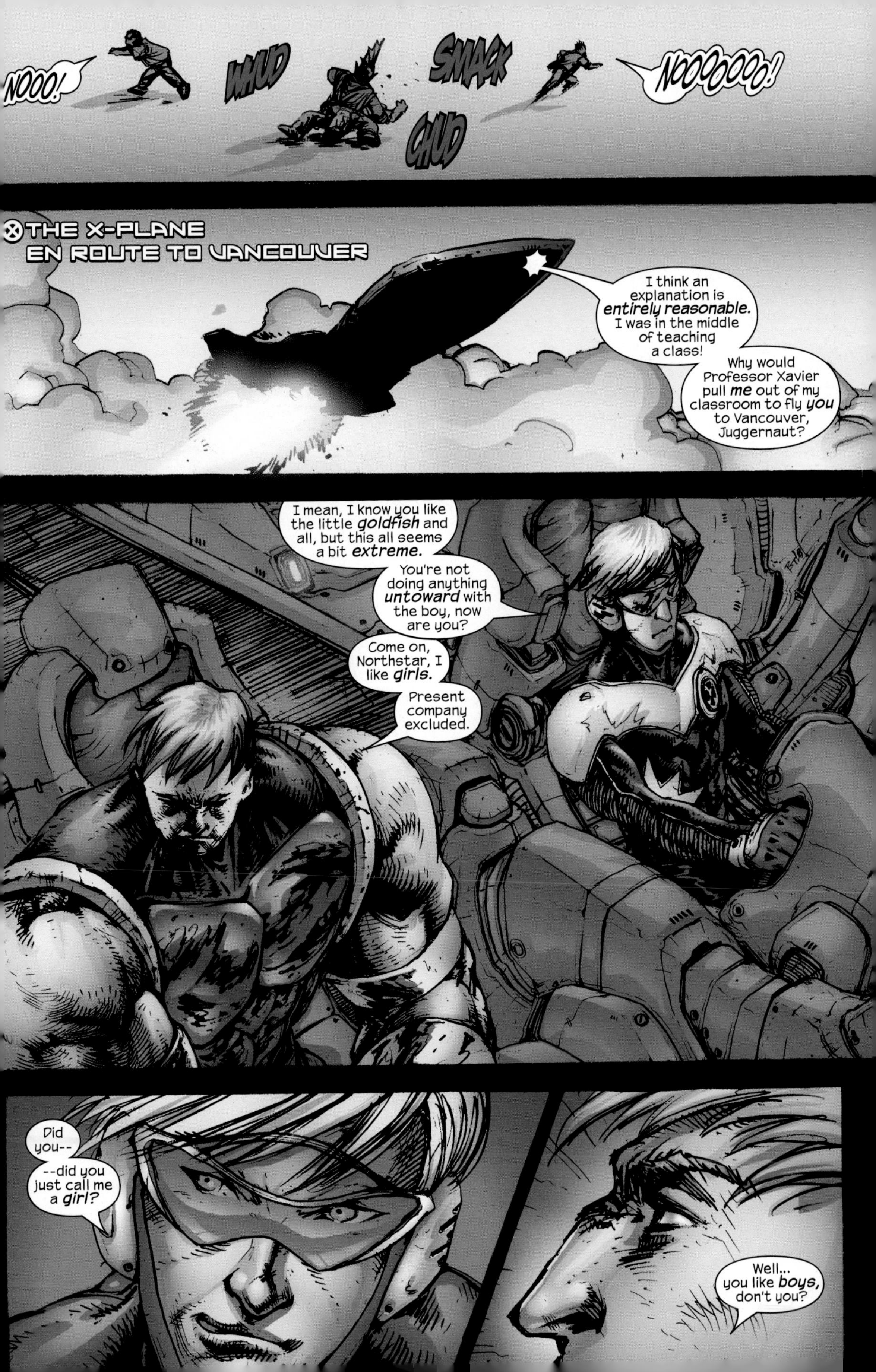
NOOO!
WHUD
SMACK
CHUD
NOOOOOOO!
THE X-PLANE
EN ROUTE TO VANCOUVER
I think an explanation is entirely reasonable. I was in the middle of teaching a class!
Why would Professor Xavier pull me out of my classroom to fly you to Vancouver, Juggernaut?
I mean, I know you like the little goldfish and all, but this all seems a bit extreme.
You're not doing anything untoward with the boy, now are you?
Come on, Northstar, I like girls.
Present company excluded.
Did you--
--did you just call me a girl?
Well... you like boys, don't you?

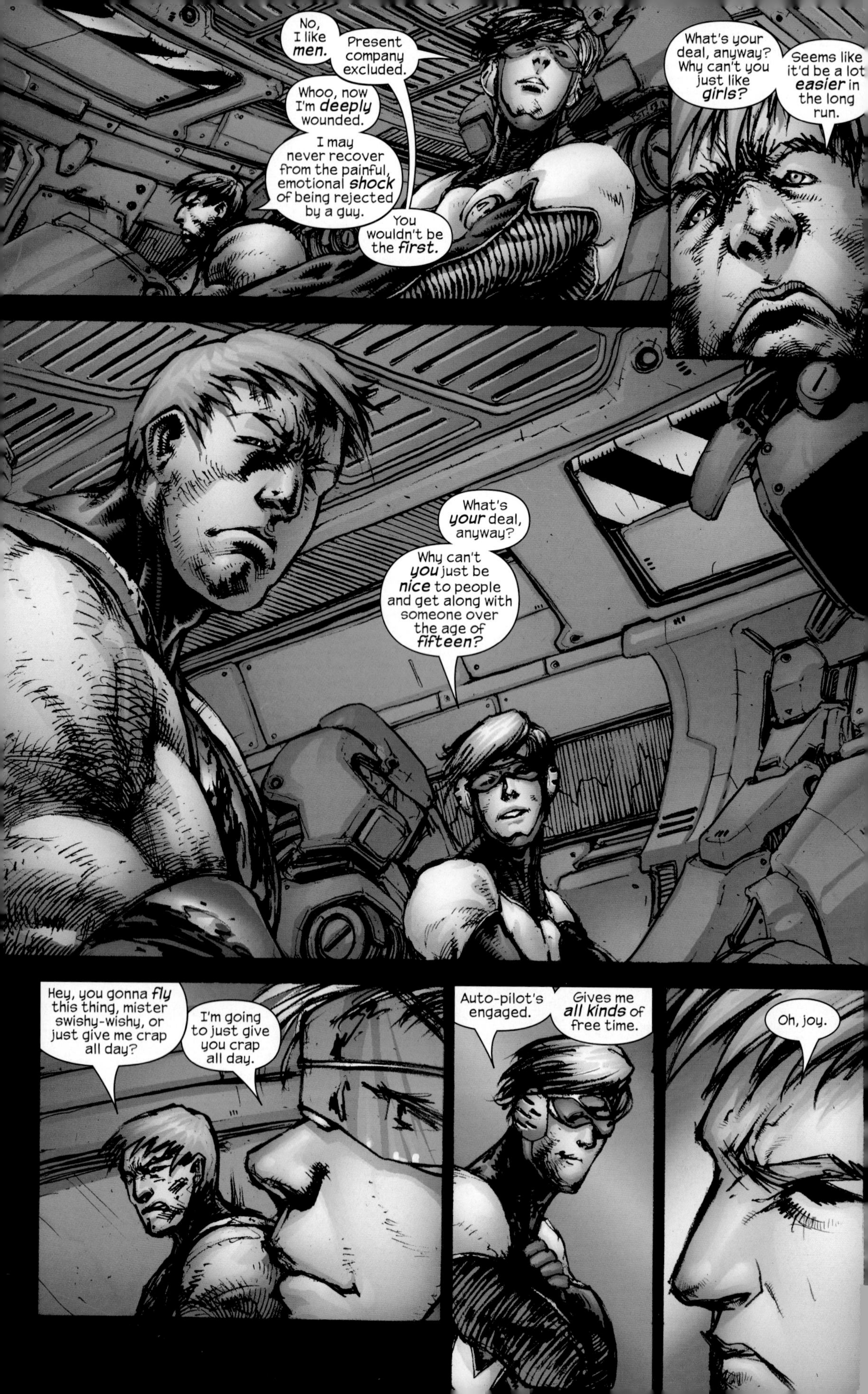
No, I like men.
Present company excluded.
Whooo, now I'm deeply wounded.
I may never recover from the painful, emotional shock of being rejected by a guy.
You wouldn't be the first.
What's your deal, anyway? Why can't you just like girls?
Seems like it'd be a lot easier in the long run.
What's your deal, anyway?
Why can't you just be nice to people and get along with someone over the age of fifteen?
Hey, you gonna fly this thing, mister swishy-wishy, or just give me crap all day?
I'm going to just give you crap all day.
Auto-pilot's engaged.
Gives me all kinds of free time.
Oh, joy.

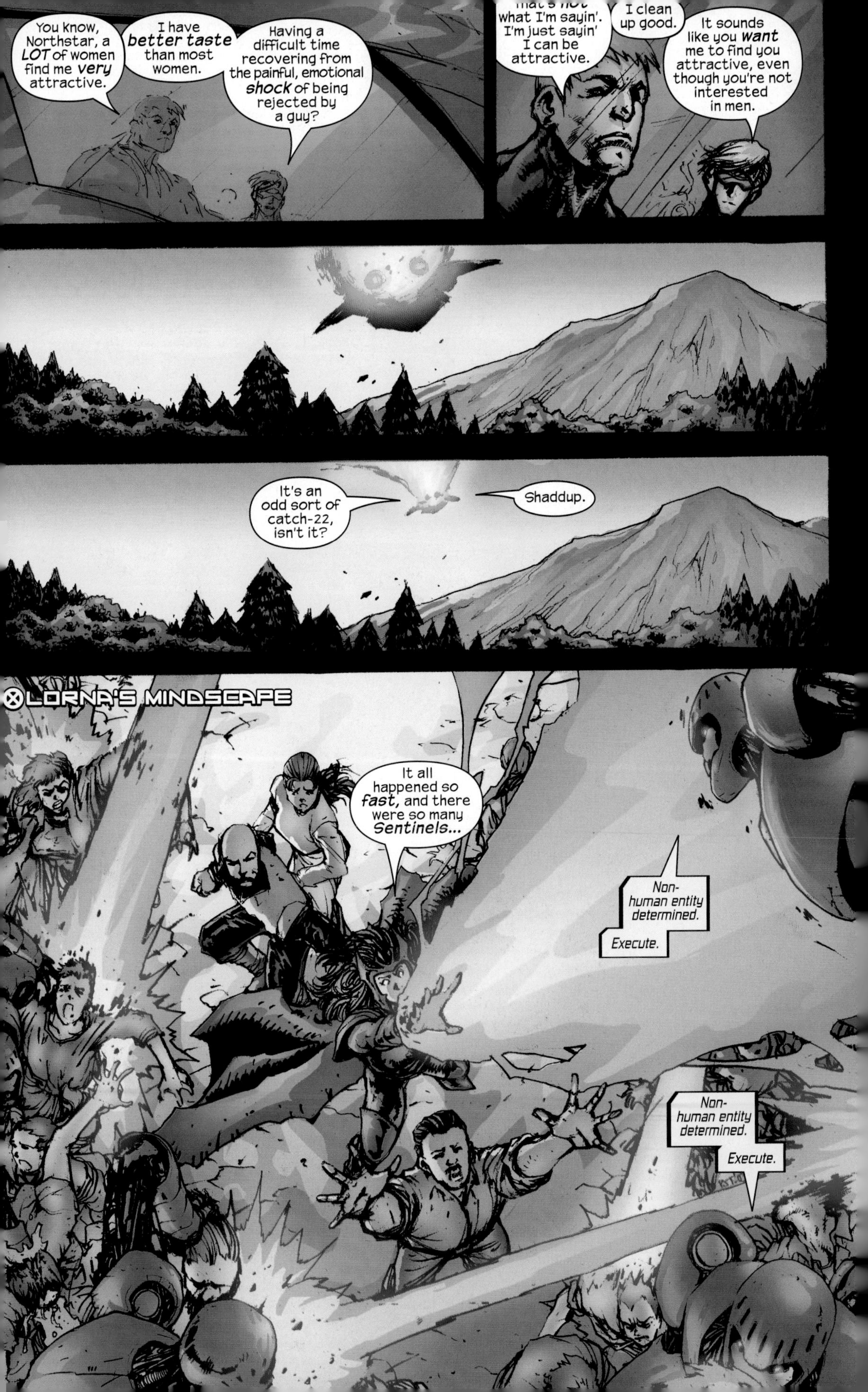
You know, Northstar, a LOT of women find me very attractive.
I have better taste than most women.
Having a difficult time recovering from the painful, emotional shock of being rejected by a guy?
what I'm sayin'. I'm just sayin' I can be attractive.
I clean up good.
It sounds like you want me to find you attractive, even though you're not interested in men.
It's an odd sort of catch-22, isn't it?
Shaddup.
LORNA'S MINDSCAPE
It all happened so fast, and there were so many Sentinels...
Non-human entity determined.
Execute.
Non-human entity determined.
Execute.

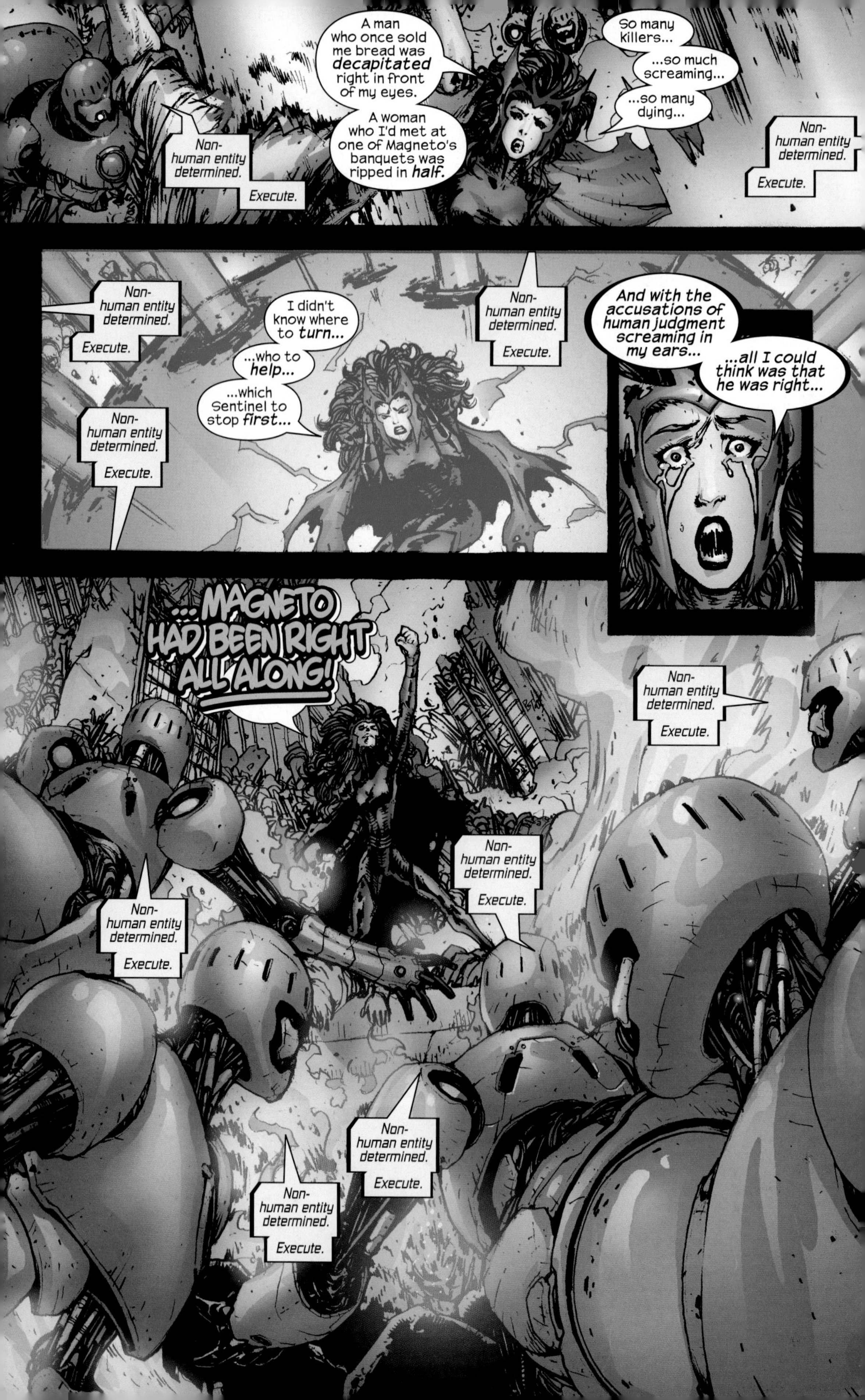

A man who once sold me bread was *decapitated* right in front of my eyes.
A woman who I'd met at one of Magneto's banquets was ripped in *half*.
So many killers...
...so much screaming...
...so many dying...
Non-human entity determined.
Execute.
Non-human entity determined.
Execute.
Non-human entity determined.
Execute.
I didn't know where to *turn*...
...who to *help*...
...which Sentinel to stop *first*...
Non-human entity determined.
Execute.
Non-human entity determined.
Execute.
And with the accusations of human judgment screaming in my ears...
...all I could think was that he was right...
...MAGNETO HAD BEEN RIGHT ALL ALONG!
Non-human entity determined.
Execute.
Non-human entity determined.
Execute.
Non-human entity determined.
Execute.
Non-human entity determined.
Execute.
Non-human entity determined.
Execute.

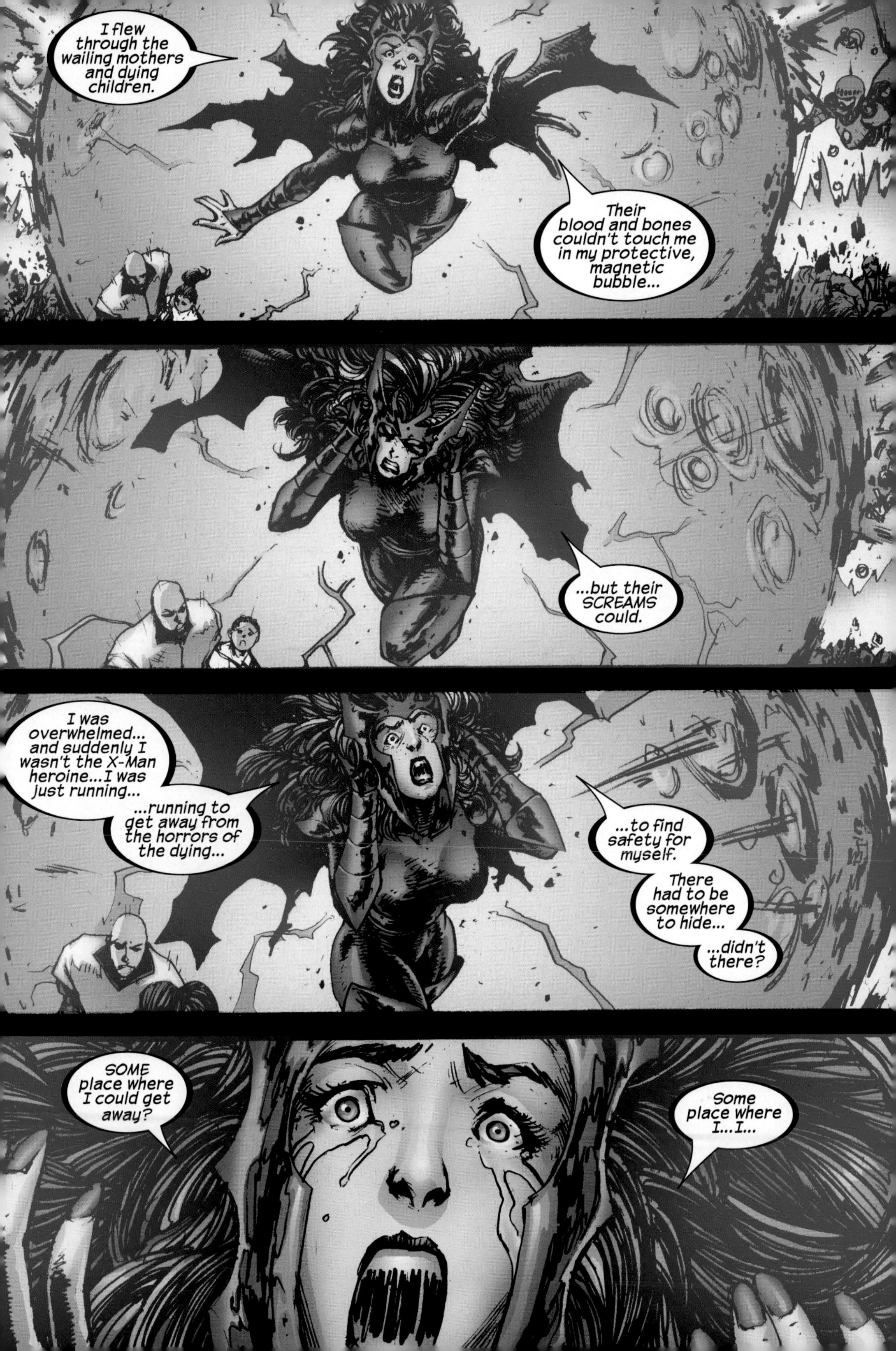
I flew through the wailing mothers and dying children.
Their blood and bones couldn't touch me in my protective, magnetic bubble...
...but their SCREAMS could.
I was overwhelmed... and suddenly I wasn't the X-Man heroine...I was just running...
...running to get away from the horrors of the dying...
...to find safety for myself.
There had to be somewhere to hide...
...didn't there?
SOME place where I could get away?
Some place where I...I...

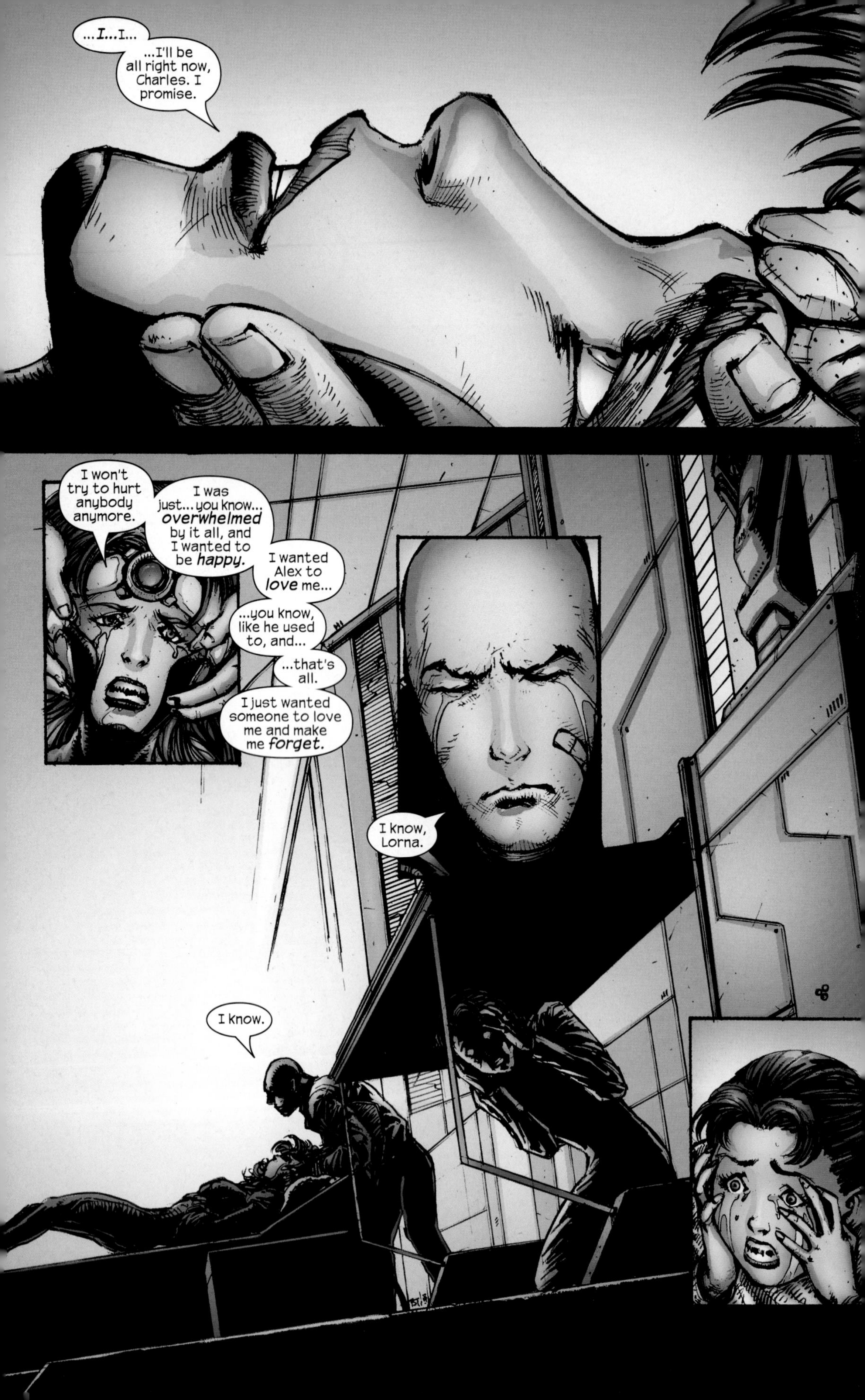
...I...I...
...I'll be all right now, Charles. I promise.
I won't try to hurt anybody anymore.
I was just... you know... overwhelmed by it all, and I wanted to be happy.
I wanted Alex to love me...
...you know, like he used to, and...
...that's all.
I just wanted someone to love me and make me forget.
I know, Lorna.
I know.

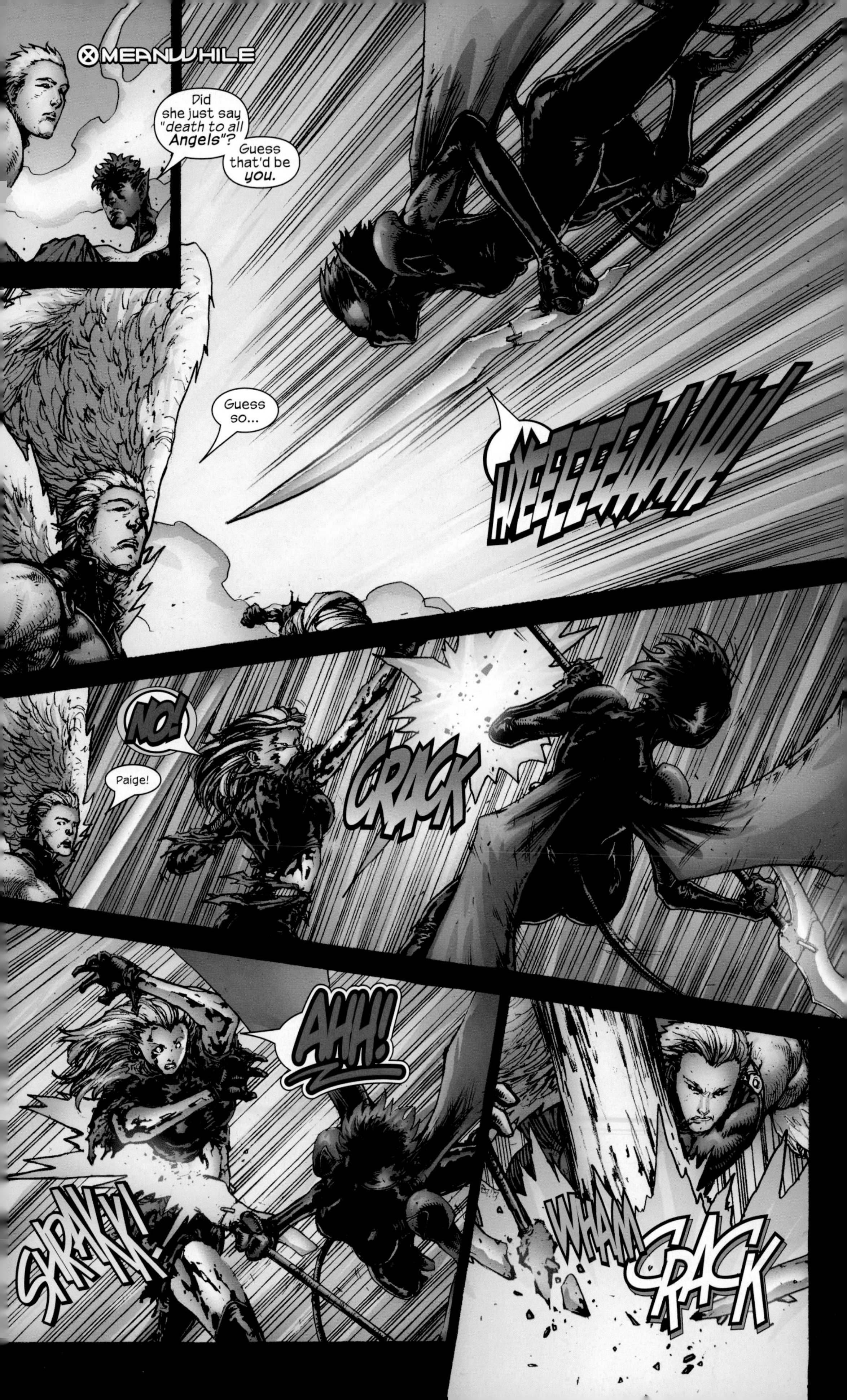
MEANWHILE
Did she just say "death to all Angels"?
Guess that'd be you.
Guess so...
HWEEEEEAAAH!
NO!
Paige!
CRACK
AHH!
SHRAKK!
WHAM
CRACK

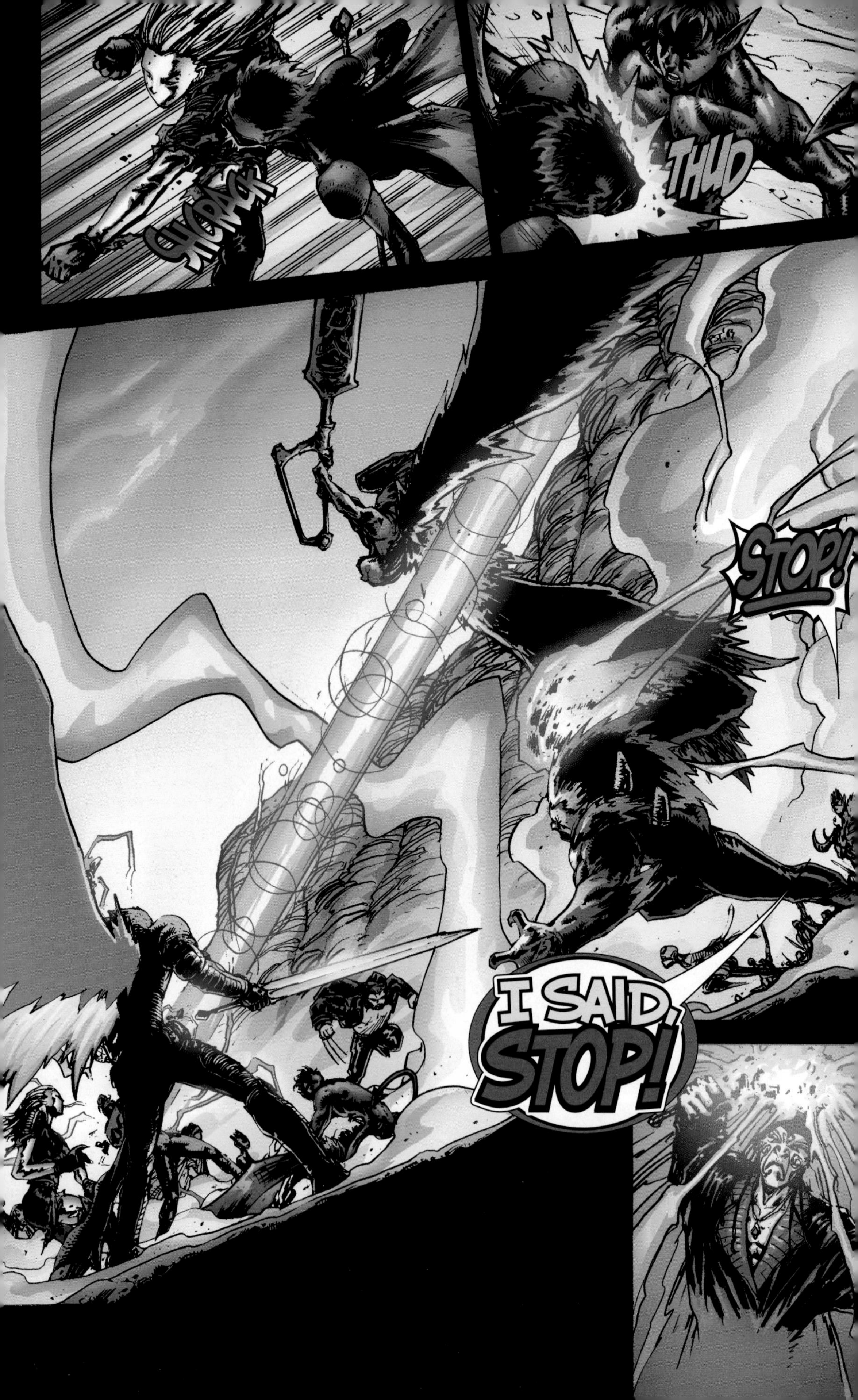
SHCRACK
THUD
STOP!
I SAID, STOP!

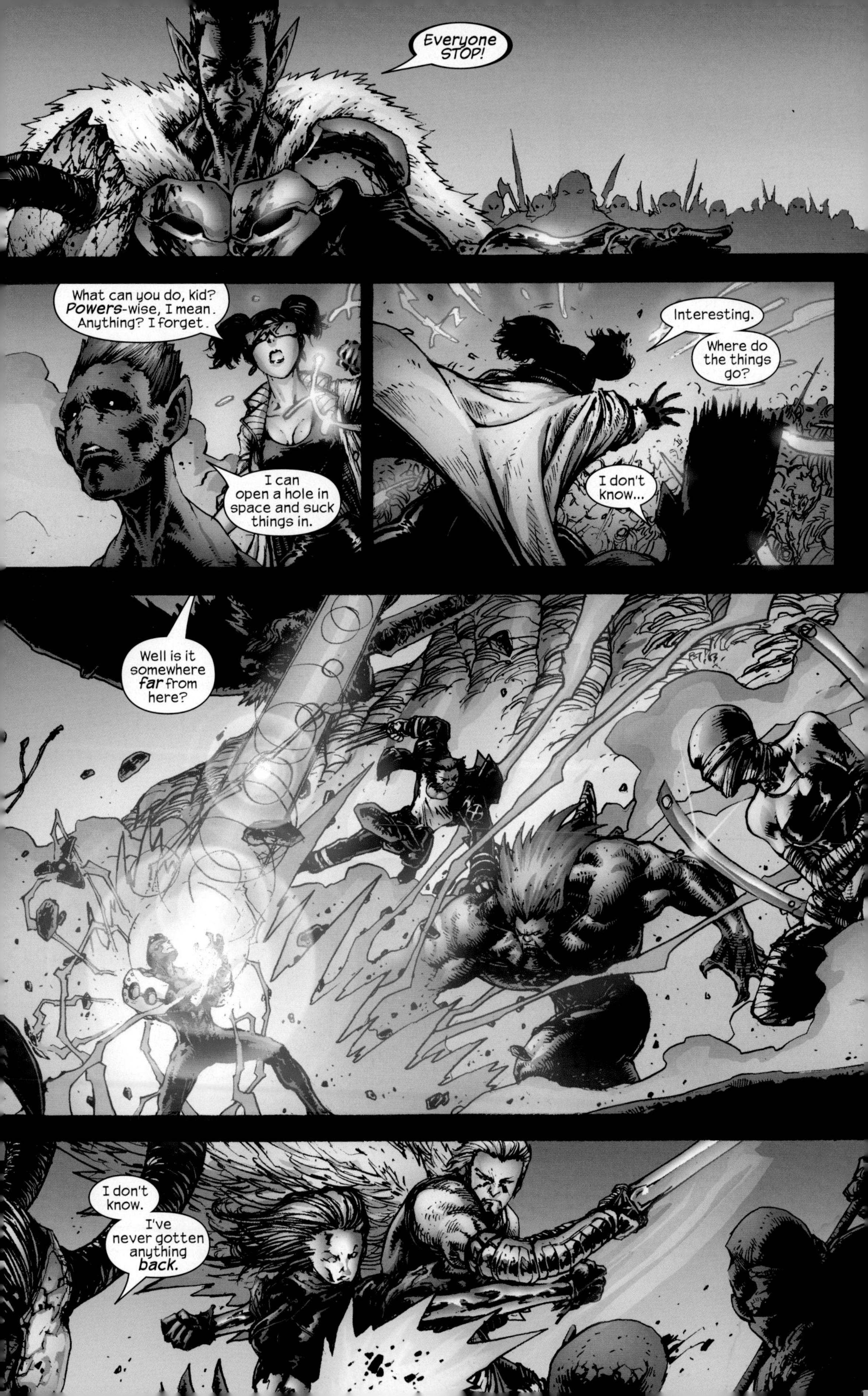
Everyone STOP!
What can you do, kid? Powers-wise, I mean. Anything? I forget.
I can open a hole in space and suck things in.
Interesting.
Where do the things go?
I don't know...
Well is it somewhere far from here?
I don't know.
I've never gotten anything back.

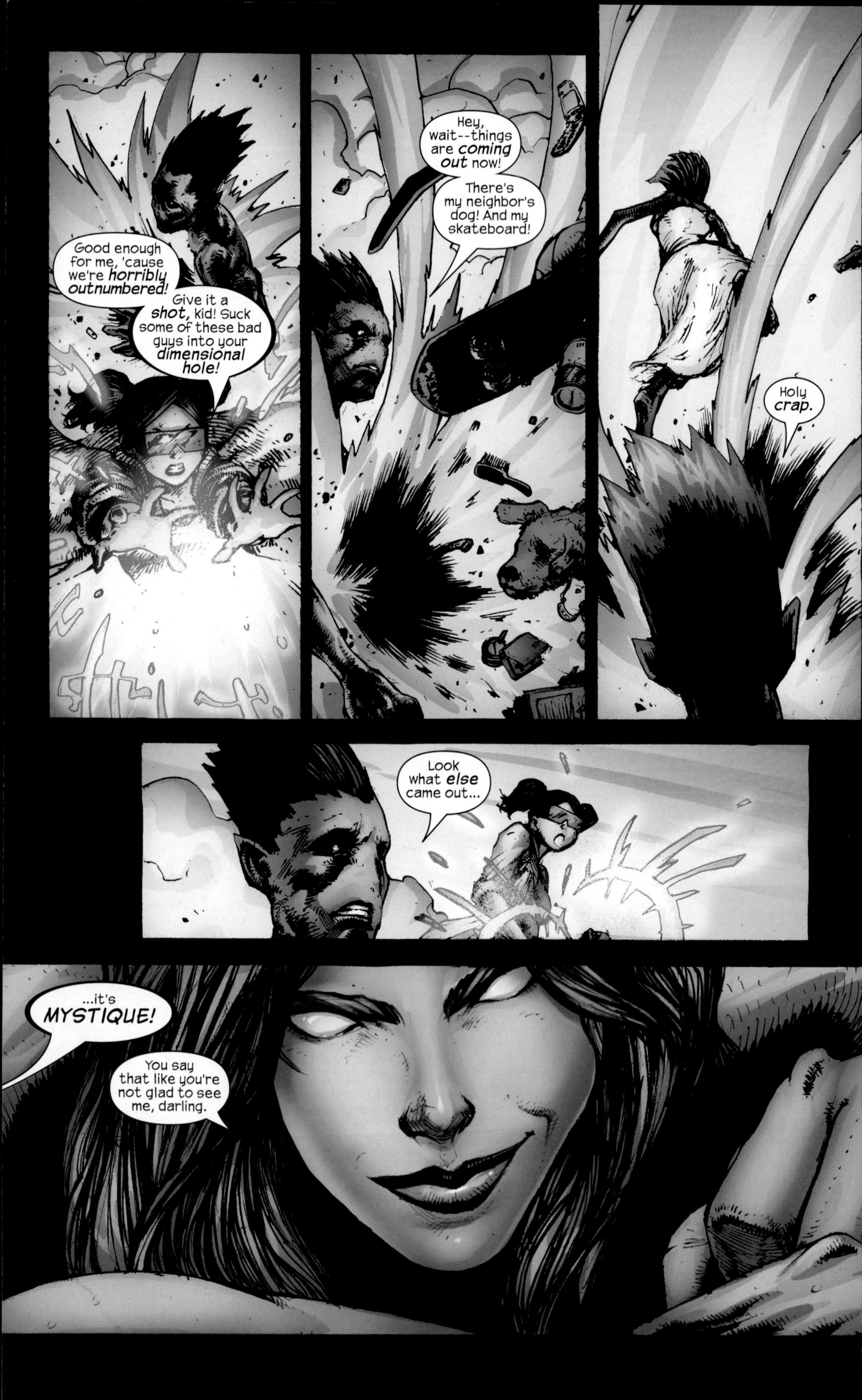
Good enough for me, 'cause we're horribly outnumbered!
Give it a shot, kid! Suck some of these bad guys into your dimensional hole!
Hey, wait--things are coming out now!
There's my neighbor's dog! And my skateboard!
Holy crap.
Look what else came out...
...it's MYSTIQUE!
You say that like you're not glad to see me, darling.

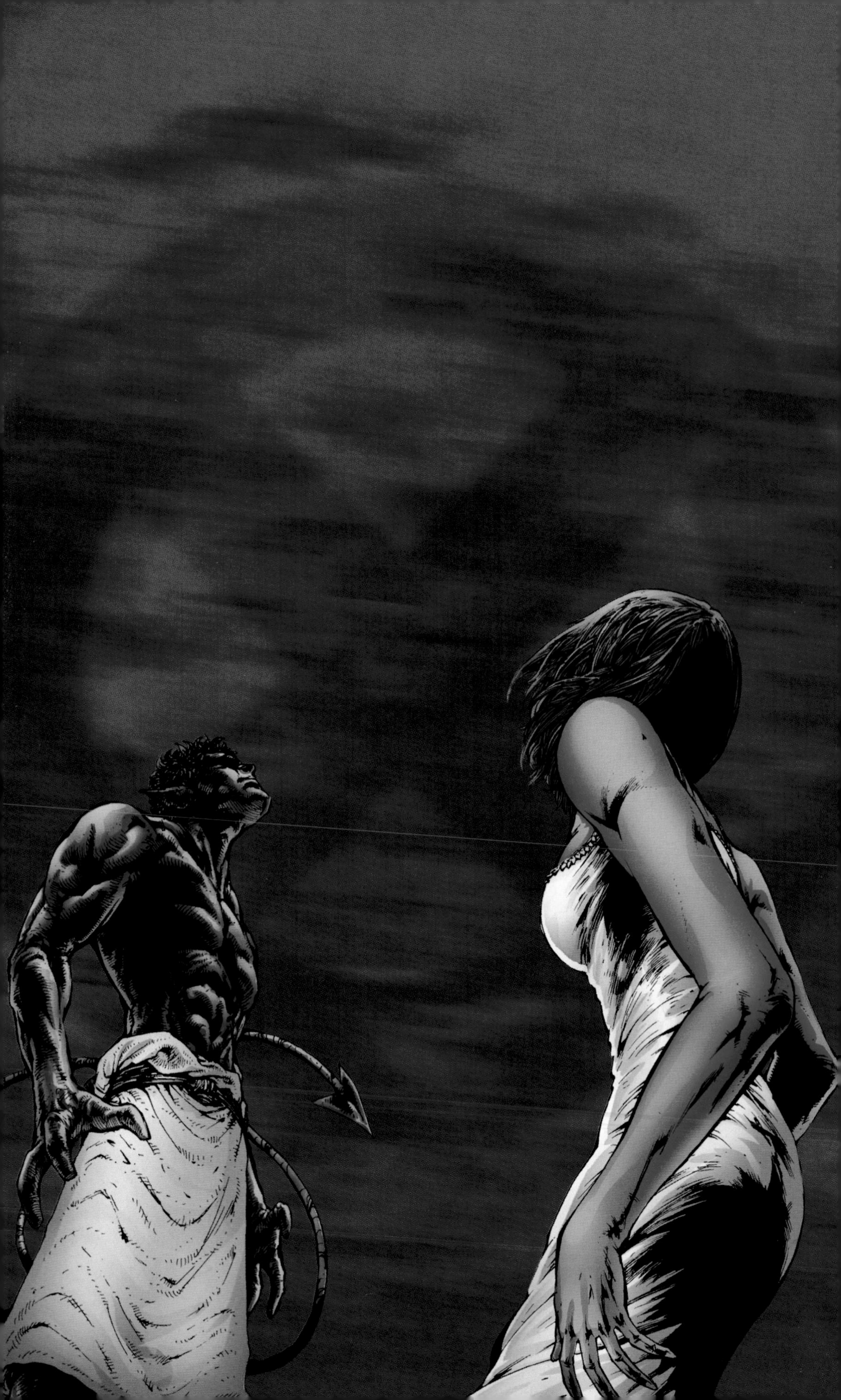

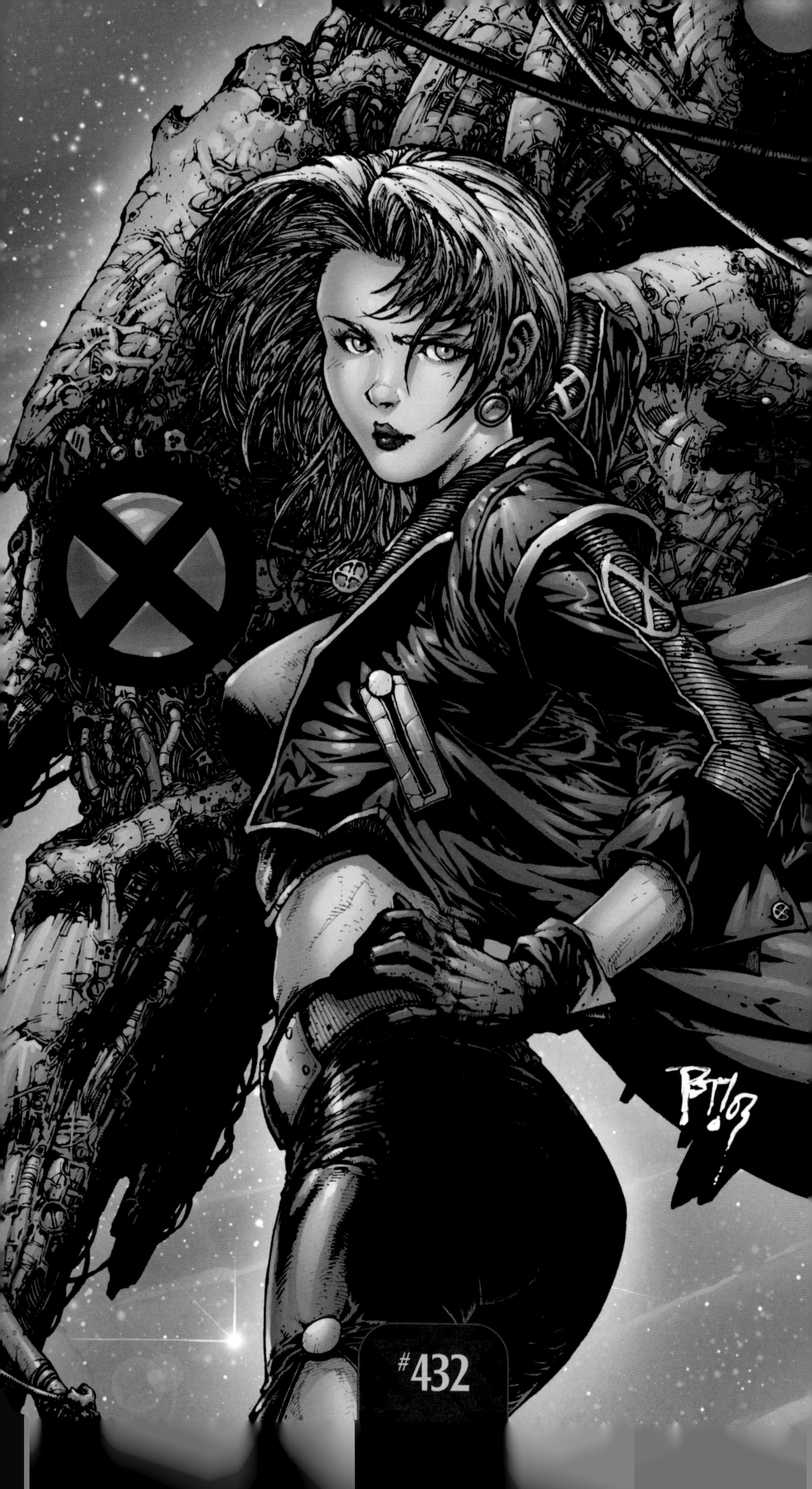
#432

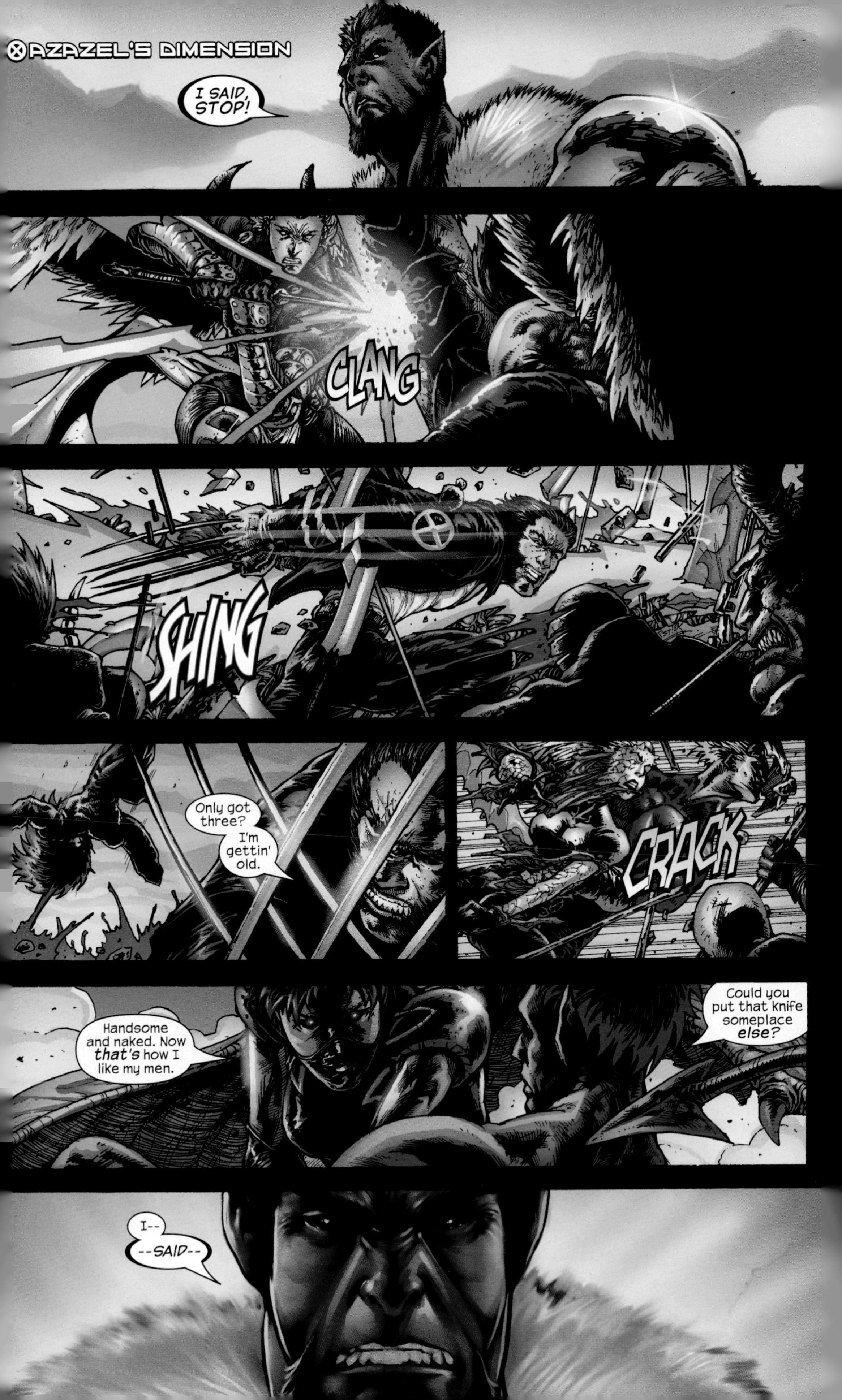
AZAZEL'S DIMENSION
I SAID, STOP!
CLANG
SHING
Only got three? I'm gettin' old.
CRACK
Handsome and naked. Now *that's* how I like my men.
Could you put that knife someplace *else?*
I--
--SAID--

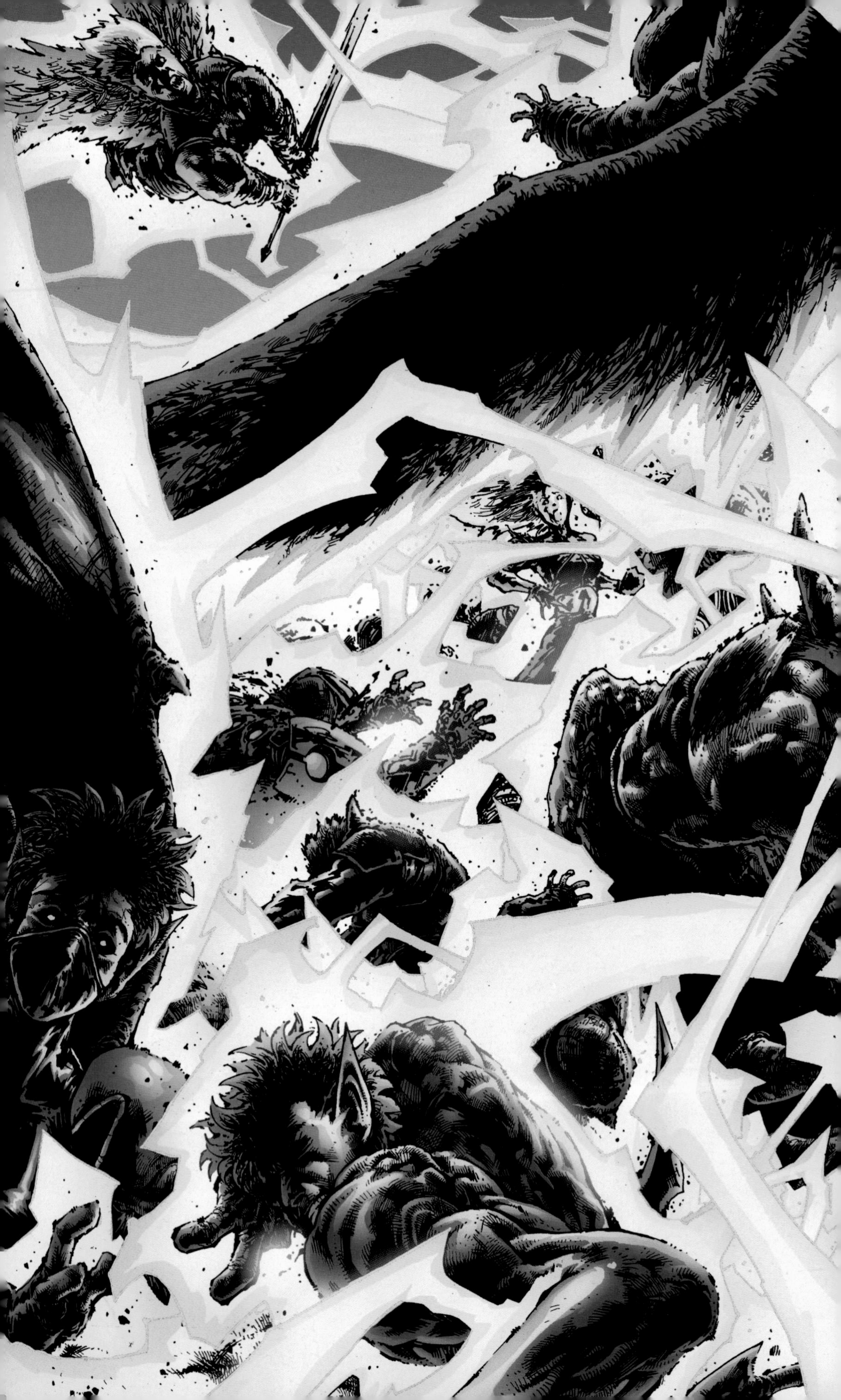

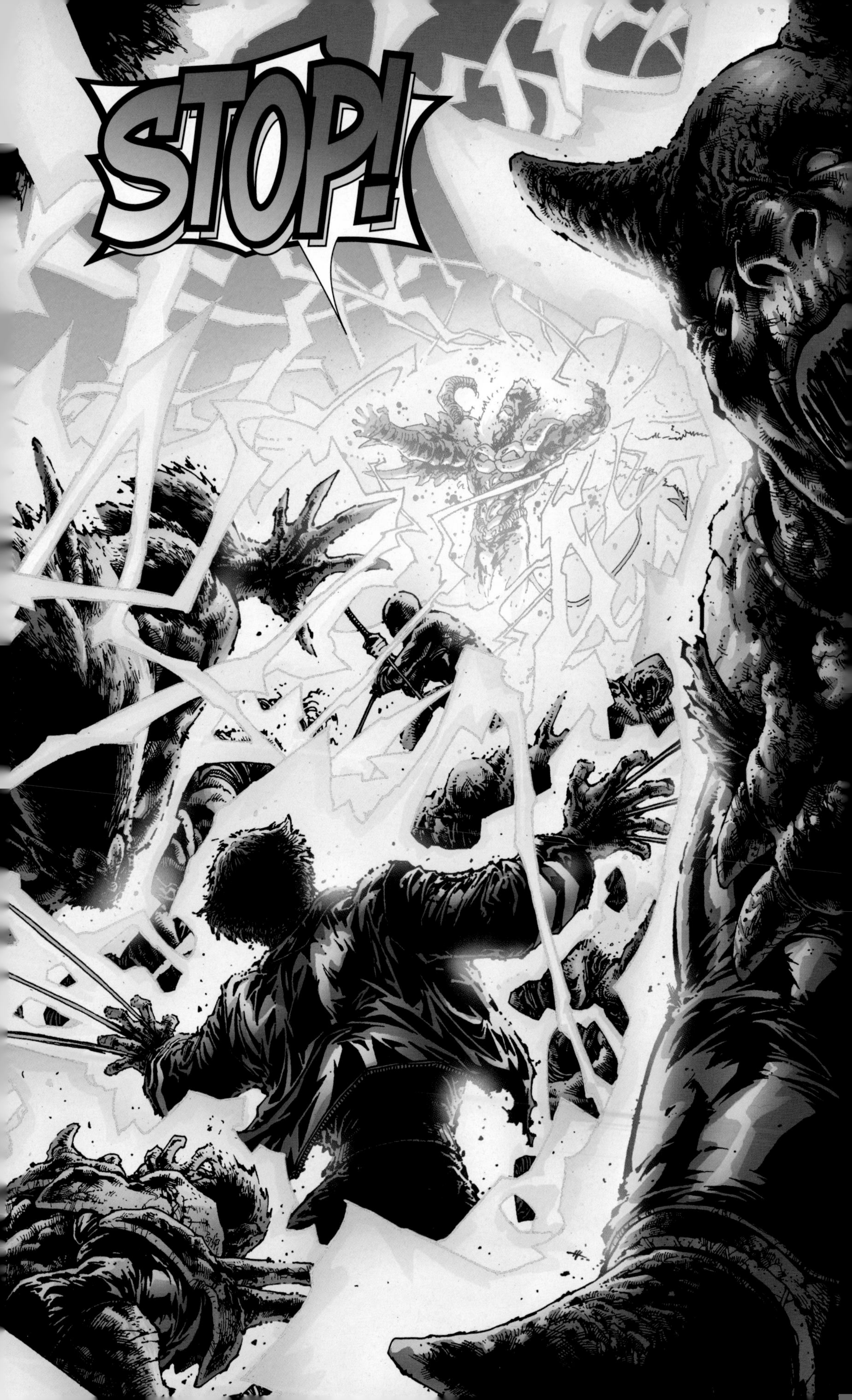
STOP!

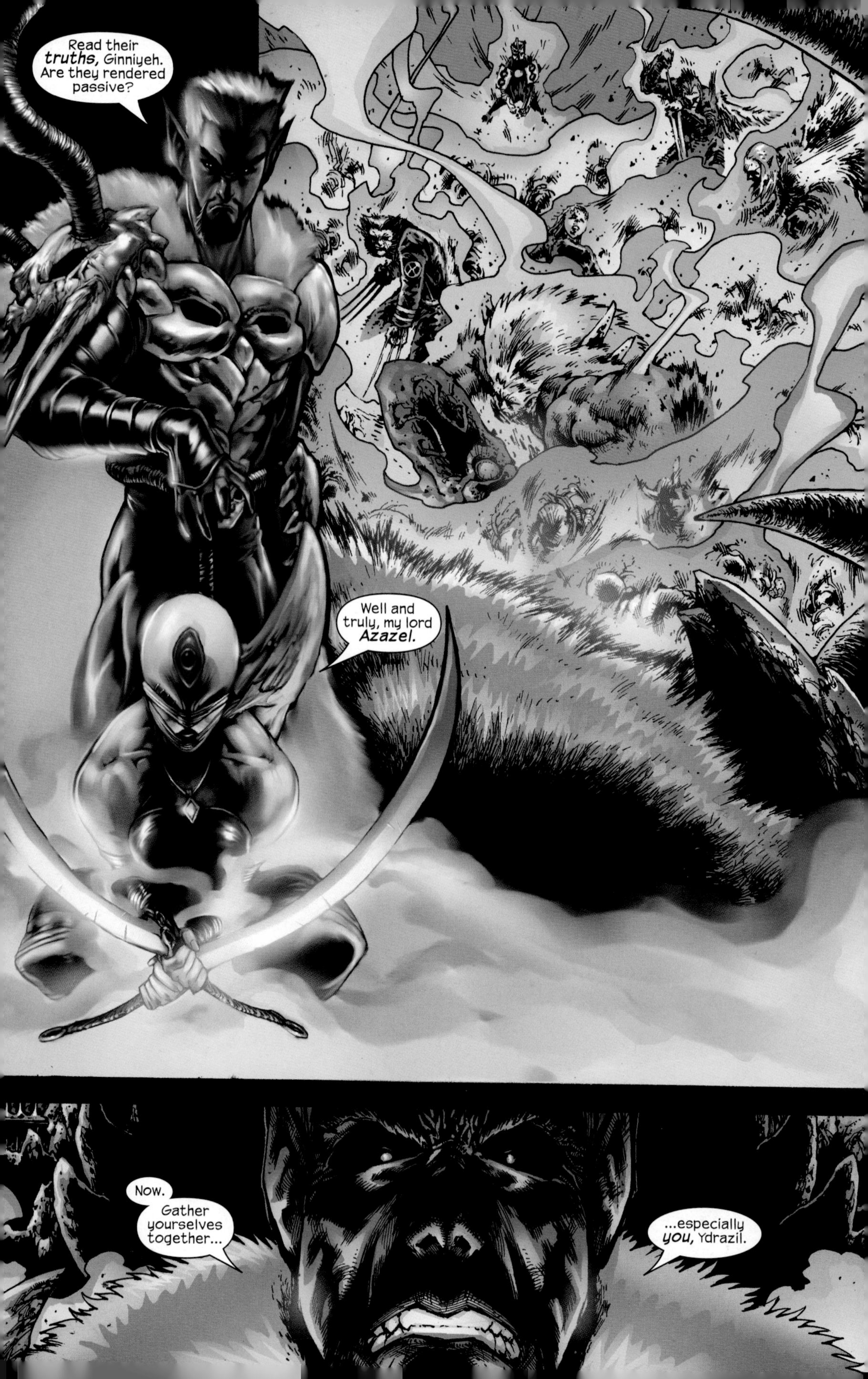
Read their truths, Ginniyeh. Are they rendered passive?
Well and truly, my lord Azazel.
Now.
Gather yourselves together...
...especially you, Ydrazil.

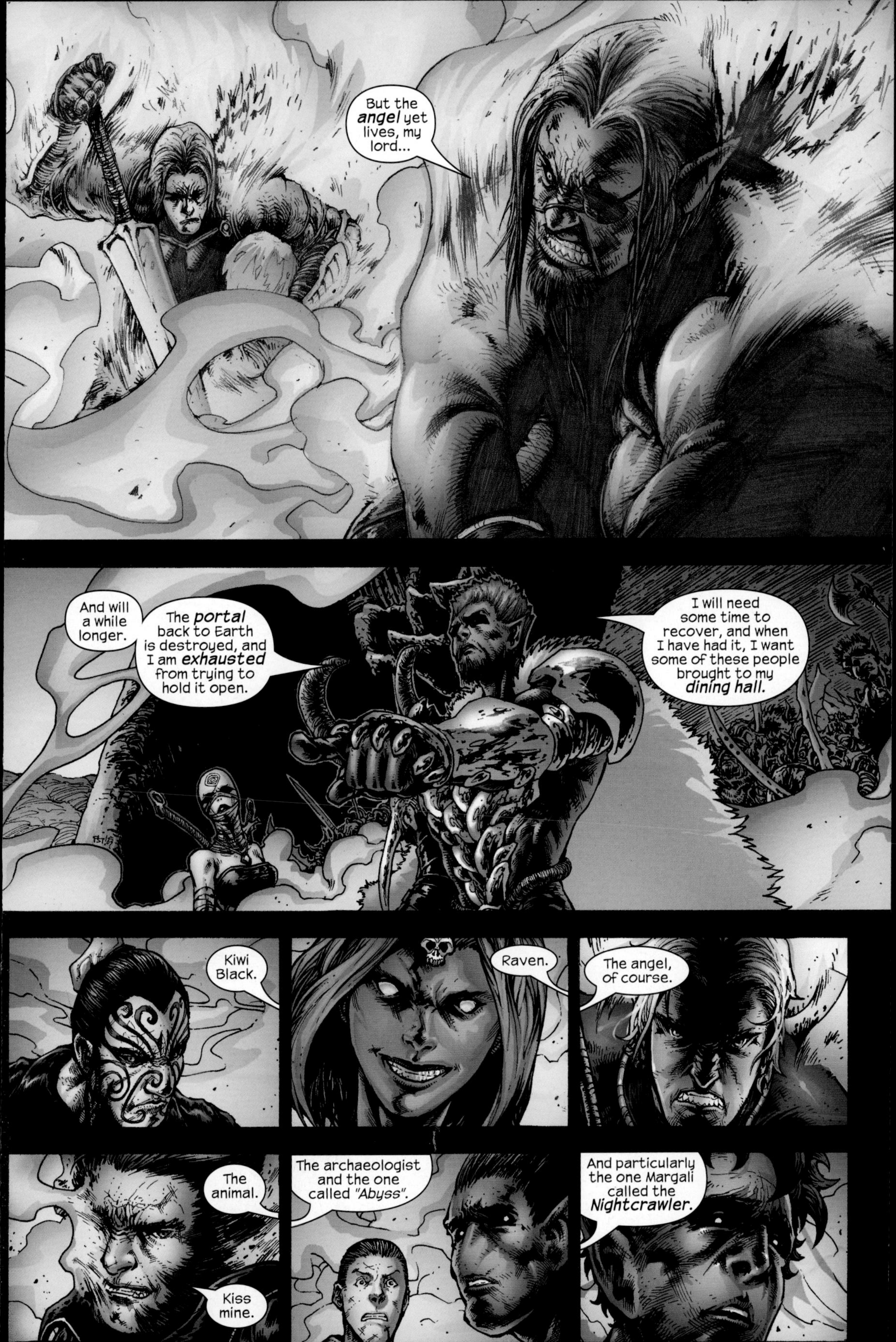
But the *angel* yet lives, my lord...
And will a while longer.
The *portal* back to Earth is destroyed, and I am *exhausted* from trying to hold it open.
I will need some time to recover, and when I have had it, I want some of these people brought to my *dining hall.*
Kiwi Black.
Raven.
The angel, of course.
The animal.
Kiss mine.
The archaeologist and the one called *"Abyss"*.
And particularly the one Margali called the *Nightcrawler*.

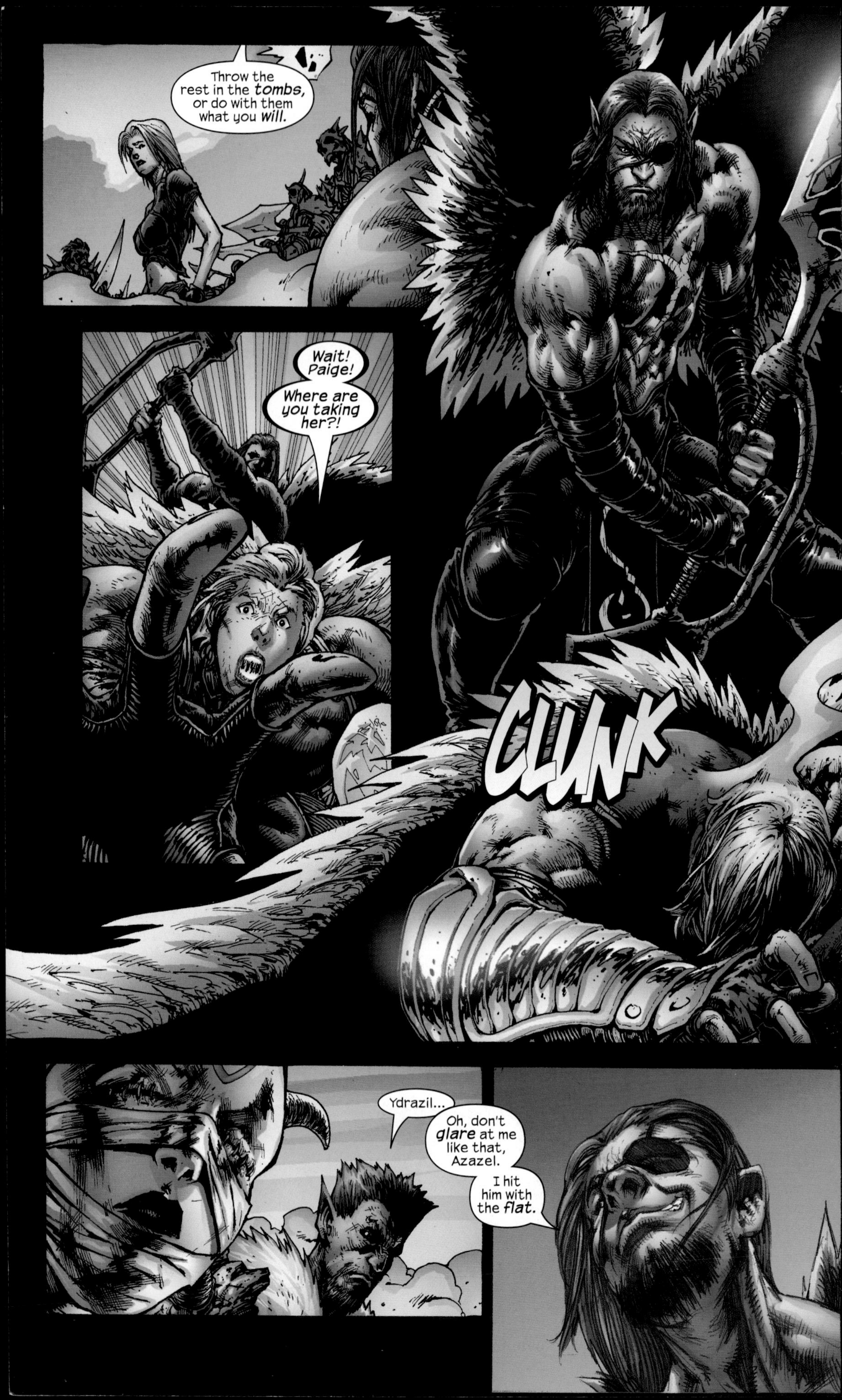

Throw the rest in the tombs, or do with them what you will.
Wait! Paige!
Where are you taking her?!
CLUNK
Ydrazil...
Oh, don't glare at me like that, Azazel.
I hit him with the flat.

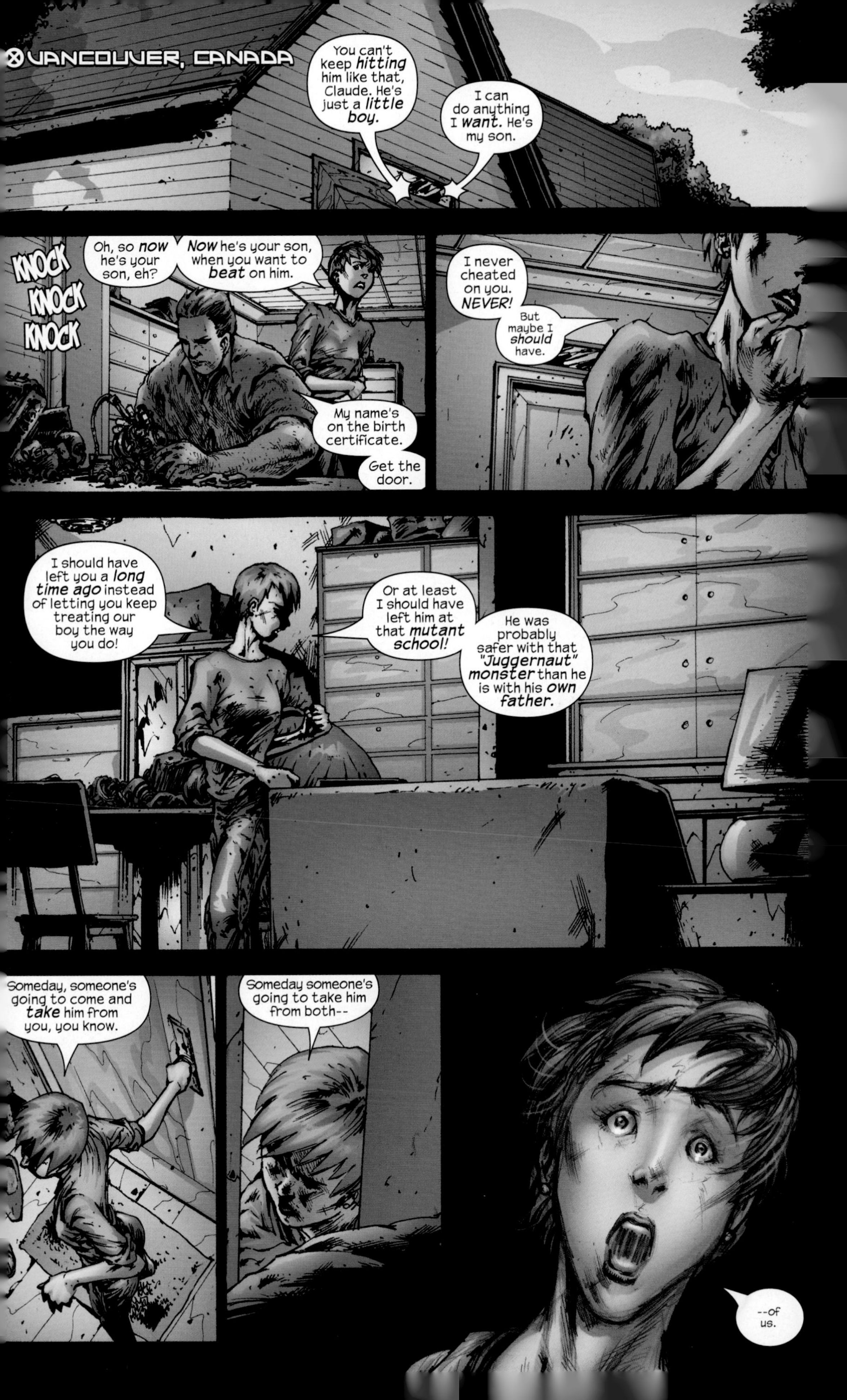
VANCOUVER, CANADA
You can't keep hitting him like that, Claude. He's just a little boy.
I can do anything I want. He's my son.
KNOCK KNOCK KNOCK
Oh, so now he's your son, eh?
Now he's your son, when you want to beat on him.
My name's on the birth certificate.
Get the door.
I never cheated on you. NEVER!
But maybe I should have.
I should have left you a long time ago instead of letting you keep treating our boy the way you do!
Or at least I should have left him at that mutant school!
He was probably safer with that "Juggernaut" monster than he is with his own father.
Someday, someone's going to come and take him from you, you know.
Someday someone's going to take him from both--
--of us.

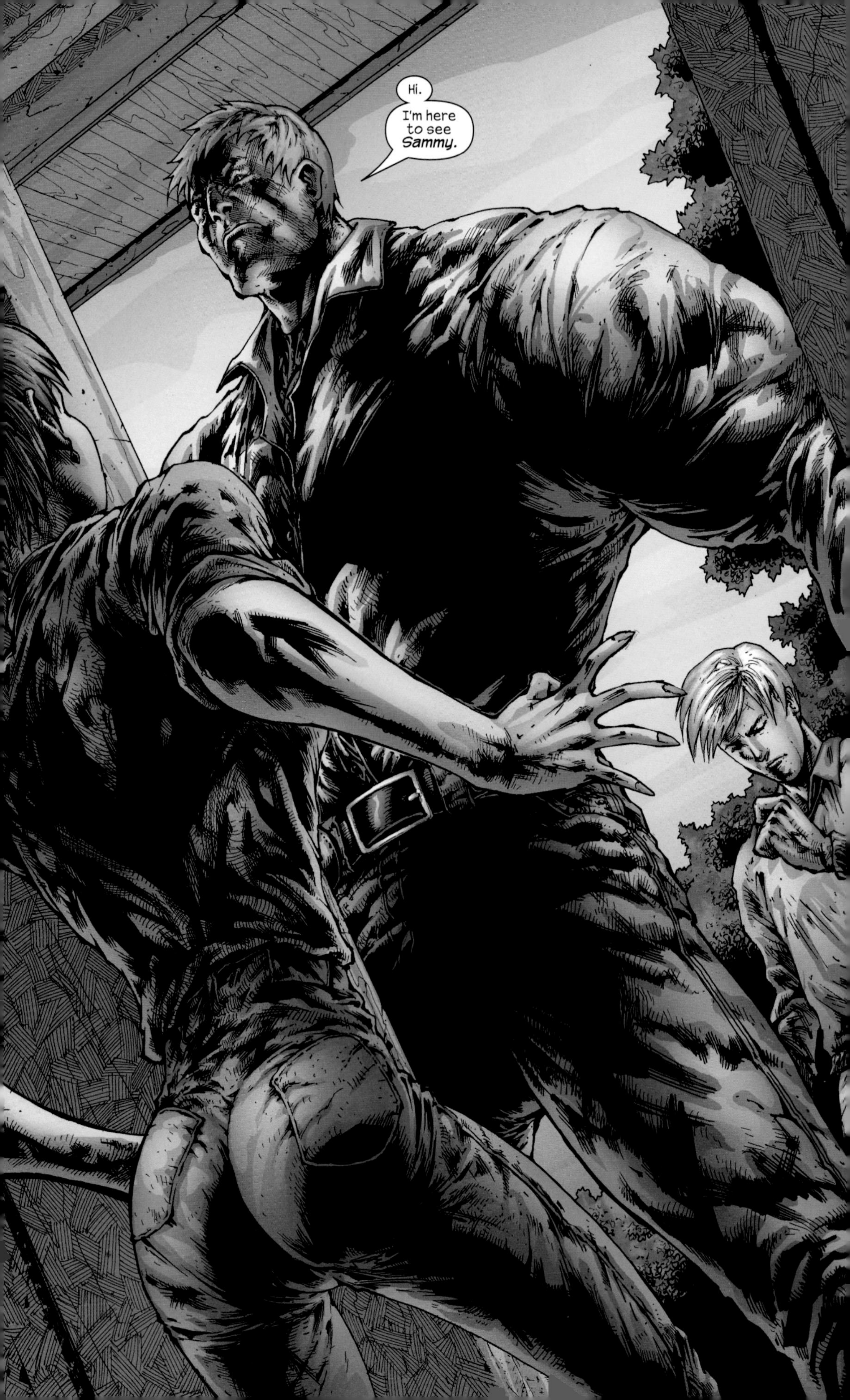
Hi.
I'm here to see *Sammy*.

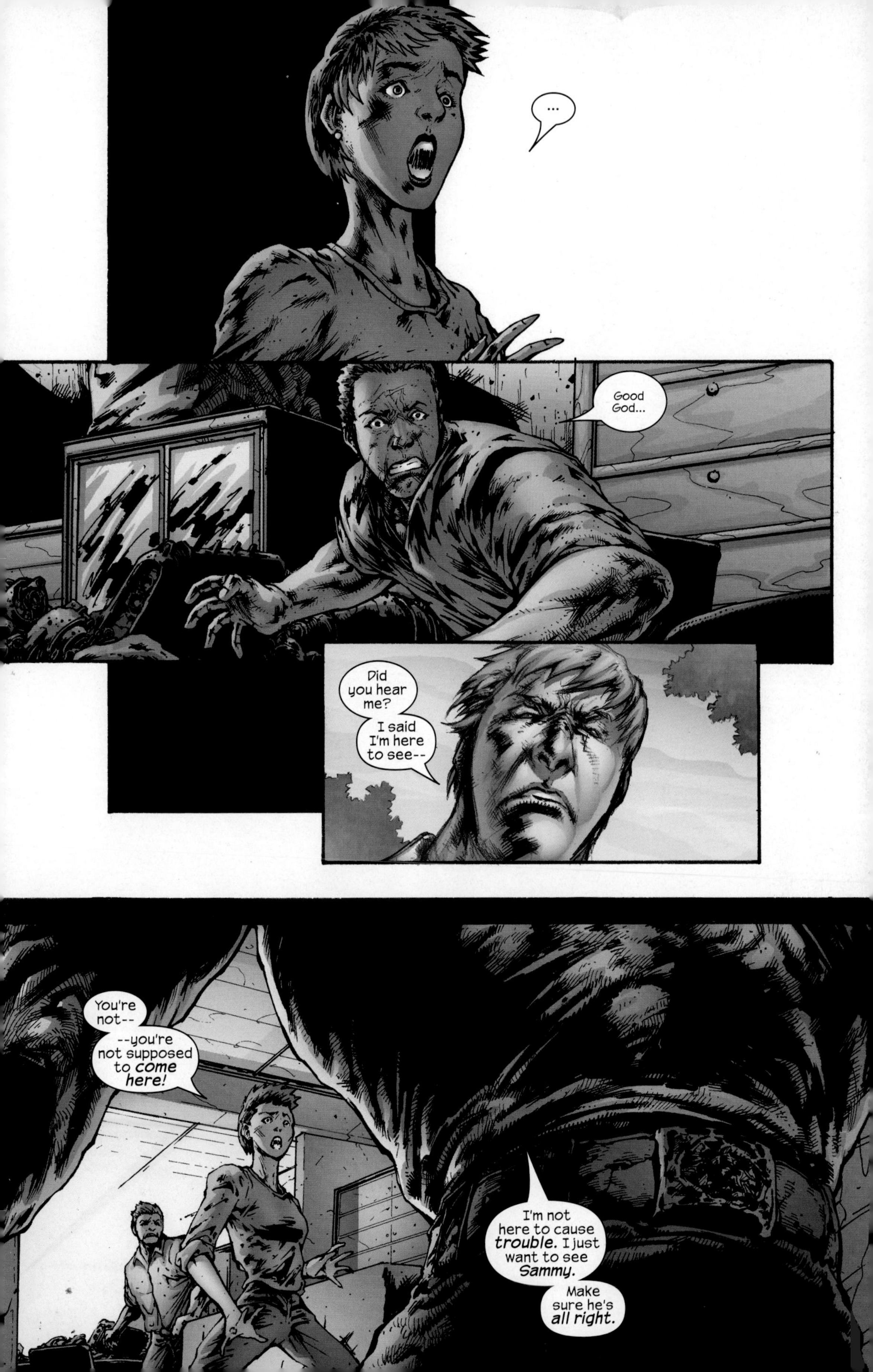
...
Good God...
Did you hear me?
I said I'm here to see--
You're not--
--you're not supposed to *come here!*
I'm not here to cause *trouble.* I just want to see *Sammy.*
Make sure he's *all right.*

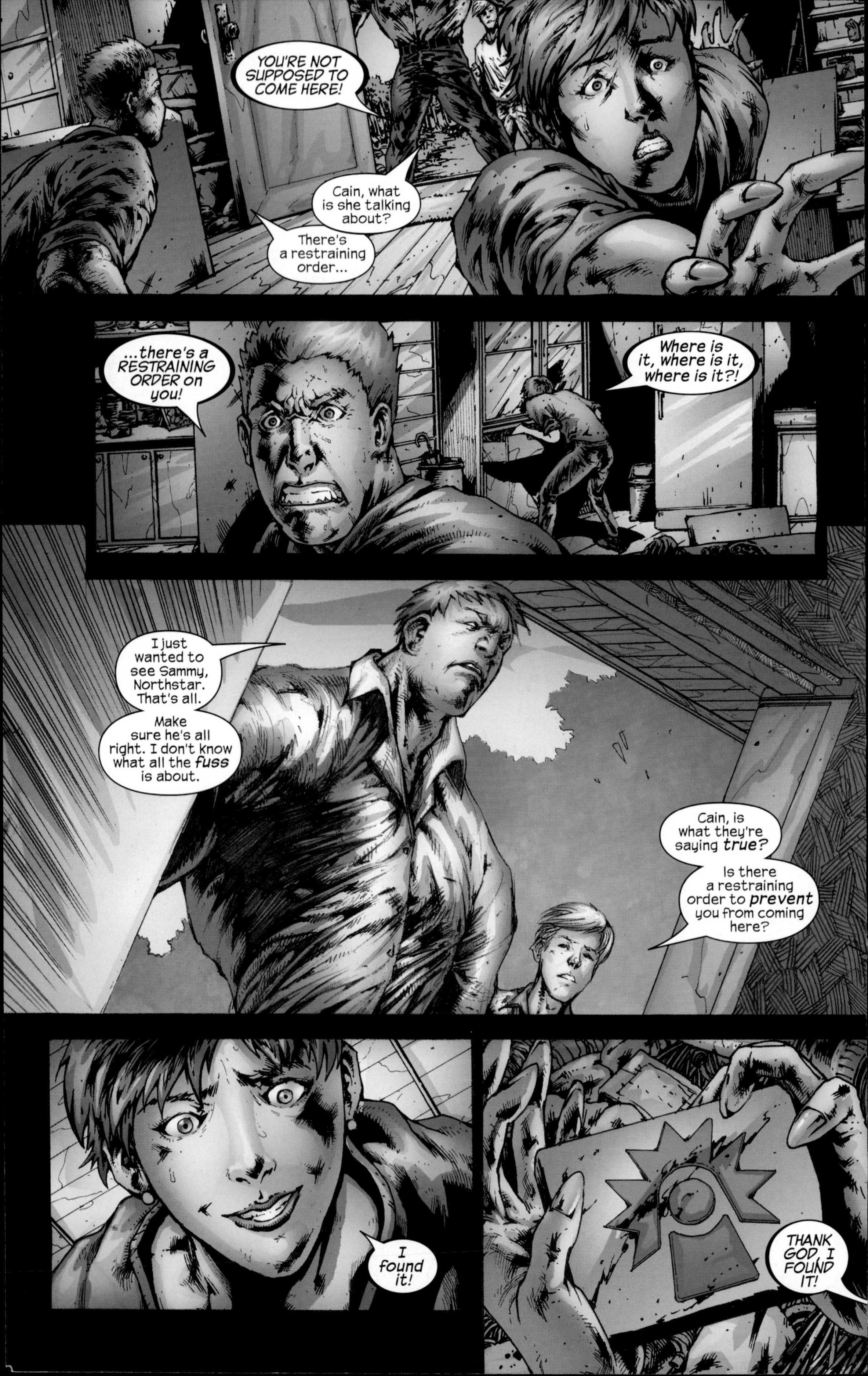
YOU'RE NOT SUPPOSED TO COME HERE!
Cain, what is she talking about?
There's a restraining order...
...there's a RESTRAINING ORDER on you!
Where is it, where is it, where is it?!
I just wanted to see Sammy, Northstar. That's all.
Make sure he's all right. I don't know what all the *fuss* is about.
Cain, is what they're saying *true*?
Is there a restraining order to *prevent* you from coming here?
I found it!
THANK GOD, I FOUND IT!

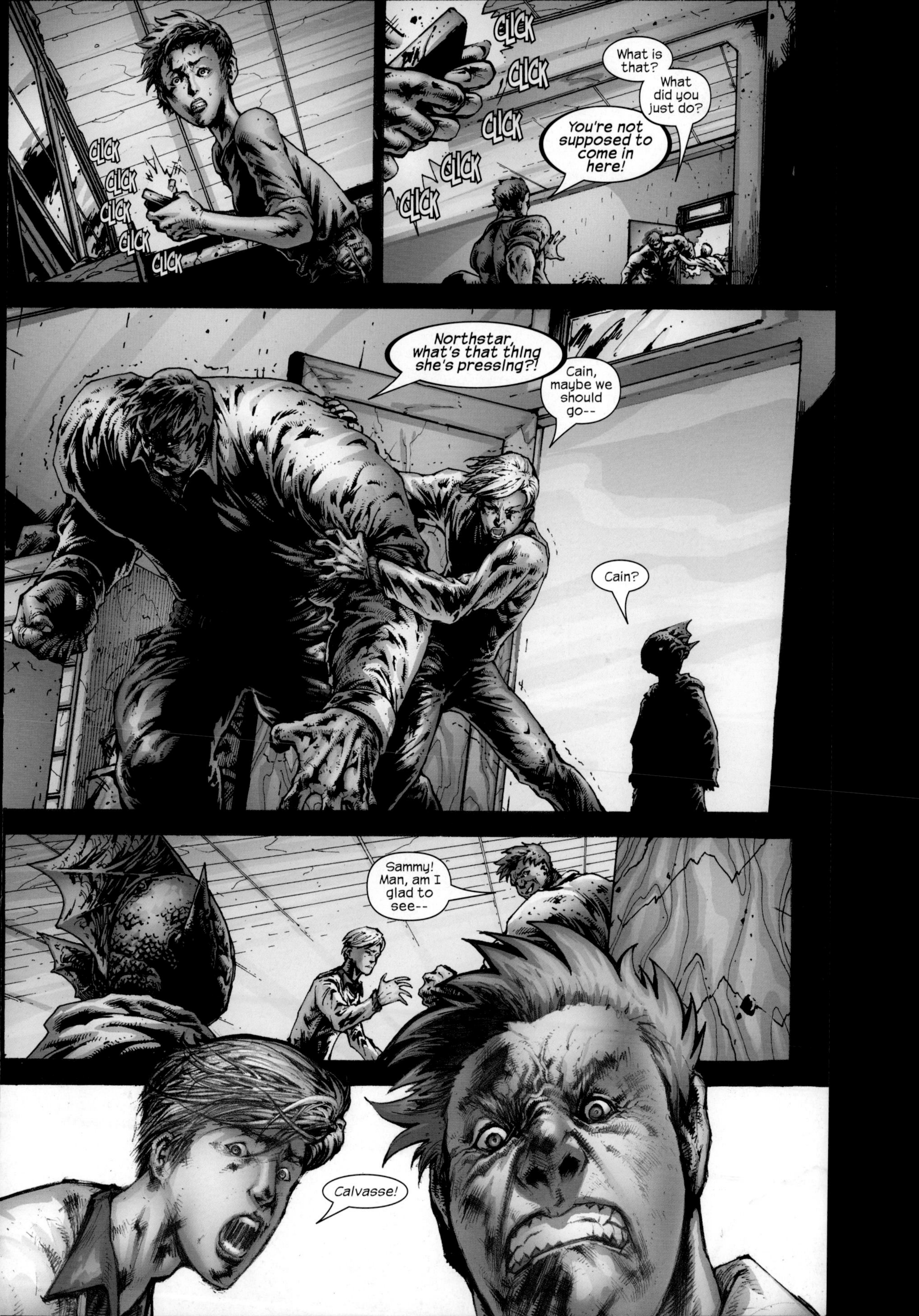
CLICK
CLICK
CLICK
CLICK
CLICK
CLICK
CLICK
CLICK
CLICK
CLICK
What is that?
What did you just do?
You're not supposed to come in here!
Northstar, what's that thing she's pressing?!
Cain, maybe we should go--
Cain?
Sammy! Man, am I glad to see--
Calvasse!

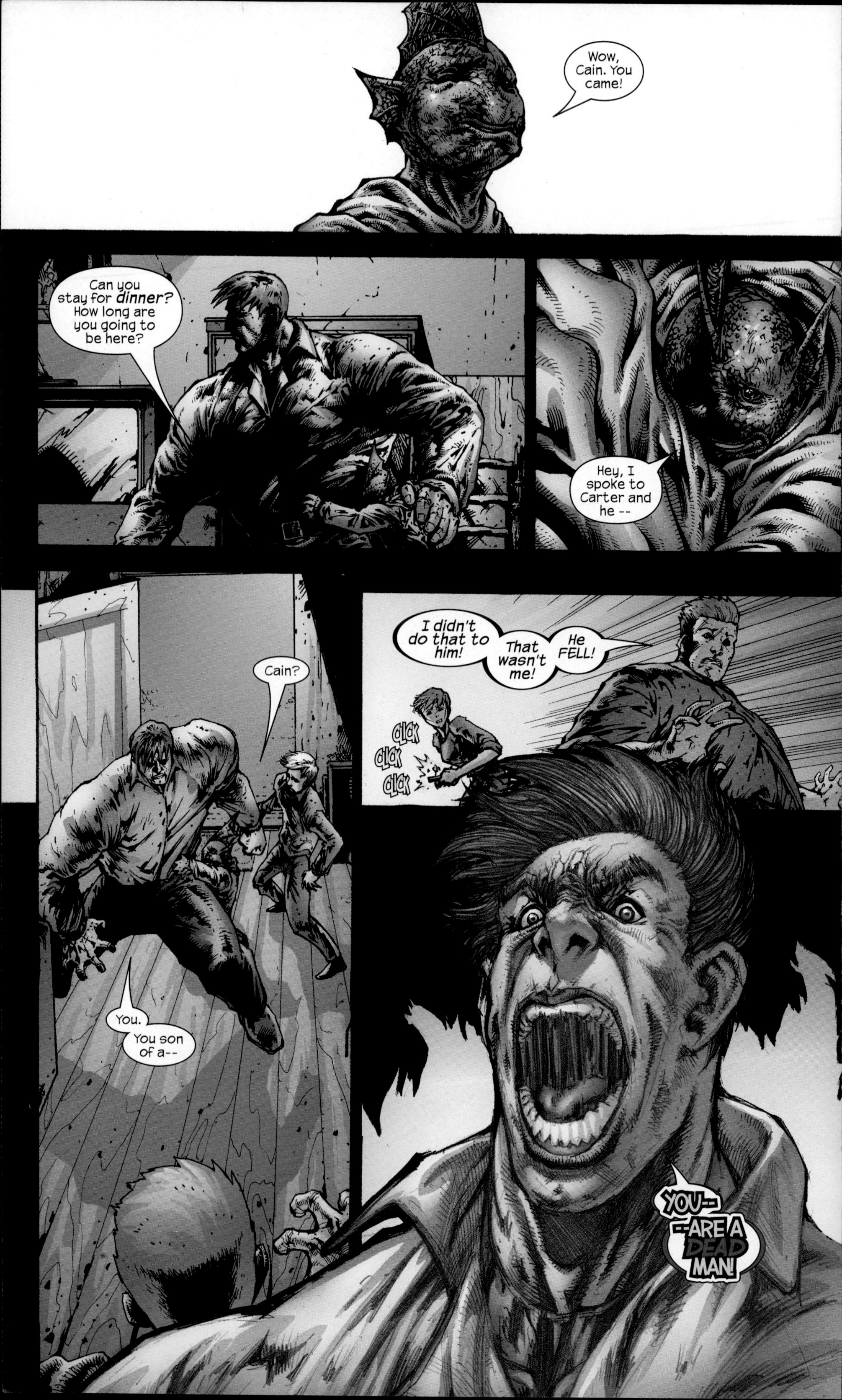
Wow, Cain. You came!
Can you stay for *dinner?* How long are you going to be here?
Hey, I spoke to Carter and he --
Cain?
I didn't do that to him!
That wasn't me!
He FELL!
CLICK
CLICK
CLICK
You.
You son of a--
YOU--
--ARE A DEAD MAN!

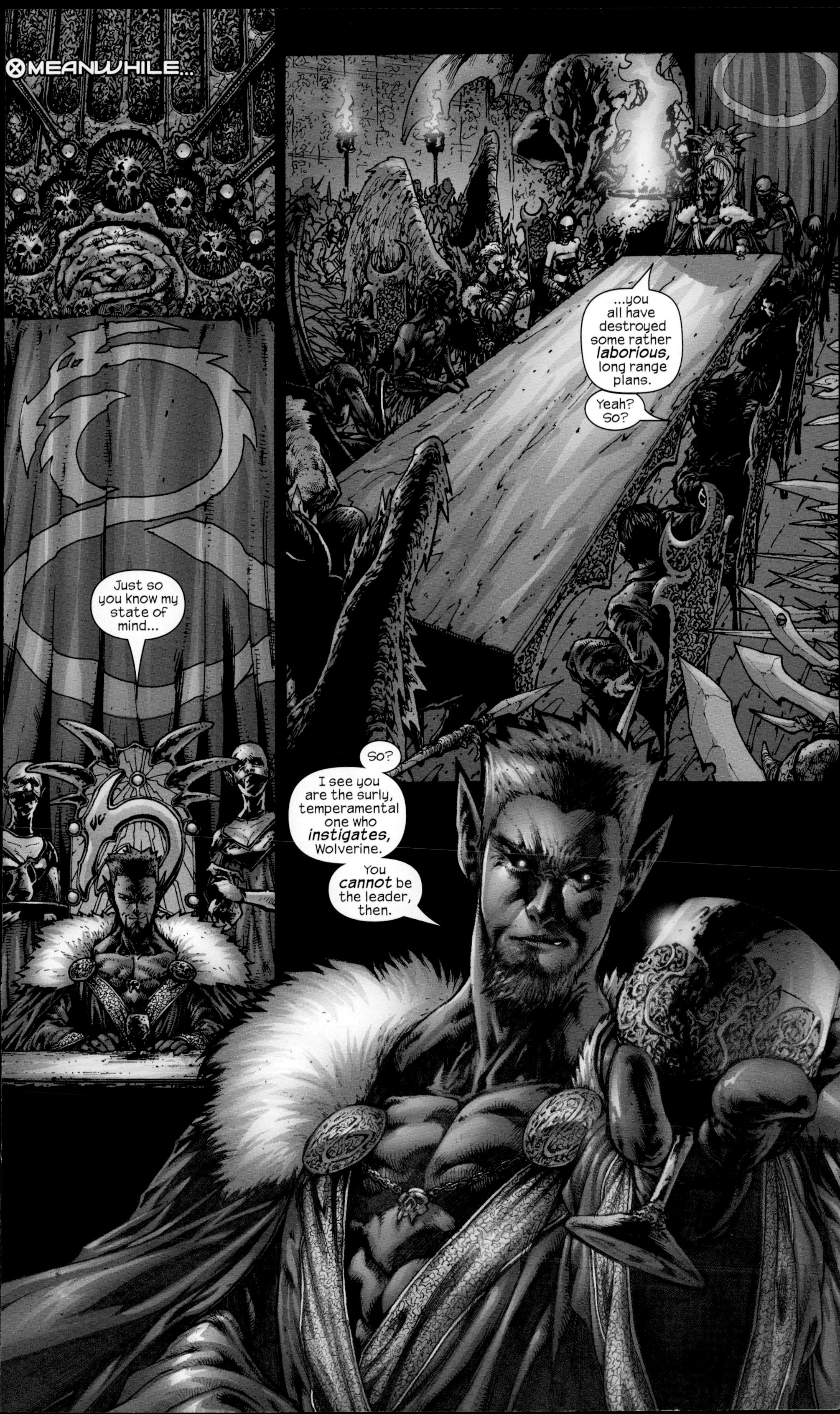
MEANWHILE...
...you all have destroyed some rather *laborious,* long range plans.
Yeah? So?
Just so you know my state of mind...
So?
I see you are the surly, temperamental one who *instigates,* Wolverine.
You *cannot* be the leader, then.

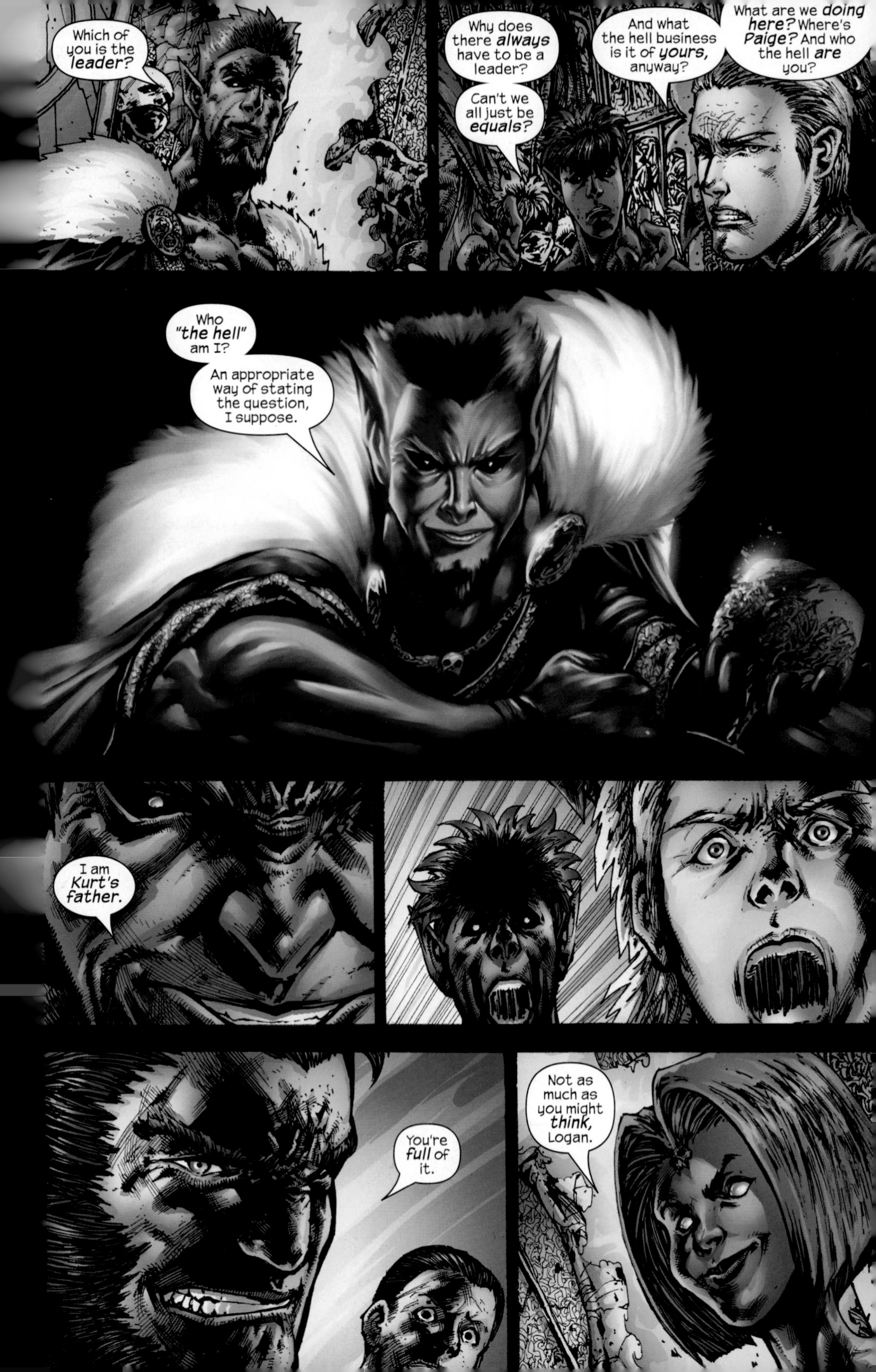
Which of you is the leader?
Why does there always have to be a leader?
Can't we all just be equals?
And what the hell business is it of yours, anyway?
What are we doing here? Where's Paige? And who the hell are you?
Who "the hell" am I?
An appropriate way of stating the question, I suppose.
I am Kurt's father.
You're full of it.
Not as much as you might think, Logan.

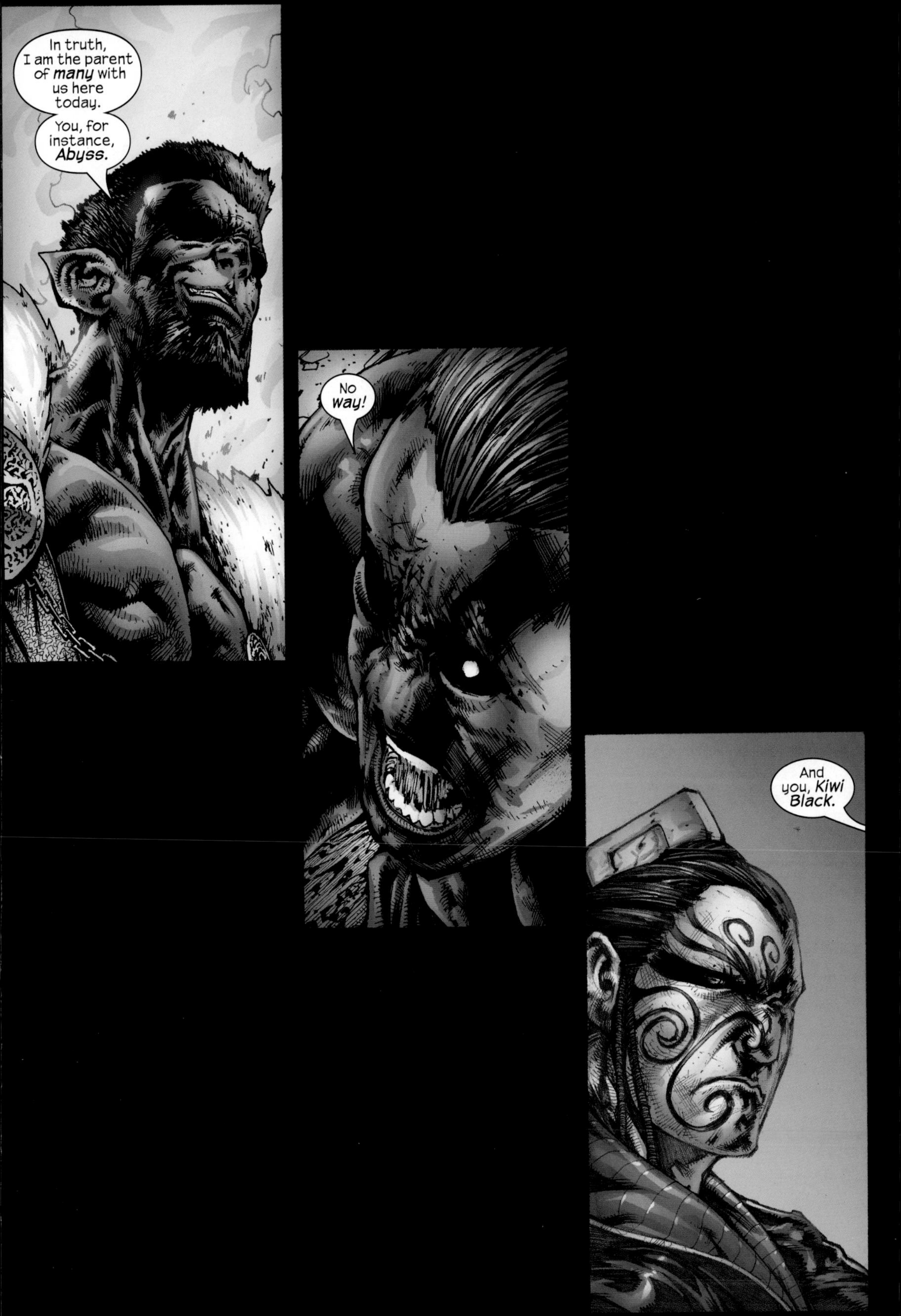
In truth, I am the parent of *many* with us here today.
You, for instance, *Abyss.*
No *way!*
And you, *Kiwi Black.*

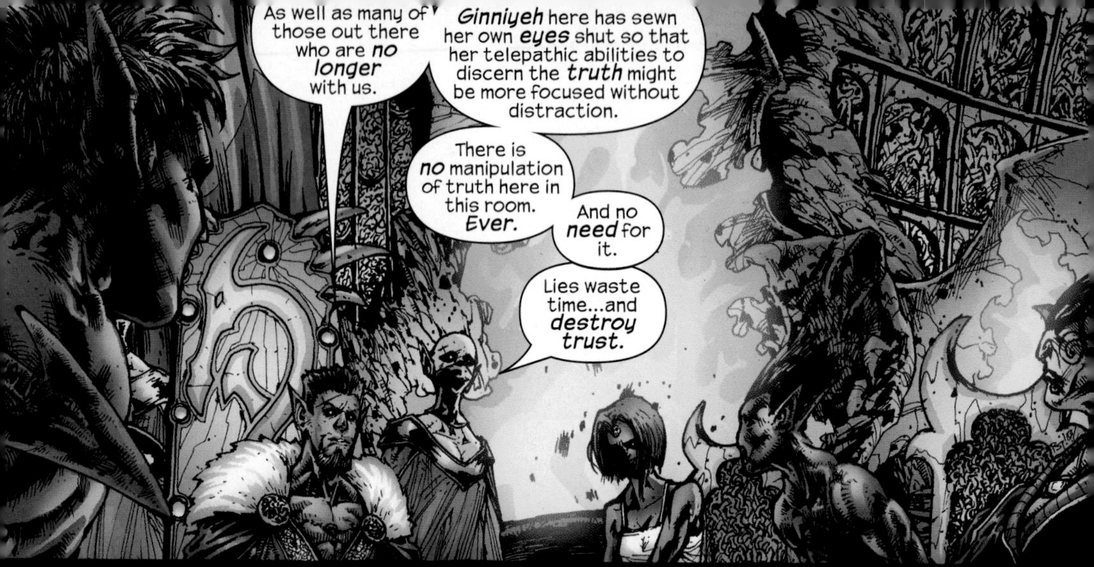

As well as many of those out there who are *no longer* with us.
Ginniyeh here has sewn her own *eyes* shut so that her telepathic abilities to discern the *truth* might be more focused without distraction.
There is *no* manipulation of truth here in this room. *Ever.*
And no *need* for it.
Lies waste time...and *destroy trust.*

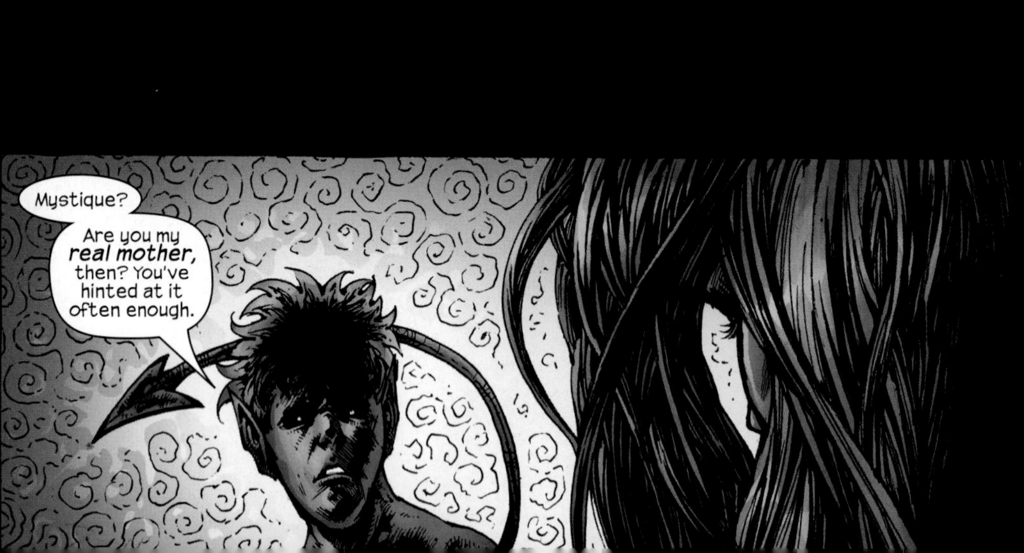

Mystique?
Are you my *real mother,* then? You've hinted at it often enough.

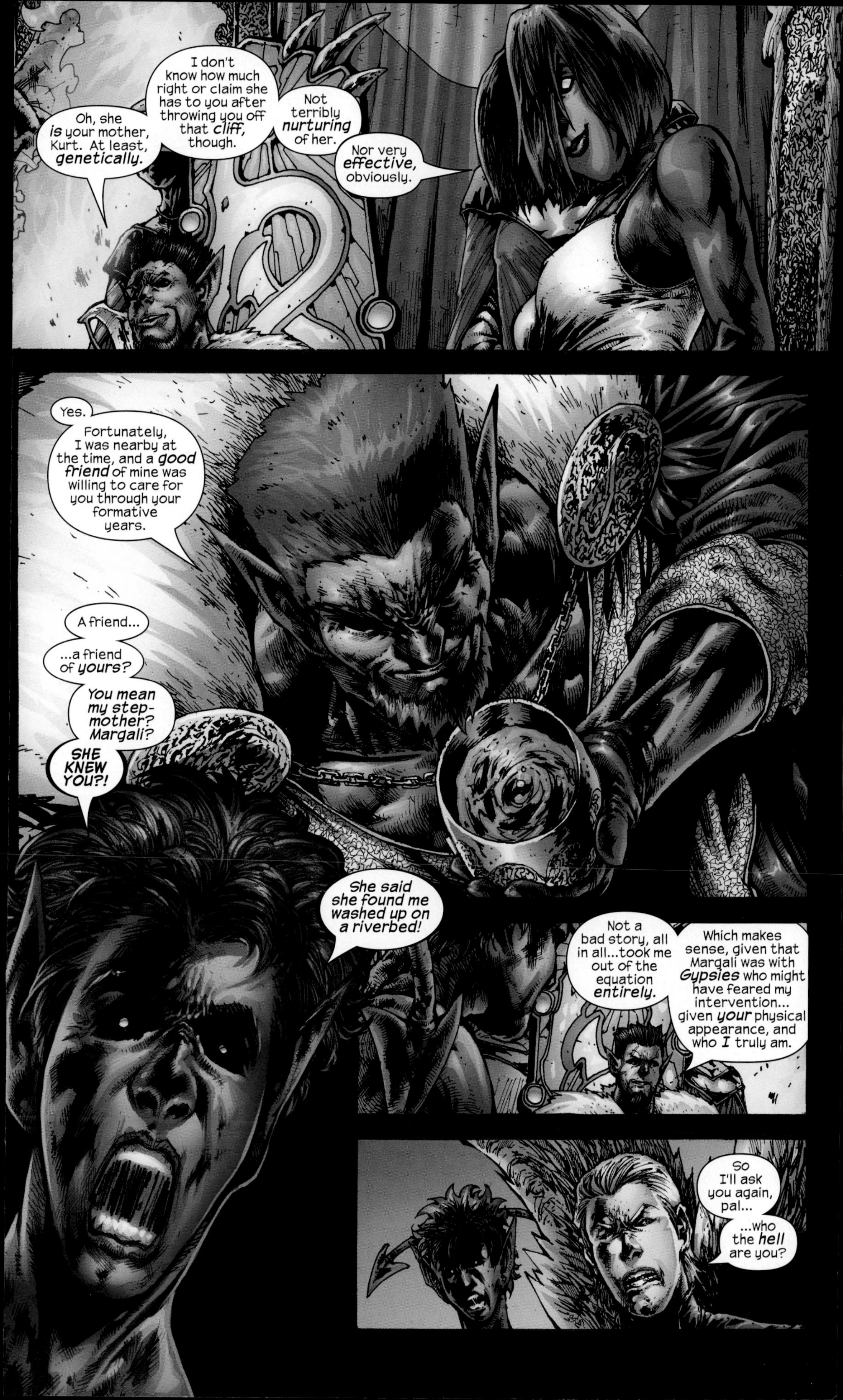

Oh, she *is* your mother, Kurt. At least, ***genetically.***
I don't know how much right or claim she has to you after throwing you off that ***cliff,*** though.
Not terribly ***nurturing*** of her.
Nor very ***effective,*** obviously.
Yes.
Fortunately, I was nearby at the time, and a ***good friend*** of mine was willing to care for you through your formative years.
A friend...
...a friend of ***yours?***
You mean my step-mother? Margali?
SHE KNEW YOU?!
She said she found me washed up on a riverbed!
Not a bad story, all in all...took me out of the equation ***entirely.***
Which makes sense, given that Margali was with ***Gypsies*** who might have feared my intervention... given ***your*** physical appearance, and who ***I*** truly am.
So I'll ask you again, pal...
...who the ***hell*** are you?

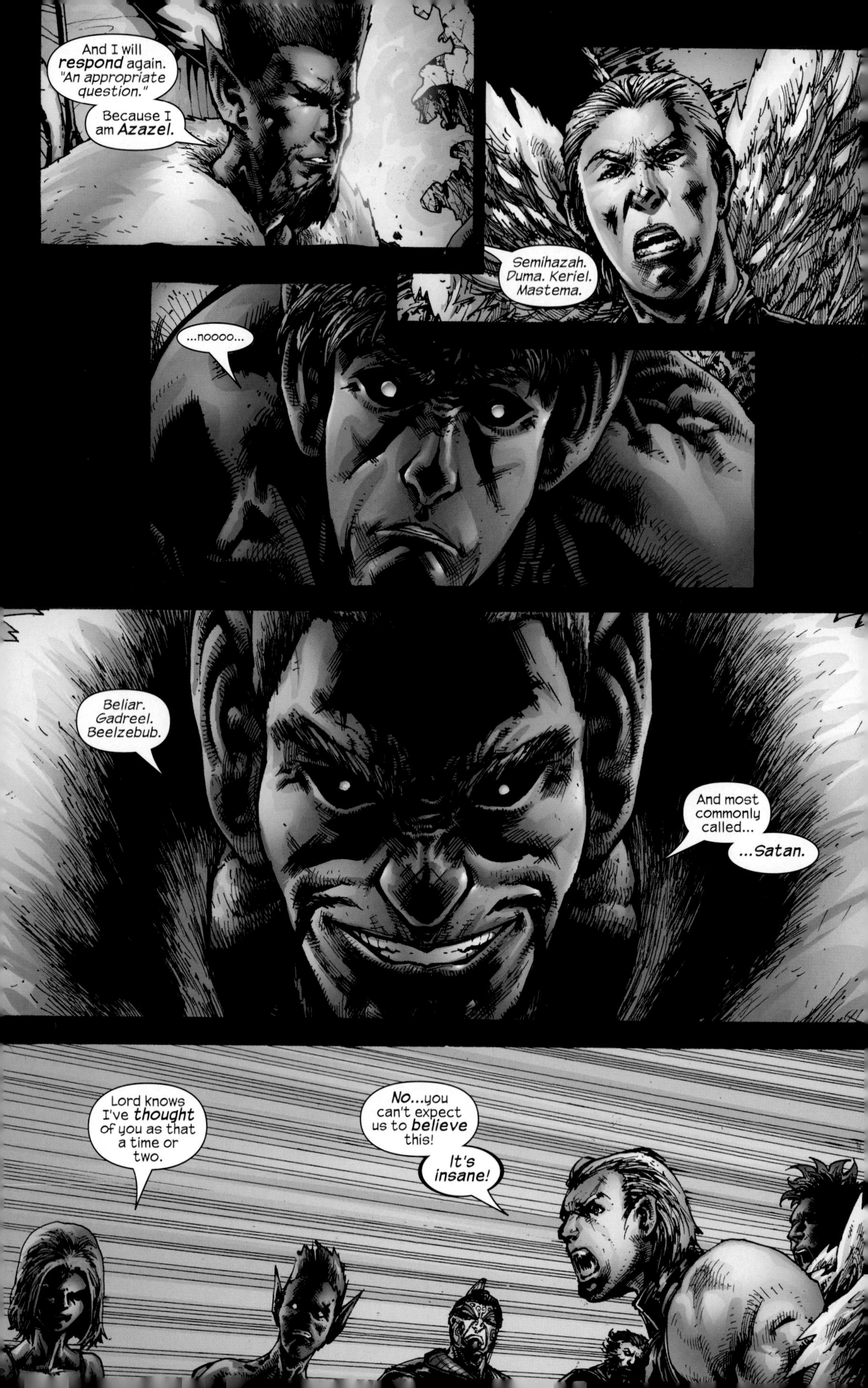
And I will **respond** again. *"An appropriate question."*
Because I am ***Azazel.***
Semihazah. Duma. Keriel. Mastema.
...noooo...
Beliar. Gadreel. Beelzebub.
And most commonly called...
...Satan.
Lord knows I've ***thought*** of you as that a time or two.
No...you can't expect us to ***believe*** this!
*It's **insane!***

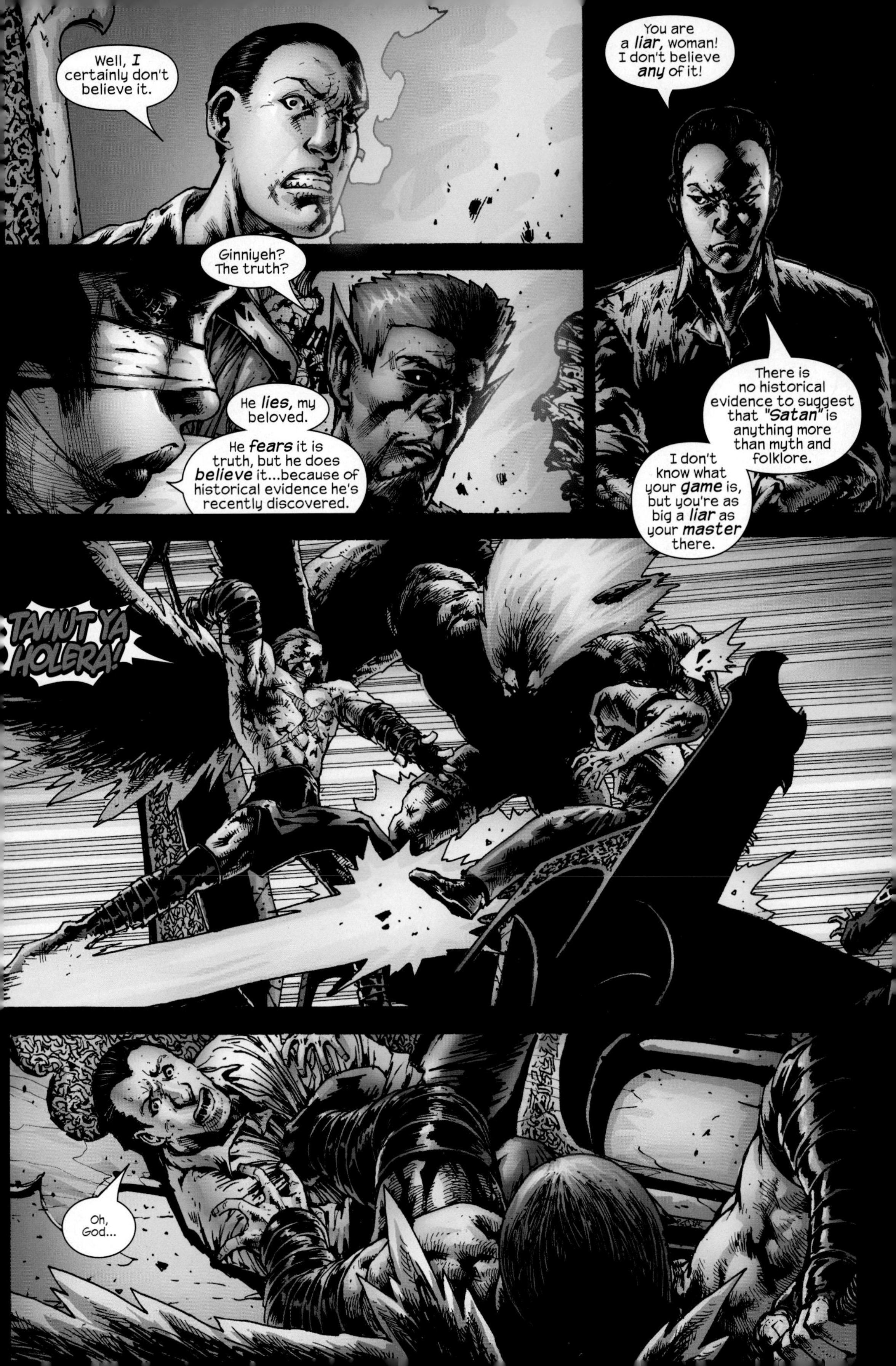
Well, I certainly don't believe it.
You are a liar, woman! I don't believe any of it!
Ginniyeh? The truth?
He lies, my beloved.
He fears it is truth, but he does believe it...because of historical evidence he's recently discovered.
There is no historical evidence to suggest that "Satan" is anything more than myth and folklore.
I don't know what your game is, but you're as big a liar as your master there.
TAMUT YA HOLERA!
Oh, God...

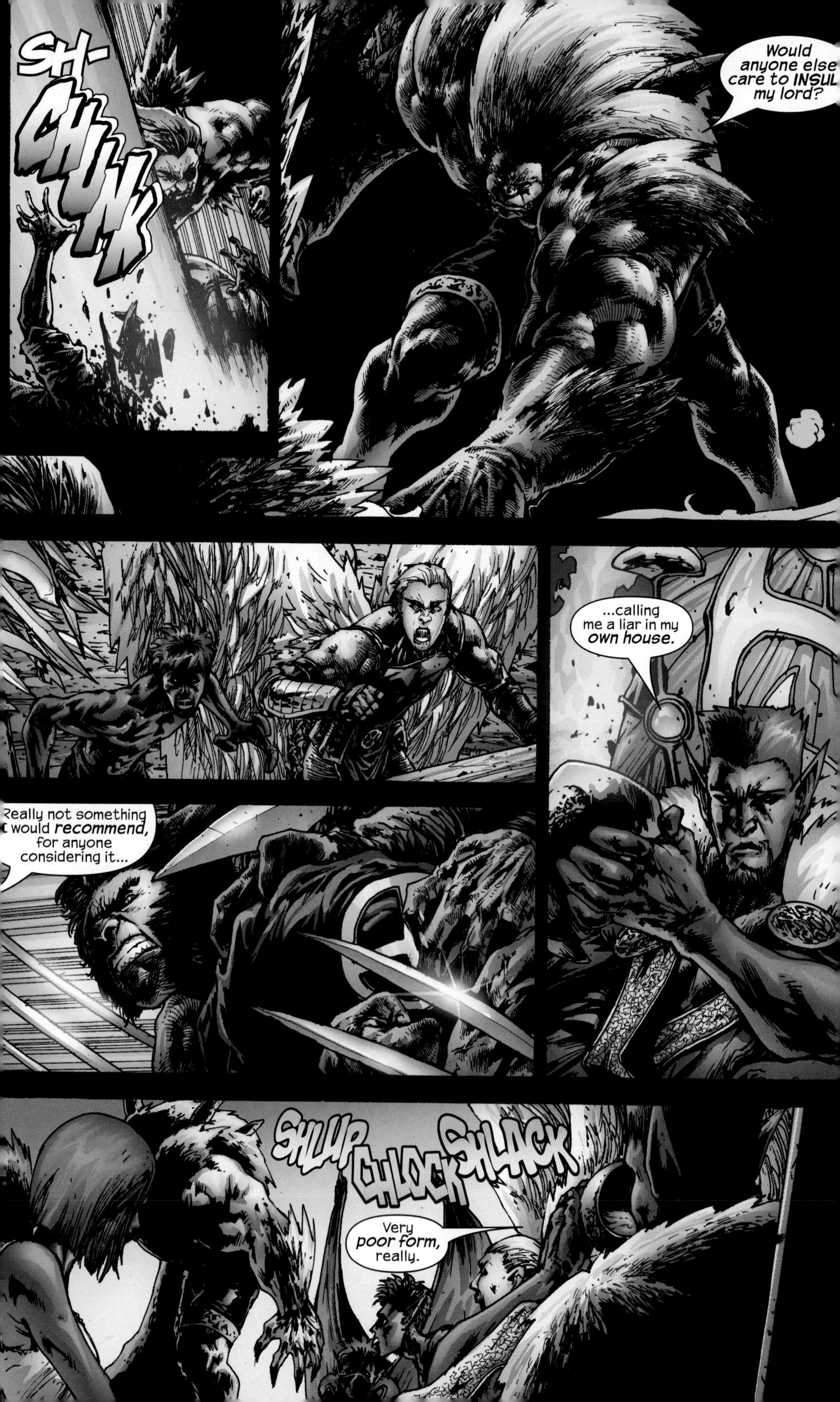
SH-CHUNK
Would anyone else care to INSUL my lord?
...calling me a liar in my own house.
Really not something I would recommend, for anyone considering it...
SHLUP CHLOCK SHLACK
Very poor form, really.

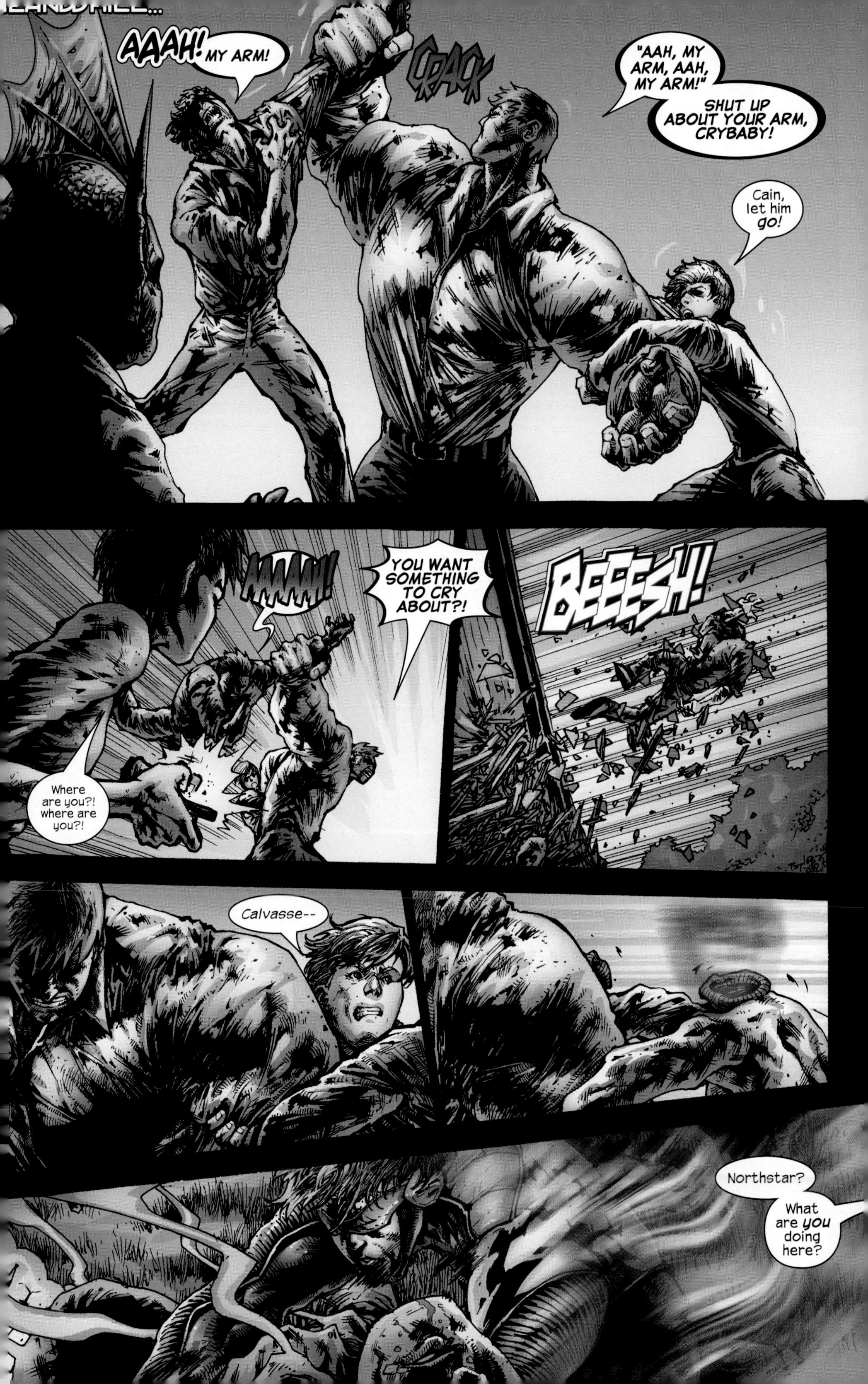
AAAH! MY ARM!
CRACK
"AAH, MY ARM, AAH, MY ARM!"
SHUT UP ABOUT YOUR ARM, CRYBABY!
Cain, let him go!
AAAAH!
YOU WANT SOMETHING TO CRY ABOUT?!
Where are you?! where are you?!
BEEESH!
Calvasse--
Northstar?
What are you doing here?

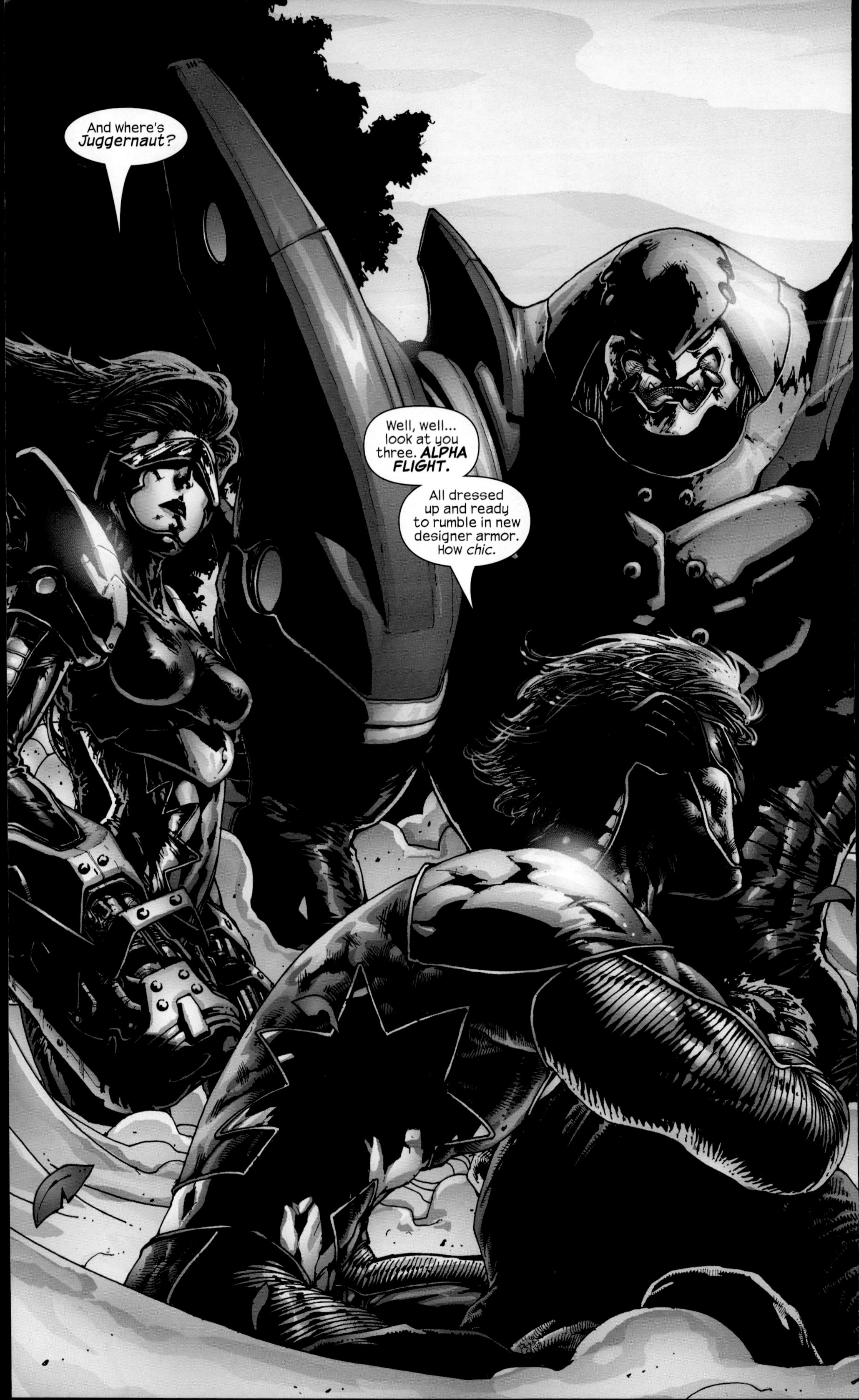
And where's Juggernaut?
Well, well... look at you three. ALPHA FLIGHT.
All dressed up and ready to rumble in new designer armor. How chic.

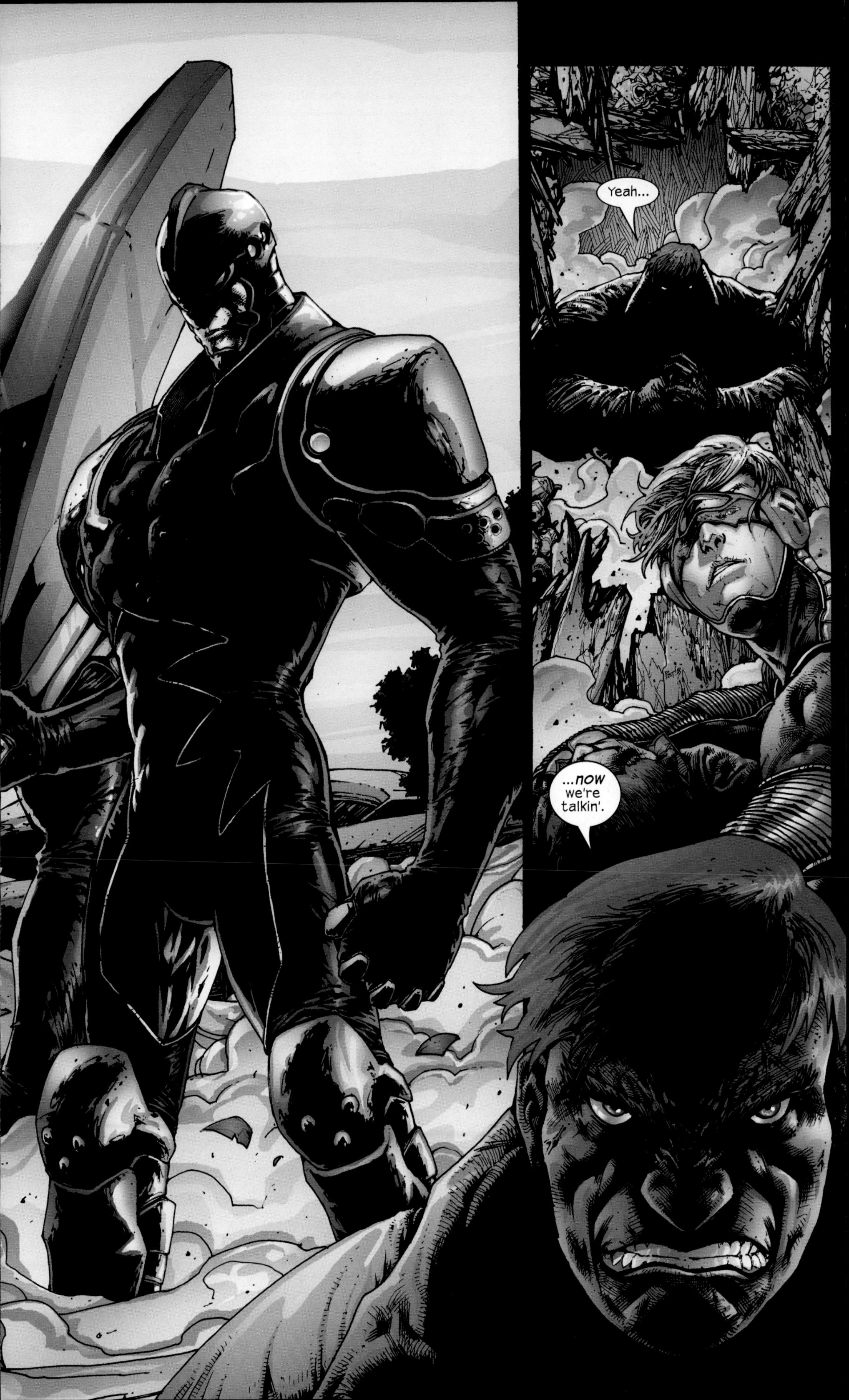
Yeah...
...*now* we're talkin'.

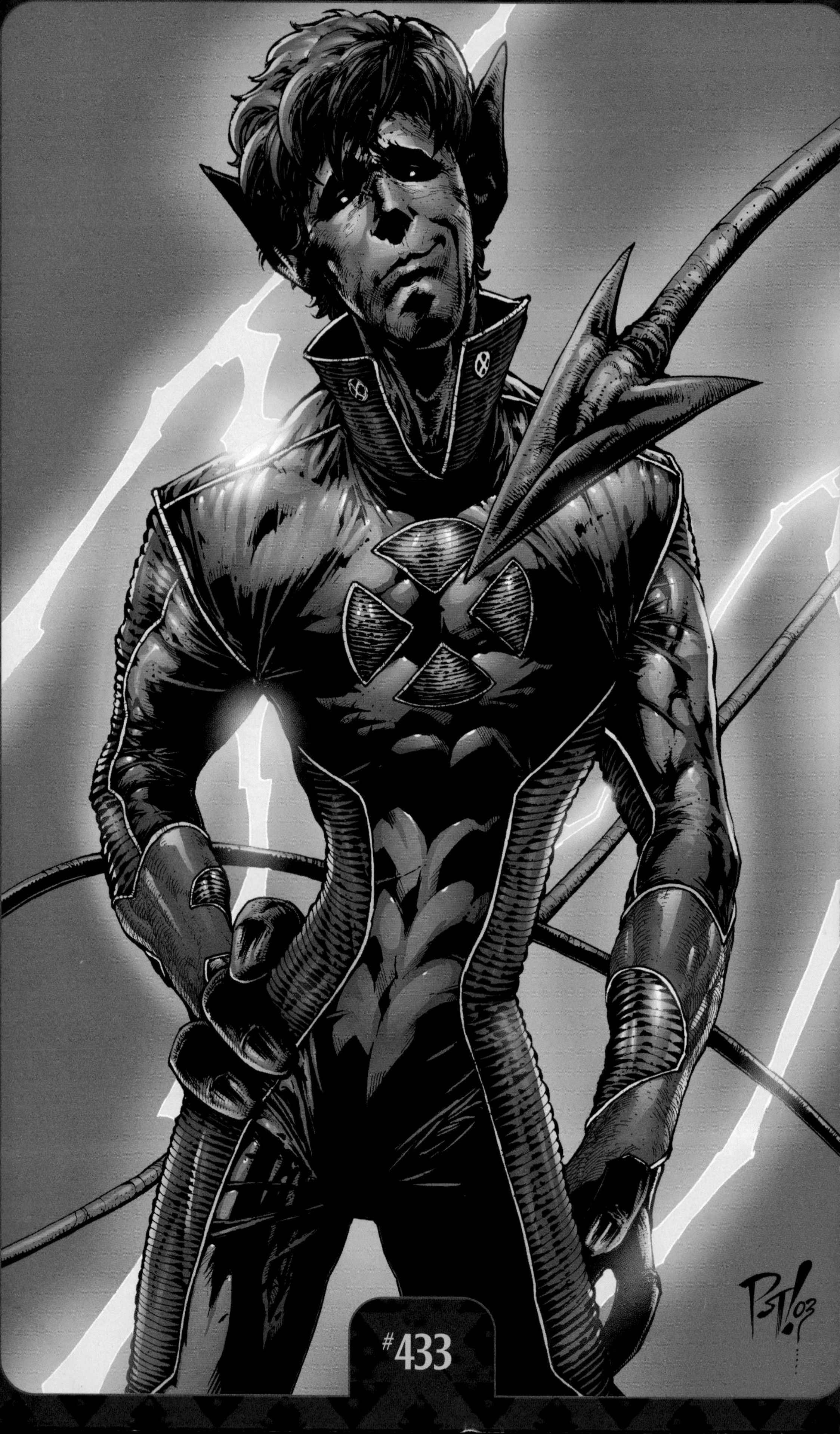
#433

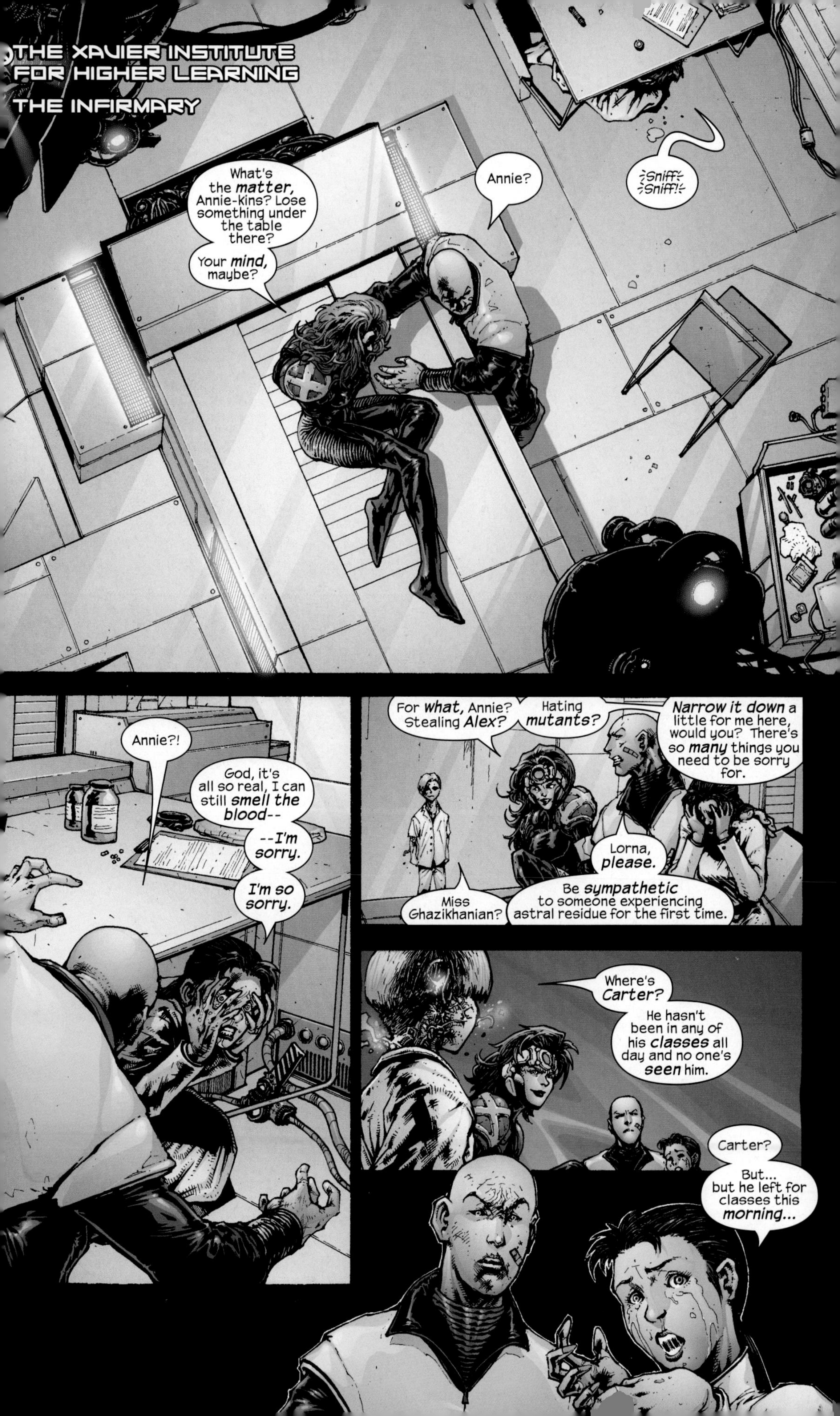
THE XAVIER INSTITUTE FOR HIGHER LEARNING
THE INFIRMARY
What's the matter, Annie-kins? Lose something under the table there?
Your mind, maybe?
Annie?
Sniff! Sniff!
Annie?!
God, it's all so real, I can still smell the blood--
--I'm sorry.
I'm so sorry.
For what, Annie? Stealing Alex?
Hating mutants?
Narrow it down a little for me here, would you? There's so many things you need to be sorry for.
Lorna, please.
Miss Ghazikhanian?
Be sympathetic to someone experiencing astral residue for the first time.
Where's Carter?
He hasn't been in any of his classes all day and no one's seen him.
Carter?
But... but he left for classes this morning...

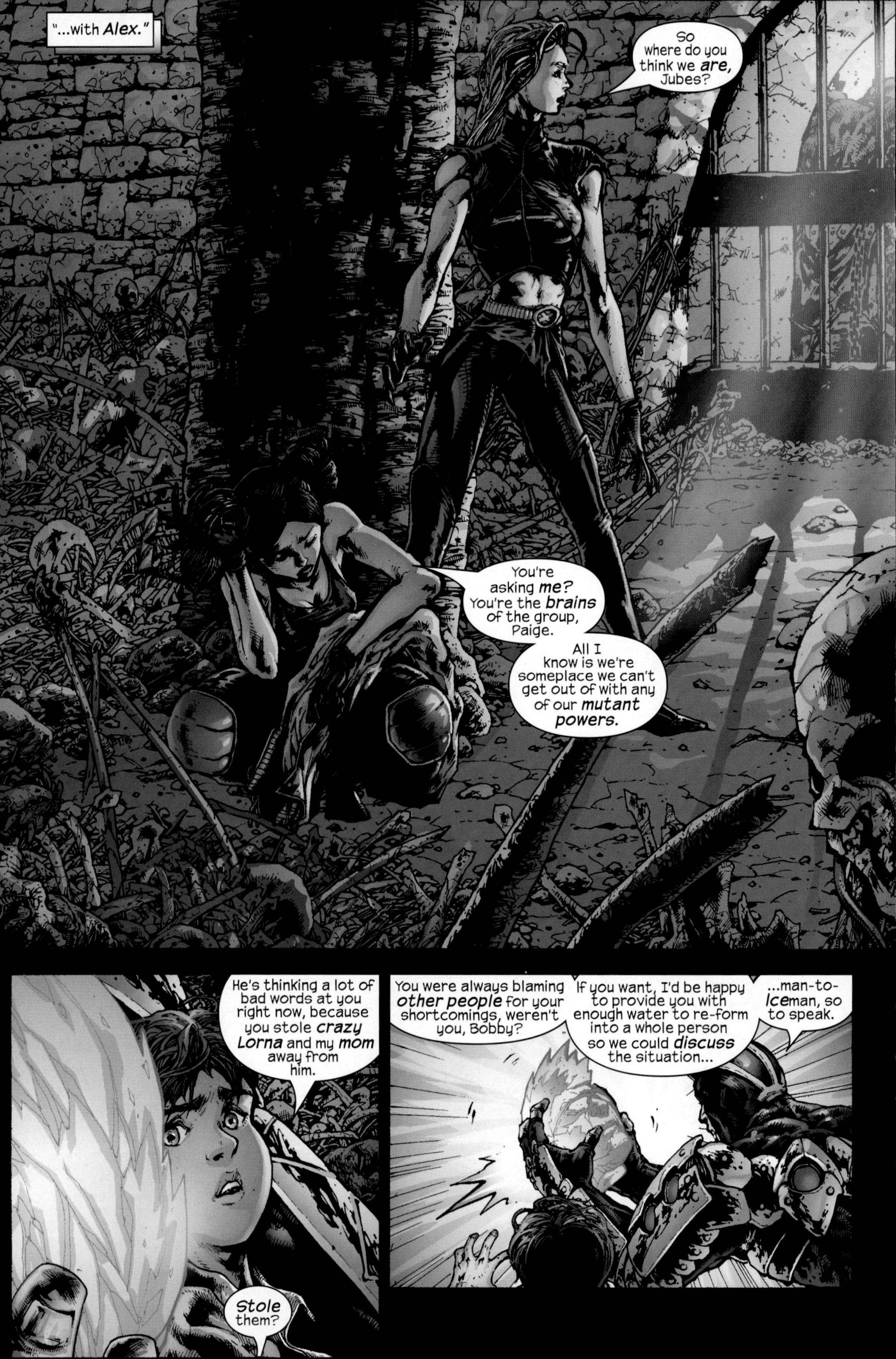
"...with Alex."
So where do you think we are, Jubes?
You're asking me? You're the brains of the group, Paige.
All I know is we're someplace we can't get out of with any of our mutant powers.
He's thinking a lot of bad words at you right now, because you stole crazy Lorna and my mom away from him.
Stole them?
You were always blaming other people for your shortcomings, weren't you, Bobby?
If you want, I'd be happy to provide you with enough water to re-form into a whole person so we could discuss the situation...
...man-to-Iceman, so to speak.

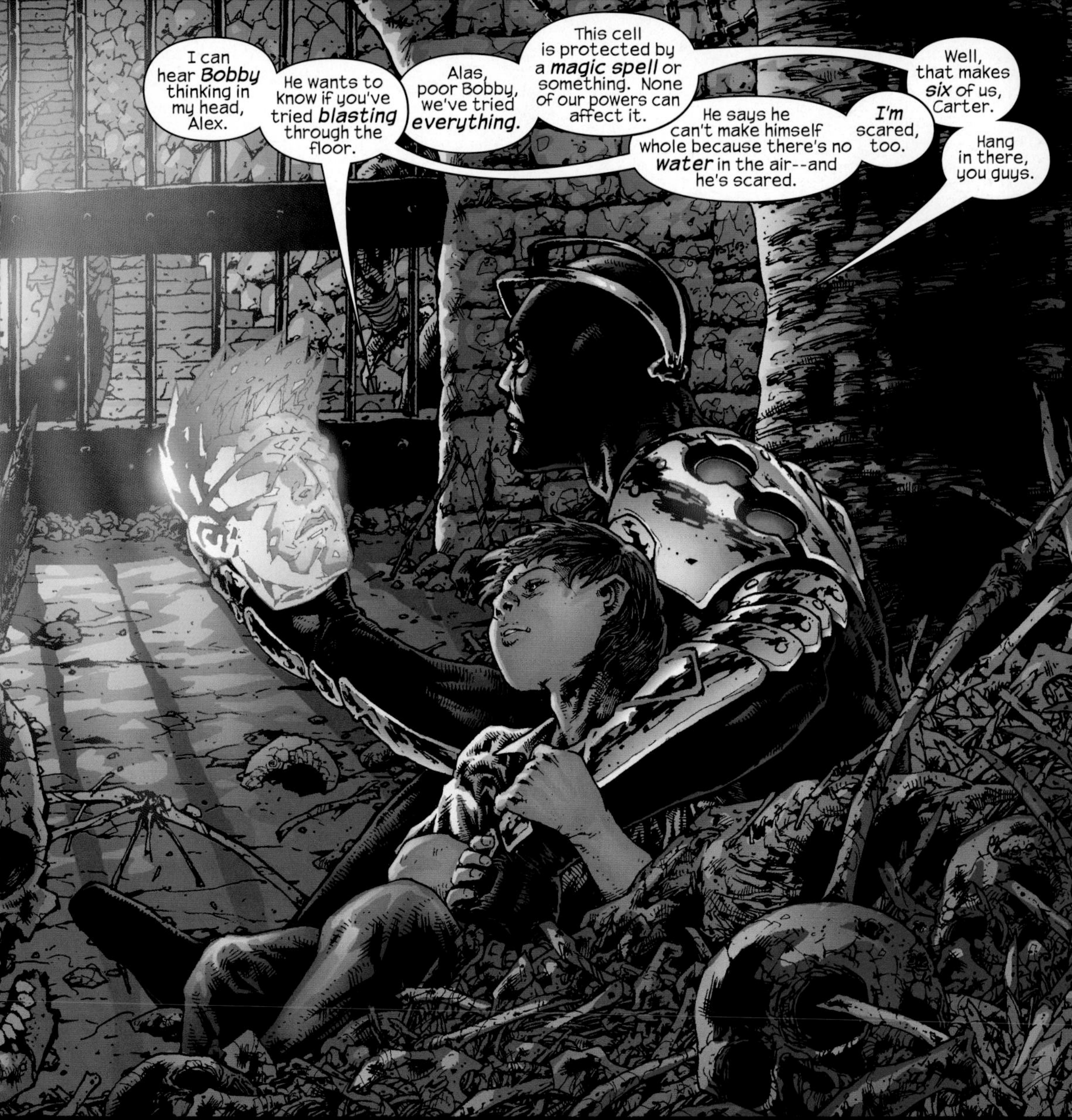
I can hear *Bobby* thinking in my head, Alex.
He wants to know if you've tried *blasting* through the floor.
Alas, poor Bobby, we've tried *everything.*
This cell is protected by a *magic spell* or something. None of our powers can affect it.
He says he can't make himself whole because there's no *water* in the air--and he's scared.
I'm scared, too.
Well, that makes *six* of us, Carter.
Hang in there, you guys.

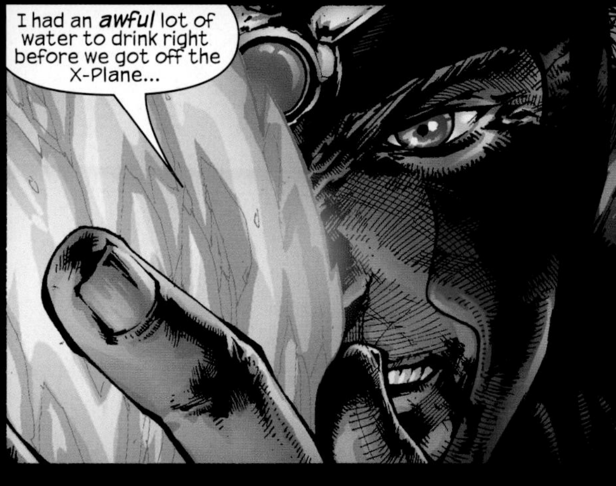
I had an *awful* lot of water to drink right before we got off the X-Plane...

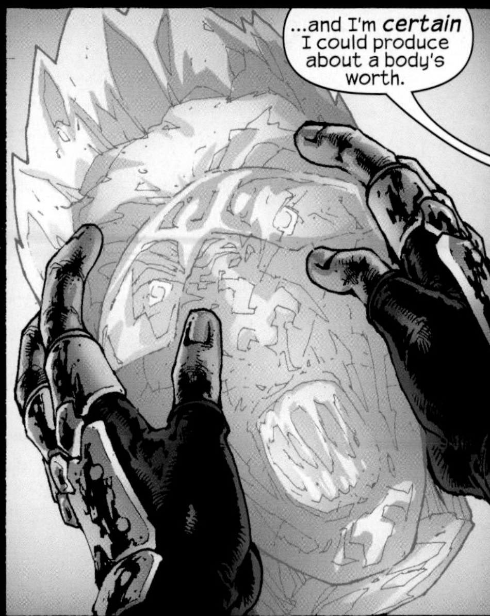
...and I'm *certain* I could produce about a body's worth.

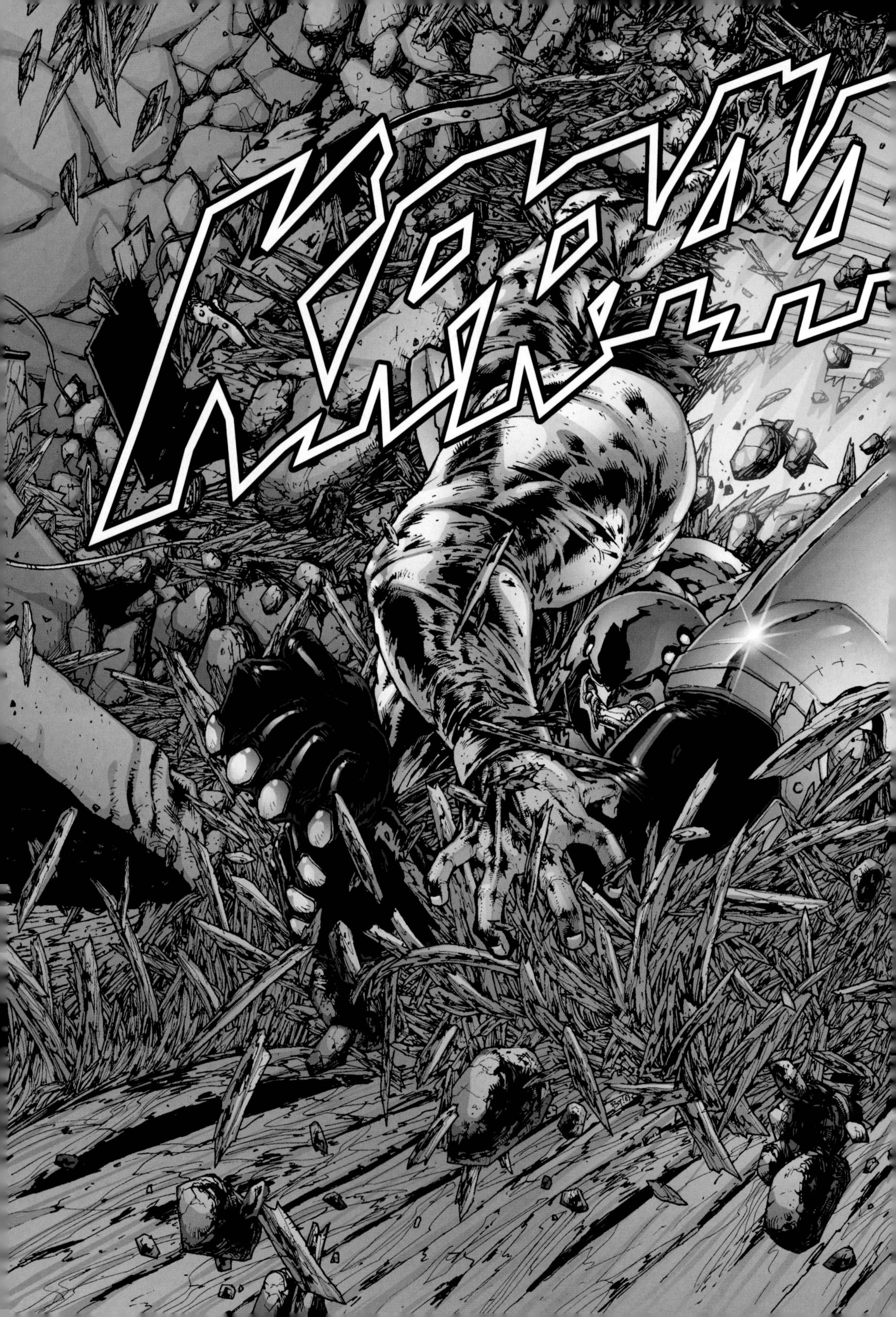

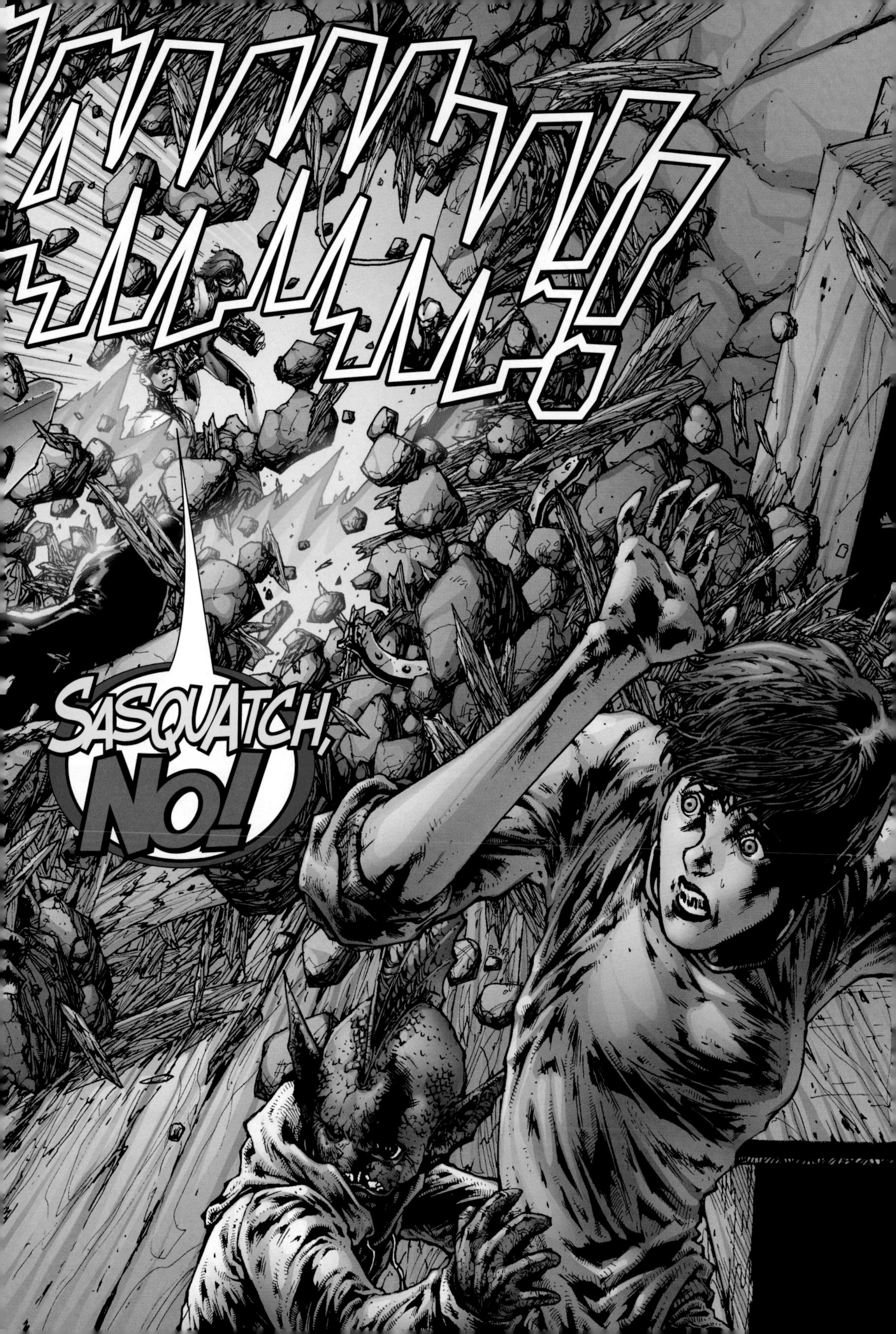
SASQUATCH, NO!

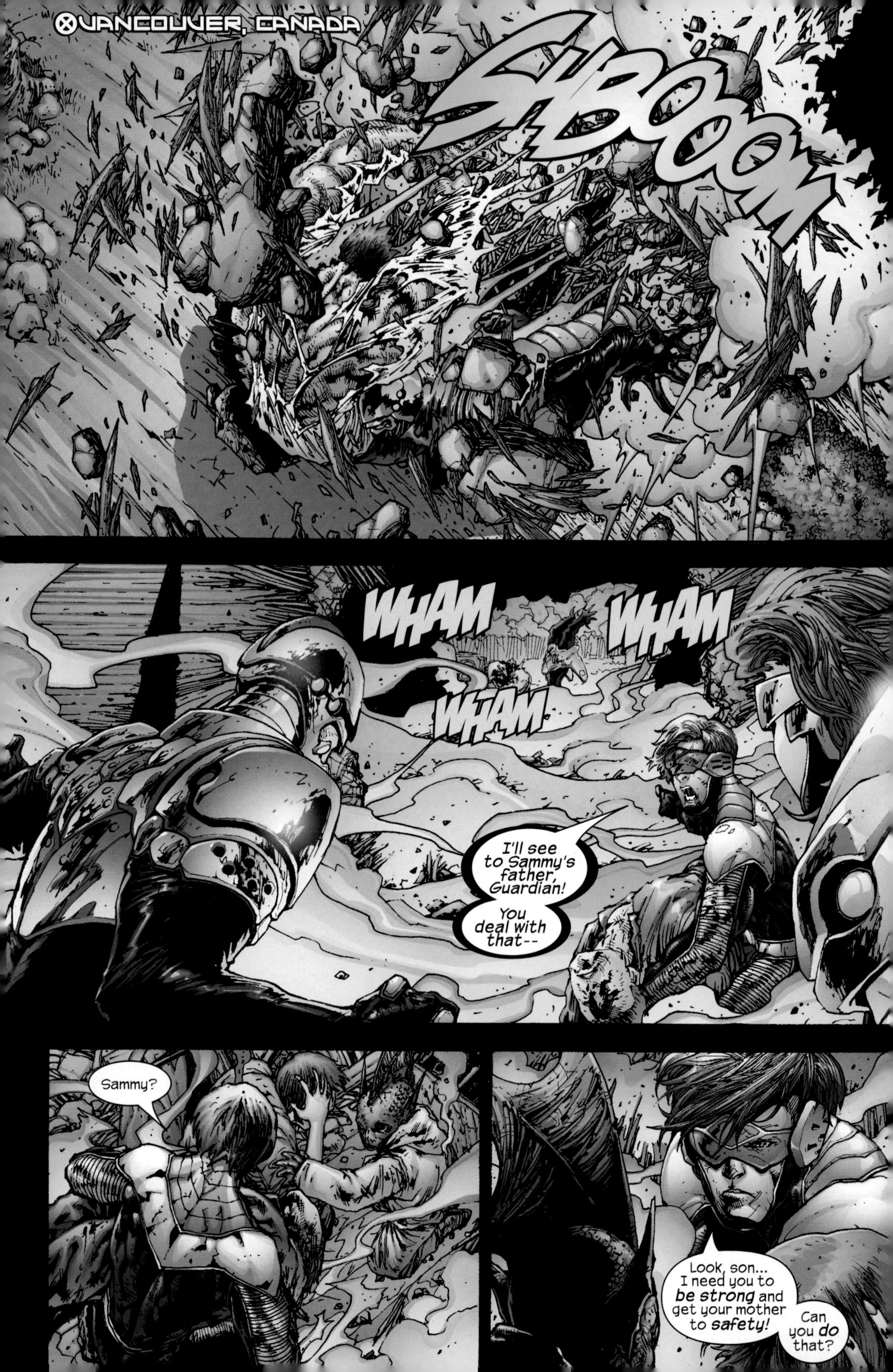
VANCOUVER, CANADA
SHBOOM
WHAM
WHAM
WHAM
I'll see to Sammy's father, Guardian!
You deal with that--
Sammy?
Look, son... I need you to be strong and get your mother to safety!
Can you do that?

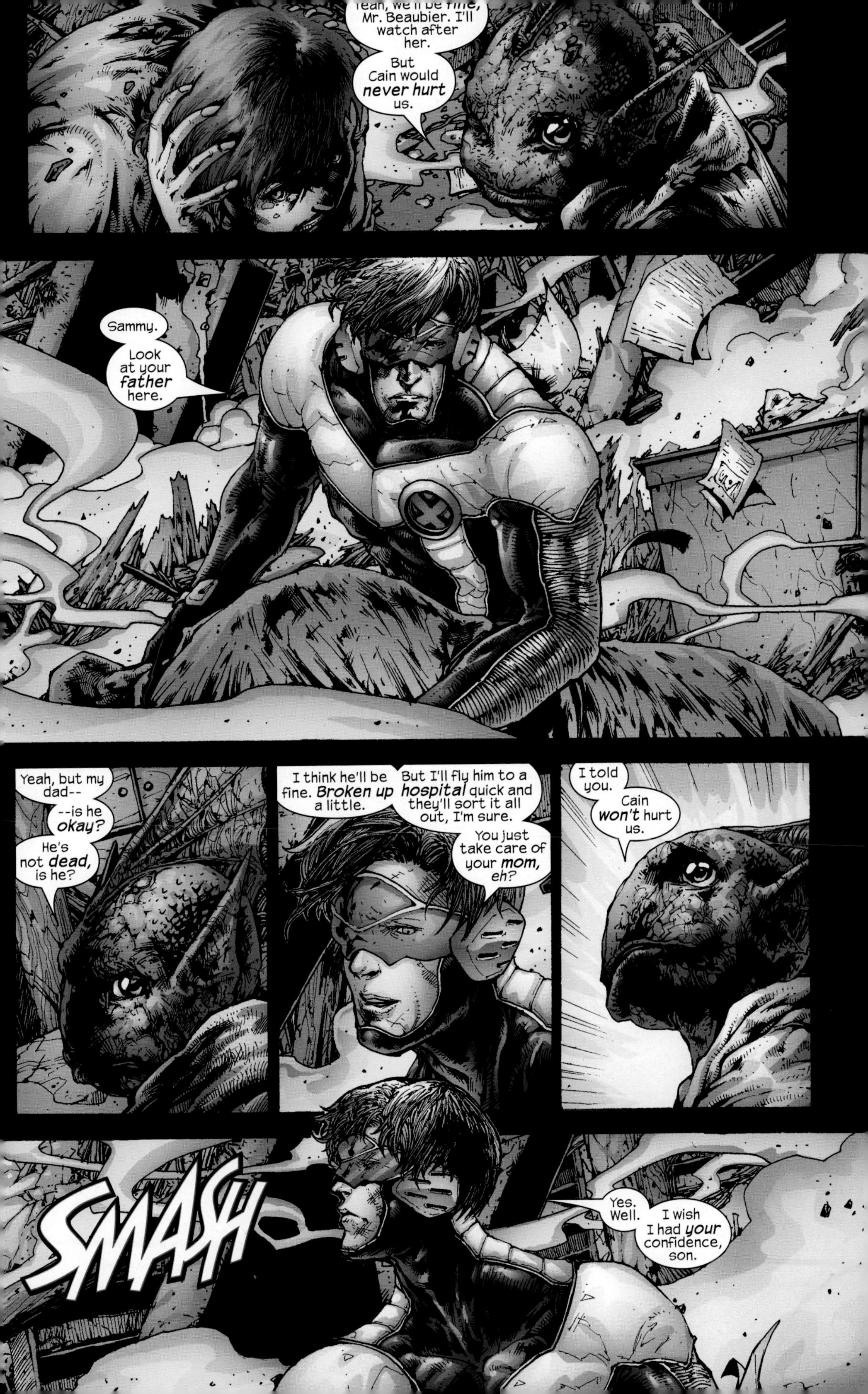

Yeah, we'll be fine, Mr. Beaubier. I'll watch after her.
But Cain would never hurt us.
Sammy.
Look at your father here.
Yeah, but my dad--
--is he okay?
He's not dead, is he?
I think he'll be fine. Broken up a little.
But I'll fly him to a hospital quick and they'll sort it all out, I'm sure.
You just take care of your mom, eh?
I told you.
Cain won't hurt us.
SMASH
Yes. Well.
I wish I had your confidence, son.

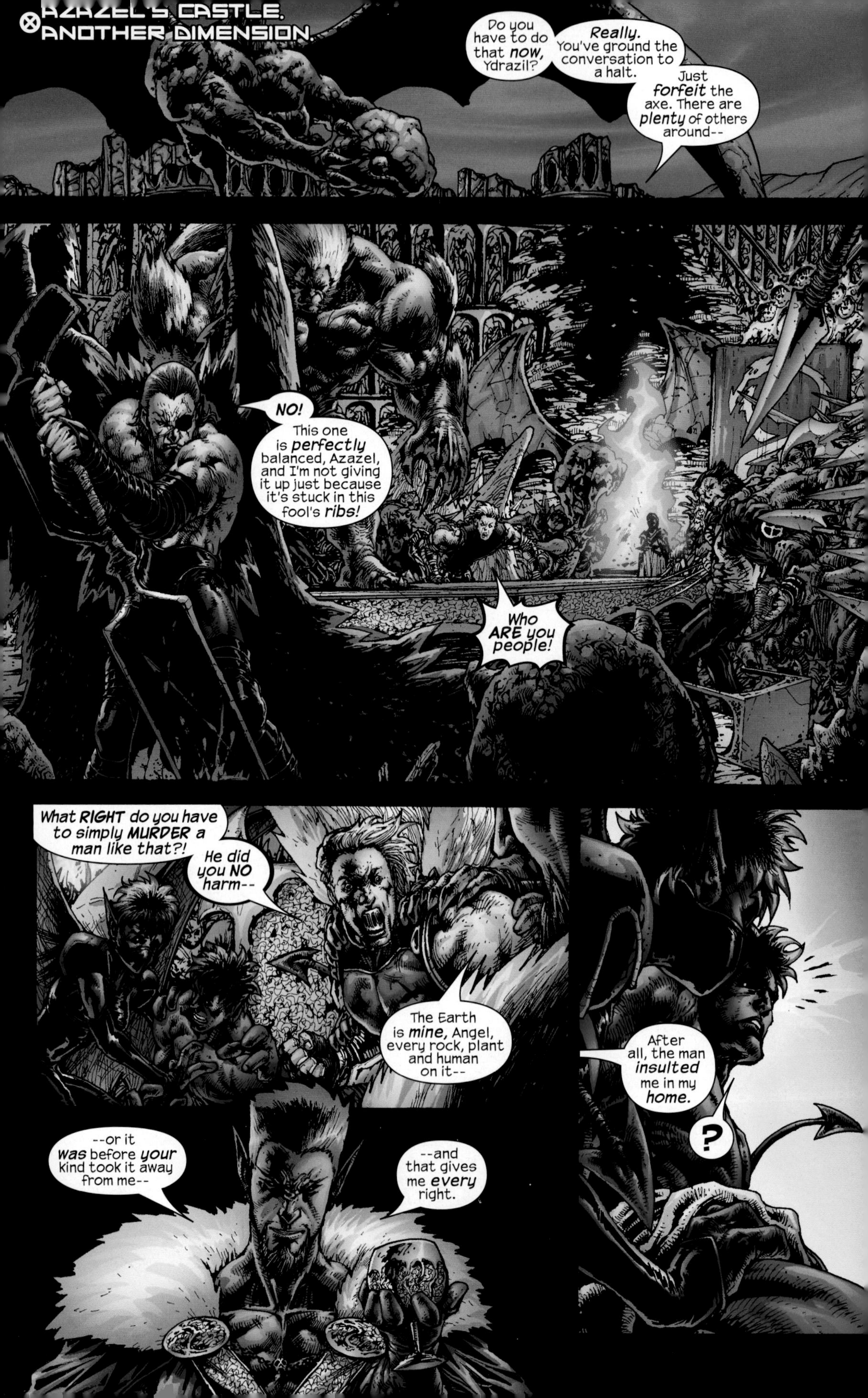
AZAZEL'S CASTLE. ANOTHER DIMENSION.
Do you have to do that now, Ydrazil?
Really. You've ground the conversation to a halt.
Just forfeit the axe. There are plenty of others around--
NO! This one is perfectly balanced, Azazel, and I'm not giving it up just because it's stuck in this fool's ribs!
Who ARE you people!
What RIGHT do you have to simply MURDER a man like that?!
He did you NO harm--
The Earth is mine, Angel, every rock, plant and human on it--
After all, the man insulted me in my home.
?
--or it was before your kind took it away from me--
--and that gives me every right.

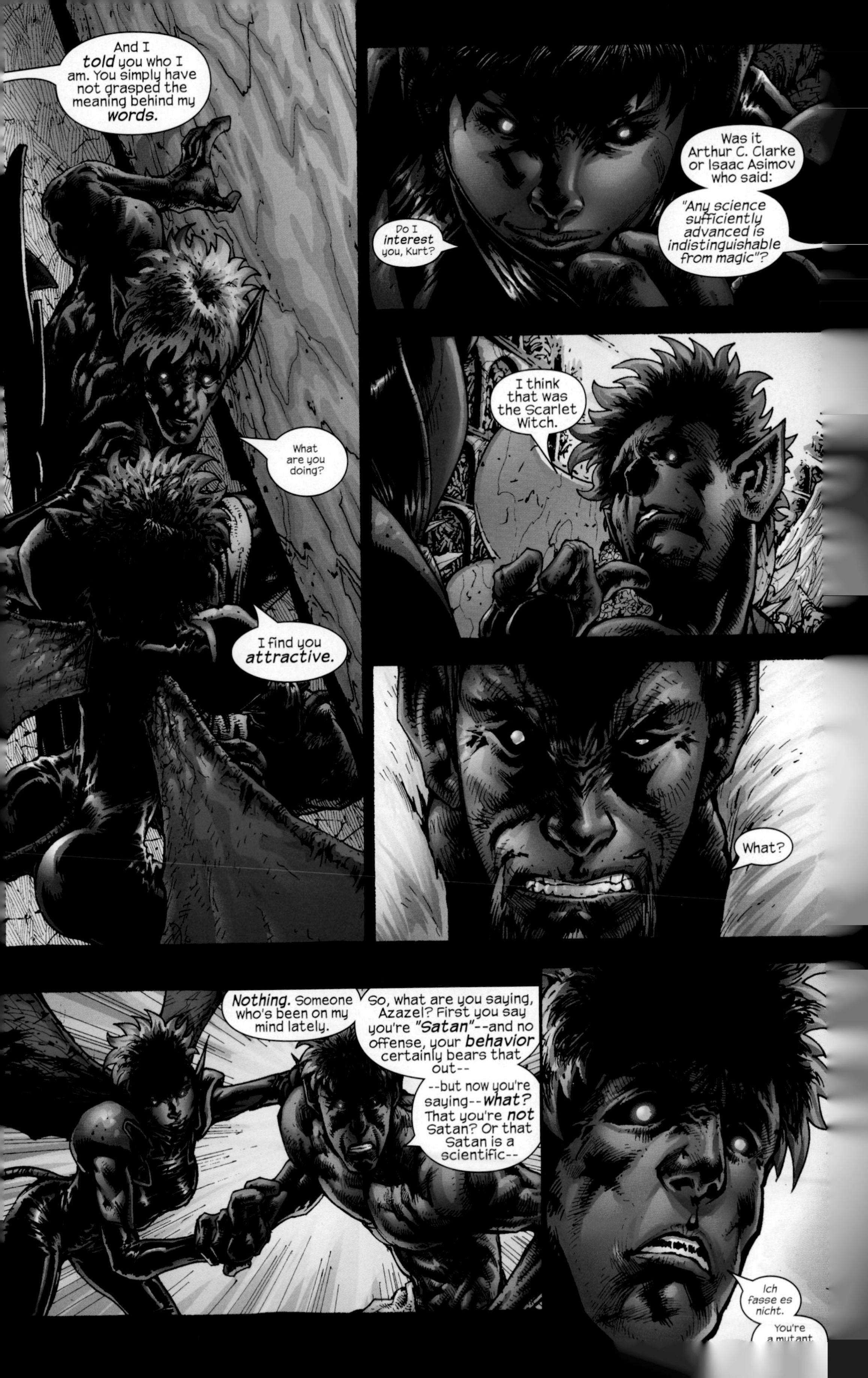

And I told you who I am. You simply have not grasped the meaning behind my words.
Do I interest you, Kurt?
Was it Arthur C. Clarke or Isaac Asimov who said:
"Any science sufficiently advanced is indistinguishable from magic"?
What are you doing?
I think that was the Scarlet Witch.
I find you attractive.
What?
Nothing. Someone who's been on my mind lately.
So, what are you saying, Azazel? First you say you're "Satan"--and no offense, your behavior certainly bears that out--
--but now you're saying--what? That you're not Satan? Or that Satan is a scientific--
Ich fasse es nicht.
You're

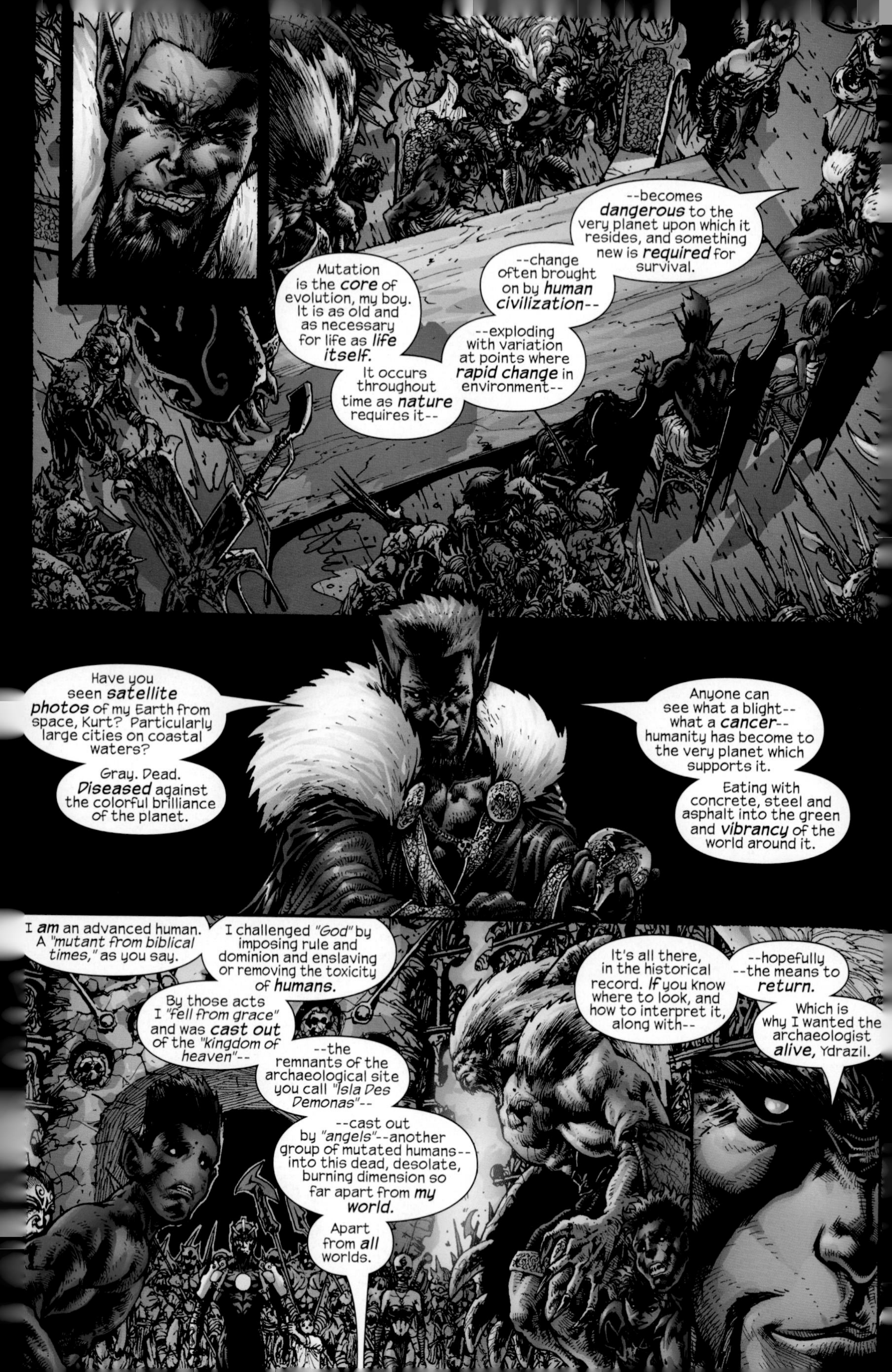

Mutation is the *core* of evolution, my boy. It is as old and as necessary for life as *life itself*.
It occurs throughout time as *nature* requires it--
--exploding with variation at points where *rapid change* in environment--
--change often brought on by *human civilization*--
--becomes *dangerous* to the very planet upon which it resides, and something new is *required* for survival.
Have you seen *satellite photos* of my Earth from space, Kurt? Particularly large cities on coastal waters?
Gray. Dead. *Diseased* against the colorful brilliance of the planet.
Anyone can see what a blight--what a *cancer*--humanity has become to the very planet which supports it.
Eating with concrete, steel and asphalt into the green and *vibrancy* of the world around it.
I *am* an advanced human. A *"mutant from biblical times,"* as you say.
I challenged *"God"* by imposing rule and dominion and enslaving or removing the toxicity of **humans.**
By those acts I *"fell from grace"* and was **cast out** of the *"kingdom of heaven"*--
--the remnants of the archaeological site you call *"Isla Des Demonas"*--
--cast out by *"angels"*--another group of mutated humans--into this dead, desolate, burning dimension so far apart from *my* **world.**
Apart from *all* worlds.
It's all there, in the historical record. *If* you know where to look, and how to interpret it, along with--
--hopefully--the means to *return.*
Which is why I wanted the archaeologist *alive,* Ydrazil.

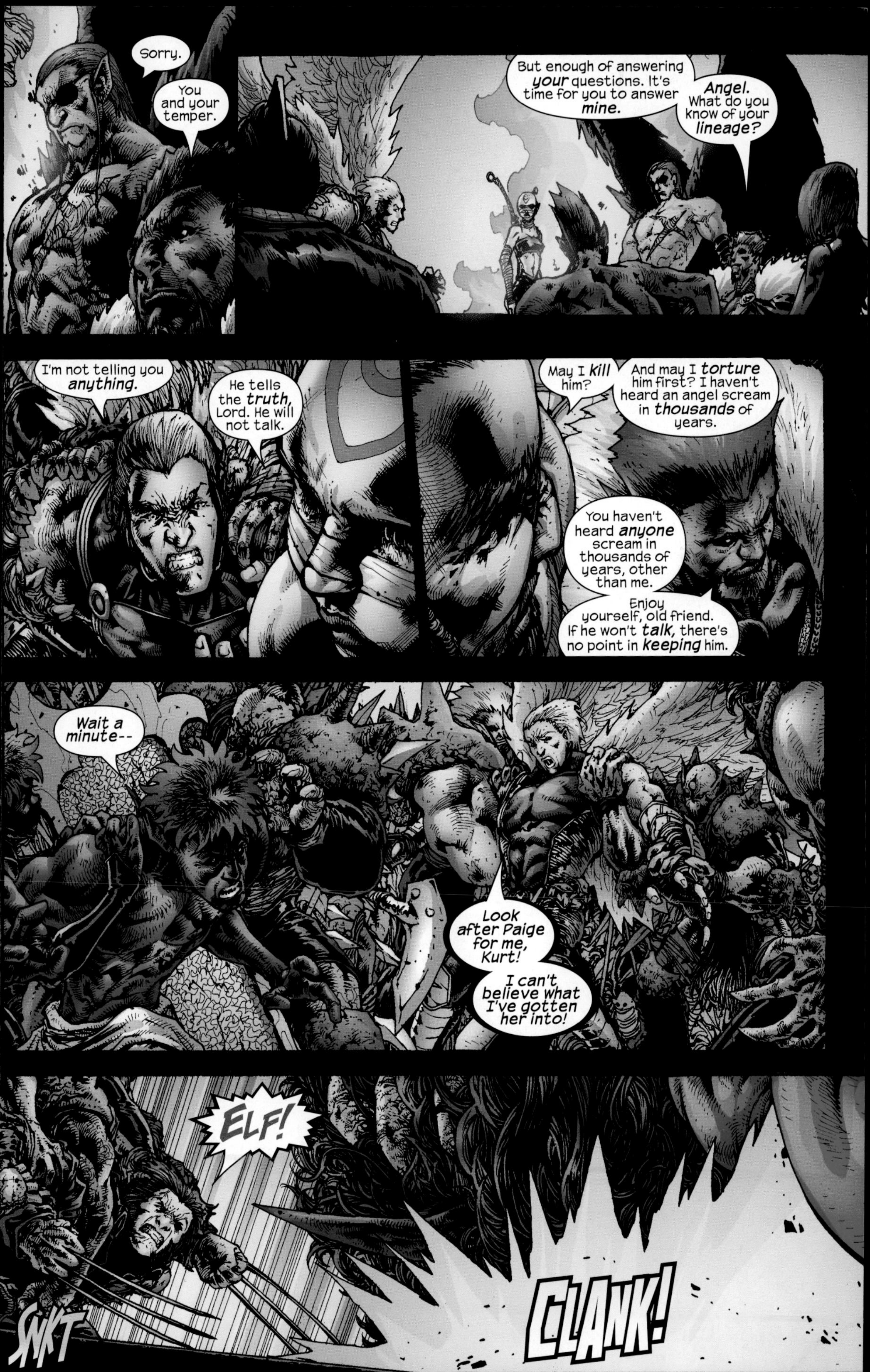
Sorry.
You and your temper.
But enough of answering *your* questions. It's time for you to answer *mine.*
Angel. What do you know of your *lineage?*
I'm not telling you *anything.*
He tells the *truth,* Lord. He will not talk.
May I *kill* him?
And may I *torture* him first? I haven't heard an angel scream in *thousands* of years.
You haven't heard *anyone* scream in thousands of years, other than me.
Enjoy yourself, old friend. If he won't *talk,* there's no point in *keeping* him.
Wait a minute--
Look after Paige for me, Kurt!
I can't believe what I've gotten her into!
ELF!
SNKT
CLANK!

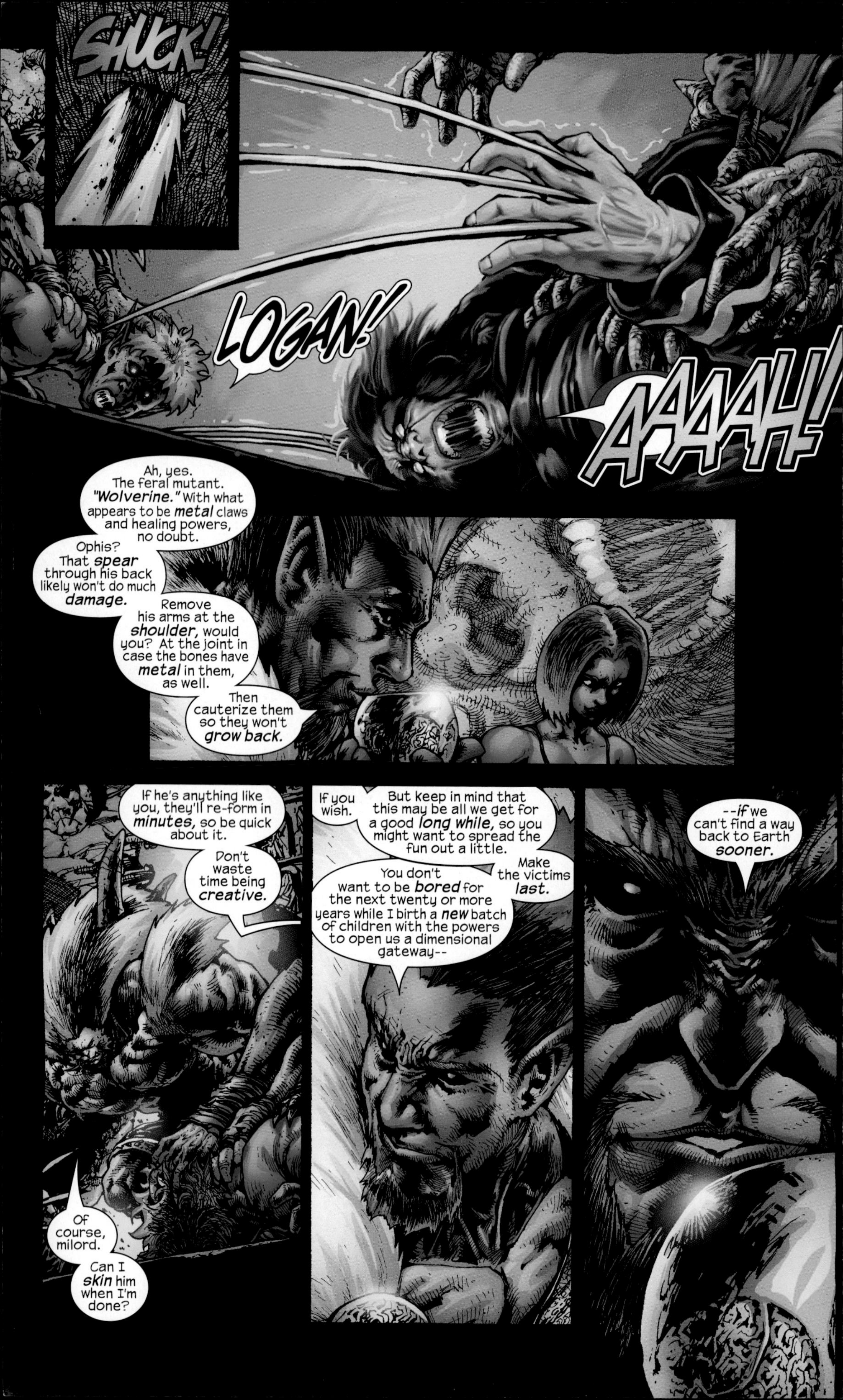
SHUCK!
LOGAN!
AAAAH!
Ah, yes. The feral mutant. "Wolverine." With what appears to be metal claws and healing powers, no doubt.
Ophis? That spear through his back likely won't do much damage.
Remove his arms at the shoulder, would you? At the joint in case the bones have metal in them, as well.
Then cauterize them so they won't grow back.
If he's anything like you, they'll re-form in minutes, so be quick about it.
Don't waste time being creative.
Of course, milord.
Can I skin him when I'm done?
If you wish.
But keep in mind that this may be all we get for a good long while, so you might want to spread the fun out a little.
Make the victims last.
You don't want to be bored for the next twenty or more years while I birth a new batch of children with the powers to open us a dimensional gateway--
--if we can't find a way back to Earth sooner.

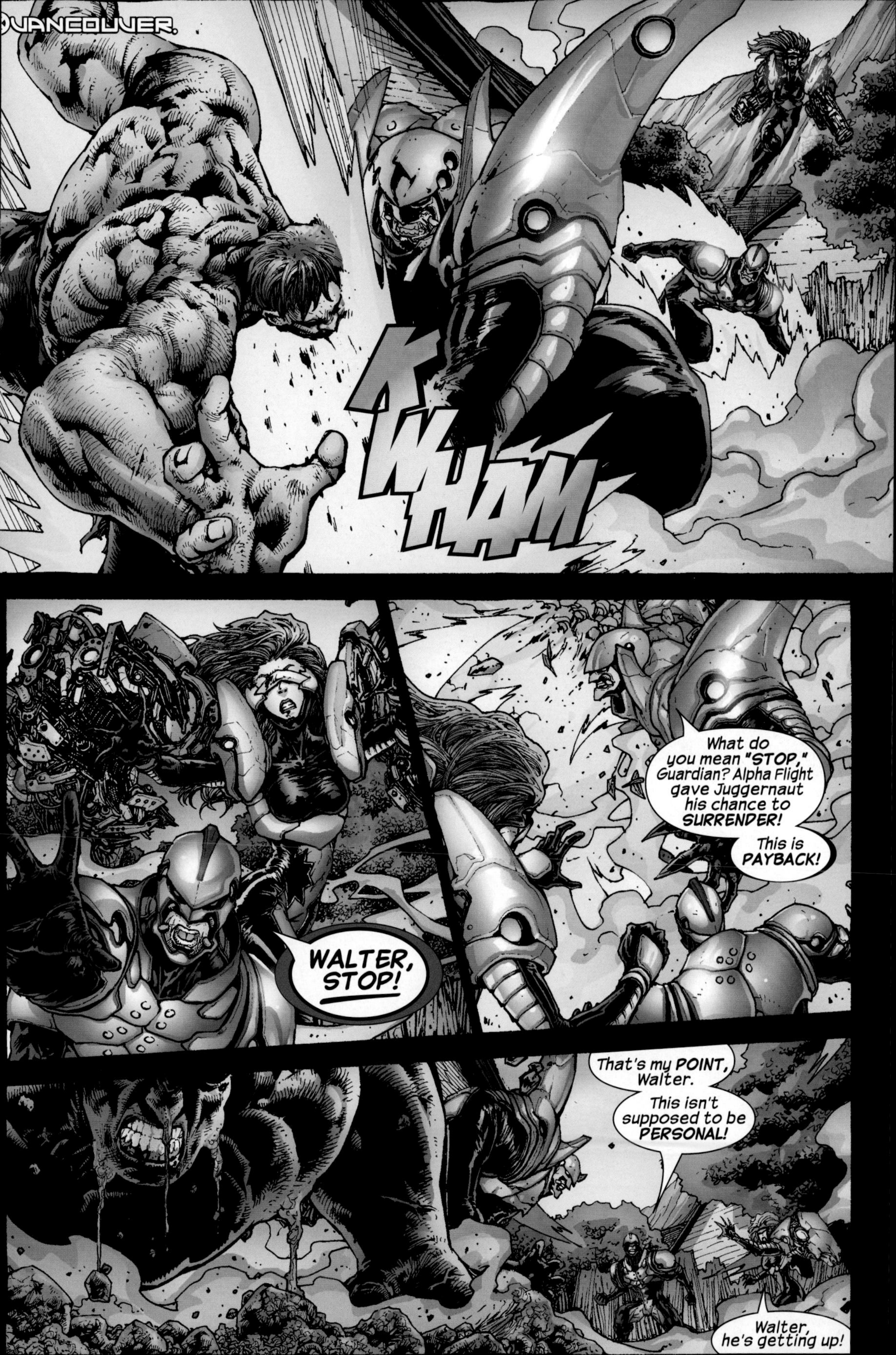
VANCOUVER.
KWHAM
WALTER, STOP!
What do you mean "STOP," Guardian? Alpha Flight gave Juggernaut his chance to SURRENDER!
This is PAYBACK!
That's my POINT, Walter.
This isn't supposed to be PERSONAL!
Walter, he's getting up!

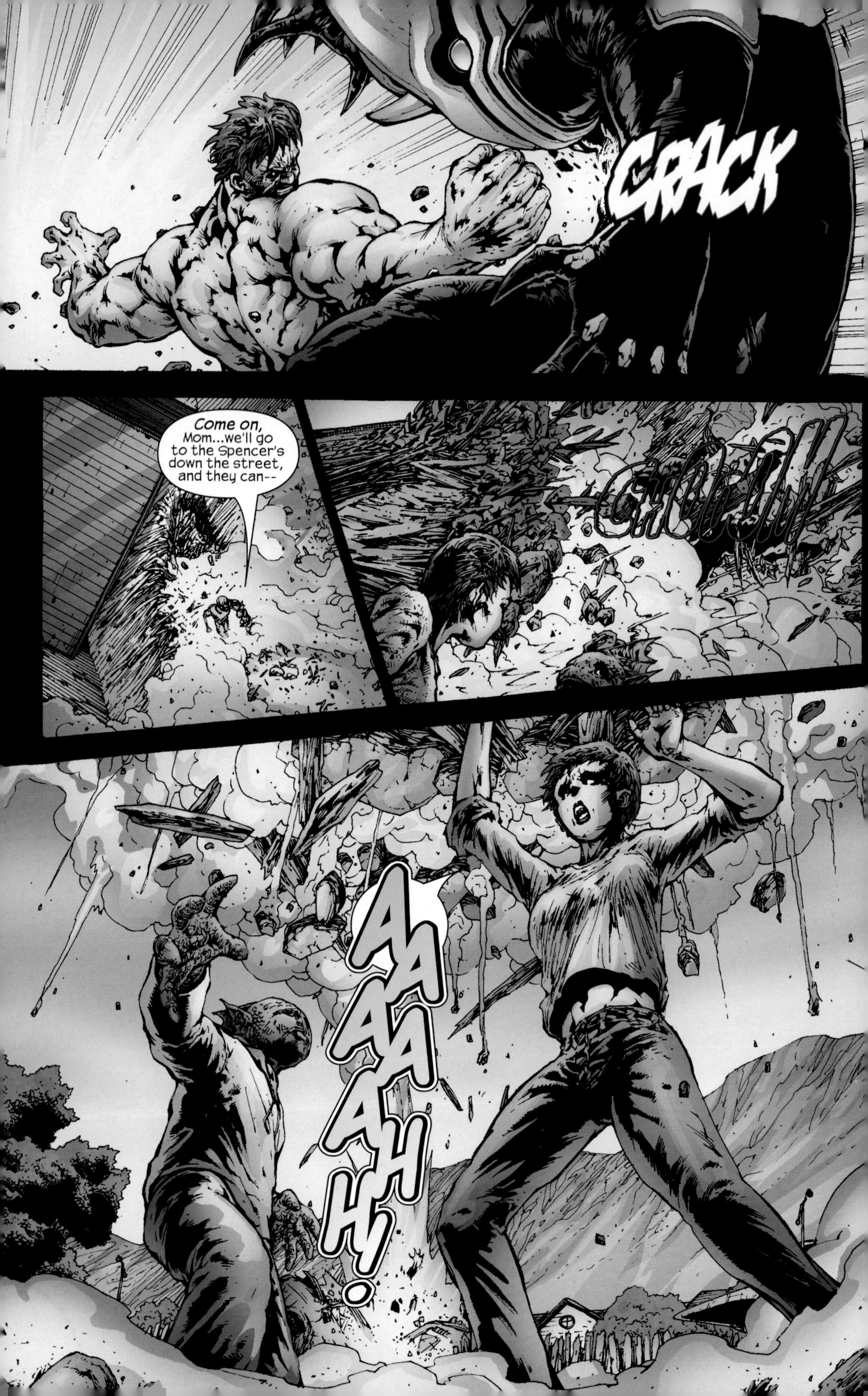
CRACK
Come on, Mom...we'll go to the Spencer's down the street, and they can--
AAAAAHH!

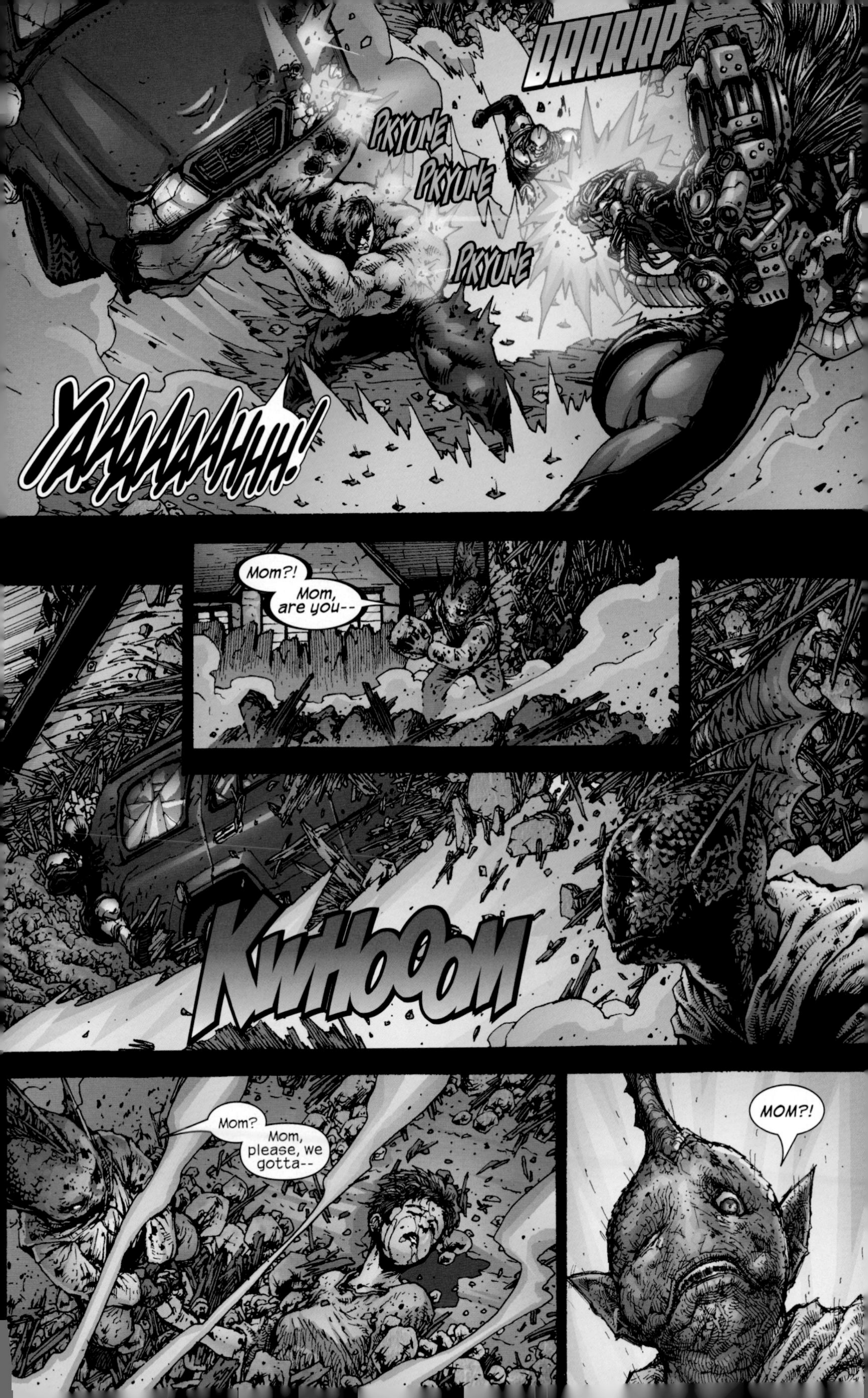
BRRRRP
PKYUNE
PKYUNE
PKYUNE
YAAAAAAHHH!
Mom?!
Mom, are you--
KWHOOOM
Mom?
Mom, please, we gotta--
MOM?!

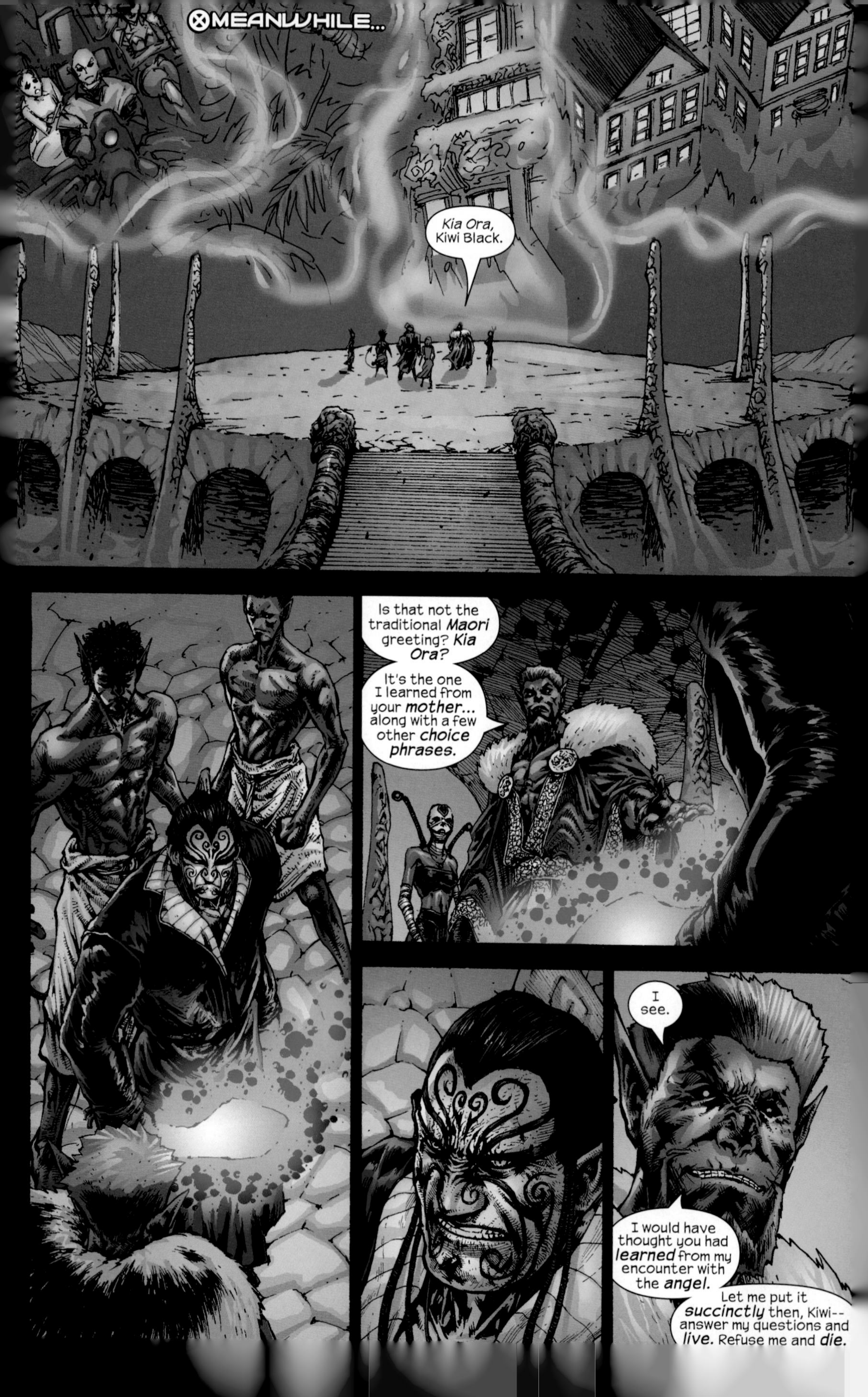
MEANWHILE...
Kia Ora, Kiwi Black.
Is that not the traditional *Maori* greeting? *Kia Ora?*
It's the one I learned from your *mother*... along with a few other *choice phrases.*
I see.
I would have thought you had *learned* from my encounter with the *angel.*
Let me put it *succinctly* then, Kiwi-- answer my questions and *live.* Refuse me and *die.*

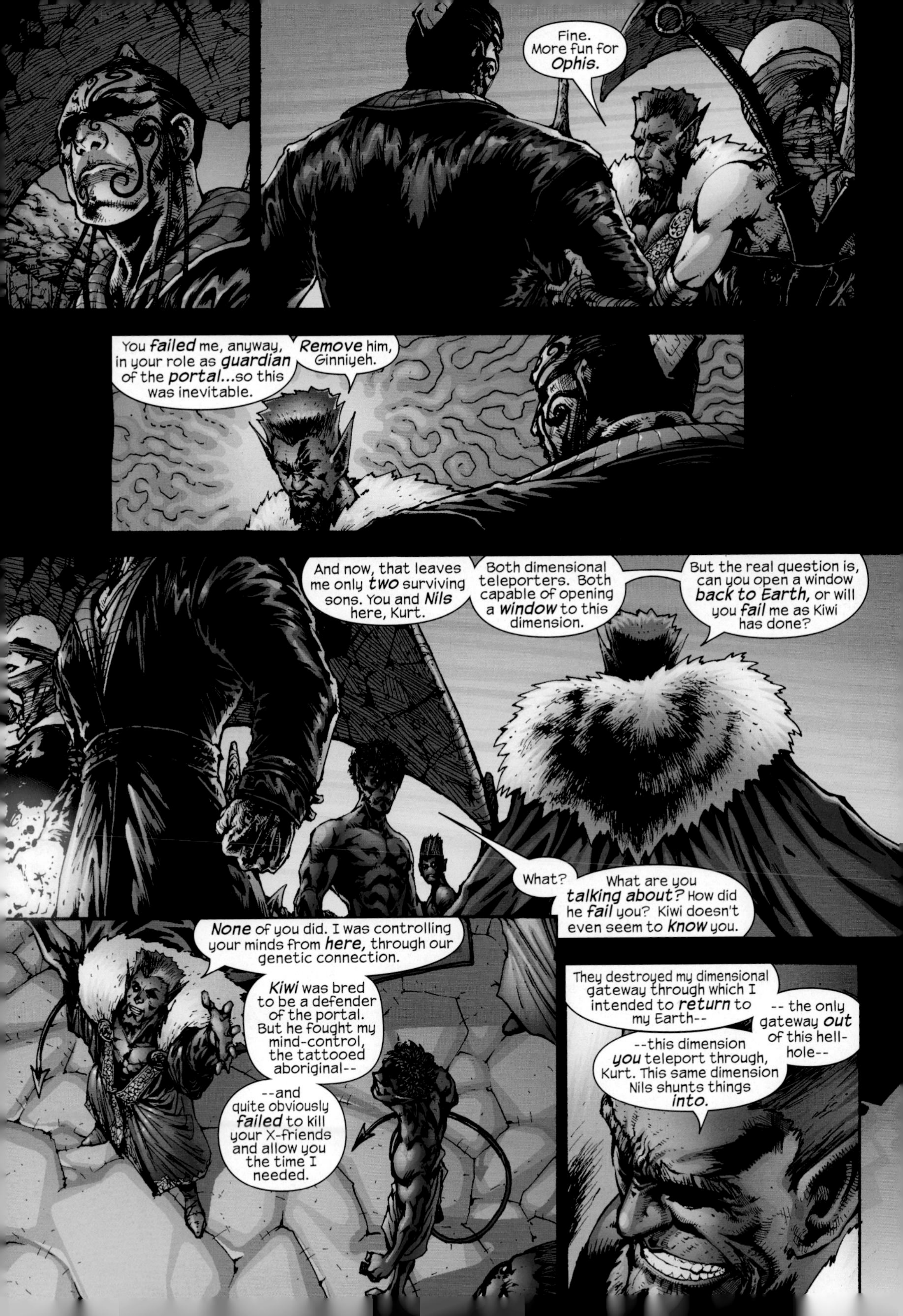
Fine. More fun for Ophis.
You failed me, anyway, in your role as guardian of the portal...so this was inevitable.
Remove him, Ginniyeh.
And now, that leaves me only two surviving sons. You and Nils here, Kurt.
Both dimensional teleporters. Both capable of opening a window to this dimension.
But the real question is, can you open a window back to Earth, or will you fail me as Kiwi has done?
What?
What are you talking about? How did he fail you? Kiwi doesn't even seem to know you.
None of you did. I was controlling your minds from here, through our genetic connection.
Kiwi was bred to be a defender of the portal. But he fought my mind-control, the tattooed aboriginal--
--and quite obviously failed to kill your X-friends and allow you the time I needed.
They destroyed my dimensional gateway through which I intended to return to my Earth--
-- the only gateway out of this hell-hole--
--this dimension you teleport through, Kurt. This same dimension Nils shunts things into.

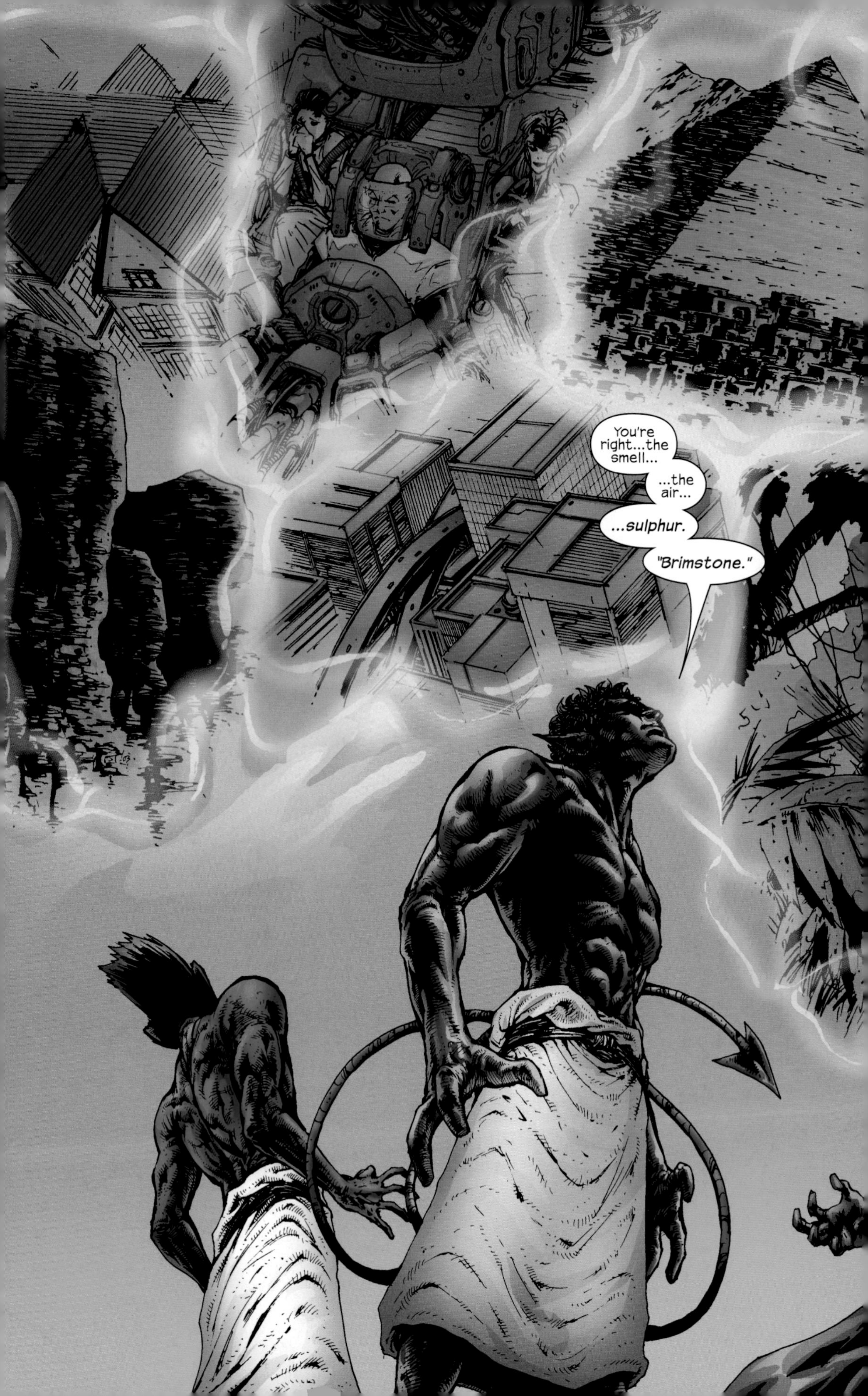

You're right...the smell...
...the air...
...sulphur.
"Brimstone."

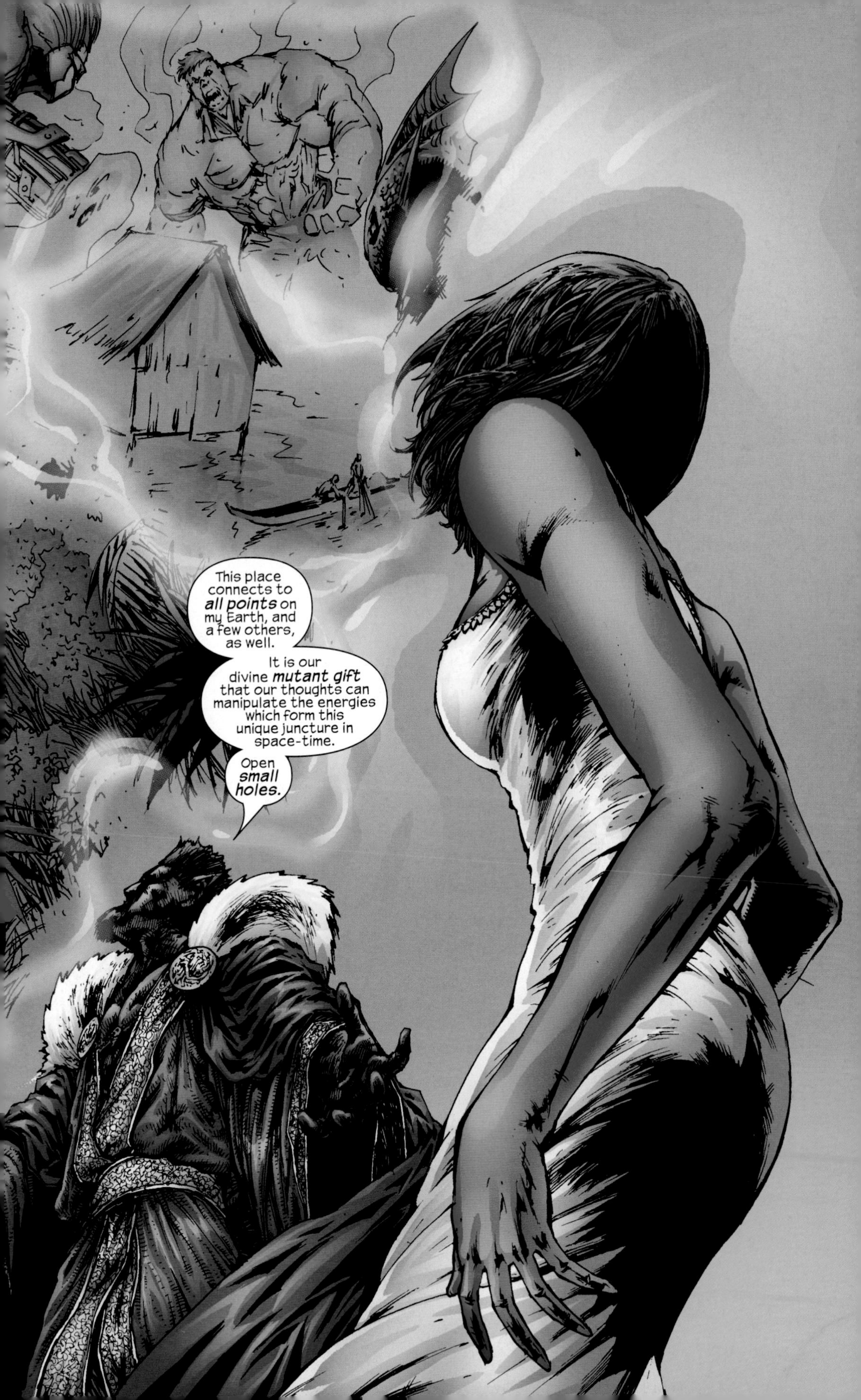
This place connects to *all points* on my Earth, and a few others, as well.
It is our divine *mutant gift* that our thoughts can manipulate the energies which form this unique juncture in space-time.
Open *small holes.*

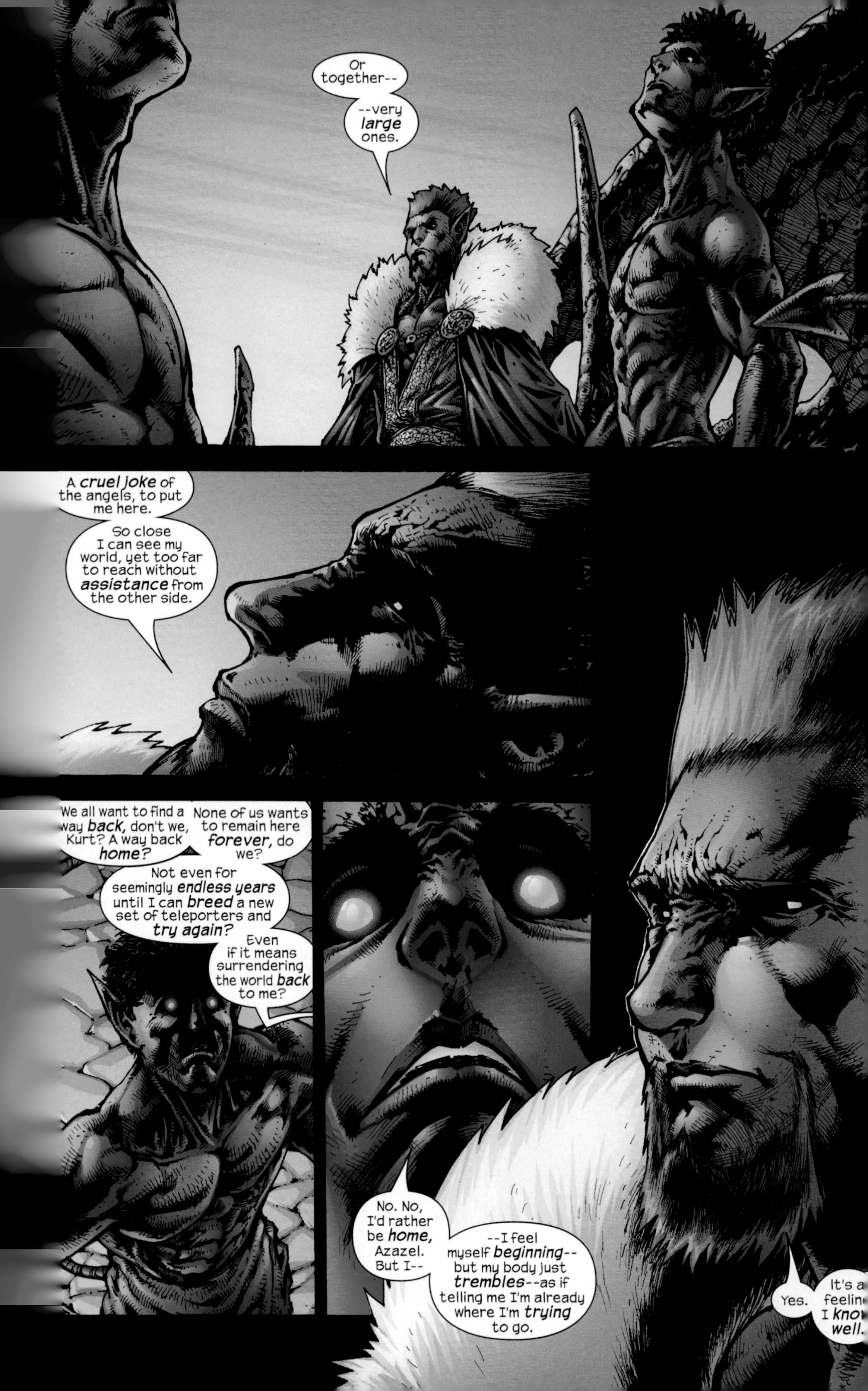
Or together--
--very large ones.
A cruel joke of the angels, to put me here.
So close I can see my world, yet too far to reach without assistance from the other side.
We all want to find a way back, don't we, Kurt? A way back home?
None of us wants to remain here forever, do we?
Not even for seemingly endless years until I can breed a new set of teleporters and try again?
Even if it means surrendering the world back to me?
No. No, I'd rather be home, Azazel. But I--
--I feel myself beginning--but my body just trembles--as if telling me I'm already where I'm trying to go.
Yes.

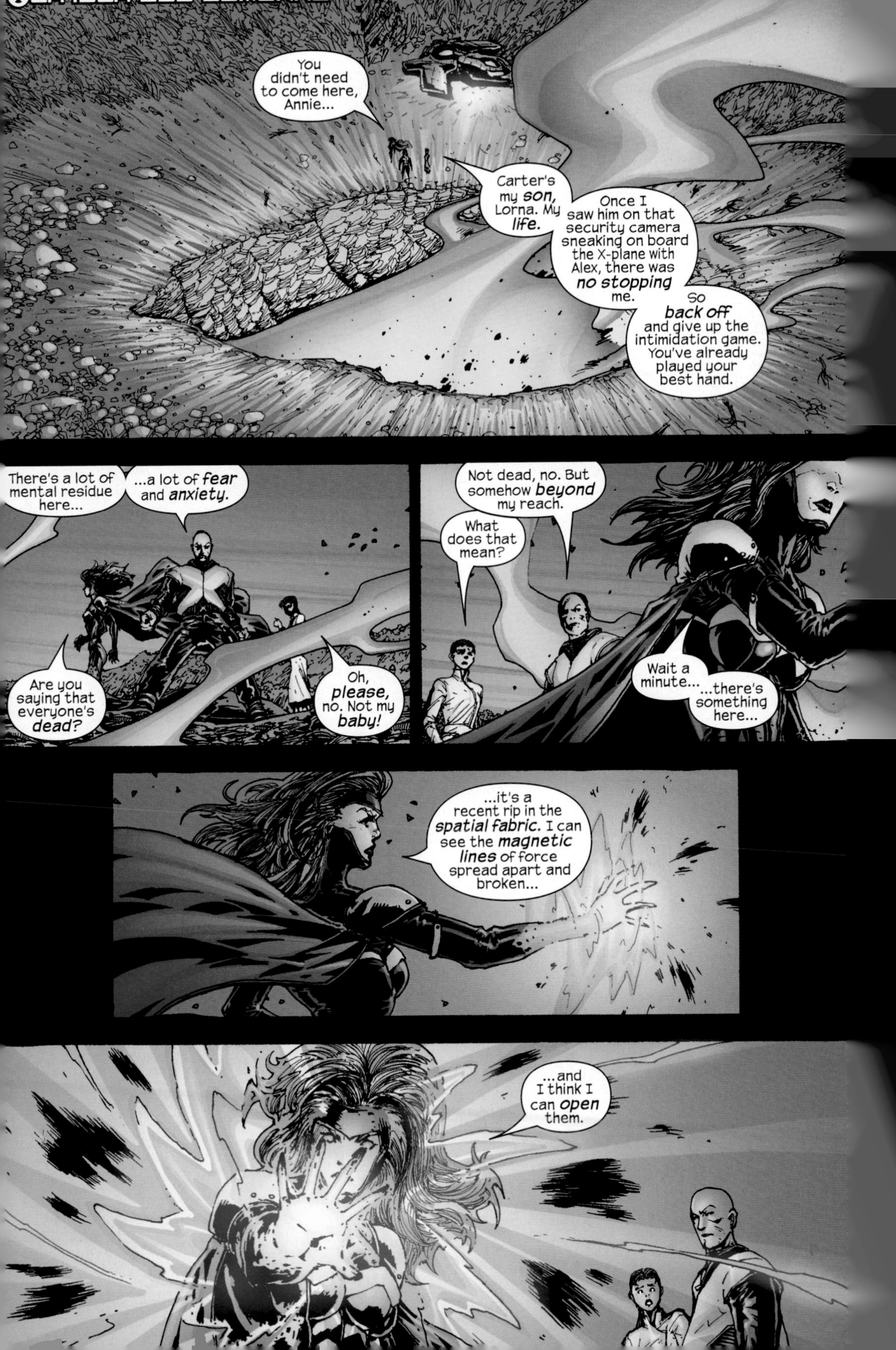
You didn't need to come here, Annie...
Carter's my son, Lorna. My life.
Once I saw him on that security camera sneaking on board the X-plane with Alex, there was no stopping me.
So back off and give up the intimidation game. You've already played your best hand.
There's a lot of mental residue here...
...a lot of fear and anxiety.
Are you saying that everyone's dead?
Oh, please, no. Not my baby!
Not dead, no. But somehow beyond my reach.
What does that mean?
Wait a minute...
...there's something here...
...it's a recent rip in the spatial fabric. I can see the magnetic lines of force spread apart and broken...
...and I think I can open them.

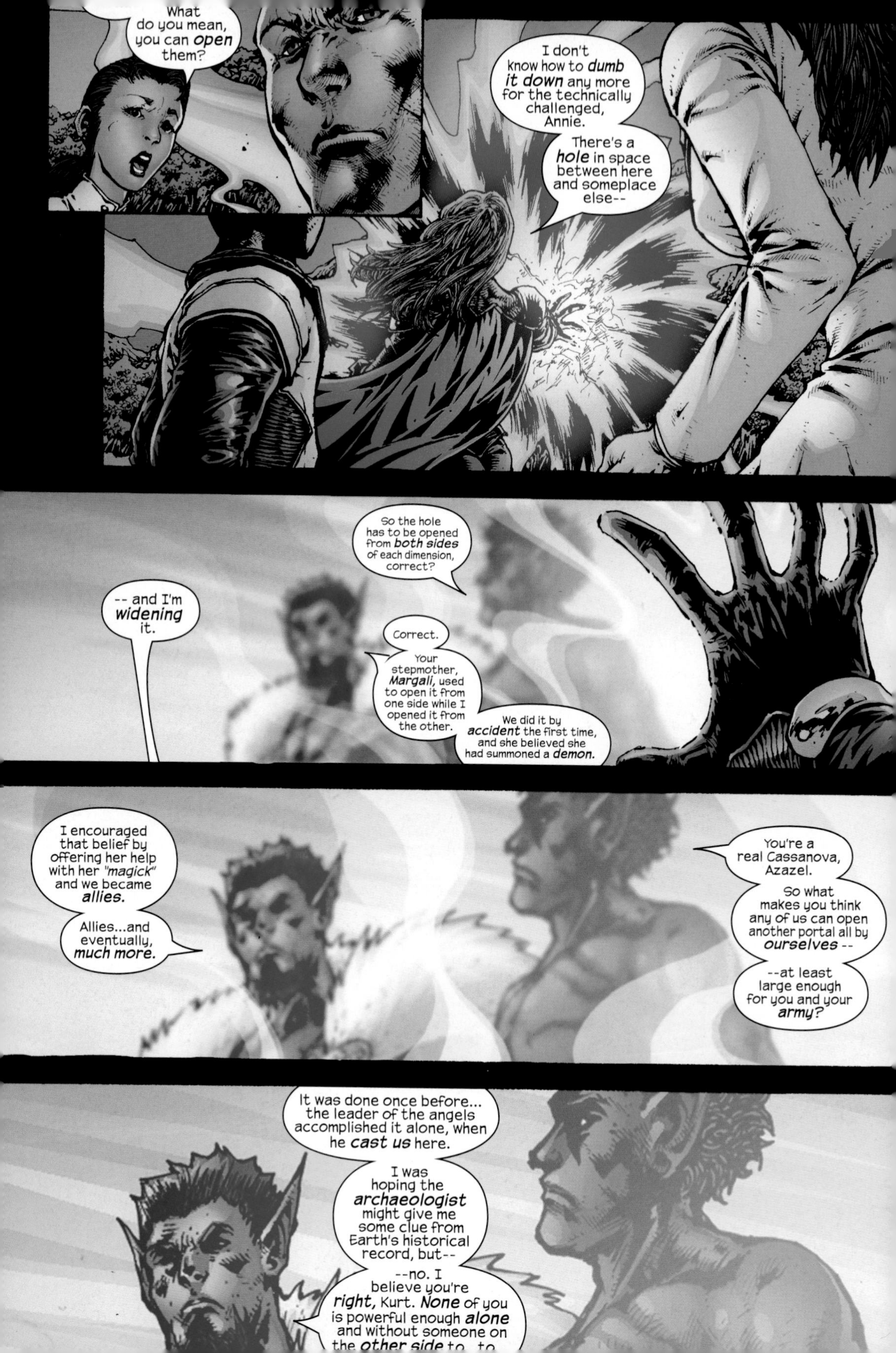
What do you mean, you can *open* them?
I don't know how to *dumb it down* any more for the technically challenged, Annie.
There's a *hole* in space between here and someplace else--
-- and I'm *widening* it.
So the hole has to be opened from *both sides* of each dimension, correct?
Correct.
Your stepmother, *Margali*, used to open it from one side while I opened it from the other.
We did it by *accident* the first time, and she believed she had summoned a *demon.*
I encouraged that belief by offering her help with her "magick" and we became *allies.*
Allies...and eventually, *much more.*
You're a real Cassanova, Azazel.
So what makes you think any of us can open another portal all by *ourselves* --
--at least large enough for you and your *army?*
It was done once before... the leader of the angels accomplished it alone, when he *cast us* here.
I was hoping the *archaeologist* might give me some clue from Earth's historical record, but--
--no. I believe you're *right,* Kurt. *None* of you is powerful enough *alone* and without someone on the *other side* to... to

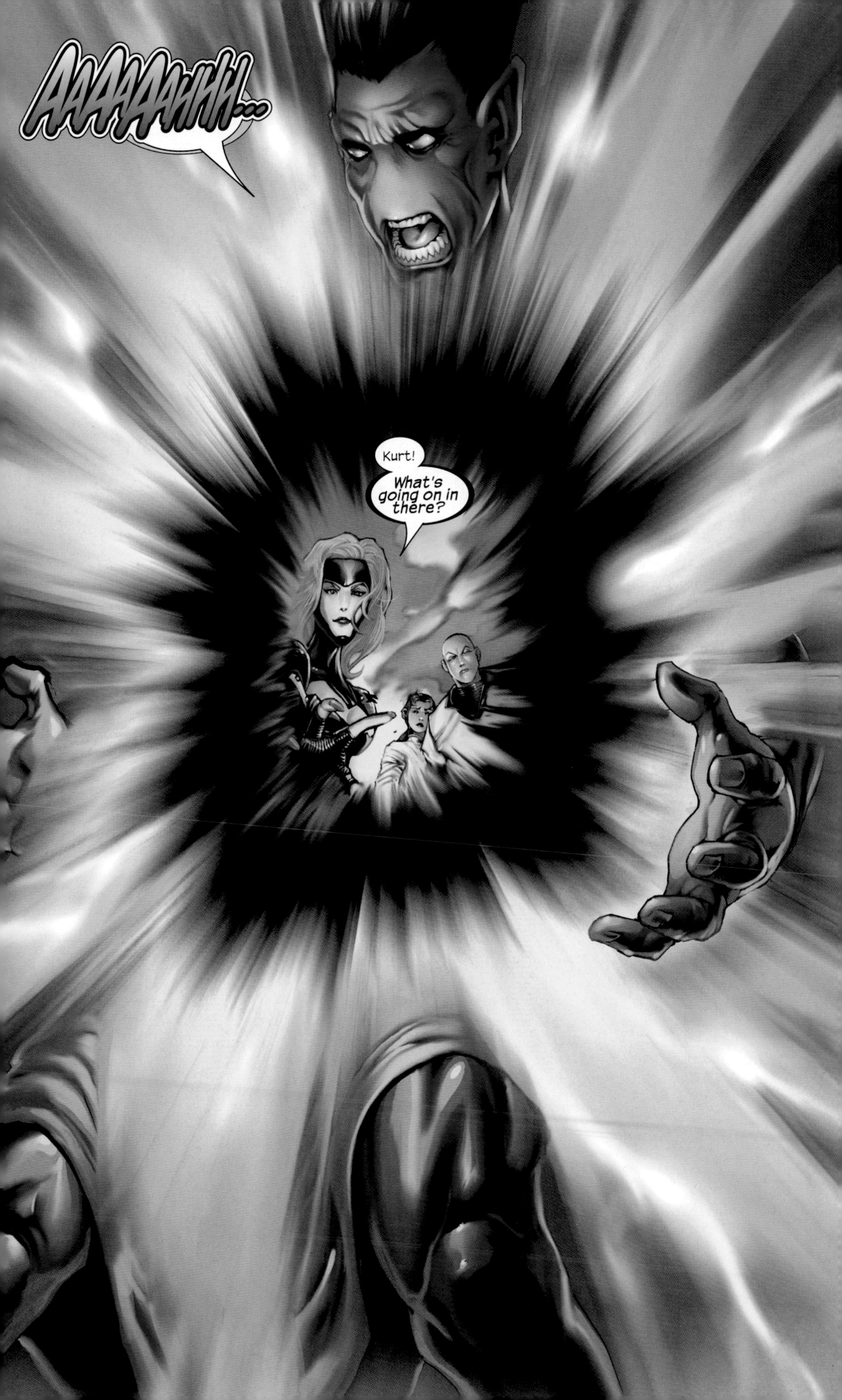
AAAAAAHHH...
Kurt!
What's going on in there?

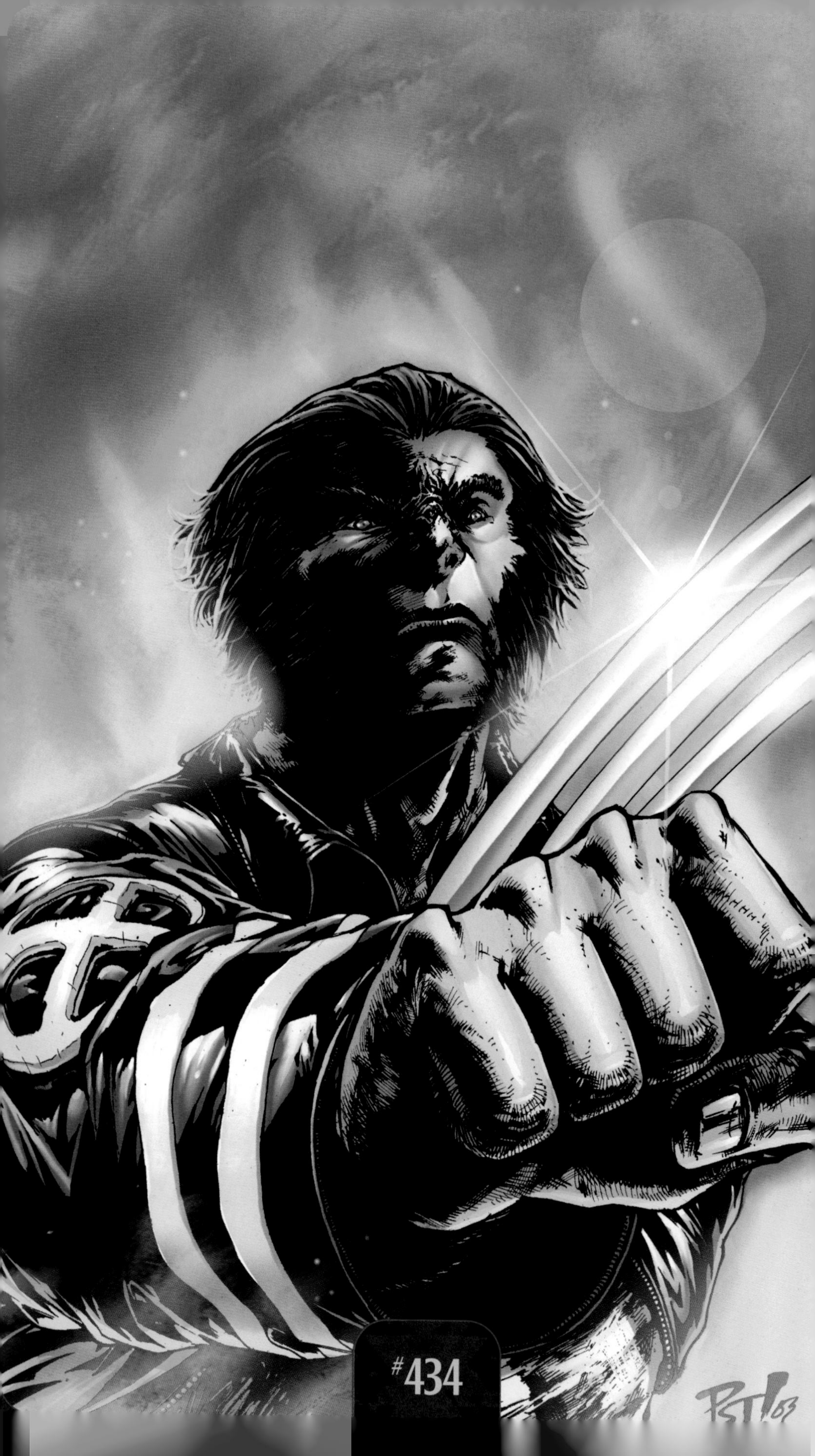
#434

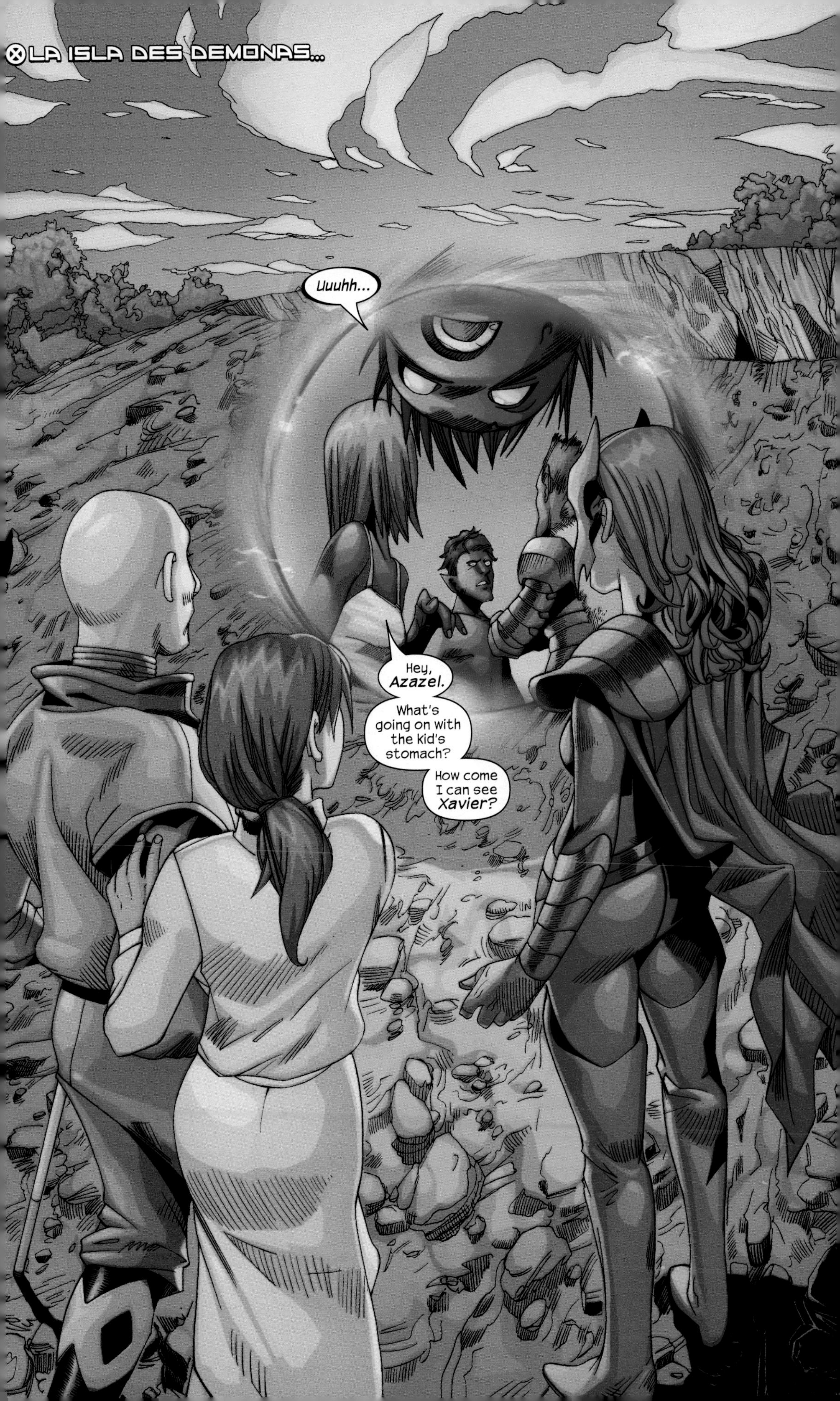
LA ISLA DES DEMONAS...
Uuuhh...
Hey, Azazel.
What's going on with the kid's stomach?
How come I can see Xavier?

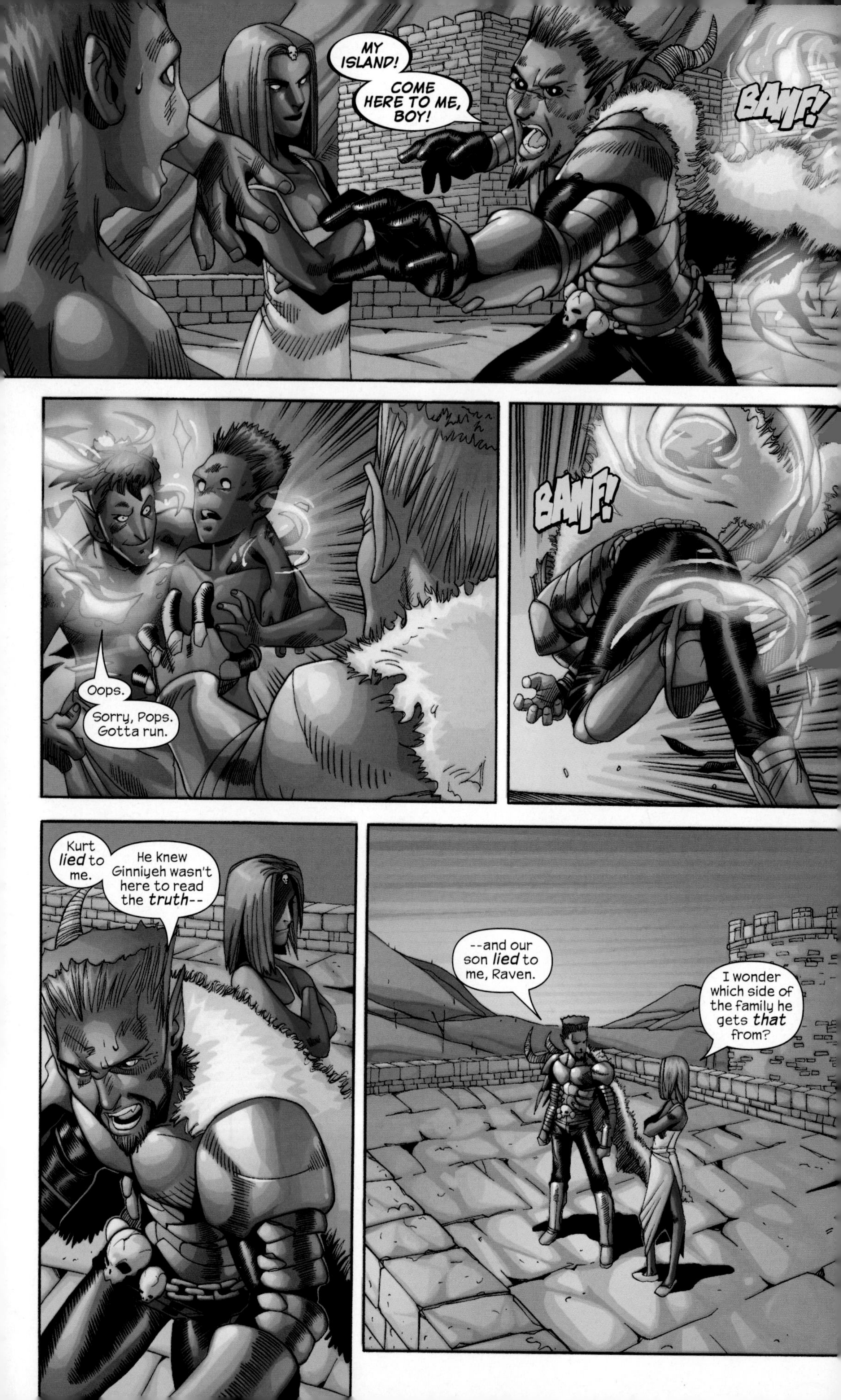

MY ISLAND!
COME HERE TO ME, BOY!
BAMF!
Oops.
Sorry, Pops. Gotta run.
BAMF!
Kurt *lied* to me.
He knew Ginniyeh wasn't here to read the *truth*--
--and our son *lied* to me, Raven.
I wonder which side of the family he gets *that* from?

Mom?

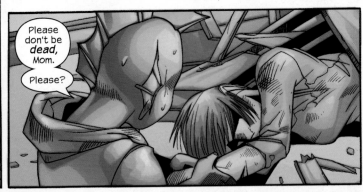

Please don't be *dead*, Mom.

Please?

SHBAM-CHEEEESH!

COME ON!

IS THAT ALL YOU GOT?!

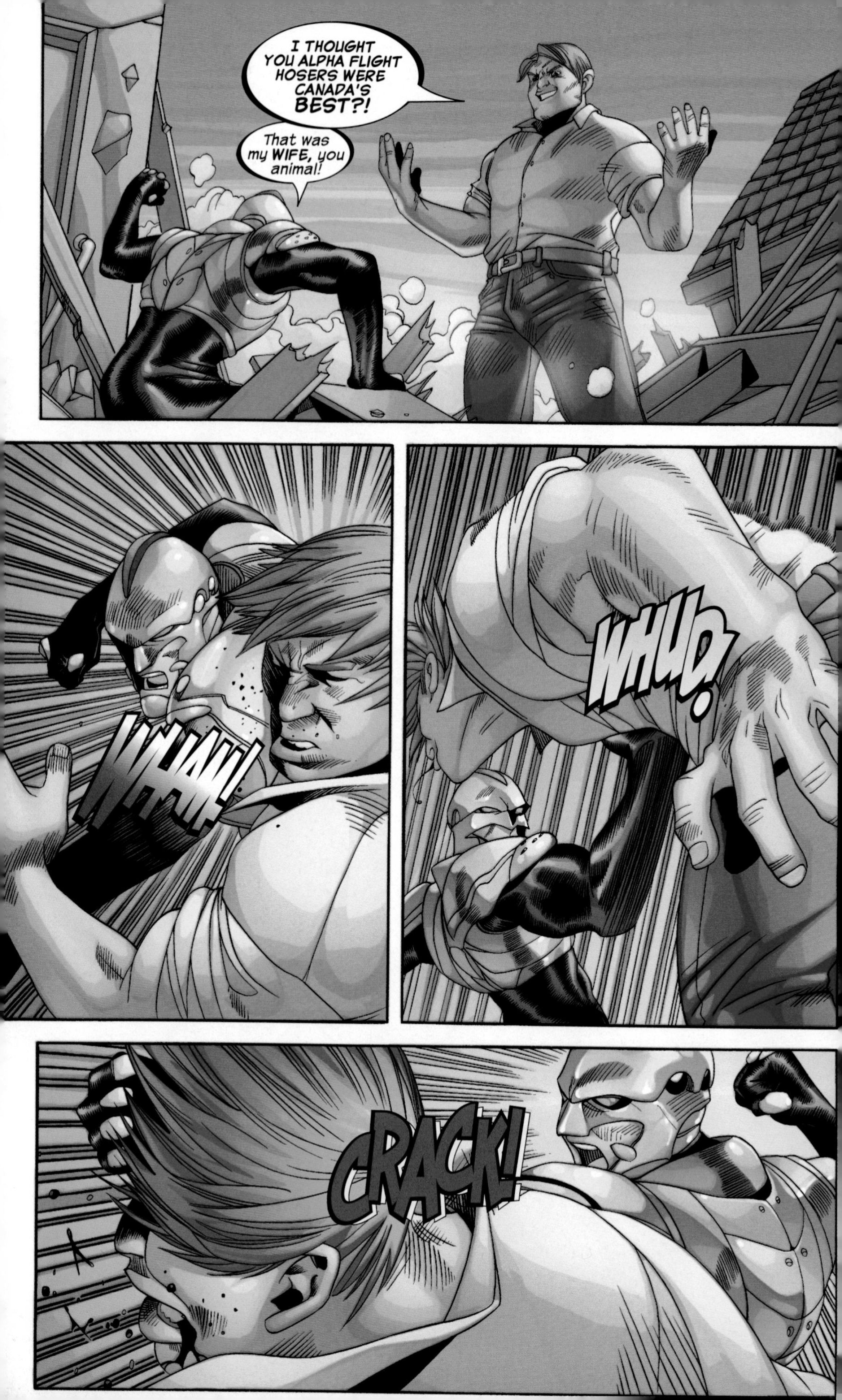
I THOUGHT YOU ALPHA FLIGHT HOSERS WERE CANADA'S BEST?!
That was my WIFE, you animal!
WHAM!
WHUD!
CRACK!

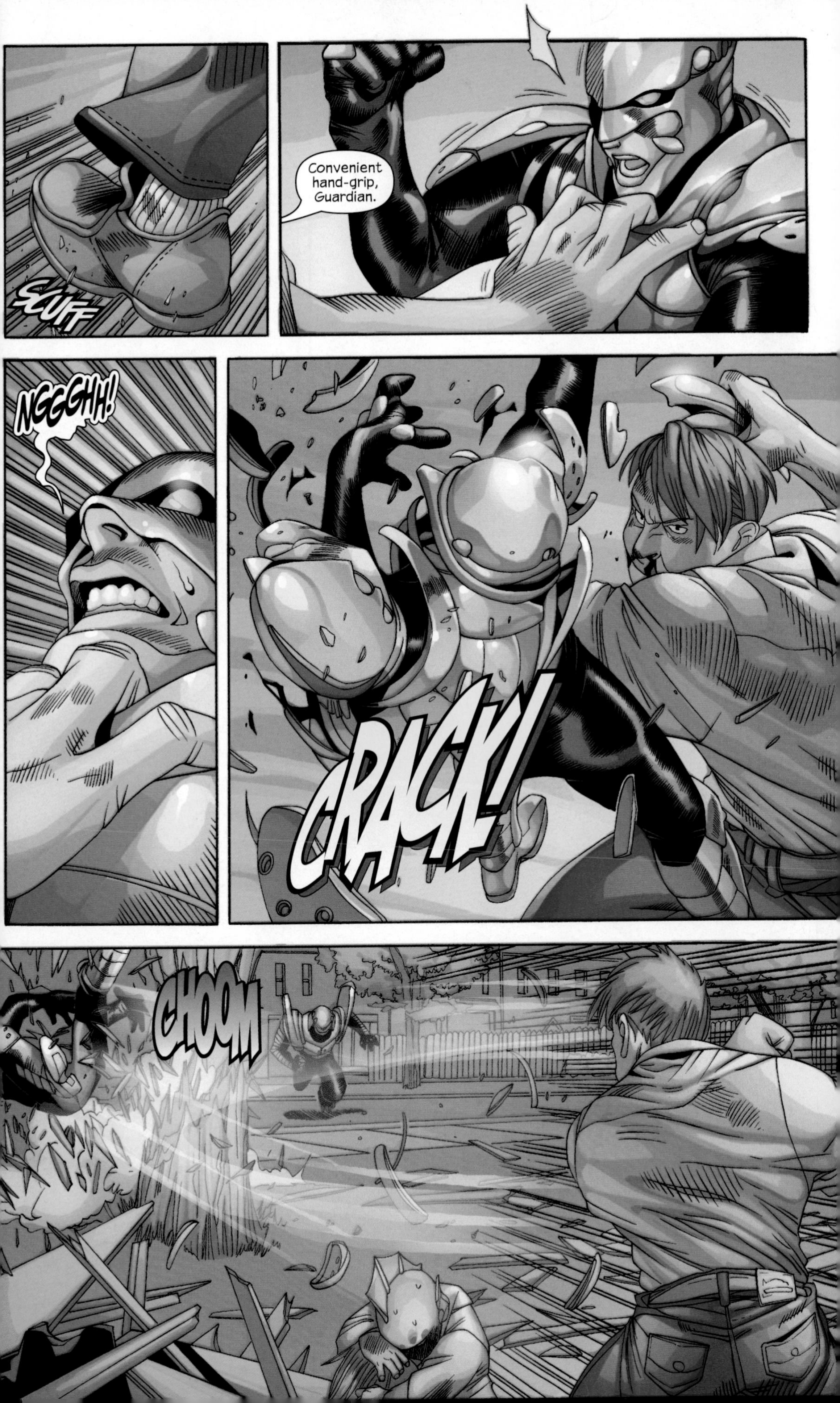

SCUFF
Convenient hand-grip, Guardian.
NGGGHH!
CRACK!
CHOOM

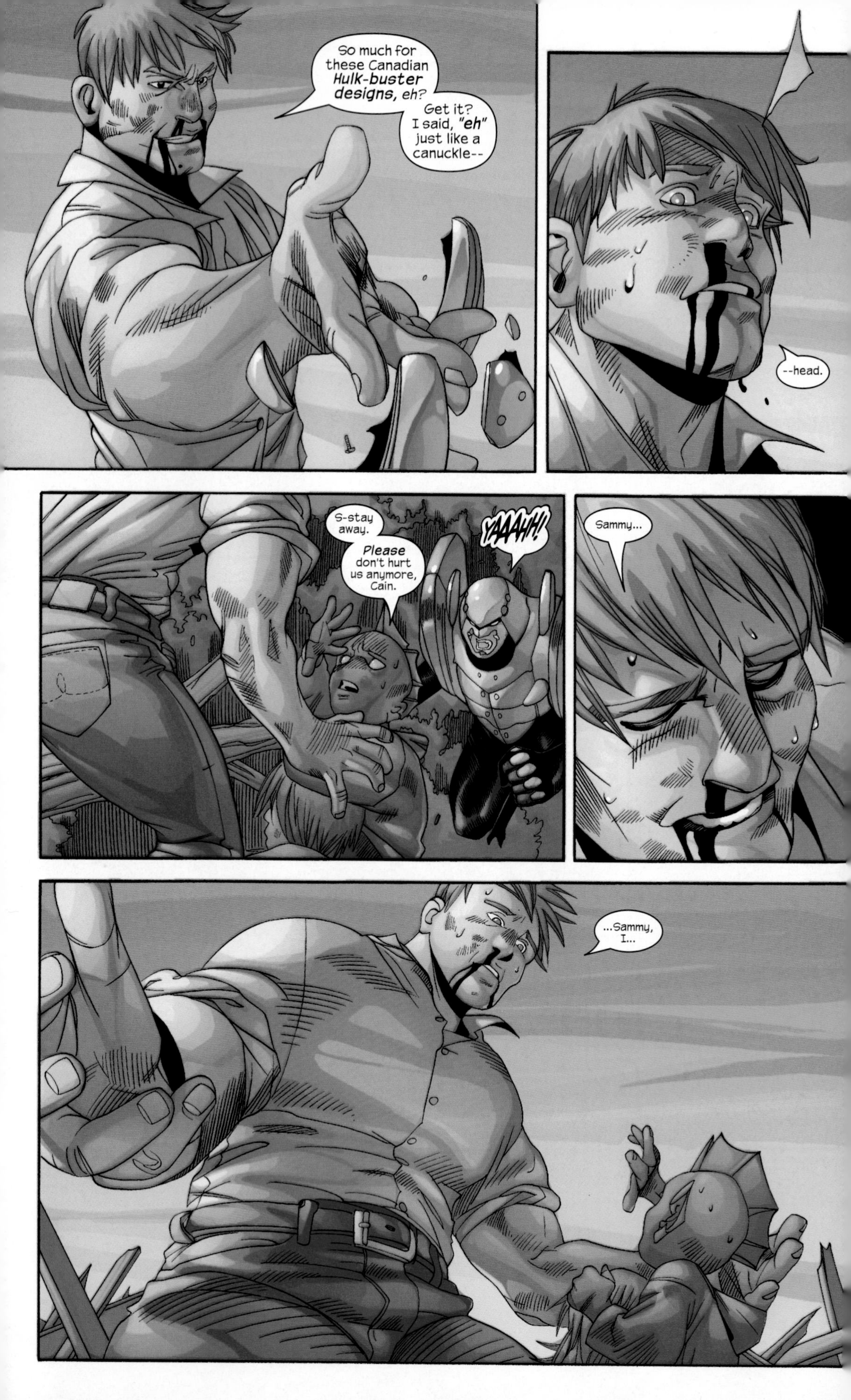
So much for these Canadian Hulk-buster designs, eh?
Get it? I said, "eh" just like a canuckle--
--head.
S-stay away.
Please don't hurt us anymore, Cain.
YAAAHH!
Sammy...
...Sammy, I...

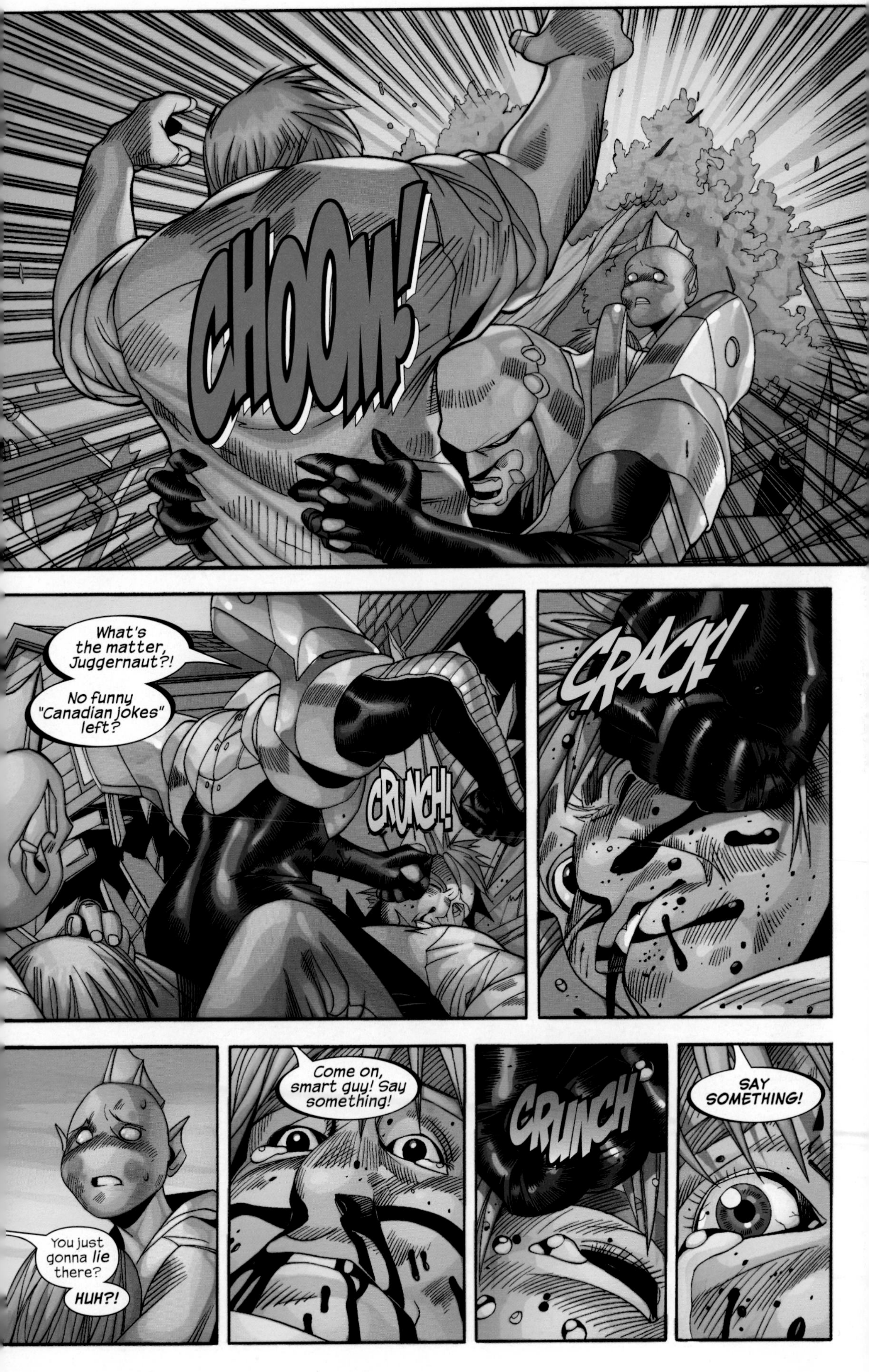
CHOOM!
What's the matter, Juggernaut?!
No funny "Canadian jokes" left?
CRUNCH!
CRACK!
You just gonna *lie* there?
HUH?!
Come on, smart guy! Say something!
CRUNCH
SAY SOMETHING!

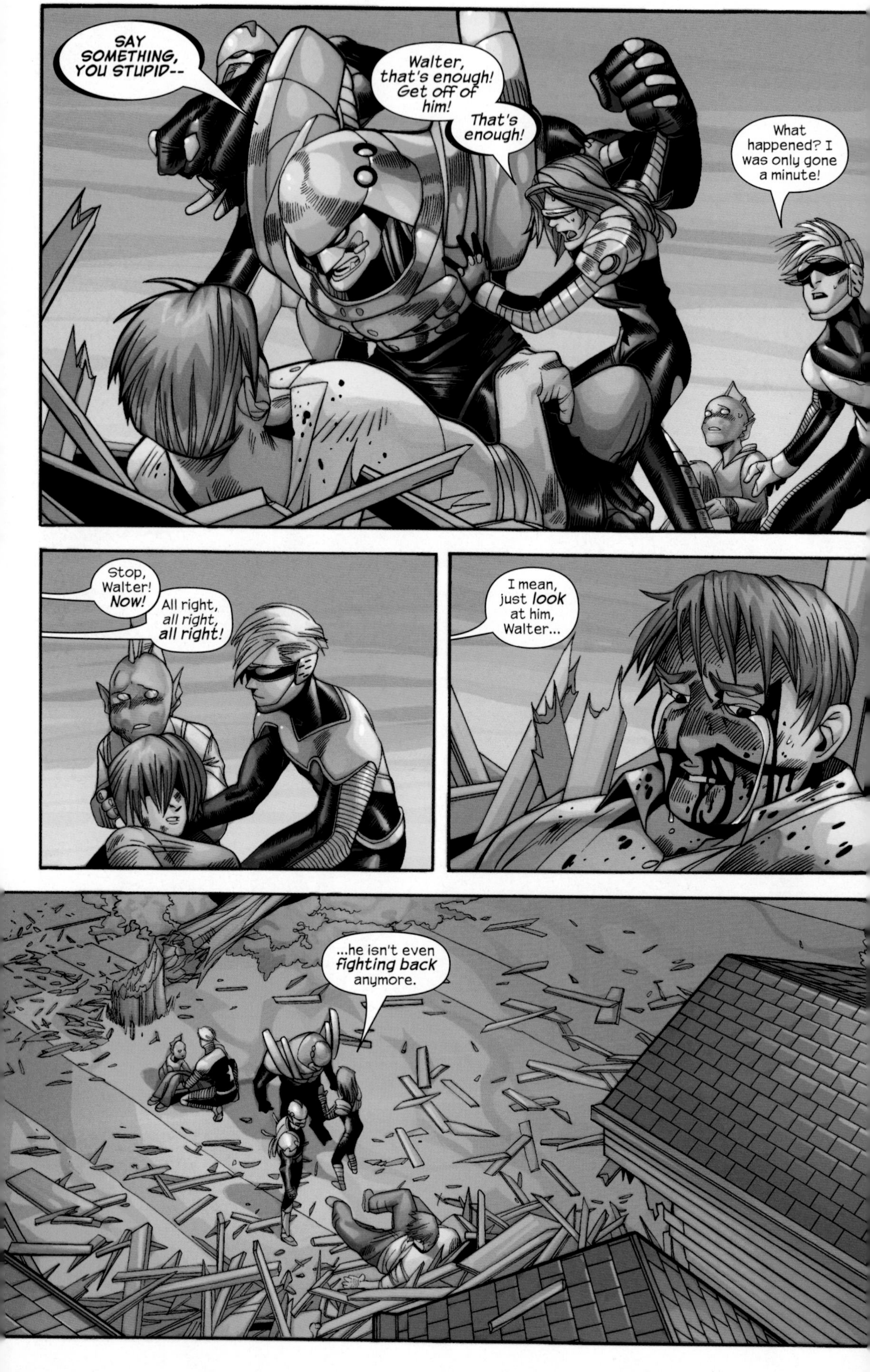
SAY SOMETHING, YOU STUPID--
Walter, that's enough! Get off of him!
That's enough!
What happened? I was only gone a minute!
Stop, Walter! Now!
All right, all right, all right!
I mean, just look at him, Walter...
...he isn't even fighting back anymore.

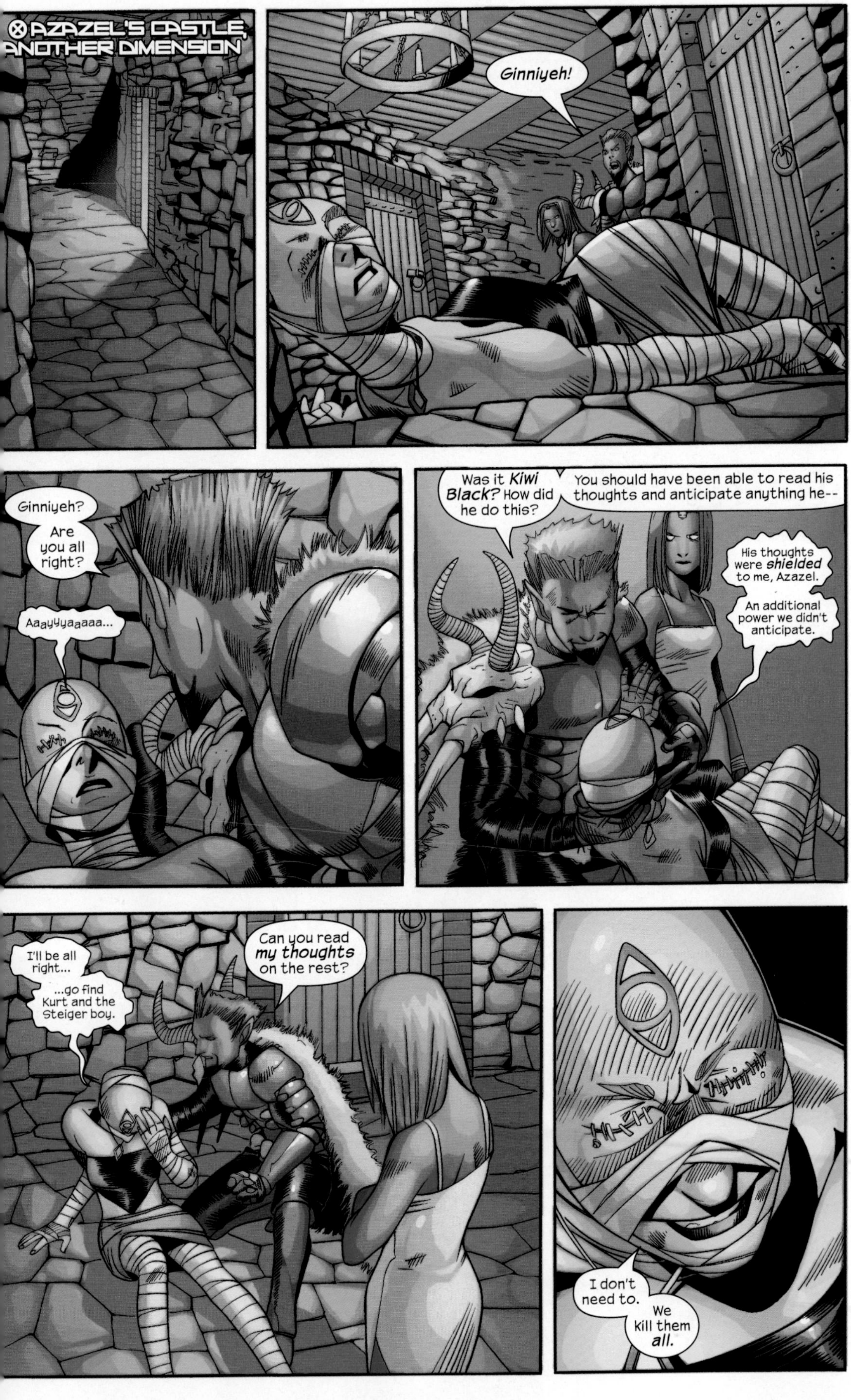
AZAZEL'S CASTLE, ANOTHER DIMENSION
Ginniyeh!
Ginniyeh? Are you all right?
Aaayyyaaaa...
Was it Kiwi Black? How did he do this?
You should have been able to read his thoughts and anticipate anything he--
His thoughts were shielded to me, Azazel.
An additional power we didn't anticipate.
I'll be all right...
...go find Kurt and the Steiger boy.
Can you read my thoughts on the rest?
I don't need to.
We kill them all.

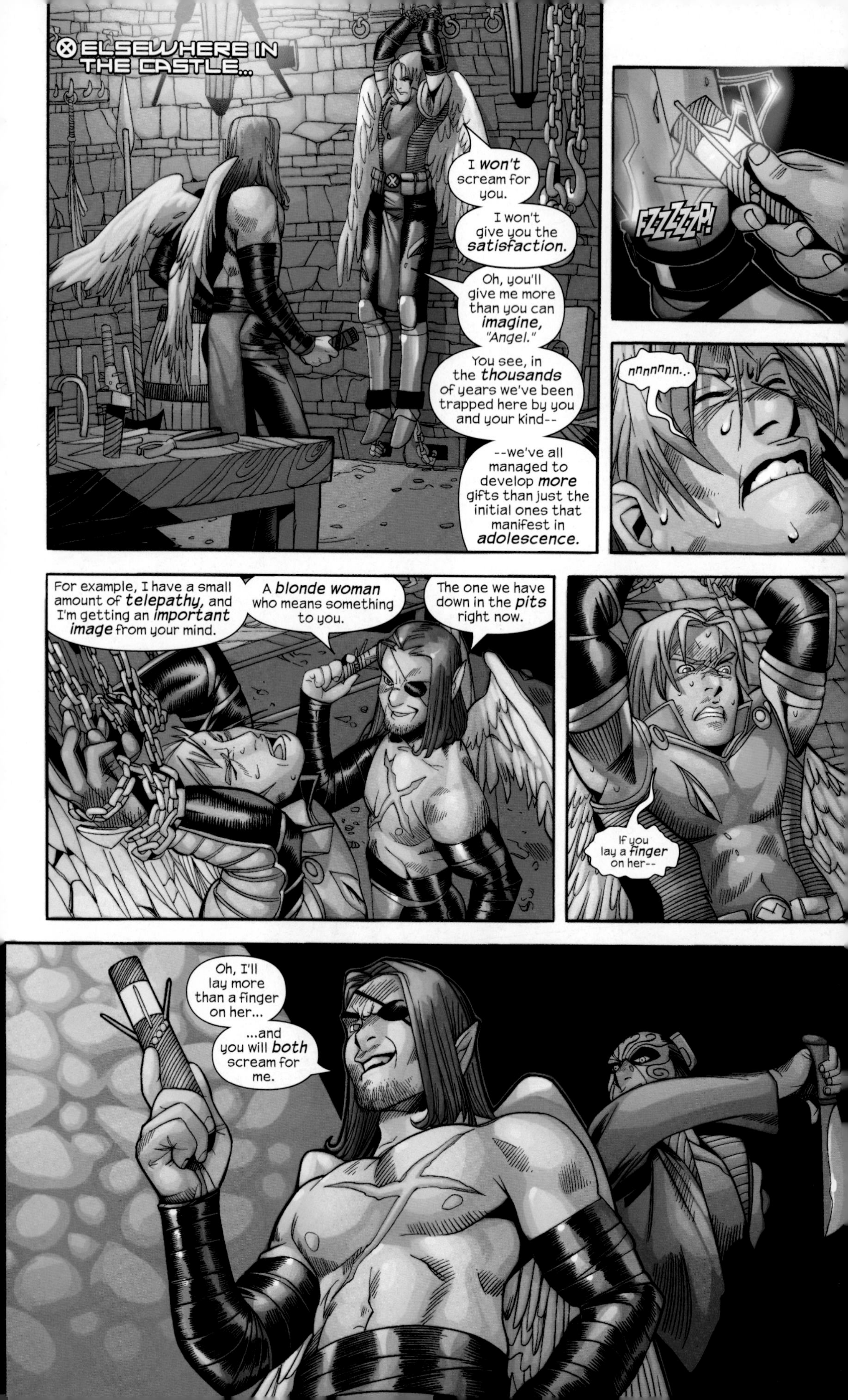
ELSEWHERE IN THE CASTLE...
I won't scream for you.
I won't give you the satisfaction.
Oh, you'll give me more than you can imagine, "Angel."
You see, in the thousands of years we've been trapped here by you and your kind--
--we've all managed to develop more gifts than just the initial ones that manifest in adolescence.
FZZZZZP!
nnnnnnn...
For example, I have a small amount of telepathy, and I'm getting an important image from your mind.
A blonde woman who means something to you.
The one we have down in the pits right now.
If you lay a finger on her--
Oh, I'll lay more than a finger on her...
...and you will both scream for me.

Bobby wants me to tell you that he's ready to take some of the water from our bodies to *reform*.

Any. water.

I'm sorry for that comment, Bobby. *Really.*

But if you can get enough water from the rest of us to become *whole* again, I'm willing to *let* you.

Yeah, Bobby. I'm game.

Take whatever you need from me.

Yeah, Bobby. Take whatever you need from *Paige.*

Okay, okay...he can take whatever he needs from *me*, too.

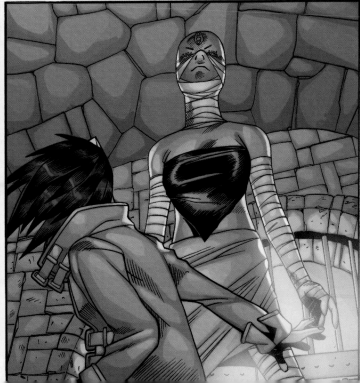

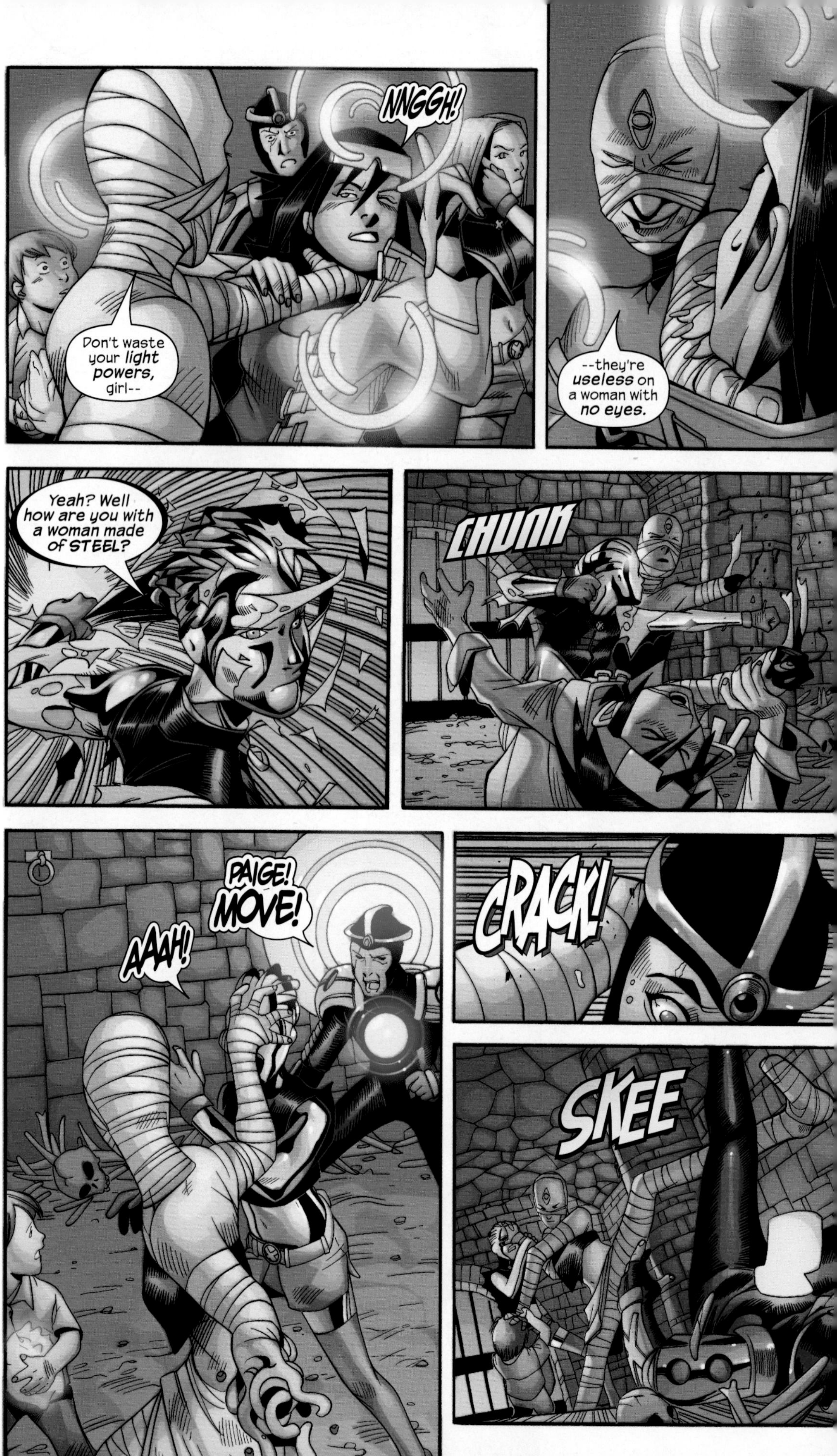
NNGGH!
Don't waste your light powers, girl--
--they're useless on a woman with no eyes.
Yeah? Well how are you with a woman made of STEEL?
CHUNK
PAIGE! MOVE!
AAAH!
CRACK!
SKEE

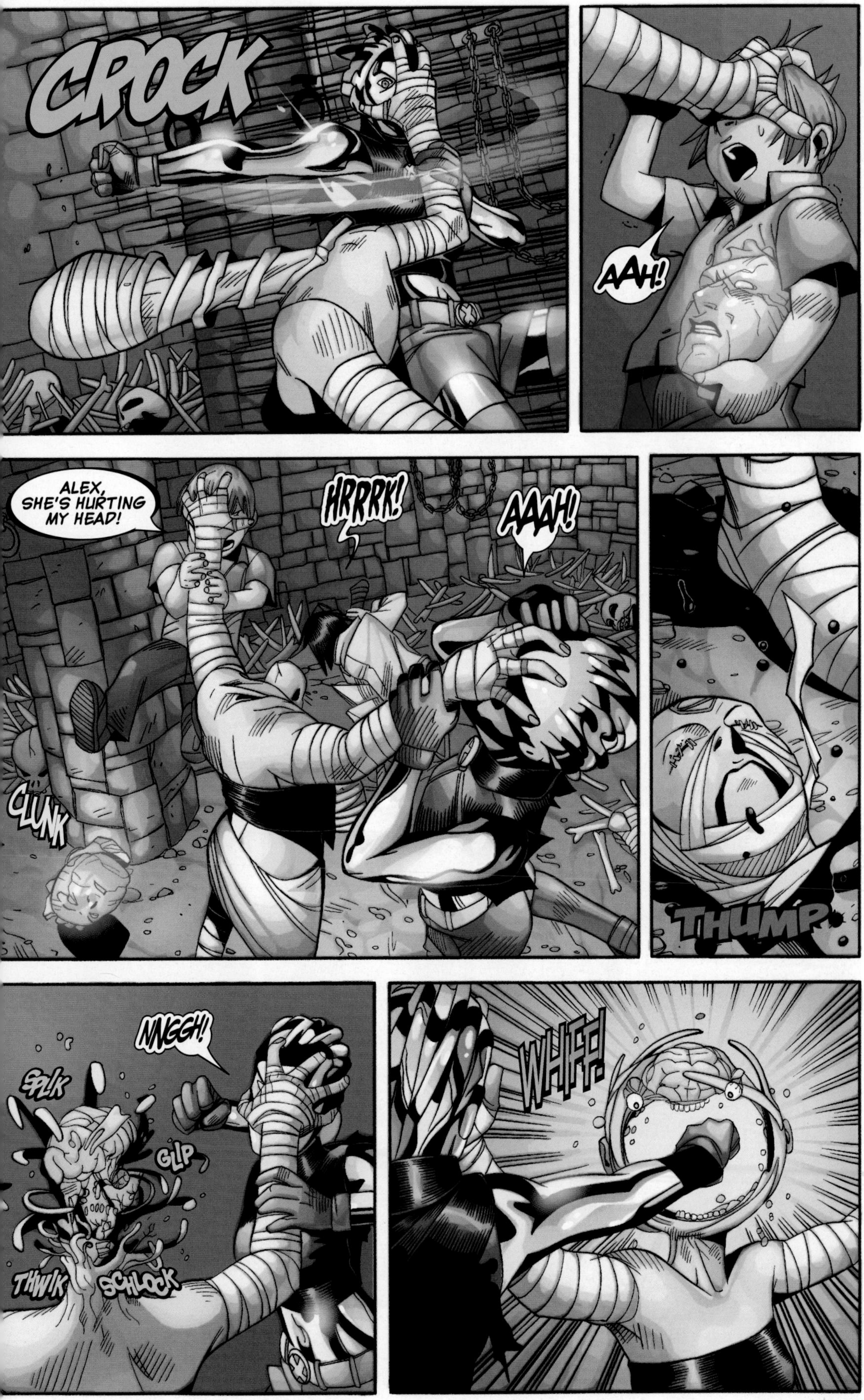
CROCK
AAH!
ALEX, SHE'S HURTING MY HEAD!
HRRRK!
AAAH!
CLUNK
THUMP
NNGGH!
SPLIK
GLIP
THWIK
SCHLOCK
WHIFF!

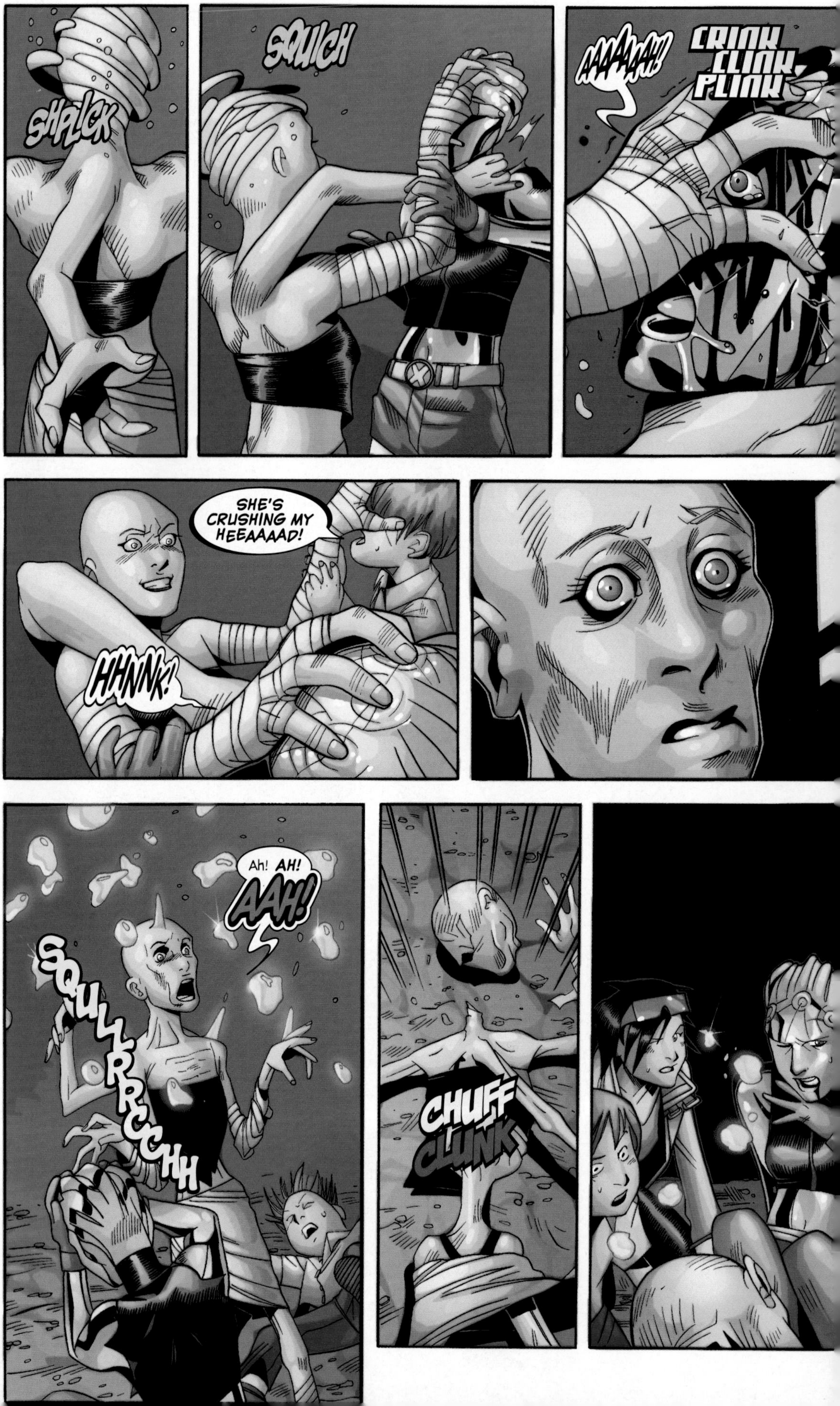
SHPLICK
SQUICH
AAAAAAAH!
CRINK CLINK PLINK
SHE'S CRUSHING MY HEEAAAAD!
HHNNK!
Ah! AH! AAH!
SQUILRRCCHH
CHUFF
CLUNK

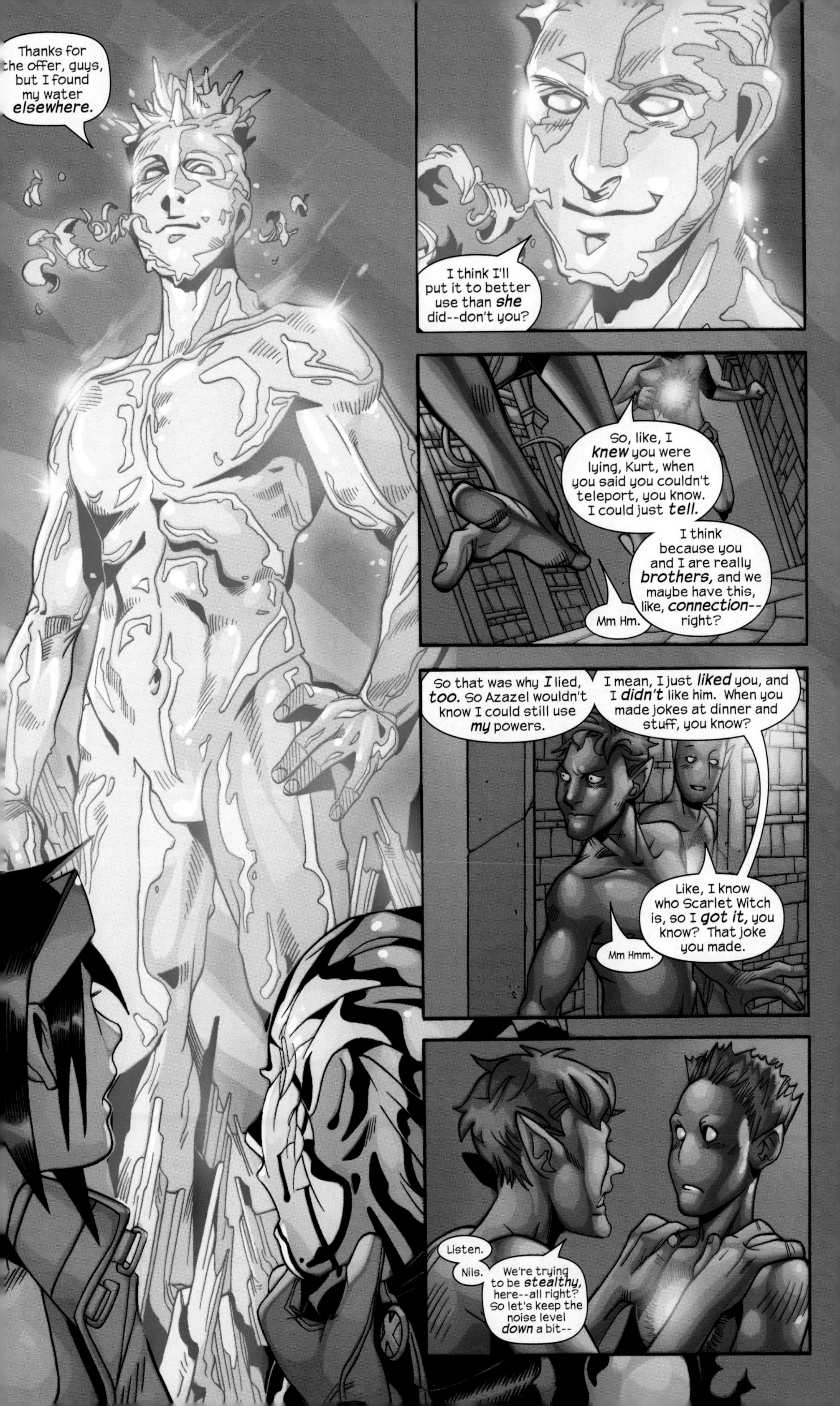
Thanks for the offer, guys, but I found my water *elsewhere.*
I think I'll put it to better use than *she* did--don't you?
So, like, I *knew* you were lying, Kurt, when you said you couldn't teleport, you know. I could just *tell.*
I think because you and I are really *brothers,* and we maybe have this, like, *connection*--right?
Mm Hm.
So that was why *I* lied, *too.* So Azazel wouldn't know I could still use *my* powers.
I mean, I just *liked* you, and I *didn't* like him. When you made jokes at dinner and stuff, you know?
Like, I know who Scarlet Witch is, so I *got it,* you know? That joke you made.
Mm Hmm.
Listen.
Nils.
We're trying to be *stealthy,* here--all right? So let's keep the noise level *down* a bit--

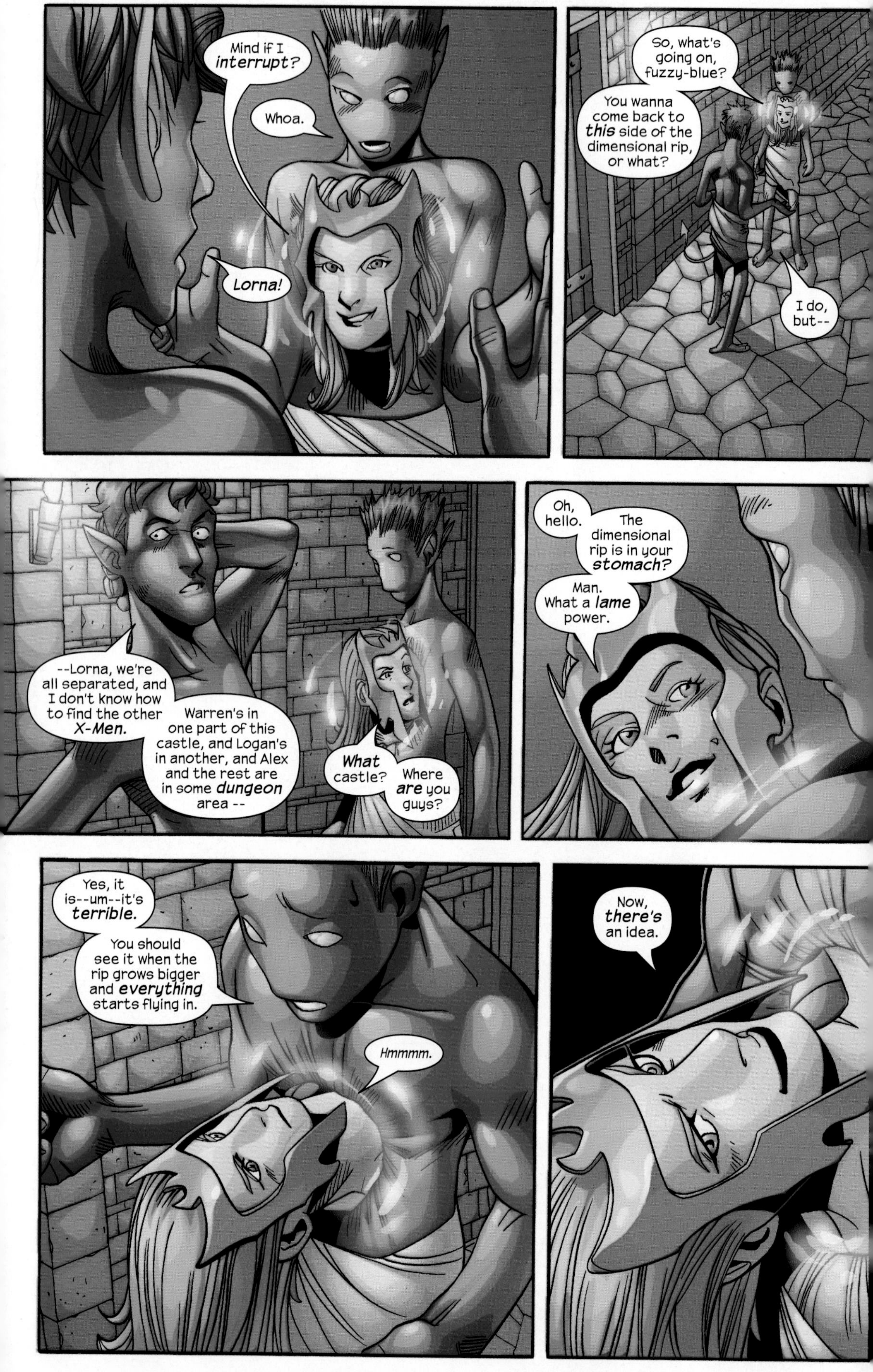
Mind if I interrupt?
Whoa.
Lorna!
So, what's going on, fuzzy-blue?
You wanna come back to this side of the dimensional rip, or what?
I do, but--
--Lorna, we're all separated, and I don't know how to find the other X-Men.
Warren's in one part of this castle, and Logan's in another, and Alex and the rest are in some dungeon area --
What castle?
Where are you guys?
Oh, hello.
The dimensional rip is in your stomach?
Man. What a lame power.
Yes, it is--um--it's terrible.
You should see it when the rip grows bigger and everything starts flying in.
Hmmmm.
Now, there's an idea.

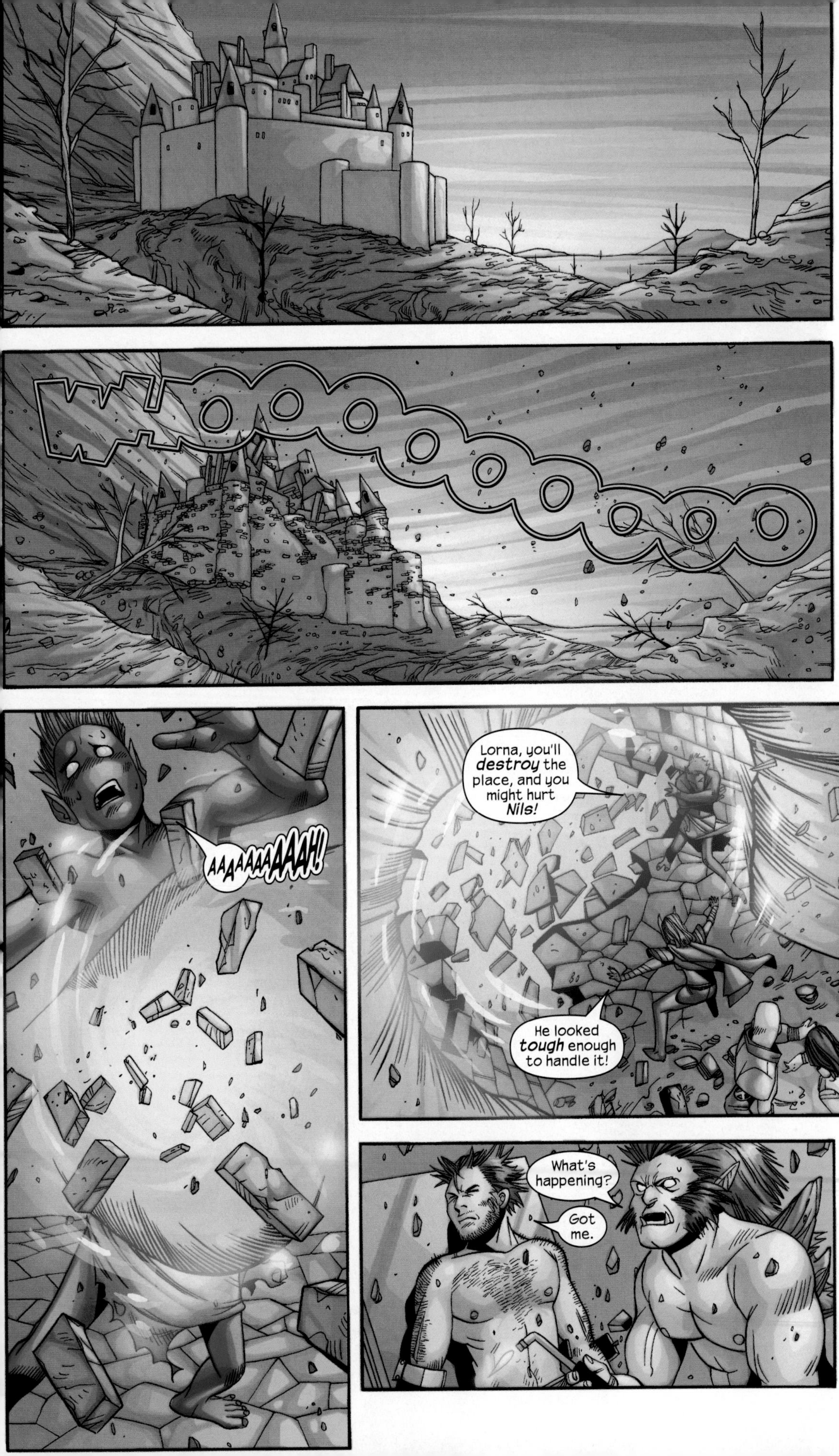
WHOOOOOOOOOOO
AAAAAAAAAAH!
Lorna, you'll destroy the place, and you might hurt Nils!
He looked tough enough to handle it!
What's happening?
Got me.

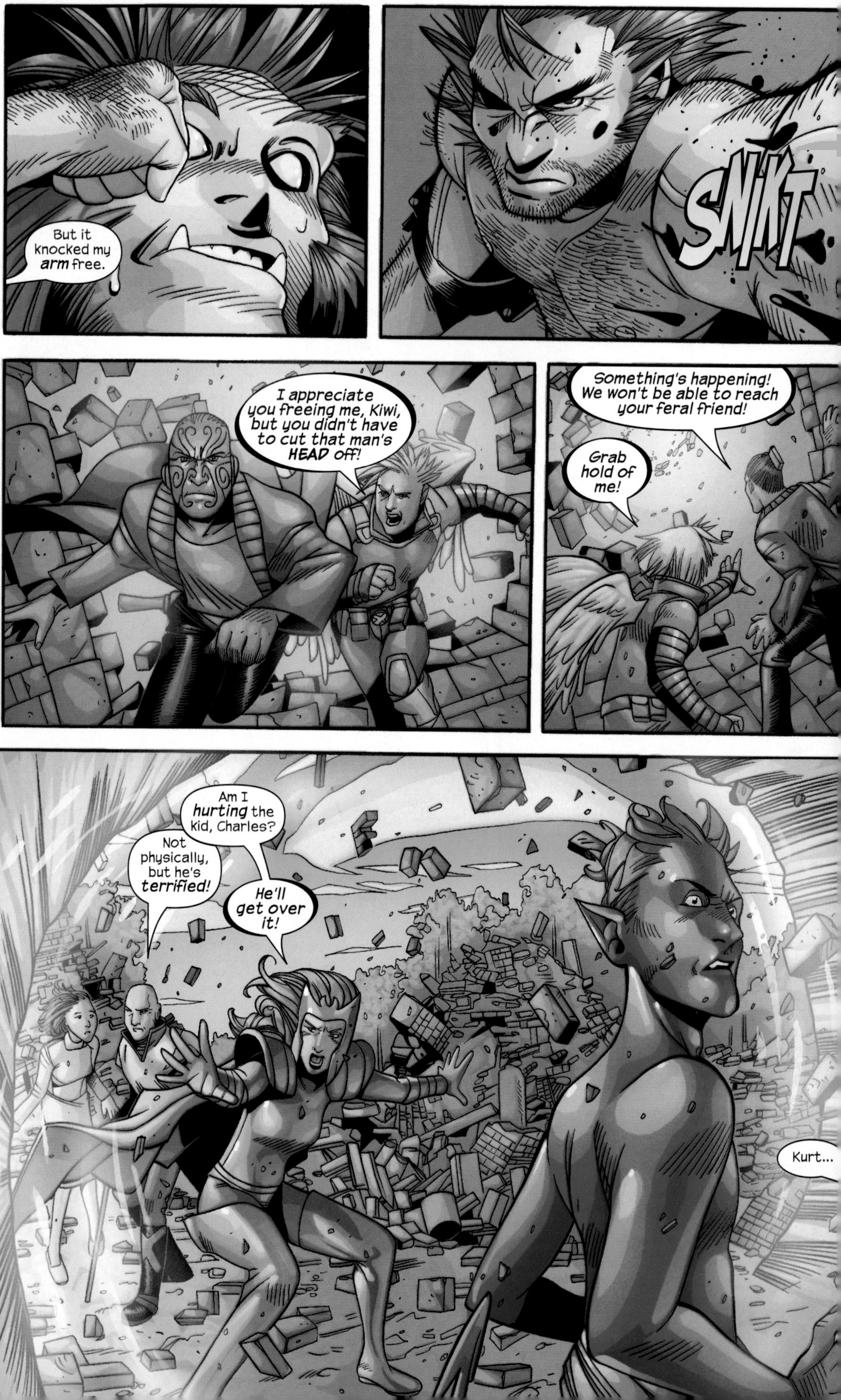
But it knocked my arm free.
SNIKT
I appreciate you freeing me, Kiwi, but you didn't have to cut that man's HEAD off!
Something's happening! We won't be able to reach your feral friend!
Grab hold of me!
Am I hurting the kid, Charles?
Not physically, but he's terrified!
He'll get over it!
Kurt...

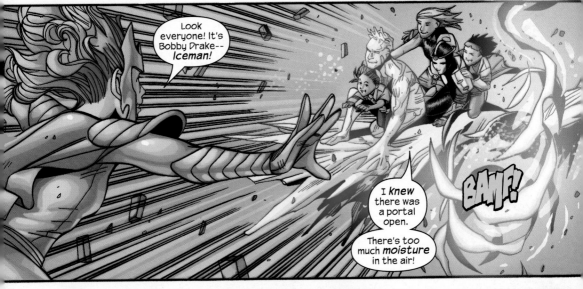

Look everyone! It's Bobby Drake-- *Iceman!*

I *knew* there was a portal open.

There's too much *moisture* in the air!

BAMF!

Oh, Carter, my baby!

Mom, it was so *cool!* You shoulda seen it!

Thank you, Bobby. Thank you *so* much.

Don't, uh--

--don't mention it.

The whole castle's coming through the portal...

...it's all *collapsing* around us!

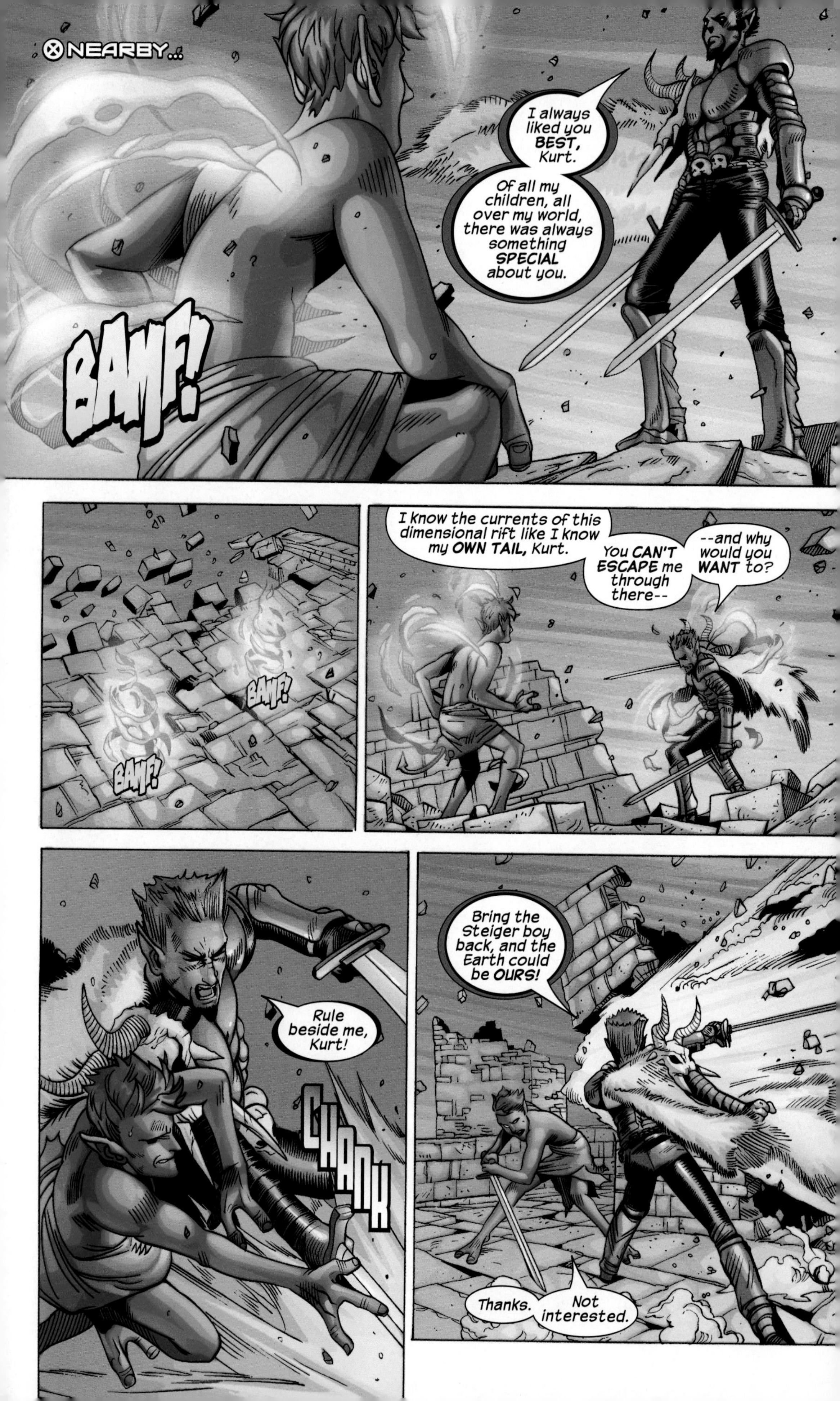
NEARBY...
I always liked you BEST, Kurt.
Of all my children, all over my world, there was always something SPECIAL about you.
BAMF!
BAMF!
BAMF!
I know the currents of this dimensional rift like I know my OWN TAIL, Kurt.
You CAN'T ESCAPE me through there--
--and why would you WANT to?
Rule beside me, Kurt!
CHANK
Bring the Steiger boy back, and the Earth could be OURS!
Thanks.
Not interested.

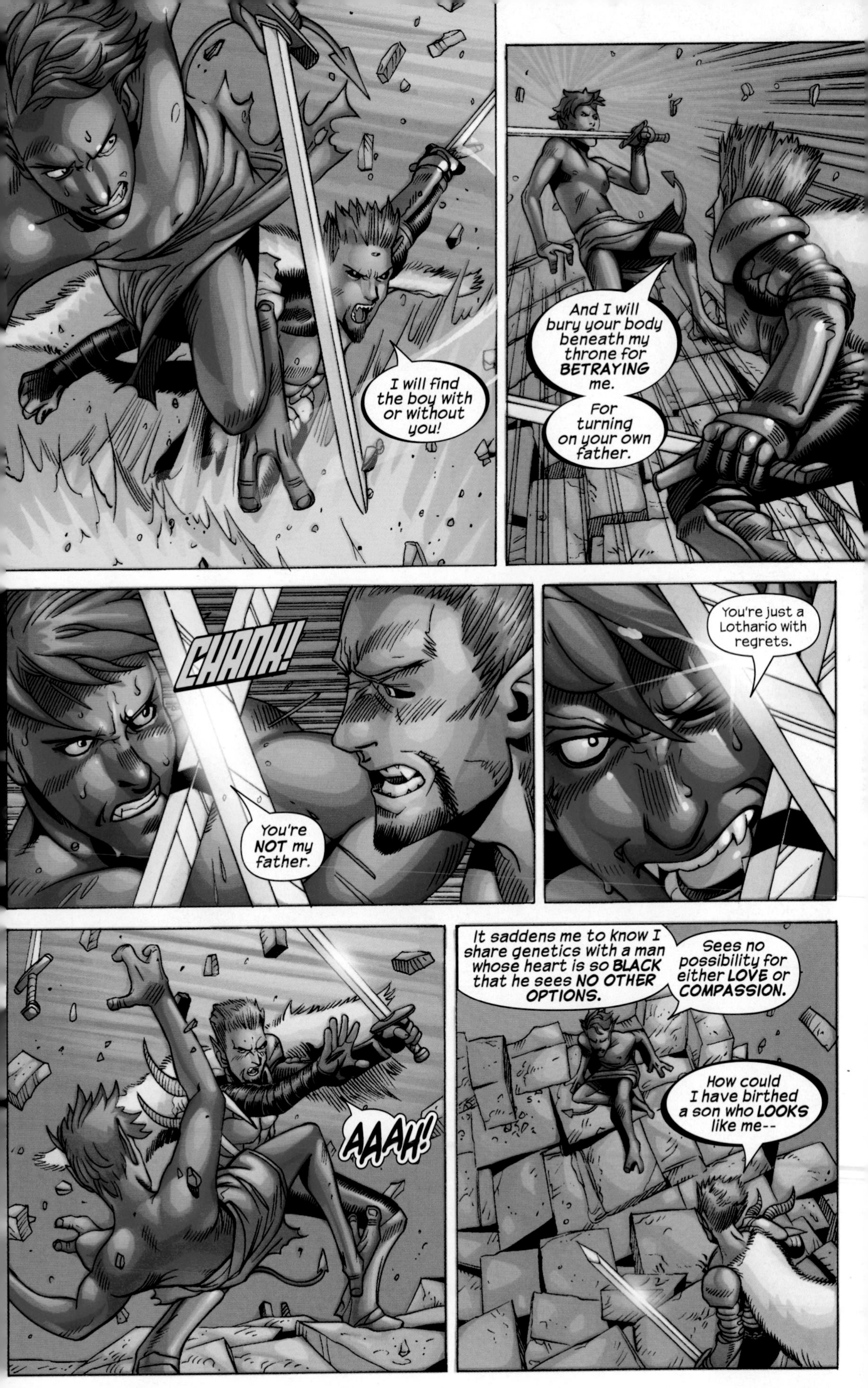
I will find the boy with or without you!
And I will bury your body beneath my throne for BETRAYING me.
For turning on your own father.
CHANK!
You're NOT my father.
You're just a Lothario with regrets.
AAAH!
It saddens me to know I share genetics with a man whose heart is so BLACK that he sees NO OTHER OPTIONS.
Sees no possibility for either LOVE or COMPASSION.
How could I have birthed a son who LOOKS like me--

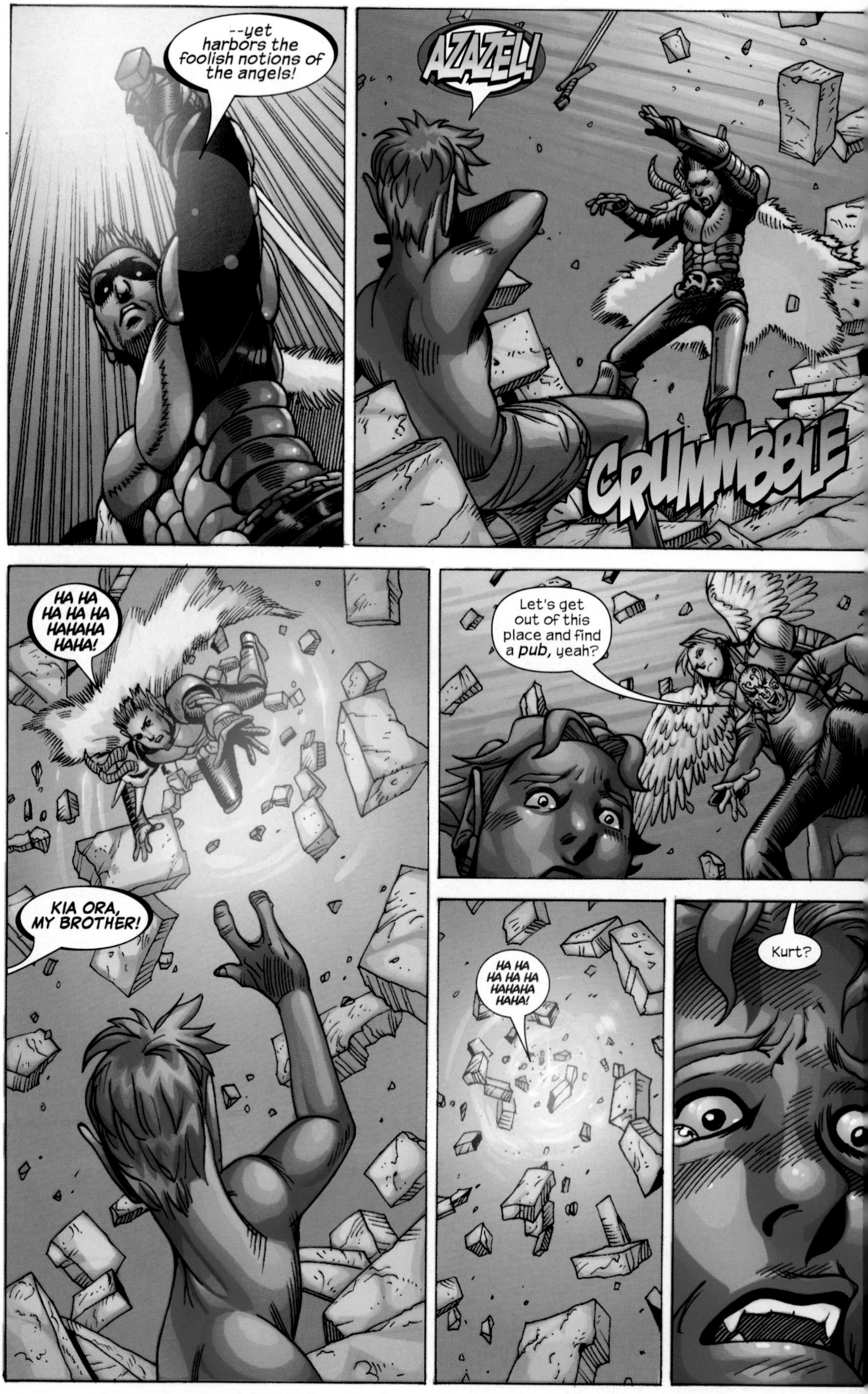
--yet harbors the foolish notions of the angels!
AZAZEL!
CRUMMBBLE
HA HA HA HA HA HAHAHA HAHA!
KIA ORA, MY BROTHER!
Let's get out of this place and find a *pub*, yeah?
HA HA HA HA HA HAHAHA HAHA!
Kurt?

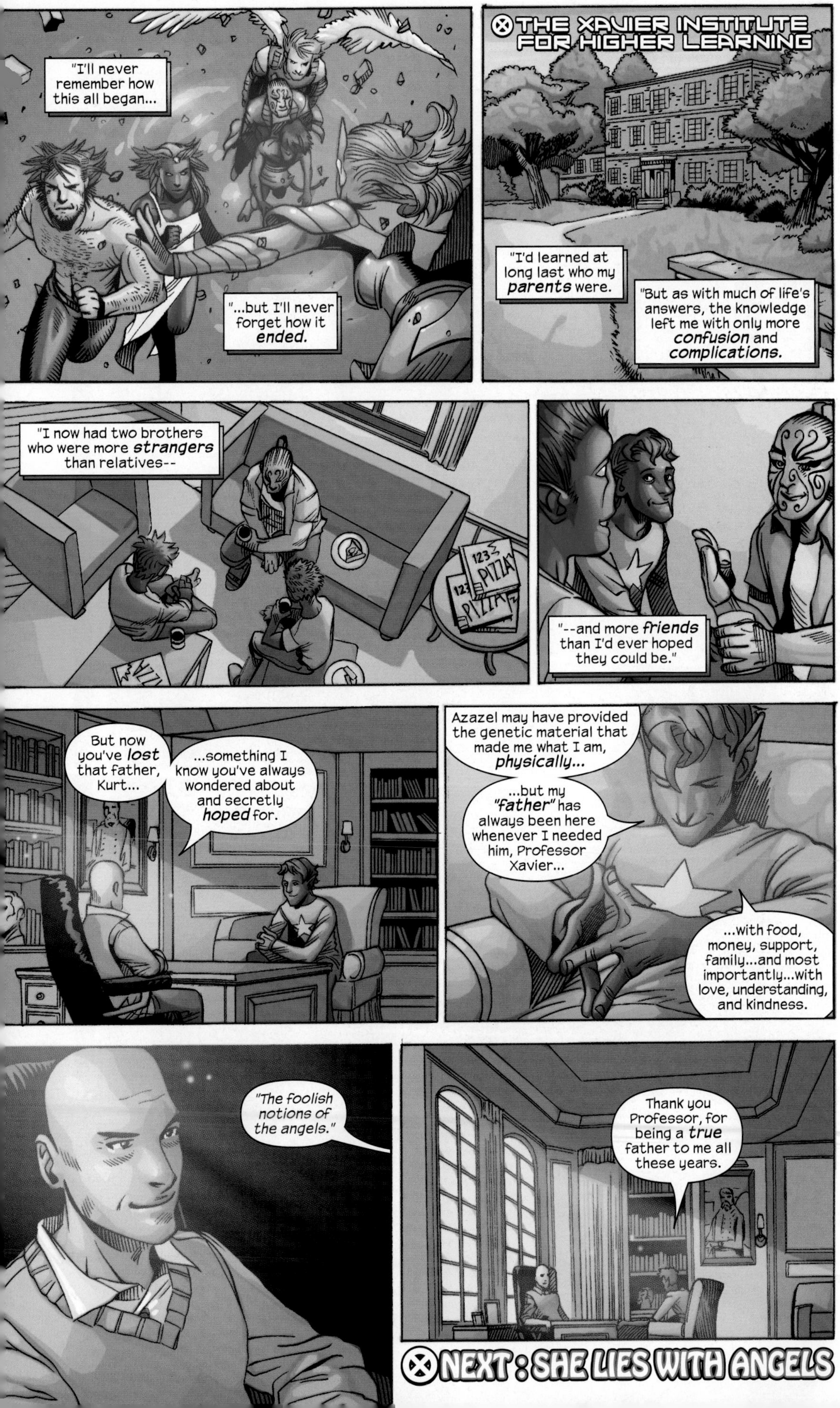
"I'll never remember how this all began...
"...but I'll never forget how it ended.
THE XAVIER INSTITUTE FOR HIGHER LEARNING
"I'd learned at long last who my parents were.
"But as with much of life's answers, the knowledge left me with only more confusion and complications.
"I now had two brothers who were more strangers than relatives--
123 PIZZA
"--and more friends than I'd ever hoped they could be."
But now you've lost that father, Kurt...
...something I know you've always wondered about and secretly hoped for.
Azazel may have provided the genetic material that made me what I am, physically...
...but my "father" has always been here whenever I needed him, Professor Xavier...
...with food, money, support, family...and most importantly...with love, understanding, and kindness.
"The foolish notions of the angels."
Thank you Professor, for being a true father to me all these years.
NEXT: SHE LIES WITH ANGELS

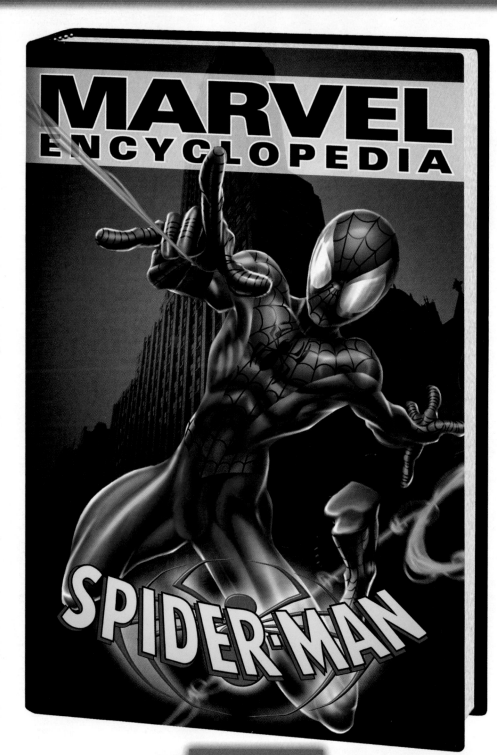

**EVERYTHING You Ever Wanted to Know About Spider-Man...
And Weren't Afraid to Ask!**

Mary Jane

A novel by Judith O'Brien

MARVEL

Marvel's First Young Adult Prose Novel In Hardcover!

Written by Popular Romance Writer Judith O'Brien with Illustrations by Mike Mayhew

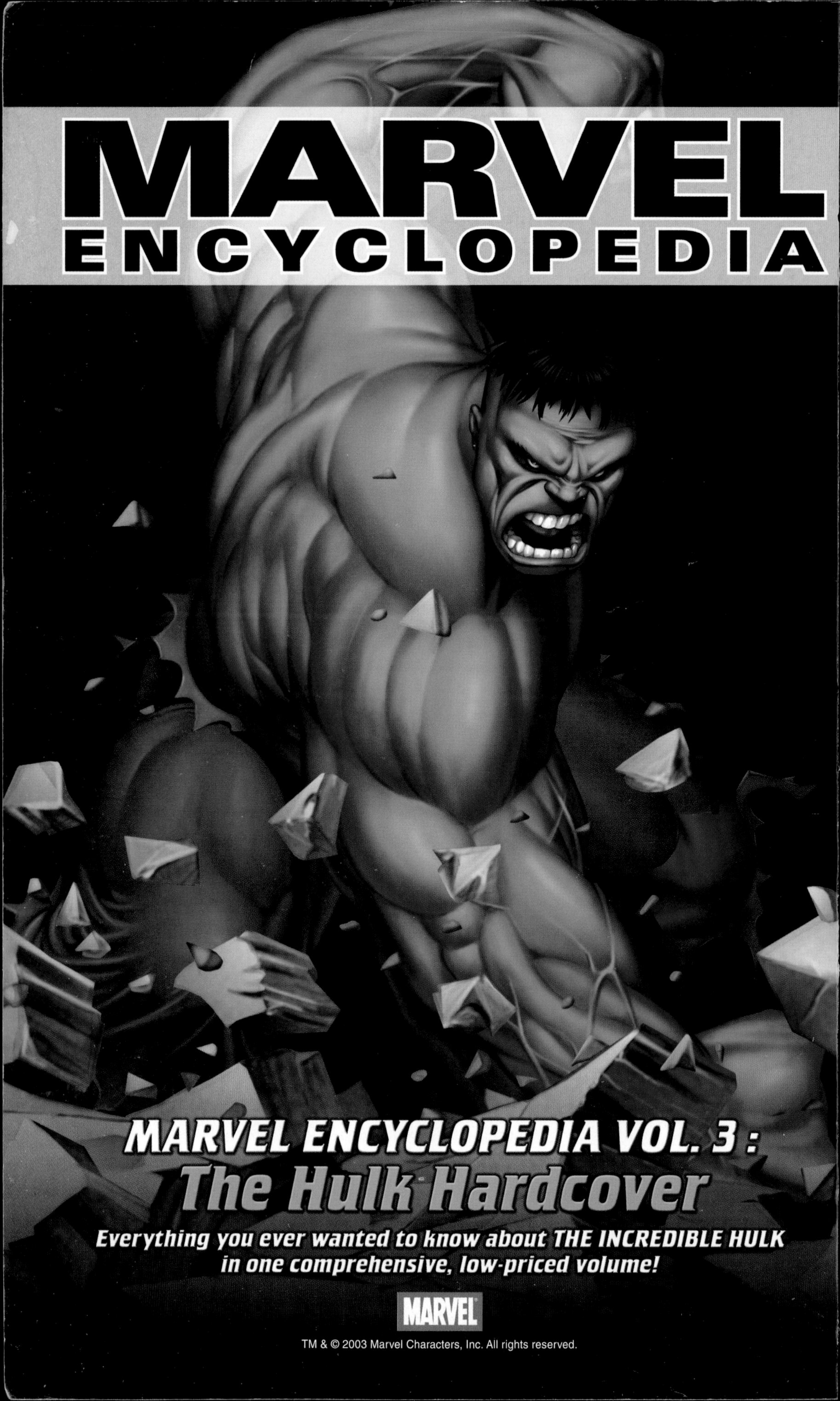
MARVEL
ENCYCLOPEDIA
MARVEL ENCYCLOPEDIA VOL. 3 :
The Hulk Hardcover
Everything you ever wanted to know about THE INCREDIBLE HULK
in one comprehensive, low-priced volume!
MARVEL
TM & © 2003 Marvel Characters, Inc. All rights reserved.